Globalize Liberation

How to uproot the system and build a better world

Edited by David Solnit

Individual essays © each author
See pages 486-487 for a list of photo/illustration credits.

Cover and book design by Jason Justice:

www.justicedesign.com
GRAPHIC DESIGN FOR SOCIAL CHANGE!

Front cover photo (top) by Linda Panetta. Front cover photo (center) by
Karl Seifert. Front cover photo (bottom) by David Hanks. Spine photo by
Mariana Mora. Back cover photo (top) by Eric Wagner. Back cover photo
(bottom) by Linda Panetta.

Library of Congress Cataloging-in-Publication Data

Globalize Liberation: how to uproot the system and build a better world /
edited by David Solnit
p. cm.
  ISBN 0-87286-420-0
  1. Anti-globalization movement. 2. Social justice. 3. Globalization—
Economic aspects. 4. Globalization—Social aspects. 5. International
business enterprises—Political aspects. I. Solnit, David.

HN17.5 .G584 2003
303.48'4—dc21
                          2002041265

City Lights Books

Visit our website: www.citylights.com

City Lights Books are edited by Lawrence Ferlinghetti and Nancy J. Peters
and published at the City Lights Bookstore, 261 Columbus Avenue, San
Francisco, CA 94133.

Acknowledgements

Thanks to my mother Terry Allen, who models positive values that make being a revolutionary inevitable in the present order.

Much appreciation to my awesome sister Rebecca, who initially encouraged me to take on this project, and helped immensely at each step with encouragement, editing, late night phone conversations, and support.

Many thanks to all of the authors, photographers and artists in the book who generously donated their energy, inspiration, ideas, support, and hard work to make this book happen. And to Elaine Katzenberger for believing in the project and working hard to make it real, along with all the City Lights workers. And Jason Justice for his tireless, inspired design efforts on this book and for all the work he does for the movements. ·

I'm grateful for all the help , advice and encouragement I received from Marina Sitrin, Patrick Reinsborough, Jennifer Whitney, Chris Gray, Chris Crass, Graciela, Chris Carlsson, Kristen Gardner, my brothers Steve and Daniel, Aryeh Shell, Sasha Wright, and all the other folks in my communities and movements who made it possible.

This book comes out of shared struggles and creative uprisings with friends and allies everywhere, but especially with friends in the Art and Revolution Collective (particularly Alli Starr), Direct Action Network folks, Freedom Rising Affinity Group, Action for Local Global Justice, Anti-Capitalist/Imperialist Cluster, Direct Action to Stop the War, 54th Street Collective House in Oakland, and the Code Orange (for Liberation) Affinity Group.

A NOTE ABOUT THIS BOOK

Globalize Liberation weaves together diverse voices and struggles, drawing from the experience of hands-on organizers, thinkers, artists, communities and movements. It is a book by practitioners for practitioners. The essays here help make the new radicalism more explicit, and the intention is to popularize the practices, understandings, and experiments that are spreading across the globe.

Everyone and every group or community develops their own politics that is a reflection of their life experience—who they are, where they live, who they work with, and what inspires them. This book reflects the people, movements, and ideas that I (as a white Jewish-Irish male carpenter who has spent the last two decades organizing in the direct action movements of the San Francisco Bay Area and the western United States) am connected to and that have influenced or inspired me. It does not for a moment pretend to be objective or comprehensive, nor to include all of the voices that need to be heard. Everyone's web of resistance is different, depending on who we are, where we live, and to whom we are connected. What is yours?

As a carpenter, I have packed this book like a tool belt, with the most useful and practical tools: ideas and understandings of how to uproot the system causing our problems and build a better world. The ideas and writings of the people in this book have been incredibly useful to me over the last few years—sources of hope and help in clarifying my own understanding—and I have circulated photocopies and e-mails of many of them.

This book is a resource, but does not offer a repeatable blueprint, roadmap, or recipe for the changes our planet so desperately needs. No one size fits all. It is up to each of us to engage with our community, think strategically, be creative, follow our intuition, look for possibilities, and take action.

The hope is that the ideas, experiences, and passions in this book will spread like dandelion seeds in the wind, like fire in dry grass.

TABLE OF CONTENTS

SECTION 2

HOW TO CHANGE THINGS

photo spread: Karl Seifert

SECTION 3

IDEAS IN ACTION

HOW TO USE THIS BOOK

Globalize Liberation was created as a resource of hands-on tools, ideas, and examples to aid in our efforts to gain control of our lives and our communities, and ultimately to change the world we live in. It is intended to help individuals, groups, and movements to deepen their understanding of what's wrong and why, to create a vision of alternatives, and to develop strategies for creating change.

This book was written by activists, organizers, and movement people who draw from their experience, experiments, and passionate desire for a better world. From various perspectives, they offer analysis of the underlying causes of our current problems, along with strategies for uprooting them, examples of people who are doing this in their own community, and visions of what a better world might look like.

The book is divided into three sections:

WHAT'S THE PROBLEM
Answers to the question: "What is at the root of our problems?"
Designed to help you develop your own analysis.
If we want to get at the causes of our social and ecological problems and better understand their symptoms, we have to know where the roots lie. There are many different ways of approaching this question. Who we are, where we live, and what experiences we have all shape how we view the world. Understanding how other people and communities answer this question is essential if we hope to make alliances and build a movement of movements.

HOW TO CHANGE THINGS
Tools, reflections, and visions.
Designed to help us effectively change our communities and the world.
These essays can help us develop a theory of how to effect change. They can also be used to inform our actions and grassroots organizing, making them more effective and strategic. An understanding of how to make change and a vision of where we're heading can sustain us through tough times and help us achieve our goals.

IDEAS IN ACTION
Examples of how people organize effectively to improve our lives in the short term while pursuing a long-term vision of liberation.
Drawn from a wide range of struggles in North America, Argentina, and beyond, most of these essays document activities that are very recent, but a few (Poll Tax, Italy's Disobedients, and Civil Rights) trace the rich history from which today's new radical movements have grown.

STUDY/DISCUSSION GROUPS: Most of us are hungry for quality discussion and shared thinking about what's happening in the world and how to make change, ideas about what our lives and the world could be like, and how to be effective in our efforts while sustaining ourselves and our movements. Governments, corporations, the military, and the elite have countless foundations and think tanks that devote huge amounts of time and resources to the development of analysis and strategies for concentrating power and wealth and maintaining the status quo. Please consider making time for a study group in your organization, with your fellow activists, schoolmates, co-workers, housemates, neighbors, or friends. Invite people to participate, choose, and copy relevant articles to be read, have discussion questions ready, spend some time to relate what you read to your group's own situation/s, and above all, aim for equal participation.

A Study Group Manual for Globalize Liberation with suggestions for how to pull together a study group, select readings, and facilitate discussion is available at:

www.globalizeliberation.org

background photo: Josh Warren White

Introduction

The New Radicalism: Uprooting the System and Building A Better World

By David Solnit

A twenty-year veteran of mass direct-action organizing, street confrontations, and jails, David Solnit has used creativity and strategy to help build radical mass movements for positive change and common-sense social revolution in the United States and globally. He helped to initiate and was an organizer of the direct-action shutdown of the World Trade Organization in Seattle in 1999. He cofounded Art and Revolution, and as a puppeteer and arts organizer, he has helped to popularize the use of street theater, culture, and puppets as an innovative form of resistance in social-change movements and street actions throughout North America. In global justice, antiwar, environmental justice, workers', antiauthoritarian, international solidarity, human rights, and community struggles he has worked to popularize the use of direct democracy and direct action. He works with Code Orange Affinity Group, a part of Direct Action to Stop the War, which coordinated the shutdown of San Francisco's Financial District on March 20, 2003, the day after the full-scale U.S. invasion of Iraq, and is currently waging an ongoing direct-action campaign for "Democracy, Not Empire." He lives and works as a carpenter in Oakland, California.

A new radicalism has risen up across the globe.

It offers the hope of building a better world by actively confronting, and uprooting the system that is the cause of our social and ecological problems. (Radical, like radish, comes from the Latin *rad* and means *to get to the root of.*) In many places this new world is already under construction.

The new radicalism has many names or no name at all. It often operates below the official radar, unacknowledged by the world of corporate media soundbites, politicians, official policies and politics. Because it is hard to name, more complex than a headline, and seeks to make fundamental changes rather than superficial reforms, it often goes unrecognized, sometimes even by its own participants.

Its common-sense principles and rebellious spirit have always been with us, but this new radicalism is a dramatic departure from previous efforts to effect change. It transcends simplistic generalizations about form or method: It has no international headquarters, no political party, no traditional leaders or politicians running for office, and no uniform ideology or ten-point platform. Rather, it takes many forms and expresses itself differently in different places and communities across the globe. Not only is the new radicalism increasingly popular and widespread, it is also incredibly innovative in fostering a wide range of creative new ways to struggle for change.

From the streets of San Francisco:
"They succeeded this morning—they shut the city down," said San Francisco cop Drew Cohen, as 20,000 outraged residents occupied and blockaded intersections and corporate and government headquarters across San Francisco's downtown financial district on March 20, 2003—the day after the U.S. full-scale invasion of Iraq. "They're highly organized, but they are totally spontaneous. The protesters are always a few steps ahead of us," he added.

to the neighborhoods of Buenos Aires:
"We are nothing. We will be everything" and "Parque Lezama Asamblea" read the banners hung out the second-story windows of the occupied bank. The neighbors had broken into and taken over the former bank building as I arrived in the Parque Lezama neighborhood in Buenos Aires, Argentina. Middle-aged and scruffy young neighbors carried out debris together, scrubbed windows and floors, and hooked up the electricity without permission. At dusk, when it was clean and the fluorescent lights above turned on, they all gathered inside for an "assembly" to discuss how best to use the former bank to benefit the neighborhood. Ideas ranged from providing services like healthcare, food, classes, and cultural events for the neighborhood to making it a center where they and other

neighborhoods that had formed assemblies in the wake of Argentina's economic collapse could meet together.

to the fields of South Florida:
"Consciousness plus action equals change," explained Lucas in the well-worn, mural-covered storefront center in the low-income farmworker town of Immokalee. The group he is a part of, the Coalition of Immokalee Workers (CIW), was organized with other Mexican, Guatemalan, and Haitian immigrant workers in conditions that established unions won't deal with. Their actions have included three communitywide general strikes, a nationwide boycott of Taco Bell (owned by the largest restaurant corporation in the world and the biggest buyer of the tomatoes picked by workers in Immokalee), and three crosscountry "truth tours," culminating in massive protests at Taco Bell's headquarters in Southern California. They showed us the simple drawings about work conditions that they put up around town and use in discussions with other workers about their situation. They explained to me how they use popular education and develop participants' leadership skills ("We are all leaders," they say.), and how through political action they have won dignity and concrete improvements while linking to other movements and looking toward deeper changes.

These and countless other movements, uprisings, and living examples of people asserting their power to control their own lives, all constitute the new radicalism. Though very different, these struggles share some basic principles in common and understand that they are joined in a shared struggle to create a better world. More and more, movements in different sectors of society and in different parts of the world are seeing the fight in their community as part a bigger global battle.

If we are to move beyond old, tried-and-failed methods of attempting to create change and respond to our rapidly evolving world it is essential that we examine the effective forms of resistance and communication, and the positive alternatives that are emerging and flourishing around the world. These movements could well be our last best hope—our only way out of an ugly future of misery, endless war, social and ecological collapse. This book is an effort to give voice to this movement of movements and to consciously recognize and articulate the ideas and spirit that unite these diverse efforts and tactics into a new and profound radicalism. The essays included here outline an understanding of the nature and root causes of our problems, highlight new ways of making changes at a deep level, and provide inspiring examples of how people everywhere are implementing this new radicalism where they live.

A Movement of Movements

The new radicalism is a movement of movements, a network of networks, not merely intent on changing the world, but—as the Zapatistas describe—making a new one in which many worlds will fit. It is a patchwork quilt of hope sewn together with countless hands, actions, songs, e-mails, and dreams into a whole that is much greater than the sum of its pieces.

These movements, with their new ways of organizing, resistance, communication, and new forms of alternative institutions, represent a dramatic departure from the last century's prevailing strategies of working for change. A common theme within the new radicalism is the practice of letting the means determine the ends. Unless the community or world we want is built into and reflected by the struggle to achieve it, movements will always be disappointed in their efforts. Groups, political parties, or movements that are hierarchically structured themselves cannot change the antidemocratic and hierarchical structures of governments, corporations, and corporate capitalism. Many of the twentieth-century's major efforts—reforming existing institutions or governments in order to make them kinder and gentler, or overthrowing them and then occupying and replicating those same or similar structures of power—were ultimately not successful, and in the worst cases they left a legacy of disaster and betrayal for those who gave their sweat and blood in the fight for a better world. The term "Left," has sadly lumped authoritarian groups, parties, governments, and dictators together with genuinely democratic social movements, and "Left" and "Right" are no longer adequate to describe the complex political spectrum of the twenty-first century.

Unless positive new ideas and methods are more clearly articulated and widely explored, people and movements striving for a better world will remain trapped in the failed models of the past. Without a creative break from these patterns we doom ourselves to stagnant movements, another generation of disheartened radicals, and a world unchanged. It is desperately clear that we need to articulate new ways of making change. The new radicalism has been birthed from this desire to popularize and self-organize mass movements from the ground up using these new ways.

It's time to throw out the old mythology that a single organization, ideology, or network can effectively change the world. The era of monolithic movements and international political parties is over. "Correct" political lines, one-ideology-fits-all, rigid blueprints, and cookie-cutter solutions won't work. Instead, the new radicalism finds its hopeful possibilities in the diverse interconnected movement of movements that has risen up around the planet. These movements are distinct in each culture, community, and place, and this diversity is at the heart of the new radicalism's strength and appeal. This movement of movements represents the evolution of a new model of unity and expanded definitions of solidarity. This is the unity of acting in concert, finding points of convergence, making alliances and building networks, and networks of networks, that articulate a "NO" to the system, louder and more effectively than the sum of all our individual "NO's." The new radicalism has emerged organically as the impacted peoples of the world have listened to and connected with each other's experience. Out of this instinct has come mutual respect and a common understanding of the interlocking systems that keep us all down in different ways. This is the healthy biodiversity of an ecosystem of resistance.

The corporate globalized system attempts to impose a rigid homogeneity on the world—everywhere the same food, prepackaged culture, and products. In contrast, the strength of our movements lies in their fluidity and difference.

Perceptions and priorities are different based on who and where people are in the world, and this is healthy. Women, people of color, queers/lesbians/gay men, indigenous people, rural people, inner city folks, youth, unemployed, students, and so, on all have their own interests and perspectives. By linking local movements to regional struggles to global battles, and by doing the hard work of recognizing our different inheritance of relative privilege and oppression, we can build alliances across divides of culture, identity, belief, and place, and maybe we can transcend the limitations of single issues or isolated resistance.

This movement of movements encompasses endless communities: cultural resistance workers, community organizations, unions, those fighting for clean air and water, against prison expansion or police brutality, or for living wages, health care, and education. The new radicalism is contesting power on many fronts—creatively liberating political space from the system's hold to allow our dreams of real democracy, a just society, and a hopeful future to take root.

Common Principles

New radical movements, while they are different everywhere, seem to share some common principles and spirit. Some of these are: the commitment to uprooting the system that is the cause of our social and ecological problems; doing it ourselves with people power and direct action; making change without taking power; practicing direct democracy in our resistance and in the world we create; and making our efforts a laboratory of resistance, creating new language and new forms of struggle.

Uprooting the System

Our problems are systemic. They did not start and won't end with one particular injustice, politician, political party, government administration, corporation, or financial institution. Patrick Reinsborough writes in his contribution to this book, "Decolonizing the Revolutionary Imagination," "The blatancy of the corporate power grab and the accelerating ecological meltdown is evidence that we do not live in an era where we can afford the luxury of fighting the symptoms." This crisis calls for "a dramatic divergence from the slow progression of single-issue politics, narrow constituencies, and Band-Aid solutions." Reinsborough warns that "Too often the framework of issue-based struggle needs to affirm the existing system in order to win concessions and thus fails to nurture the evolution of more systemic movements."

This is not to say we don't need to fight for day-to-day short-term survival and dignity, but that those struggles can and should be understood in the context of a bigger systemic struggle so that our various efforts become cumulative rather than competitive.

Corporate globalization, which attacks nearly every sector of society and the environment in every country across the planet, provides an incredible opportunity to move our local, regional, and national struggles into a global framework for systemic change. In organizing for the Seattle resistance to the WTO, the Direct Action Network articulated this systemic analysis in its call to action:

> War, Low Wages, Deforestation, Gentrification, Gridlocked Cities, Genetic Engineering, The Rich Getting Richer, Cuts in Social Services, Increasing Poverty, Meaningless Jobs, Global Warming, More Prisons, Sweatshops. . . . All this didn't just spring from nowhere, but is the result of an economic and political system that is GOING GLOBAL. The resistance to it, if it is to be effective, must also be global.

Different movements, communities, and people have different ways of naming and looking at the system. In this book you will encounter many different names for the system: corporate capitalism, doomsday economy, patriarchy, white supremacy, neoliberalism, corporate globalization, colonialism, imperialism, industrialism, empire, militarism, the State, the money king, and so on.

I remember the first meeting of San Francisco's Direct Action to Stop the War in October 2002, when the group agreed that we would work to stop the war and also to uproot the system behind it. We chose not to define "the system" more specifically because people had different ways of naming it. By leaving it open we were able to work together with a diversity of perspectives and not have to agree on a single framework for how we saw the system. Many of us, I think, see the system as a number of interlocking institutions and oppressive social relations.

Later on, in May 2003 after the full-scale U.S. invasion of Iraq, we wanted to articulate a deeper systemic understanding of the war. We modified our goals to more clearly articulate the system, calling it "empire," and created a framework of resistance that would be inclusive of all the different struggles against it in our community. The goal we adopted was: "End the war for empire and uproot the system behind it." We then defined empire as including three interlocking parts:

Military war and occupation, including U.S. military presence throughout the world and support for war and occupation through other regimes;

Economic war to impose corporate globalization on the world, including the IMF, World Bank, WTO, NAFTA, FTAA, CAFTA, and Middle East Free Trade Agreement;

War at home, including racial injustice, sexism and patriarchy, cuts in and privatization of basic services, environmental injustice and ecological destruction, and attacks on civil liberties, immigrants, low-income communities, communities of color, unions, waged and unwaged workers.

Direct Action
Strikes, occupations, blockades, civil disobedience, sit-ins, boycotts, street parties, shut downs and mass non-cooperation, are on the rise everywhere as people give up on the crisis-ridden established channels for change—elections, law enforcement and regulatory agencies, and attempts at corporate reform. Direct action is the wide range of do-it-yourself forms of people-power that allow communities and movements to assert their power to make change themselves.

In his essay "Organizing Communities: Building Neighborhood Movements for Radical Change," Tom Knoche defines direct action:

Direct actions are those that take the shortest route toward realization of the ends desired, without depending on intermediaries. A simple example might help to clarify. If a group of tenants is having a problem with a landlord refusing to make needed repairs, they can respond in several ways. They could take the landlord to court. They could get the housing and health inspectors to issue violations and pressure the landlord to make repairs. Or they could withhold rent from the landlord themselves, and use the money withheld to pay for the repairs. Along the same vein, they might picket the landlord's nice suburban home and leaflet all of his neighbors with information about how he treats people. The first two options put responsibility for getting something done in the hands of a government agency or law enforcement official. The latter courses of action keep the tenants in control of what happens.

Direct action has been instrumental in the struggles for dignity of all manner of oppressed and marginalized peoples and it continues to be central to the new radicalism.

As George Lakey recounts the impacts of mass nonviolent direct action in his article "Strategizing for a Living Revolution," "the Philippine dictator Marcos was overthrown by 'people power' in 1986; Communist dictatorships had been overthrown by people power in East Germany, Czechoslovakia, Hungary, and Poland in 1989; commanders in the KGB, the Soviet Army and the Communist Party were prevented by people power from establishing a coup in Russia in 1991; a mass uprising in Thailand prevented a top military general from consolidating his power in 1993; the South African whites' monopoly on political rule was broken in 1994 after a decade of people's struggle. In all these places the power-holders found their power slipping away because those they depended on refused any longer to follow the script." Lakey adds that mass nonviolent action played a decisive role in ousting one-party states and dictatorships in Argentina, Haiti, the Baltic States, Mali, Malawi, Madagascar, and Benin. Most recently the government of Bolivia, after attempting to "privatize" or give away to corporations the nation's natural gas, was overthrown with strikes, highway and road blockades, and mass protests in October 2003.

Direct action operates on a different analysis than a conventional view of power. The conventional view of power sees some people holding power— politicians, CEOs, bosses, generals—whom the rest of us need to influence, pressure, or even replace if we want to change things. People-power sees power as a fragile relationship. Those in positions of power are dependent on the cooperation and acquiescence of the people they hold power over. When people organize themselves to withdraw their cooperation the power holders' grasp on power begins to weaken and crumble. If people sustain their resistance they can force changes or even topple those in power.

Direct action works most effectively when it is part of an ongoing campaign and is planned strategically to maximize popular participation and support, in order to be able to respond well to attempts to marginalize, co-opt or repress it. As Lakey says, "Campaigns put us on the offensive. A campaign is a focussed mobilization of energy with a clear objective, often in the form of a demand."

Direct action has always been the fuel of grassroots movements and is key to the successes of the new radicalism. From winning concrete improvements in people's lives to toppling governments, direct action wins concrete victories as it aims for underlying changes.

Making Change Without Taking Power
The world cannot be changed for the better by taking power.

Capturing positions of state power, either through elections or insurrection, misses the point that the aim of uprooting the system is to fundamentally change the relations of power at the root of our problems.

"To pose a truly radical alternative to the system, it must challenge not just who holds power, but the very nature of power as well," explains Starhawk in her essay, "A Feminist View of Global Justice." The old hierarchical model of power, often called power-over is articulated by Starhawk, "Power-over, domination or control, is the power wielded by an individual or elite who can control the resources and choices of others, and impose punishment on them if they do not acquiesce."

The alternative model of power has many names—power-with, counter-power, horizontalism—all referring to the restructuring of power relations so that everyone has power over the things that matter in their own life and communities. There is a vast and growing area throughout many societies of do-it-yourself (DIY) activity directed toward changing the world that does not have the state as its focus and does not aim at gaining positions of power. This is the hopeful way in which a radically new society is being experimented with and constructed, based on a fundamentally different model of organization, decisionmaking, and definitions of power.

Challenging the model of power-over also means understanding and dismantling all forms of oppression—including oppression and privilege based on race, class, and gender. Helen Luu in her essay "Discovering a Different Space of Resistance: Personal Reflections on Anti-Racist

Organizing" says, "a movement/coalition of movements that is dedicated to bringing down all forms of oppression simultaneously with challenging global capitalism is the kind of movement we must endeavor to work toward if we are truly serious about fighting for a world that is free and just for all." The system is not just our external social relationships, but it is also internalized in our movements, and in ourselves.

The Zapatistas were perhaps the first massive social movement to explicitly articulate this model of making change without taking power. Elizabeth (Betita) Martínez, explaining the Zapatista rejection of taking power explains they are, "Not proposing to take power but rather to contribute to a vast movement that would return power to civil society, using different forms of struggle." Manuel Callahan explains in "Zapatismo Beyond Chiapas," " 'Everything for everyone, nothing for ourselves' underscores the Zapatistas' commitment to define struggle not by taking state power, but imagining a new world, 'a world where many worlds fit.' "

In Argentina the popular rebellion that arose in the wake of the IMF-World Bank economic collapse embraced this notion of a new model of power. As Patricio McCabe writes in his essay "Argentina's New Forms of Resistance," "The refusal to delegate to others the solutions to the problems in our lives is extending to sectors of the population and allows experiences of self-management previously unthinkable in this corner of the world."

John Holloway's recent book *Change the World Without Taking Power* helps contextualize this trend within the evolution of contemporary social movement. Holloway writes:

> For most of the last century, efforts to create a better world worthy of humanity were focussed on the state and the winning of state power. The main controversies (between reformists and revolutionaries) were about how to win state power, whether by parliamentary or extra-parliamentary means. The history of the twentieth century suggests the question of how to win state power was not very important. In all cases the winning of state power failed to bring about the changes the militants hoped for. Neither reformist nor revolutionary governments succeeded in changing the world. It's easy to accuse the leaderships of these movements of "betraying" the movements which they led. So many betrayals suggest however, that the failure of radical, socialist or communist governments lies much deeper. We can now see that the idea that the world could be changed through the state was an illusion. We are fortunate to be living at the end of that illusion.

The institution of national governments (and the even more blatantly antidemocratic corporations) is part of the root of our social and ecological problems. State power has a logic and momentum of its own. The state is hard-wired to hold on to and keep power concentrated in its hands. This, coupled with the logic of a corporate-ruled global economy, has meant that even good-hearted, well-intentioned leaders are almost powerless to radically solve problems and improve their society.

An increasing number of movements are taking the direct-action analysis of power and extending it beyond oppositional resistance into how they will reorganize society based on a different model of power.

Direct Democracy
Real, direct democracy gives everyone power over the decisions and resources in our lives— in our neighborhoods, towns, schools, workplaces, and the world we pass on to our children. The arenas where people directly participate in the decisions that affect them are growing: community and neighborhood organizations, social change movements, and alternative institutions, are on the rise. Direct democracy means voting with our feet, our hands, our voices, and our imagination, every day of the year.

Direct democracy is the how the people apply the alternative "power-with" model of power to reorganize their communities and society, creating positive alternatives to the dominant undemocratic institutions. As Cindy Milstein describes in "Democracy is Direct," "directly democratic institutions open a public space in which everyone, if they so choose, can come together in a deliberative and decisionmaking body; a space where everyone has the opportunity to persuade or be persuaded; a space where no discussion or decision is ever hidden, and where it can always be returned to for scrutiny, accountability, or rethinking." Marina Sitrin in her essay, "Weaving Imagination and Creation: The Future in the Present" writes, "The Zapatistas in Mexico, the collectives and assemblies, occupied factories and movements of the unemployed in Argentina, the movements in South Africa, are all movements and struggles that are inspiring attempts at direct democracy and collective decisionmaking. They also reflect various forms of a future vision of a society free from need, yet full of desire."

Direct democracy can be realized both in how we organize our resistance to an antidemocratic system and in the better world we construct to take its place. The affinity groups—the small five-to-twenty-person basic planning and decisionmaking groups for the mass direct actions of many social movements in North America and Europe—and the spokescouncils through which they coordinate are examples of directly democratic organizing of oppositional struggle. George Lakey tells the stories of student radicals in Serbia and Burma who catalyzed direct action uprisings to remove their respective dictators. The students in Serbia "would be the first to admit that a mass insurgency that brings down a dictator is not enough—not enough to establish full democracy, respect for diversity, economic institutions in harmony with the earth, or other parts of their vision. It's one thing to open up a power vacuum through noncooperation (and that is a great and honorable achievement). It's another thing to firmly establish the democratic community we deserve. For that, the strategy must go deeper. We need to create a strategy that builds at the same time as it destroys. We need a strategy that validates alternatives, supports the experience of freedom, and expands the skills of cooperation."

Sometimes called dual power or parallel institutions, these living laboratories of a directly democratic community and world are essential to not just envision but to create viable organized models that create spaces of freedom in the existing world and act to prefigure the world we want to create to replace the present undemocratic order.

Reorganizing our communities to be directly democratic does not mean that we will not still have to publicly debate and struggle for decisions that affirm everyone's humanity, dignity, life, and protect our air, water, and land. Milstein continues, "Embryonic within direct democracy are values such as equality, diversity, cooperation, and value for human worth— hopefully the building blocks of a liberatory ethics as we begin to self manage our communities, our economy, and society, in an ever-widening circle of confederated citizen assemblies."

Laboratory of Resistance
New forms of resistance, communication, and organizing have been key to the successes of the new radicalism. Mixing innovation, intuition and strategy, new movements have developed new language, new actions, and new ideas of change. Imagine if the Zapatista uprising had used the language of the old Left (or the old New Left) instead of coming up with fresh ways of expressing their ideas through poetic communiqués and fables. In the introduction to the book, *Zapatistas* Harry Cleaver says, "For growing numbers of people the old words have grown stale. And as they reject the old words, they are searching for new ones. They are rethinking not only their vocabulary, but the world." The new radicalism is rethinking not only its rhetoric and its actions but also the way we organize ourselves and the alternatives we strive to create.

When we shift our thinking to see our organizing and actions as a laboratory then we can see our actions and projects as experiments. In keeping with this spirit, much of the value of the experiment is in the evaluation and discussion of what we learned. If we learn something from an experiment it is a success. Without experimentation we condemn ourselves to repeat the same tactics, forms of resistance, communication, and organization. To do so is to risk our movements becoming stagnant, our actions boring, and our resistance predictable. By infusing our political work with the humility and curiosity that comes with experimentation we create new political opportunities and make it that much more difficult for the powers that be to contain, co-opt, marginalize, or repress us.

Now is the Time

Throughout the world, two projects of globalization are in dispute: The one from above that globalizes conformity, cynicism, stupidity, war, destruction, death, and amnesia. And the one from below, that globalizes rebellion, hope, creativity, intelligence, imagination, life, memory, building a world where many worlds fit. —Subcomandante Marcos, Zapatista Army of National Liberation, Statement to Via Campesina, Cancun, Mexico, September 2003

We live in a global crisis. Human misery and displacement, ecological meltdown, the antidemocratic concentration of power and wealth, and a state of endless war have reached an unprecedented scale. It is a time with disastrous and possibly apocalyptic consequences if we do not uproot and replace the current system. There is no guarantee that positive social movements based on solidarity and community will win. Racist, fascist, and religious fundamentalist forces are also on the move, attempting to harness the widespread discontent and stoking fears.

We also live in a time with great opportunity for deep, positive, radical changes in the world. Social movements are bigger, more democratic, and more connected than at any time in the past. The biggest worldwide demonstration in history of over 12 million people protesting against the U.S. invasion of Iraq took place on February 15, 2003 and was organized in less than two months by interconnected social movements on every continent. At the same time, the global economic system, the corporations, and the U.S. government are facing a historic loss of legitimacy around the world. When a tyrant, system, or empire loses it legitimacy or its perceived "right to govern" in the eyes of the governed it is only a matter of time before it is overthrown or collapses.

We in the United States are in a unique position to contribute to making a better world as well as the betterment of our own lives and communities. We saw with the direct action shutdown of the WTO in Seattle that our resistance, because of where and who we are, can have massive global consequences. It showed how quickly history can shift.

What happens here in the United States and the northern industrialized countries is key. We are in the control room of the doomsday machine. Can we stop it? Can we work with our neighbors, coworkers, and communities to organize widespread open resistance and practical alternative institutions in the United States? If so, we can have a massive impact in checking our government's global reach and giving breathing space to movements around the world. Can we in the United States help create a new movement of movements to catalyze a long-term, effective uprising in the heart of the empire? Will we step up to the plate and join with movements around the world? Do we have the guts and imagination? Many people around the world are waiting for the people of the United States to join them in serious rebellion against the empire.

The future is up for grabs and the potential for a better world is within our grasp. Tastes of what a better world would be like are all around us, and models of how society can be reorganized to favor people and the planet exist in some of our alternative community institutions and in parts of our social change movements at home and around the world. All we have to do is change everything. Let's take a step and keep walking there together.

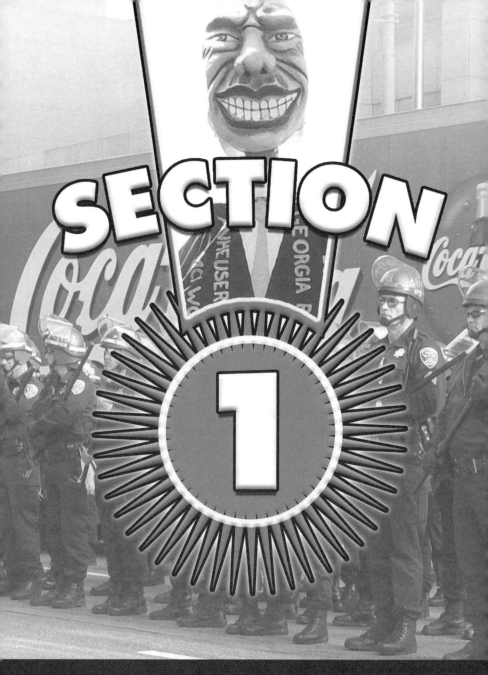

SECTION

1

WHAT'S THE PROBLEM?

photos: David Hanks

Photo: David Hanks; Puppet: David Morely and K Ruby of Wise Fool Puppet Intervention

The Money King Is Only an Illusion

U'wa Traditional Authorities

A message from the U'wa Traditional Authorities, delivered on May 7, 2002, from Cubará, Boyacá, Colombia, to the national and international public, issued upon the withdrawal of Occidental Petroleum from U'wa sacred territory.

Today we invite all of our fellow children of the earth to join us in telling the world that Mother Earth is alive, that the U'wa are alive, and that the joining of many voices, hands, cries, writings, meditations, and thoughts are what set people free from aggressors and destroyers.

We all belong to the divine creation, and as such we deserve respect. Mother Earth, despite being violated, continues to silently feed and sustain us. She doesn't feel envy. She speaks but very few listen to her voice. She cries out insistently but everything continues the same. This worries us, but we the U'wa and friends of the U'wa will continue to defend her with our voice, our sacred fasts, our songs, our faith.

photo top: Terrence Freitas

INDIGENOUS

Brothers and sisters, the air, water, sun, and moon are contaminated and they are being destroyed. This worries us because if humanity wants to continue to live we should be making decisions to prevent our self-destruction. No one destroys man. Man destroys himself. The U'wa want to avoid the destruction of the world because we want to continue to live.

Terrence Freitas

The money king is only an illusion. Capitalism is blind and barbaric. It buys consciences, governments, peoples, and nations. It poisons the water and the air. It destroys everything. And to the U'wa, it says that we are crazy, but we want to continue being crazy if it means we can continue to exist on our dear Mother Earth.

Brother and sisters of the world, the U'wa will continue defending Mother Earth. We invite you to join us.

How The U'wa and People's Globalization Beat Big Oil

By Patrick Reinsborough

Patrick Reinsborough is a long-term U'wa supporter and indigenous rights activist committed to amplifying earth-centered voices within the global justice movement.

When the story of Colombia's indigenous U'wa people first hit the world stage in the mid-nineties it was an all-too-familiar tragic tale: a ruthless multinational oil company invades the homelands of a traditional culture, threatening their way of life and a fragile ecosystem. It was a new twist on the same 500-year-old story of conquistadors, invasion, and genocide that shaped the Americas, only this time the gold that the invaders were willing to kill for was black.

For the U'wa (a name that means "the thinking people"), oil is *ruira*, meaning "the blood of Mother Earth," and to extract it would violate their most sacred beliefs. For Los Angeles–based Occidental Petroleum (OXY), oil is the lucrative drug of choice for industrial society and the fast track to record profits.

But on May 3, 2002, at the Occidental shareholders' meeting in Los Angeles the inspiring story of U'wa resistance turned a historic page when OXY announced that they were abandoning their concessions on U'wa land. Despite assuring investors for eight years of a major oil strike and only pursuing one drill site in the region, OXY was now suddenly claiming that there was no oil in the region. In other words, when you strip away the corporate PR, the uncompromising resistance of the U'wa and the pressure of the international solidarity campaign had worked to drive OXY out of U'wa land!

The announcement came nearly a year after OXY retreated from the Gibraltar 1 drill site, which thousands of U'wa, local campesinos, trade unionists, and students had occupied to prevent oil drilling. After using the Colombian military to brutally evict the protesters and militarize the region, OXY was unable to find oil at the site. This came as no surprise to the U'wa, whose Werjayas ("wise elders") had been doing spiritual work for months to "move" the oil away from OXY's drills.

OXY's largest institutional investor, mutual fund giant Fidelity Investments, was targeted for demonstrations and direct actions at over seventy-five locations around the world, including London, Tokyo, and forty cities across the United States. Within six months Fidelity had dumped over 60 percent of their holdings in the oil company. During the 2000 presidential elections, U'wa supporters in the United States confronted OXY's most politically connected shareholder, former vice president Al Gore (who has long-standing personal ties to OXY), and disrupted over 100 of his campaign appearances, including several nationally televised events. Across the planet there was a tidal wave of actions that showed people from all different movements and communities stood in solidarity with the U'wa.

The significance of this victory cannot be overstated. It was a victory not only for the U'wa and their thousands of allies but also a victory for all impacted communities fighting the devastation of resource extraction around the world. Although it is not the final victory for the U'wa, it is a major milestone in their decade-long struggle to defend their culture and homeland and teach the outside world that "if we kill the earth then no one will live."

But as with all victories this one has come with losses. We must remember the spirits of those who gave their lives as part of the struggle to defend

INDIGENOUS

the U'wa land and culture. Remember Terrence Frietas, Ingrid Washinawatok, and Lahe'ena'e Gay, three indigenous rights activists who were kidnapped from U'wa territory and murdered by Revolutionary Armed Forces of Columbia (FARC) guerrillas in March 1999. Remember the three indigenous children who were killed in February 2000 when the military attacked U'wa blockades. Remember the twenty noncombatants who are being murdered in Colombia's U.S.-funded war every day, as well as the numerous cultures, species, and ecosystems that have already been lost across the region.

The U'wa struggle for survival has become a symbol of resistance to oil exploration, corporate-led globalization, and American militarism. Over the last five years, the U'wa call for people of all races and cultures to unite their struggles into "a global crusade to defend life" has sparked a massive international solidarity campaign. Hundreds of demonstrations were organized in dozens of countries around the world by groups ranging from U.S.-based Rainforest Action Network to London's Reclaim the Streets, the Italian Green Party, and the movement to stop the Narmada Dam in India.

The growing connections between different resistance movements around the planet allows new opportunities for activists from the global North to use their privilege and access as tools for justice and change. The corporate-rule system relies on a gulf of ignorance and complacency to separate the communities who benefit from resource extraction from those communities whose cultures and homelands are destroyed by it. But as the U'wa campaign and others like it have shown, when global North activists frame struggles for peace, justice, and ecology around amplifying the voices of impacted communities, some of the world's most powerful corporations can be stopped. The example of the U'wa struggle reveals the potential of people's globalization campaigns to break the silence about who pays the price for corporate greed and overconsumption.

The U'wa struggle to defend their cloud-forest home is the embodiment of the clash of worldviews that defines the globalization era. Across the planet cultures with ancient spiritual traditions of living in balance with the earth are under attack by soulless multinational corporations that see the earth's resources only as commodities to exploit. The time has come for all of us to choose sides: Are we with those who fight to defend the earth or with those who would destroy it for personal profit?

In a communiqué from 1998 the U'wa wrote: "We are seeking an explanation for this 'progress' that goes against life." In their victory communiqué the U'wa speak of the illusion they eloquently call the

INDIGENOUS

David Hanks

U'wa rights activists occupy a Los Angeles intersection during the 2000 Democratic Convention, exposing presidential candidate Al Gore's ties to Occidental Petroleum, July 2000.

"money king." These simple profound words remind us that the World Bank economists, Wall Street financiers, corporate CEO's and their counterparts on Capitol Hill and at the Pentagon are blinded by the flawed assumptions of modern finance capitalism. Their schemes to globalize exploitation, environmental devastation, and corporate profits under the banner of "progress" misrepresent stock portfolios as prosperity while they liquidate the true biological wealth of the planet.

As we work for a different world—globalizing solidarity, dignity, justice, and ecological sanity—we must look to indigenous resistance to help us relearn and articulate earth-centered values. For over 500 years peoples like the U'wa have fought to protect their land and way of life from waves of invaders. Let us learn from their example and place standing in solidarity, with all the planet's indigenous cultures at the center of our strategies to build a better world.

The U'wa will continue to need our support and we will continue to need their leadership, clarity, and inspiring example as we show the oil industry that they can no longer invade pristine ecosystems, violate the rights of indigenous cultures, and destabilize the global climate. United as diverse peoples' movements, we can put a stop to corporate rule, wars for oil, and

INDIGENOUS

the doomsday economics that puts the interests of a few multinational corporations ahead of the future of life on planet earth.

So celebrate the U'wa victory and let it fuel your passion to defend the earth, knowing that our work is far from done. But with each milestone, each victory, each action, each celebration, we are getting closer and closer. Most important, let us work to magnify the inspiring voices of frontline resistance communities. For in their courage, defiance, and wisdom we see that indeed another world is possible! *Qué viva los U'wa!*

CHAPTER

2

Our Resistance Is as Transnational as Capital

By John Jordan

John Jordan is a longtime arts and direct–action organizer. He worked for nearly a decade with the performance-social intervention group Platform. He has been involved in the British antiroad movement and was an active participant in Reclaim the Streets' pioneering street parties, international days of action in '98 and '99, and their imaginative and gutsy catalyzing of direct-action anticapitalism. He is a coeditor of We Are Everywhere: The Irresistible Rise of Global Anticapitalism.

Capital has always been global. From the slave trade of earlier centuries to the imperial colonization of lands and cultures across the world, its boundless drive for expansion—for short term financial gain—has recognized no limits. Backed up by state power, capitalist accumulation has created widespread social and ecological devastation wherever it has extended.

But now, capitalism is attempting a new strategy to reassert and intensify its dominance over us. Its name is economic

GLOBALIZATION

globalization, and it consists of the dismantling of national limitations to trade and to the free movement of capital. It enables companies, driven by the demands of the rapacious gambling of money markets, to ransack the entire globe in search for ever higher profits, lowering wages and environmental standards in their wake. Globalization is arguably the most fundamental redesign of the planet's political and economic arrangements since the Industrial Revolution.

—Global Street Party agitprop, May 16, 1998

Recognizing the Common Enemy

International solidarity and global protest is nothing new—from the European revolutions of 1848 to the upheavals of 1917–18 following the Russian Revolution to the lightning flashes that erupted nearly everywhere in 1968, struggle has long been able to connect globally. But what is perhaps unique to our times is the speed and ease with which we can communicate, and the fact that globalization means that diverse people living in very different cultures around the world now share a common enemy. As this enemy becomes increasingly less subtle and more excessive—"capitalism with its gloves off"—it therefore becomes easier to recognize, understand, and ultimately dismantle.

Before the onslaught of globalization, "the system" was sometimes hard to recognize with all of its many manifestations and policies. But the reduction of diversity in the corporate landscape and the concentration of power within international institutions such as the International Monetary Fund (IMF), the World Trade Organization (WTO), and the financial markets has clarified things and offered a focal point for protest and opposition. It's a lot easier to oppose a concentrated uniform power structure than it is to confront diffuse and flexible forms.[1]

Diversity versus Uniformity

As power becomes more and more concentrated, those opposing it are becoming more diverse and fluid, hence much harder to defuse and undermine. Moreover, as the elite, their transnational corporations, and their puppets the IMF and WTO attempt to impose "free market" policies on every country on the planet, they are unwittingly creating a situation where previously separate movements are able to recognize each other's struggles as related, and they are beginning to work together on an unprecedented scale.[2]

GLOBALIZATION

Andrew Stern / www.andrewstern.net

On the final day of the protests against the WTO, the Korean delegation attached ropes to the fence and the crowd pulled at the ropes until the fence was completely demolished. Cancun, Mexico. September 2003.

The global "race to the bottom" in which workers, communities, and whole countries are forced to compete by lowering wages, standards for working conditions, environmental protections, and social spending to facilitate maximum profit is stimulating resistance all over the world. People everywhere are realizing that this resistance is pointless if done in isolation. For example, say your community manages, after years of tireless campaigning, to shut down your local toxic waste dump, what does the transnational company that owns the dump do? They simply move it to wherever the costs are less and the resistance weaker, probably somewhere in the Third World or eastern Europe.[3] Under this system, communities have a stark choice; either compete fiercely with each other or cooperate in resisting the destruction of lives, land, and livelihoods by rampaging capital.[4]

Herbert Read in *The Philosophy of Anarchism*[5] wrote, "Progress is measured by the degree of differentiation within a society." The president of the Nabisco Corporation would obviously disagree; he's "looking forward to the day when Arabs and Americans, Latinos and Scandinavians, will be munching Ritz crackers as enthusiastically as they already drink Coke or brush their teeth with Colgate."[6] Progress in the present system is measured by economic growth, which inevitably means monoculture. To accelerate profit and create economies of scale, global capital imposes

11

GLOBALIZATION

Mariana Mora

Zapatista women set up protective encirclement of community.

monoculture on the world, making everywhere look and feel like everywhere else, with the same restaurants, the same hotels, the same supermarkets filled with the same Muzak. But by embracing each other in their diversity, emerging social movements are posing powerful challenges to capital's addiction to uniformity.

Space for Utopian Thinking

Capital was only able to become truly global after the fall of the Berlin Wall and the breakup of the Eastern bloc. But although the end of the European experiment with communism opened up the space for unrestrained capitalism, it also gave a new lease on life to radical movements.[7] For more than seventy years, Soviet socialism had been held up as the model of revolutionary society, and although it was a total social and ecological disaster, its shadow lingered over most radical movements. Those who wished to discredit any forms of revolutionary thinking simply had to point to the Soviet model to prove the inevitable failure of any utopian project.

Now that the Soviet Union has ceased to exist, it has become easier for those working in radical movements to conceive of different models for society. Ideas of utopia can blossom in the space that has been cleared, and the power of radical imagination is back at the center of revolutionary struggle, freed from the framework of a monolithic ideology. It's been recognized that universal rules don't work, that there is not just one way, one utopia to apply globally. The radical social movements that are joining together now don't want to seize power, but rather, to dissolve it. They are not vanguards but catalysts in the revolutionary process. They are dreaming up many alternative forms of social organization, celebrating variety and rejoicing in autonomy.

The Ecology of Struggle

Murray Bookchin, in *Post Scarcity Anarchism*[8] wrote that "in almost every period since the Renaissance the development of revolutionary thought has been heavily influenced by a branch of science." He gives the examples of mathematics and mechanics for the Enlightenment, and evolutionary biology and anthropology for the nineteenth century. Ecology has influenced many of today's social movements, and that is perhaps why their model of organization and coordination resembles an ecological one, why it works like an ecosystem. Highly interconnected, it thrives on diversity, works best when imbedded in its own locality and context, and develops most creatively at the edges, the overlap points, the in-between spaces where different cultures meet, such as the coming together of Earth First! and the logging unions in the United States, or London's subway workers and Reclaim the Streets. The societies that these movements dream of creating will also be like ecosystems, diversified, balanced, and harmonious.[9]

An awareness of ecological crisis influences the way that many of these movements think and act. Kirkpatrick Sale illustrates the scale of the biological meltdown: "More goods and services have been consumed by the generation alive between 1950 and 1990, measured in constant dollars and on a global scale, than by all the generations in all of human history before."[10] The level of ecological destruction is mind-boggling, and the current generation of activists feels an incredible urgency about the future.[11] They know that mere reform is useless because the whole basis of the present system is profoundly antiecological, and they also know that there is no longer any argument for waiting for the right historical conditions for revolution, because time is rapidly running out. Radical creative and subversive change must happen now, simply because there is no time left for anything else.

Transnational Resistance

Capital's loudest message in the early nineties was that there is no alternative to the status quo, and that humanity had reached its highest

GLOBALIZATION

David Hanks

Immigrant rights march, Los Angeles, July 2000.

level. The end of history had arrived. In the 1920s and 1950s this same message was proclaimed by the elites, and the decades that followed, the radical upheavals of the 1930s and the 1960s, showed them that as soon as the end of history is declared it is time for radical change to occur.

On New Year's Day 1994, the day the North American Free Trade Agreement (NAFTA) came into effect, 2,000 indigenous peoples from several groups emerged from the mountains and forests of Chiapas, Mexico. Masked, armed, and calling themselves Zapatistas, their battle cry was *Ya Basta!*, "Enough is Enough!" An extraordinary popular uprising, which was to change the landscape of global resistance forever, had begun. Five towns were occupied and twelve days of fighting ensued. This was not an isolated act of local rebellion— through the Zapatistas' imaginative use of the Internet, people all over the world soon heard of the uprising. These masked rebels from poverty-stricken communities were not simply demanding that their own land and lives be given back, neither were they just asking for international support and solidarity, but they were talking about neoliberalism, about the "death sentence" that NAFTA and other free trade agreements would impose on indigenous people. They were demanding the dissolution of state-corporate power and the development of "civil society," and they were encouraging others all over the world to take up the fight against the enclosure of our lives by capital. Public sympathy in Mexico and abroad was overwhelming. The communiqués[12] coming out of Chiapas were rapidly circulated on the Internet, and there was a new sense of possibility—the Zapatistas and their supporters were weaving an electronic fabric of struggle to carry revolution around the world.[13]

Revolutionary epochs are periods of convergence, when apparently separate processes converge to form a socially explosive crisis.[14] On that cold, misty New Year's Day the Zapatista rebels probably had little idea that their revolt would eventually transform itself into the beginnings of a global revolution. No one realized that the breath of inspiration would travel so far, so quickly, but there are moments when hope is ignited, the hope that everything can be transformed. A critical mass is building— every year, every month, every day it gets bigger and stronger—and reports of strikes, direct actions, protests, and occupations all around the

world flow along the same lines of communication that move the trillions of dollars involved in the reckless, unsustainable money game of transnational capital.

During the May 1968 insurrection in Paris, a message was scrawled on the walls of the Theatre de L'Odeon: "Dare to go where none has gone before you. Dare to think what none has ever thought." Despite capital's rapacious attempts to enclose everything, a space has now been opened up and we can pay attention to that message.

A version of this essay was originally published in Do or Die: Voices from Ecological Resistance, *8, summer 1999.*

GLOBALIZATION

Notes

[1] The engines of capital, the financial markets, may be "anarchic," flexible, and fluid—but they are still governed by one unbreakable law: profit.

[2] A further irony is that the same tools that enable capital to disregard borders and produce commodities thousands of miles away from their markets—the Internet and cheap air travel—are the same tools that are helping global social movements to meet and work with each other. Of course, I am aware of the ecological and social costs of the computer industry and air travel. The only way I can resolve this contradiction is by applying a homeopathic metaphor to it. The word *homeopathy* comes from the Greek and means "similar suffering." The idea is that a substance that can produce symptoms in a healthy person can cure those symptoms in a sick person. For instance, if you suffer from hay fever, with running nose and eyes, then you take a minute dose of onion, because onion juice produces a similar effect. The concept of the minimum dose states that we must use as little medicine as possible to stimulate the body's own healing mechanism. So if we apply this to the use of destructive technologies to enable social change, it is clear that the amount of air travel and Internet used by activists is minute, compared with that used for capitalist gain, and perhaps this minute amount of "poisonous" substance may stimulate the healing capacities of the social body.

[3] See Dr. S. Lewis, "Networks of Struggle," *Corporate Watch*, 8, (spring 1999).

[4] See Jeremy Brecher and Tim Costellos's excellent book about global struggle, *Global Village or Global Pillage: Economic Reconstruction from the Bottom Up,* (Cambridge, Mass: South End Press, 1998).

[5] Read, Herbert, *The Philosophy of Anarchism,* (London: Freedom Press, 1940).

[6] *Trilaterism,* edited by Holly Sklar, 1980, quoted in *The Case Against the Global Economy* and *For a Turn Toward the Local,* Mander and Goldsmith, ed. (San Francisco: Sierra Club Books, 1996).

[7] See "A Handicap Removed" by Dominique Vidal, *Le Monde Diplomatique,* May 1998.

[8] Murray Bookchin, *Post Scarcity Anarchism,* (Montreal: Black Rose Books, 1971).

[9] Ibid.

[10] Kirkpatrick Sale, *Rebels Against the Future: Lessons for the Computer Age* (Quartet Books, 1996).

[11] The generations of the 1950s to 1980s had the threat of nuclear apocalypse hanging over them, but that was a question of probability: if there was a nuclear war. The question is no longer if, because there is certainty that as long as business continues as normal the biosphere will be irrevocably damaged, if it hasn't already been so.

[12] Emanating from Subcommandante Marcos's now legendary battered Olivetti.

[13] See the excellent writings of U.S. academic Harry Cleaver about the Zapatistas and computer-linked social movements at http://www.eco.utexas.edu/faculty/Cleaver/hmchtmlpapers.html

[14] Subcommandante Marcos said, "We ask in the name of all men and women that you save a moment, a few days, a few hours, enough minutes to find the common enemy."

Global Capitalism versus Global Community

By Walden Bello

Walden Bello is executive director of Focus on the Global South, a research, analysis, and advocacy organization based in Bangkok, Thailand, and professor of sociology and public administration at the University of the Philippines. The author of several books, including The Future in the Balance: Essays on Globalization and Resistance, *he is also active in the movement against corporate-driven globalization.*

Capitalism and community have always stood in contradiction to one another. As social analysts from Marx to Karl Polanyi to John Gray have pointed out, capitalist relations are the acid dissolving communal bonds and reconfiguring people into individual atoms whose relations to one another become mediated principally by the market. Under capitalism there is nothing is so sacred that it cannot be converted into a commodity, and traditional beliefs and norms preventing the commodification of land, labor, and life itself have often fought a losing battle.

photo top: Jeff Conant

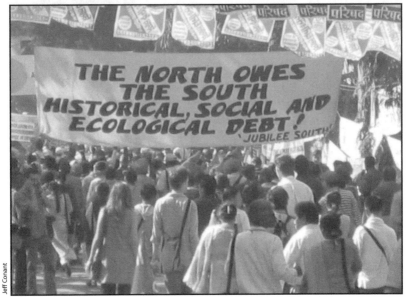

Jeff Conant

World Social Forum in Mumbai/Bombai, India. January 2004.

The Two Moments of Globalization

In what is now known as the first age of globalization that spanned the nineteenth century and ended with World War I in 1914, a massive reconstruction of social relations accompanied the "freeing" of land, labor, and wealth from their precapitalist nexus. The process of "disembedding" the market from society was marked by rapid economic growth and rapid capital accumulation, as well as by massive impoverishment and the emergence of sharp disparities in the distribution of income and assets. This contradictory process provoked a countervailing push from society, especially the lower and middle classes, an attempt to resubordinate the market—the economy—to the needs of the community.

In retrospect, socialism, communism, social democracy, and national liberation movements can all be seen as expressions of this countervailing thrust. However, not all of the responses to globalization were progressive. For example, fascism, which Karl Polanyi defined as "the reform of the market economy achieved at the price of the extirpation of all democratic institutions," was also part of this countervailing drive, one that hijacked the search for community in the service of reaction, counterrevolution, and racism.

After the defeat of fascism in World War II, it was the struggle between two responses to unbridled free-market capitalism—Keynesian capitalism and state socialism—that dominated most of the second half of the twentieth century. The Keynesian economic paradigm was a social compromise among contending classes that placed limits on the operation of the market. Its widespread adoption in the postwar period by elites in both the global North and South was explained by the need to create a stable social base in order to contain the potential for global social revolution.

In the 1980s, with the rise of Margaret Thatcher in Britain and Ronald Reagan in the United States, the process of releasing the market from the bonds of society was renewed—a process that came to be known as the "neoliberal revolution" in the North and "structural adjustment" in the South. This process accelerated in the 1990s with the collapse of the state socialist regimes in eastern Europe and Russia. The Bretton Woods institutions—the World Bank and the International Monetary Fund (IMF)—which had originally been Keynesian-inspired, were transformed into wrecking crews battering down state-assisted, protectionist capitalism in the South and the post-Soviet East to create the so-called "even global playing field" that transnational corporations demanded. With the establishment of the World Trade Organization (WTO) in 1995, the third pillar of the multilateral system was created, and the stage was set for the swiftest possible transition to a global economy driven by transnational corporations with minimal restrictions on the flow of goods, services, and capital.

Overreach

But just as it had done during the first wave of globalization that ended with World War I, capital overreached, and by the mid-nineties there were disturbing signs in both the North and South of increasing poverty and inequality, and the institutionalization of economic stagnation in scores of developing countries that had faithfully followed the tenets of structural adjustment.

Despite the availability of data on these growing problems from such institutions as the U.N. Development Program, such facts were not treated as realities deserving of attention; instead, they remained buried under the triumphalism accompanying the collapse of the socialist economies of eastern Europe and the Soviet Union. But in the late nineties, the Asian financial crisis finally transformed those facts into a reality that the global elite was forced to recognize. The economies of East Asia had liberalized their financial sectors in response to pressure from the IMF and the U.S. Treasury Department, and $100 billion of speculative capital flowed into

CAPITAL

CAPITAL

the key "tiger economies" from 1994 to 1997. Then, in the summer of 1997, $100 billion flooded out even more quickly when investors panicked over the collapse of land and stock prices that the oversupply of funds had created.

With a million people in Thailand and 22 million in Indonesia suddenly plunging below the poverty line, the Asian financial collapse triggered a reexamination of the record of the IMF and the World Bank in other parts of the global South. Almost all serious studies documented a sharp increase in inequality in the last quarter of the twentieth century; the number of people living in extreme poverty—that is, on less than $1 a day—rose from 1.1 billion in 1985 to 1.3 billion in 2000. World Bank researchers Mattias Lundberg and Lyn Squire summed up the new consensus when they wrote that "the poor are far more vulnerable to shifts in relative international prices, and this vulnerability is magnified by the country's openness to trade. . . . [A]t least in the short run, globalization appears to increase both poverty and inequality."

Rising Opposition

Social resistance to corporate-driven globalization, which had been scattered and disorganized in the early 1990s, began to come together in bigger and bigger protests. Community was being forged in resistance to the institutions of a system that had overreached itself, and in December 1999, massive street mobilizations triggered the collapse of the WTO's Third Ministerial in Seattle, dealing the proglobalization side its second biggest reversal after the Asian financial crisis. Reflecting on the meaning of what happened in Seattle, C. Fred Bergsten, head of the Institute of International Economics and a partisan of globalization, told the Trilateral Commission in Tokyo in April 2000 that "the antiglobalization forces are now in the ascendancy." Similarly, the doctrinaire *Economist* informed its readers that globalization was "not irreversible."

By the beginning of the twenty-first century, the system of global capitalism was suffering a full-blown crisis of legitimacy. Increasing numbers of people no longer saw its key institutions—which include the multilateral financial and trade system, the transnational corporations, the political system of liberal democracy and its protective cover of U.S. military hegemony—as legitimate or credible. Even before the eruption of the Enron scandal, 72 percent of Americans thought that business had too much power over their lives, according to a *Business Week* survey. And so widespread was the notion that the U.S. political system had been transformed from a democracy into a plutocracy—the rule of the rich— that one candidate in the elections of 2000, Republican senator John

Jeff Conant

World Social Forum in Mumbai/Bombai, India. January 2004.

McCain, nearly won his party's nomination by running almost solely on one issue: campaign finance reform.

September 11 and Its Aftermath

Just as in the 1920s and 1930s, not all of the responses to market-driven globalization in the 1980s and 1990s were progressive. One of these was radical Islamism, which viewed U.S. corporate and military hegemony as the apogee of the long-running Western effort to erode the integrity of Islamic societies. It called for the unity of the Islamic religion, people, and state, and issued a call for jihad against the United States. Like fascism, its popular impact was not unimpressive: By the end of the twentieth century, it had succeeded in rallying the loyalty of large numbers of young people throughout the Islamic world, so much so that conservative ruling elites such as those in Pakistan and Saudi Arabia had to borrow its language in order to survive.

In the wake of the attacks of September 11, radical Islamism became the prime target of the U.S. antiterrorist campaign. Calls on the world community to join the antiterrorist crusade were, however, met largely with skepticism throughout the global South. While most people were genuinely appalled by the Al Qaeda hijackers' methods, there was

CAPITAL

nevertheless a widespread feeling that "the United States had it coming." Though it was promoted as the project of a global antiterrorist coalition, the invasion of Afghanistan instead was viewed as yet another colonial expedition launched by the Anglo-American brotherhood.

The global elite took advantage of the antiterror campaign to not only target terrorists but also to attempt to rein in what many in its ranks saw as the greater threat in the long term: the anticorporate globalization movement, whose people in the streets were supported by several millions more who were profoundly skeptical about globalization's promise of prosperity. Just months before September 11, a massive mobilization of over 200,000 demonstrators in Genoa, Italy, had sent a forceful message to the global elite that this movement was on the rise.

The U.S. government's initial post-9/11 efforts to criminalize dissent were mitigated somewhat by an unending stream of financial scandals breaking out on Wall Street and the collapse of the Argentine economy. The examples of Enron and Worldcom showed plainly that doctrinal deregulation ends in massive corporate corruption, while the Argentine collapse serves as a red flag, warning developing countries against taking seriously the IMF creed of liberalization and globalization.

Another important event blunting the impact of September 11 on the movement and stoking disaffection with global capitalism was the spectacular failure of the World Summit on Sustainable Development to agree on a program to slow the rapid deterioration of the environment. One cannot underestimate the widespread feeling that the United States, which has declined to sign the Kyoto Protocol on Climate Change, now stands as the main obstacle to environmental stabilization.

But beyond the anger directed at Washington is the growing awareness that the problem is global capitalism itself. Up until a few years ago, many agreed with economist Herman Daly that ecological deterioration is due to the inexorable drive of the man-made system of production to fill too quickly the limited space created over eons by nature. From this perspective, slower growth and lower rates of consumption would be the key to environmental stabilization, and this could be achieved through policy choices supported by the public.

This analysis is now giving way to the more radical view that the real culprit is an unchecked capitalist mode of production that transforms nature's bounty into commodities and constantly creates new demands for its products. Capitalism has many "laws of motion," but one of the most destructive as far as the environment goes is Say's law, which states that

supply creates its own demand. Capitalism is a demand-creating machine that transforms living nature into dead commodities, natural wealth into dead capital. It erodes men and women's being-in-nature (creature) and being-in-society (citizen) and, even as it drains them of life energy as workers, it molds their consciousness around one role: that of consumer.

The U.S. refusal to sign the Kyoto Accord has upset the Japanese and European political and economic elites, but many environmentalists feel that what they're most upset about is the Americans' frank acknowledgment of the basic dynamic of the G7 countries' shared system: its continuing expansion can only be achieved via the continued consumption and toxification of nature. From this perspective, achieving ecological equilibrium will entail not just policy changes but a radical shift in the reigning mode of production.

CAPITAL

Pôrto Alegre and the Construction of a Global Community

As this continuing chain of events creates a crisis of legitimacy for global capitalism, the illusion of a community of interests between the promoters of corporate-driven globalization and the peoples of the world is being destroyed. Meanwhile, at the World Social Forum (WSF) in Pôrto Alegre, the growing perception of a community of interests among the latter, distinct from that of the global corporate elites, has manifested itself.

Pôrto Alegre, a medium-sized city in Brazil, has become a byword for the spirit of this burgeoning global community. Galvanized by the slogan "Another World Is Possible," some 50,000 people flocked to this coastal city in 2002—nearly five times more than the number who attended in 2001—and attendance in 2003 was equally impressive. The pilgrims included fisherfolk from India, farmers from Thailand, trade unionists from the United States, and indigenous people from Central America. In symbolic terms, while Seattle was the site of the first major victory of the transnational anticorporate globalization movement, Pôrto Alegre represents the transfer to the South of the center of gravity of that movement.

Scheduled to take place annually, the Pôrto Alegre forum might be said to perform three functions for the real global community: first, it represents a space—both physical and temporal—for this diverse movement to meet, to network, and quite simply, to feel and affirm itself; second, it's a retreat during which the movement gathers its energies and charts the directions of its continuing drive to confront and roll back the processes, institutions, and structures of global capitalism; and third, Pôrto Alegre provides the opportunity for the movement to elaborate, discuss, and debate the vision,

CAPITAL

Andrew Stern / www.andrewstern.net

A billboard advertisement seen around the city during the second World Social Forum declares "another world is possible." Pôrto Alegre, Brazil, January 2002.

values, and institutions of an alternative world order built on a real community of interests.

Pôrto Alegre, of course, is only one moment of a larger process of charting alternatives to a system that has lost its power to convince. It is a macrocosm of many smaller but equally significant enterprises being carried out throughout the world by millions who have told the reformists, the cynics, and the "realists" to move aside because indeed another world is possible. And necessary.

Among the shared understandings emerging in this enterprise are two approaches: first, at the national and community level, the direction must be to consciously subordinate the logic of the market, the pursuit of "cost efficiency," to the values of security, equity, and social solidarity. This, to use the language of the great social democratic scholar Karl Polanyi, is about reembedding the economy in society, rather than having society driven by the economy. Contrary to the claim of some critics of the movement, this priority of community does not seek to return society to the past, to the bonds of tradition, but moves forward to a truly liberated, self-conscious, and reflexive society.

Second, in order to allow this dynamic to unfold, the global context must be changed from a centralized system of global governance that imposes

one set of rules in the service of one model of economic growth—the free-market model favored by the IMF, World Bank, and the WTO—to a pluralistic system of global economic governance. For it is in such a global context—more fluid, less structured, with multiple checks and balances—that the communities of the South—and North—will be able to carve out the space to develop based on their values, their rhythms, and the strategies of their choice.

There is a global community in the making, but it is not the desocialized atoms orbiting around the impersonal market that was the vision of Adam Smith and Margaret Thatcher. It is not the false community composed of an unorganized global majority and an organized ruling elite. This community in the making is composed of many communities joined by common fundamental interests and values but whose social articulation of those values and interests are inflected by different histories and cultures. In such a world, as British philosopher John Gray puts it, the primary role of global institutions should be "to express and protect local and national cultures by embodying and sheltering their distinctive practices."

Competing with the Right

Since September 11, global capitalism has continued to lose legitimacy as a way of organizing our economic life. This is not to say that the structures of production, commerce, and distribution will collapse anytime soon. Nevertheless, history has shown that once legitimacy is lost—once a system loses its ability to convince people of its necessity—it may only be a matter of time before seemingly solid social structures begin to unravel. The crisis of global capitalism does not guarantee ultimate ascendancy for the emergent global community, however. The Right is also on the move, taking advantage of the crisis of the neoliberal establishment to concoct ideological mixtures of reaction and populism that stoke the deepest fears of the masses. Note, for instance, the mass resonance of the French fascist Jan Marie Le Pen's slogan that "Socially I am Left, economically I am Right, and politically I am for France." Note how the Netherlands, considered the most successful social and economic example of the 1990s, has recently been rocked by the electoral revolution instigated by the populist rightist Pim Fortuyn. One must also be aware of the similar origins and dynamics of religious fundamentalisms of the Al Qaeda type in the South and fascist populist movements in the North.

At the beginning of the twentieth century, Rosa Luxemburg made her famous comment that the future might possibly belong to "barbarism." Barbarism in the form of fascism nearly triumphed in the 1930s and early 1940s. Today, corporate-driven globalization is creating much of the same

CAPITAL

instability, resentment, and crisis that formed the breeding ground for fascist, fanatical, and authoritarian populist forces back then. Globalization has not only lost its promise, but it is causing many people to become embittered. If we do not want to see the vacuum filled by terrorists, demagogues, and the purveyors of irrationality and nihilism, the forces representing human solidarity and community have no choice but to step in quickly to convince the disenchanted masses that indeed a better world is possible.

Global Ecology! Global Democracy! Now!

By Patrick Reinsborough

Patrick Reinsborough is a writer, grassroots organizer, and popular educator who has worked on a wide range of issues including forest protection, nuclear power, police brutality, urban sprawl, peace in northern Ireland, indigenous rights, and numerous local and global environmental justice struggles. He has been deeply involved in global forest protection campaigns, the international network to support Colombia's indigenous U'wa people, and the antiwar and global justice movements. Patrick is the cofounder of the smartMeme Strategy and Training project.

This essay is adapted from a speech given at the World Economic Forum Counter-Summit held at Columbia University in February 2002.

The World Economic Forum claims that it's about addressing the issues of our times. It's a gathering of the political, economic, and cultural elites who claim to have the solutions to the world's problems. In that spirit, then, those of us who have gathered in resistance—those of us who were not

photo top: David Hanks

ECOLOGY

invited to the world's most exclusive cocktail party—are also here to talk about the world's problems.

I'm going to start, unfortunately, with some bad news, because from the perspective from which I see things—an earth-centered critique of the corporate global economy that puts a respect for the diversity of life at the center of my political analysis—there is a lot of very bad news.

We are living in a time of dramatic struggle—between civil society and corporate rule; between people's globalization and corporate globalization; between coercive globalization imposed from above and collaborative globalization evolving from below. But underneath these contemporary framings is the deeper arc of history. Just as globalization is not new, neither is the resistance. Now our time—our place in the struggle—is shaped by the end game of two of the grand historic forces that define the modern era. First, 500 years of conquest, colonialism, genocide and organized white supremacy. Second, 200 years of rampant industrialization, resource extraction, and unfettered economic growth. Together these forces have pushed us to the point where the life support systems of our planet are literally on the brink of collapse.

In the context of the emerging global justice or people's globalization movement, I want to talk about some of the issues around confronting the ecological crisis. First, let's begin with the world's forests. Old-growth forests. An old-growth forest is a primary, fully functioning, intact forest ecosystem—a forest that has never been impacted by human beings. Of the original old-growth forest cover on this planet, only 22 percent remains—that's less than one quarter. Some people here, particularly the urban set, might be thinking, "What does that have to do with me? I'm busy fighting for justice in my community, fighting for issues that concern me. What do large tracts of wilderness have to do with me?"

In reality, the message that we need to understand and communicate is that those forests and the remaining wilderness areas represent what's left of the intact biological wealth of the planet. They are essential components of the ecological operating systems upon which all life on this planet depends. The earth's real wealth isn't on Wall Street or tied up in stock options and corporate spreadsheets. The real wealth of this planet is in its biological and cultural diversity. That is the natural and social capital that actually allows us to live our lives, and much of it is located in that remaining fraction of the world's forests. Those 22 percent of the world's original forests contain between 50 and 75 percent of all life on planet earth—all plant and animal species. They also house around 75 percent of all traditional indigenous cultures, all of them living in those tiny chunks

ECOLOGY

of what's left of the world's old-growth forests. That is our collective heritage, the legacy of 4 billion years of evolution. That biological and cultural diversity is our greatest resource. Yet the forests continue to fall at an alarming rate.

Likewise, we are seeing the ecological crisis expressed in what is loosely called global warming, but is more accurately called global climate destabilization.

It continually amazes me that the global justice movement has not rallied around the issue of fossil fuels and the destruction they cause at every stage of their production. The climate crisis is a core symptom of out-of-control economic globalization that demands our attention. We are fortunate, despite the corporate censorship of the media, to have a lot of information at our disposal—often too much information. For folks who pay attention to the U.N. Intergovernmental Panel on Climate Change, you are probably as amazed as I am that their reports to the world—which have become increasingly frantic global alarm bells—get tucked away on page 17, page 18, or page 24 of the newspapers. The latest findings from this panel, which is made up of over 1,500 of the world's top climate scientists, state that over the next century we can expect our planet to heat up by between 3 to 10 degrees Fahrenheit. To put this into perspective, during the last ice age—a time when I believe this spot here in Manhattan was covered by glaciers—the global average temperature was about 3–7 degrees cooler. Those are the types of cataclysmic global changes we are talking about, the kind of destabilization we're looking at over the next century, happening rapidly.

Some of the folks who have an interest in tracking the impacts of global warming that are expressed through violent or extreme weather are the people in the insurance industry, and the world's largest re-insurer, Munich Re, has compiled statistics about the losses from global warming. In 1998 alone, the price tag of global warming was $87 billion, while 300 million people were displaced from their homes and 32,000 lost their lives.

That's just the beginning of the price tag we are paying for our fossil fuel addiction. Fossil fuels destroy ecosystems, threaten human rights, and impact public health at every stage of their production. From oil exploration and extraction in fragile wilderness areas like the Arctic National Wildlife Refuge that destroys habitat and violates indigenous rights; to the violence and pollution caused by massive oil pipelines and tanker spills; to the toxic price tag of environmental racism where all too often it is poor people and communities of color who suffer skyrocketing cancer rates when their neighborhoods are used as sites for refineries,

ECOLOGY

David Hanks

dumps, and chemical plants; to the looming threat of global warming as the tailpipes of clogged American highways full of single-occupancy SUVs pump out enough carbon dioxide pollution to destabilize the climate itself. It is our addiction to fossil fuels that underlies much of America's militarism and empire building around the world, and it has turned the drug pushers of Big Oil into some of the most powerful corporations on the planet. Our addiction must stop. We are long overdue to break the fossil fuel chain of destruction.

When we add up all the various corporate and industrial assaults on the natural world, we see a truly terrifying picture of the present in the context of geologic time: this is an era of extinction. We are currently living through the sixth and most rapid mass extinction in the history of planet earth. The Smithsonian Institute estimates that today, while we go about our business of trying to create a global justice movement, approximately 374 plant and animal species will become extinct. The reality is that the scientists don't really have any idea, because they have only been able to classify a tiny percentage of the planet's species, and the natural world is being bulldozed far too rapidly for us to ever know its full extent. What we do know is that the ever-expanding corporate global economy is shredding the web of life. We are living through a biological meltdown.

30

ECOLOGY

So what are the real issues underlying the symptoms that we see? This speaks to one of the most flawed assumptions of our times. We are encouraged to think that humanity is the most important species on the planet. But in reality, humanity is just one strand in the complex web of life. We are dependent on the rest of the web for clean air, clean water, for the medicines and food crops we rely upon for survival. When we engage in false debates—such as jobs versus the environment, or whether we can afford to transform our society to deal with the ecological crisis, or when we wonder why we should bother to save the snail-toed darter or some arcane species of slug—we are failing to understand a reality that should be at the core of our politics: the interdependence of all life on our tiny fragile planet.

Think of the earth as a complex machine, something that we don't fully understand how it works, say, an airplane. You would have to be a pretty foolish pilot to open up your engine and say, "I don't know what this piece does, let's pull it out of there, I don't understand this cog, let's pull it out too." Now ask yourself how long could you continue sabotaging the engine before the airplane crashes. That's exactly what corporate capitalism is doing—and it's not just taking little snips. It's taking a chain saw to the web of life.

The fundamental operating assumption of the global corporate takeover is that we humans are separate from the earth and not dependant on it, that the earth is ours to rape and pillage, to exploit and commodify for personal gain. Behind that poisonous idea is the model that our society should assess our progress in terms of unlimited economic growth. I like to think of it as a flowchart mentality: over here we have resources, in the middle we have incredibly complex systems to make lots of cool stuff, and then on the other end, pollution and waste. Resources in, cool stuff, pollution out. Of course our consumer society is obsessed with the cool stuff in the middle. We never think about the whole system. Where do the resources come from—what ecosystem; whose homeland? And where does the pollution go—whose neighborhood; whose bloodstream? As we fight for a better world we must remember that we live on a planet that is bound within certain limits, ecological limits that we fail to respect at our own peril.

As a radical ecologist I look to nature for field-tested models of organization and structure. When I look at what the global capitalist economy has created, I can see only one thing in nature with a similar logic. Ed Abbey said it best when he described capitalism as based on "the ideology of the cancer cell." We find ourselves trapped inside a system

ECOLOGY

based on unlimited growth literally pushing to the point where it kills its host. And that host is us and planet earth.

Essentially what we are looking at, what the World Economic Forum in their twisted logic is offering up as progress and prosperity, is actually a doomsday economy. They are pushing us into the largest biological and ecological crisis this planet has ever seen. Planet earth is having a going-out-of-business sale—a real liquidation sell-off—and the WEF are the ones who are cashing in while the rest of us—the entire range of life on the planet and the future generations—are paying the price.

So that was the bad news. The good news is, when you follow this metaphor through and look to the natural world, something else is happening that I think we all represent. When an organism is under attack, it will create antibodies, and those antibodies will grow and spread and identify the invader and they'll work to transform it. I think that's what we see happening all around us. We are seeing the antibodies rising, a push toward transformative culture. People are recognizing that in this generation we don't have the choice to not be radicals because we don't have time to address merely the symptoms. We have to get to the root of it. To paraphrase my favorite Thoreau quote, "For every thousand people hacking at the branches of the tree of evil, only one is hacking at the root . . ."

And that's our job, to ensure that more and more people start hacking at the root. In conclusion I want to very briefly suggest to you one place I believe we can get at the roots of the problem. I think a great starting point is the assumptions of the global financial system and the people who make up the intellectual monoculture that is running the global economy, particularly the giant private banks.

I'm involved with an international coalition running a campaign against Citigroup, which is the largest and most destructive financial institution on the planet. I have come to recognize Citi as one of the nerve centers of global destruction—the jugular of the global economy controlling the flow of money around the planet. Citigroup, in addition to being the number-one funder of fossil fuel development, one of the biggest underwriters of forest destruction, the number-one predatory and racist lender in America, a major funder of the prison industry and the number-one holder of Third World debt, is also the world's largest currency trader. That means that the Citi corporation is at the center of the flow of global capital. Roughly $1.5 trillion a day is moving around the global economy. That's $1.5 trillion every day, and that money flow is increasingly the true governance

ECOLOGY

system of the planet. It makes megabanks like Citigroup, Deutsche Bank, and ChaseManhattan the de facto judge, jury, and executioner.

The global financial system is an amoral and out-of-control machine that is largely incapable of seeing communities, ecosystems, and cultures as anything other than resources to extract. It is a cult of self-destruction with bankers and economists as its high priests, and the gathered assembly of the WEF as its main cheerleaders. Ultimately, the global economy—or corporate globalization as we often call it—is about homogenization, assimilation, and monoculture. It can be more accurately called global corporatization—the forced conversion of every institution into the corporate form. In the corporate worldview everything is on the chopping block. Education, health care, and prisons are slated for privatization. Subsistence economies are structurally adjusted to make way for resource extraction and cash crop plantations. The commons are seized, patented, and commodified right down to the building blocks of life itself—our genetic lineage. Sweeping trade agreements and institutions like the Free Trade Areas of the Americas (FTAA) and WTO create a global caste system in which the new aristocrats are the international investors and absentee landlords.

The WEF and their bought-and-paid-for cronies in government are busy strategizing right now about how to accelerate the remaking of the world in this narrow image. They are building a global corporate state based on the sole function of a corporation—the maximization of profits. Not wealth, not justice, not wisdom—profits in the most limited sense, mere financial profits. In other words, they are liquidating the planet's real wealth—biological and social capital—and transferring it into financial capital that is oftentimes no more than electronic blips on a computer screen. These people with their business Ph.D.s, government posts, and establishment credentials are out of touch with the most basic ecological realities. Perhaps we could remind them of some simple truths: grass is green, the earth is round, and you cannot have unlimited economic growth on a finite planet. No matter how rich or how greedy or how racist or how stupid you are, you still can't do it.

Why have such obviously flawed ideas come to shape the direction of global society? It is essential for our movement to recognize that the ecological crisis is a symptom of a deeper crisis, a crisis in democracy. As long as we allow the same corporations that profit off this destructive vision to write the rules of the global economy, we are never going to solve the ecological crisis. We are never going to have a democratic, just, and ecologically sane global society. We must fight the corporate coup d'etat, but not just defensively. It's time to go on the offensive. We must rise to

ECOLOGY

the challenge of playing the real "great game," which is to reassert democratic control over the flow of capital and make the shift from an economy based on extraction and exploitation to one based on restoration and equity. We must decorporatize our culture, economy, and political system and build a global society based on principles rather than blind profits; and most fundamentally, create an economy that cherishes rather than pillages the natural wealth and diversity of our planet by living within its ecological limits. I'm very excited by the movement that is emerging in this country in solidarity with the traditions of popular resistance around the world. People are recognizing that the age of single-issue politics is over. We are all in this together—environmentalists, students, people of faith, anarchists, socialists, labor organizers, your friends and neighbors, people of all classes, races, and beliefs. And together, we are struggling to create a movement that is diverse enough for all of us, yet focused enough to actually get to the root of our collective problems.

I want to end with a thought that provides a lot of inspiration for me, because I believe that hope is a radical's best ally, particularly when confronting something as apocalyptic and pathological as the global corporate system. So let me offer a bumper-sticker version of Shopenhauer, the nineteenth-century philosopher's model of truth, which says that truth goes through three different stages: the first is ridicule, and I think that a lot of us in our work have been ridiculed; the second is violent repression—that's always been the staple for suppressing new ideas and we're starting to get a real taste of it here in this country; and finally, the third stage is that the truth is accepted as self-evident.

That is what's happening—we're part of a common-sense revolution, a revolution in consciousness, a revolution that's affirming basic values in support of life and democracy and justice. And I think the awareness that these basic values are not reflected by the corporate system is spreading, and that makes me very excited about what is to come.

Let's show them that the revolution is already happening. In our hearts and minds, in the ways we do our work and live our lives, and most importantly in the dreams that we dare to dream. As the Brazilian popular educator Paulo Freire once said, "We must set our sight beyond the horizon and then make the road by walking." That's what movements are, people moving, all moving in the same direction, moving toward something better. So think big, my friends, think big. Because our times demand it.

See you in the streets!

Democracy Is Direct

By Cindy Milstein

Cindy Milstein writes for various antiauthoritarian periodicals. She designed and wrote for the booklet Bringing Democracy Home, *and is a contributor to* Confronting Capitalism *and* Anti-Capitalism: A Field Guide to the Global Justice Movement. *She is also on the board and a faculty member at the Institute for Social Ecology in Vermont, a board member of the Institute for Anarchist Studies, and coorganizer of the Renewing the Anarchist Tradition conference. In addition to studying and teaching political theory, she has long been active in community organizing, anarchist projects, and social movements.*

These days, words seem to be thrown around like so much loose change.

Democracy is no exception.

We hear demands to democraticize the World Bank, the International Monetary Fund (IMF), and the World Trade Organization (WTO). Some contend that democracy is the standard for good government. Others

DEMOCRACY

Josh Warren White

Street theater outside the presidential debates in Boston. October 2000.

allege that more, better, or even participatory democracy is the needed antidote to our woes. At the heart of these well-intentioned but misguided sentiments beats a genuine desire: to gain control over our lives.

This is certainly understandable given the world in which we live. Anonymous, often distant events and institutions—nearly impossible to describe, much less confront—determine whether we work, drink clean water, or have a roof over our heads. Most people feel that life isn't what it should be; many go so far as to complain about the government or corporations. But beyond that, the sources of social misery are so cleverly masked they may even look friendly: the Ben and Jerry's ice-cream cone of caring capitalism or the humanitarian gestures of Western superpowers.

Since the real causes appear untouchable and incomprehensible, people tend to displace blame onto imaginary targets with a face: individuals rather than institutions, people rather than power. The list of scapegoats is long: from blacks and Jews, to single mothers and gays, and so on. It's much easier to lash out at those who, like us, have little or no power. Hatred of the visible other replaces social struggle against seemingly invisible systems of oppression. Around the globe, the longing for community—a place where we can take hold of our own lives, share it with others, and build something of our own choosing—is being distorted into nationalisms, fundamentalisms, separatisms, and the resultant hate crimes, genocides, and wars. Community no longer implies a rich recognition of the self and society; it translates into a battle unto death between one tiny us and another small them, as the wheels of domination roll over us all. The powerless trample the powerless, while the powerful go largely unscathed.

We are left with a few bad choices, framed for us by the powers that be. Writer and social critic Slavoj Zizek has termed this the double blackmail in relation to the Kosovo conflict: If you opposed air strikes, you lent tacit support to Slobodan Milosevic's authoritarian regime of ethnic cleansing; if you condemned Milosevic, then you stood behind a world molded by global capital. This choiceless choice applies to many other contemporary crises as well. Genocides seem to necessitate nation-state interventions; the excesses of free trade seem to call for international regulatory bodies. If

DEMOCRACY

Jason Justice

March on Chevron Toxico's Richmond, California refinery in solidarity with anti-WTO protests in Cancun, Mexico. September 2003.

the right answer, from an ethical point of view, lies outside this picture altogether, what of it? It's all talk when people are dying or the environment is being destroyed. At least that's what common wisdom purports, from government officials to news commentators to the average person on the street.

Even much of the Left can see no other realistic choices to control an out-of-control world than those that are presented to us from on high. Given this, the leftist horizon narrows to what's allegedly achievable: nongovernmental organizations or Two-Thirds World participation in international decisionmaking bodies; accountability and openness in nation-states; the rectification of the wrongs of capitalism. These and other such demands are bare minimums within the current system. Yet they are a far cry from any sort of liberatory response. They work with a circumscribed and neutralized notion of democracy, where democracy is neither of the people, by the people, nor for the people, but rather, only in the supposed name of the people. What gets dubbed democracy, then, is mere representation, and the best that progressives and leftists can advocate for within the confines of this prepackaged definition are improved versions of a fundamentally flawed system.

DEMOCRACY

Jason Justice

Activists confront Chevron Toxico refinery. Richmond, California, 2003.

The moment a people gives itself representatives, it is no longer free, Jean-Jacques Rousseau famously proclaimed in *On the Social Contract*. Freedom, particularly social freedom, is indeed utterly antithetical to a state, even a representative one. At the most basic level, representation asks that we give our freedom away to another; it assumes, in essence, that some should have power and many others shouldn't. Without power, equally distributed to all, we renounce our very capacity to join with everyone else in meaningfully shaping our society. We renounce our ability to self-determine, and thus our liberty. And so, no matter how enlightened our leaders may be, they are governing as tyrants nonetheless, since we—the people—are servile to their decisions.

This is not to say that representative government is comparable with more authoritarian forms of rule. A representative system that fails in its promise of, say, universal human rights, is clearly preferable to a government that makes no such pretensions at all. Yet even the kindest of representative systems necessarily entails a loss of liberty. Like capitalism, a grow-or-die imperative is built into the state's very structure. As Karl Marx explained in *Capital*, capitalism's aim is—in fact, has to be—the unceasing movement of profit making. So, too, is there such an aim underlying the state: the unceasing movement of power making. The drive for profit and the drive for power, respectively, become ends in themselves. For without these drives, we have neither capitalism nor the state; these goals are part of their body constitution. Hence, the two often interlinked systems of exploitation and domination must do whatever is necessary to sustain themselves, otherwise they are unable to fulfill their unceasing momentum.

Whatever a state does, then, has to be in its own interests. Sometimes, of course, the state's interests coincide with the interests of various groups or people; they may even overlap with concepts such as justice or compassion. But these convergences are in no way central or even essential to its smooth functioning. They are merely instrumental stepping stones as the state continually moves to maintain, solidify, and consolidate its power.

Because, like it or not, all states are forced to strive for a monopoly on power. The same competition, wrote Mikhail Bakunin in *Statism and Anarchism*, which in the economic field annihilates and swallows up small and even medium-sized capital . . . in favor of vast capital . . . is also operative in the lives of the states, leading to the destruction and absorption of small and medium-sized states for the benefit of empires. States must, as Bakunin noted, devour others in order not to be devoured.

Such a power-taking game will almost invariably tend toward centralization, hegemony, and increasingly sophisticated methods of command, coercion, and control. Plainly, in this quest to monopolize power, there will always have to be dominated subjects.

As institutionalized systems of domination, then, neither state nor capital are controllable. Nor can they be mended or made benign. Thus, the rallying cry of any kind of leftist or progressive activism that accepts the terms of the nation-state, capitalism, or both is ultimately only this: No exploitation without representation! No domination without representation!

Direct democracy, on the other hand, is completely at odds with both the state and capitalism. For as rule of the people (the etymological root of democracy), democracy's underlying logic is essentially the unceasing movement of freedom making. And freedom, as we have seen, must be jettisoned in even the best of representative systems.

Not coincidentally, direct democracy's opponents have generally been those in power. Whenever the people spoke—as in the majority of those who were disenfranchised, disempowered, or even starved—it usually took a revolution to work through a dialogue about democracy's value. As a direct form of governance, therefore, democracy can be nothing but a threat to those small groups who wish to rule over others: whether they be monarchs, aristocrats, dictators, or even federal administrations as in the United States.

Indeed, we forget that democracy finds its radical edge in the great revolutions of the past, the American Revolution included. As political actors in the United States, it seems particularly appropriate to harken to those strains of a radicalized democracy that fought so valiantly and lost so crushingly in the American Revolution. We need to take up that unfinished project if we have any hope of contesting domination itself.

This does not mean that the numerous injustices tied to the founding of the United States should be ignored or whitewashed. The fact that native

DEMOCRACY

peoples, blacks, women, and others were (and often continue to be) excluded, brutalized, and exploited wasn't just a sideshow to the historic event that created this country. Any movement for direct democracy has to grapple with the relation between this oppression and the liberatory moments of the American Revolution.

At the same time, one needs to view the revolution in the context of its times and ask, In what ways was it an advance? Did it offer glimpses of new freedoms, ones that should ultimately extend to everyone? Like all the great modern revolutions, the American Revolution spawned a politics based on face-to-face assemblies confederated within and between cities.

American democratic polity was developed out of genuine community life. The township or some not much larger area was the political unit, the town meeting the political medium, and roads, schools, the peace of the community, were the political objectives, according to John Dewey in *The Public and Its Problems*. This outline of self-governance did not suddenly appear in 1776. It literally arrived with the first settlers, who in being freed from the bonds of Old World authority, decided to constitute the rules of their society anew in the Mayflower Compact. This and a host of other subsequent compacts were considered mutual promises—of both rights and duties—on the part of each person to their community, a promise initially emanating out of newfound egalitarian religious values. The idea caught on, and many New England villages drafted their own charters and institutionalized direct democracy through town meetings, where citizens met regularly to determine their community's public policy and needs.

Participating in the debates, deliberations, and decisions of one's community became part of a full and vibrant life; it not only gave colonists (albeit, mostly men) the experience and institutions that would later support their revolution but also a tangible form of freedom worth fighting for. Hence, they struggled to preserve control over their daily lives: first with the British over independence, and later, among themselves over competing forms of governance. The final constitution, of course, set up a federal republic, not a direct democracy. But before, during, and after the revolution, time and again, town meetings, confederated assemblies, and citizens' militias either exerted their established powers of self-management or created new ones when they were blocked—in both legal and extralegal institutions—becoming ever more radical in the process.

We have inherited this self-schooling in direct democracy, even if only in vague echoes like New Hampshire's "Live Free or Die" motto or Vermont's yearly Town Meeting Day. Such institutional and cultural fragments, however, bespeak deep-seated values that many in the United States still

Jason Justice

Blockade of Chevron Toxico's Richmond, California refinery in solidarity with local environmental justice groups. September 2003.

hold dear: independence, initiative, liberty, equality. They continue to create a very real tension between grassroots self-governance and top-down representation—a tension that we, as modern-day revolutionaries, need to build on.

Such values resonate through the history of the American Left: from nineteenth-century experiments in utopian communities, to the Civil Rights movement's struggle for social freedom, to the Students for a Democratic Society's demands for a participatory democracy in the 1960s, to the anarchist-inspired affinity group organizing of the 1970s' antinuke movement, as well as today's anticapitalist convergences. In both its principles and practices, the U.S. Left has been inventive and dynamic, particularly in the postwar era. We've challenged multiple "isms," calling into question old privileges and dangerous exclusions. We've created a culture within our own organizations that nearly mandates, even if it doesn't always work, an internally democratic process. We're pretty good at organizing everything from demonstrations to counterinstitutions.

This is not to romanticize the past or present work of the Left; rather, it is to point out that we, too, haven't lacked a striving for the values underpinning this country's birth. Then and now, however, one of our

DEMOCRACY

biggest mistakes has been to ignore politics per se—that is, the need for a guaranteed place for freedom to emerge.

The Clash sang years ago of rebels dancing on air, and it seems we have modeled our political struggles on this. We may feel free or powerful in the streets, at our infoshops, within our collective meetings, but this is a momentary and often private sensation. It allows us to be political, as in reacting to, opposing, countering, or even trying to work outside public policy. But it does not let us do politics, as in making public policy itself. It is only freedom from those things we don't like, or more accurately, liberation.

Liberation and freedom are not the same, contended Hannah Arendt in *On Revolution*. Certainly, liberation is a basic necessity: people need to be free from harm, hunger, and hatred. But liberation falls far short of freedom. If we are ever to fulfill both our needs and desires, if we are ever to take control of our lives, each and every one of us needs the freedom to self-develop—individually, socially, and politically. As Arendt added, [Liberation] is incapable of even grasping, let alone realizing, the central idea of revolution, which is the foundation of freedom.

The revolutionary question becomes: Where do decisions that affect society as a whole get made? For this is where power resides. It is time we opened the doors of that house to everyone. For only when we all have equal and ongoing access to participate in the space where public policy is made—the political sphere—will freedom have a fighting chance to gain a footing.

Montesquieu, one of the most influential theorists for the American revolutionists, tried to wrestle with the constitution of political freedom in his monumental *The Spirit of the Laws*. He came to the conclusion that power must check power. In the postrevolutionary United States, this idea eventually made its way into the Constitution as a system of checks and balances. Yet Montesquieu's notion was much more expansive, touching on the very essence of power itself. The problem is not power, per se, but power without limits. Or to press Montesquieu's concept, the problem is power as an end in itself. Power needs to be forever linked to freedom; freedom needs to be the limit placed on power. Tom Paine, for one, brought this home to the American Revolution in *The Rights of Man*: Government on the old system is an assumption of power for the aggrandizement of itself; on the new, a delegation of power for the common benefit of society.

Jason Justice

Blockade of Chevron Toxico's refining of Iraqi oil in solidarity with anti-WTO protests in Cancun, Mexico. September 2003.

If freedom is the social aim, power must be held horizontally. We must all be both rulers and ruled simultaneously, or a system of rulers and subjects is the only alternative. We must all hold power equally in our hands if freedom is to coexist with power. Freedom, in other words, can only be maintained through a sharing of political power, and this sharing happens through political institutions. Rather than being made a monopoly, power should be distributed to us all, thereby allowing all our varied powers (of reason, persuasion, decisionmaking, and so on) to blossom. This is the power to create rather than dominate.

Of course, institutionalizing direct democracy assures only the barest bones of a free society. Freedom is never a done deal, nor is it a fixed notion. New forms of domination will probably always rear their ugly heads. Yet minimally, directly democratic institutions open a public space in which everyone, if they so choose, can come together in a deliberative and decisionmaking body; a space where everyone has the opportunity to persuade and be persuaded; a space where no discussion or decision is ever hidden, and where it can always be returned to for scrutiny, accountability, or rethinking. Embryonic within direct democracy, if only to function as a truly open policymaking mechanism, are values such as equality, diversity, cooperation, and respect for human worth—hopefully, the building blocks of a liberatory ethics as we begin to self-manage our

communities, the economy, and society in an ever-widening circle of confederated citizen assemblies.

As a practice, direct democracy will have to be learned. As a principle, it will have to undergird all decisionmaking. As an institution, it will have to be fought for. It will not appear magically overnight. Rather, it will emerge little by little out of struggles to, as Murray Bookchin phrased it, democratize the republic, radicalize our democracy.

We must infuse all our political activities with politics. It is time to call for a second American Revolution, but this time, one that breaks the bonds of nation-states, one that knows no borders or masters, and one that draws the potentiality of libertarian self-governance to its limits, fully enfranchising all with the power to act democratically. This begins with reclaiming the word democracy itself—not as a better version of representation but as a radical process to directly remake our world.

CHAPTER

6

A Feminist View of Global Justice

By Starhawk

Starhawk has been active in direct action, peace, ecological, and global justice movements for thirty years, and has participated as a trainer, organizer, and in-the-streets activist in global justice mass actions since Seattle. She is the author of Webs of Power, The Spiral Dance, Truth or Dare, *and* The Fifth Sacred Thing, *among other books.*

Among its other faults, global corporate capitalism oppresses women. Women make up the bulk of the world's poor and the vast majority of low-paid workers in maquiladoras and sweatshops worldwide. Women and children suffer reduced life spans from lack of health care, lack of clean water, and other means of life. When education becomes costly, women lose opportunities first. Women's bodies become commodities in the international sex trade.

If the global justice movement is to pose a truly radical alternative to the system, it must challenge not just who holds power in this current system, but the very nature of power as well. Central to that challenge must be an understanding of how power interfaces with gender.

photo top: Jutta Meier-Wiedenbach

FEMINISM

The word *power* has many meanings. I like to differentiate between several kinds of power. Power-over, domination, or control is the power wielded by an individual or an elite who can control the resources and choices of others, and impose punishment on them if they do not acquiesce. We all encounter that kind of power daily, in our schools, our workplaces, in the courts and jails, and in the military might that backs our current economic system.

Power from within is closer to the root meaning of the word *power*, which comes from the Latin, *podere*, meaning ability. It refers to our inherent power to do, make, create, imagine, and change.

Power-with is our collective power, our ability to join together and take action, create change, and support each other. *Solidarity* might be another term for this kind of power.

Through organizing, action, and generally agitating, we can use our power from within and our collective power to challenge the structures of domination and control, delegitimize the institutions that support them, and eventually cause their downfall and transformation.

Patriarchy is a system designed to maximize the male capacity for violence. It divides men from women, assigns all the aggressive, active, power-over traits to men, and leaves to women all the tasks and traits associated with nurturing, compassion, caring, and emotion.

Men are then indoctrinated to be deeply ashamed of exhibiting any female traits, of being "womanlike" in any way. Women are indoctrinated to be passive, compliant, and nonassertive. Men do the "real work," and women do all the support work that is never counted as real. And men cannot afford to let women, or other men, rise above them in status or power.

The ideology of global corporate capitalism represents the triumph of power-over, of values that men have held—aggression, conquest, boldness, competition, ruthlessness—over the values that women have held— compassion, nurturing, community, and care for the next generation. I'm not saying that either set of values is innate to either gender, but that the way patriarchy has functioned for millennia is to assign certain values and qualities to each gender, and then to overvalue the "male" qualities while denigrating the "female." Over the last few decades, feminists have challenged this division. Women are allowed more than before to exemplify more "male" characteristics, to compete in the marketplace, to be aggressive. And men are, in private, allowed to exhibit more emotion, to participate more in the rearing of their children, to cry.

FEMINISM

Jutta Meier-Wiedenbach

Zapatista rebel nurses baby. Chiapas, Mexico.

But in the public sphere, we're seeing an eradication of any societal responsibility for nurturing or mutual care. Privatization removes education, health care, the provision of basic needs and services from the public sphere, absolving us of any collective responsibility. Instead, they become arenas of profitmaking, competition, and aggression.

The neoliberal agenda also promises corporations unlimited access to resources, investment opportunities, to the cheap labor of women and to women's bodies, as males have always fantasized having unlimited access to women's bodies. Life itself becomes a patentable commodity: The genetic code is another arena of plunder. Any restrictions, any demands for accountability to any values other than profitmaking, are dismissed as hampering pure, masculine competitiveness.

FEMINISM

Corporations function like freewheeling bachelor buccaneers, with no ties to mother, wife, home, or children, to community or responsibility, off roaming the world in search of adventure and profit. Any attempts to impose limits, safety or labor standards, or accountability are now brushed off as an adolescent boy rejects his mother's insistence that he be home by midnight. Any values that don't serve ruthless competition fall by the wayside, including honesty, integrity, and sound fiscal accounting: witness Enron and Worldcom.

Concern for nurturing values is seen as weakness. Care for the poor or the next generation is dismissed as an unrealistic idealism, sentimental, out of touch with the "hard" realities of the bottom line. Anyway, we are told, the system ultimately will benefit the poor by providing universal prosperity. Global corporate capitalism is a form of patriarchy, and patriarchy is integrally bound up with war. Patriarchy provides the ideology and the psychological condition that turns men into killers, that removes any softness, any empathy that would make men less willing to fight, to risk death, pain, mutilation, and to kill.

And patriarchy needs war. The exigencies of war justify the everyday cruelties men inflict on one another and their domination of women. War is the rationale for every sacrifice of human feeling and compassion. Politicians justify war as defense of women and those very female values of nurturing, security, safety, home, and children that in their everyday lives they care so little about, as well as liberty and democracy. They then proceed to assault those values, restricting liberties, siphoning away what few resources are still allocated to health care or education or social welfare or art, to a running accompaniment of gorilla-chest-beating rhetoric.

War and military power are the enforcers of global corporate capitalism. For the system does not, in reality, confer universal prosperity on all: It transfers wealth and resources away from the poor and the middle class and concentrates them in fewer and fewer hands. When the exploited resist, the military and police powers of the state are brought to bear on the rebels. The threat of that power keeps most would-be insurgents in line.

Global corporate capitalism needs a strong military, and it needs to reinforce the value system of patriarchy that sustains the military. While women may now be found in armies and on police lines, the patriarchal nature of the system has not changed. For patriarchy is not so much domination by men as it is domination by traditionally male values. Women can rise to power in a patriarchal system by serving male values. A Margaret Thatcher or a Condoleezza Rice can make the system appear liberal, but a woman who attempts to use power to serve nurturing values, as Hillary Clinton at times did, is virulently hated.

If we are to overthrow the global corporate capitalist system, we need to challenge patriarchy and develop an analysis that recognizes the key importance of gender oppression along with racism, classism, heterosexism, and all their siblings that sustain systems of oppression.

We must also take a good hard look at the ways in which our own movement reflects masculinist values. The global justice movement, which challenges corporate globalization in all its forms, has been inspired, led, and informed by many women, from Vandana Shiva to

FEMINISM

David Hanks

Protest in solidarity with Zapatistas, San Francisco, CA.

Maude Barlowe to the organizers of most of the summit actions. But there are still overt and covert ways in which men dominate and nurturing values are dismissed.

We are in a war, as those of us who have weathered actions like Québec City and Genoa have noticed. While the level of assault directed against First World protesters varies, war is ongoing in the Third World, overt in Palestine, Afghanistan, Iraq, and many other places, and looming in any country that rebels against the global order.

The exigencies of war create a strong psychic pressure—to value what is hard, tough, aggressive, unfeeling. And if fate or political necessity places you in a situation in which, say, riot cops are breaking peoples' bones all around you, survival may depend on not feeling, on shutting off fear and even empathy in order to simply survive. We necessarily place a high value on courage—a quality certainly not limited to men. But when other values are dismissed, when we are not allowed to regain compassion, to admit our fear, to share our grief and heal our sorrows, we become less effective advocates for the very things we are fighting for. Among certain sectors of the movement, "fluffy" is the term that dismisses any action not seen as hard-core enough—and what does that term mean if not "soft," "gentle," "womanlike"?

We need a commitment to value the soft as well as the hard, the compassionate as well as the hard-core, the healers as well as the fighters. We need to value our process, and how we treat each other, as well as the impact we have on the institutions we oppose.

A movement that embraces feminist values becomes more alive, more creative—for patriarchy is inherently predictable and boring. It spawns the "tactical frivolity" of the Pink Bloc snake dancing through the police lines to the Congress Center in Prague, and the magic of the Pagan Cluster taking over Grand Central Station in New York City with an impromptu spiral dance. It empowers both women and men to live the full spectrum of human capacities for action and compassion, for fighting and for loving. It embodies the world we want to create: a world where we can all be whole.

Racism: The U.S. Creation Myth and Its Premise Keepers

By Elizabeth (Betita) Martínez

Elizabeth (Betita) Martínez, a Chicana antiracist activist since 1960, has taught Ethnic Studies and Women's Studies as an adjunct professor since 1989. She lectures around the country and is the author of six works on struggles for social justice in Las Américas, including two books on Chicano/a history. Her best-known work is the bilingual volume 500 Years of Chicano History in Pictures, *used by teachers, community groups, and youth since 1976. Currently she is director of the Institute for MultiRacial Justice, a resource center for building alliances between peoples of color.*

What Is White Supremacy?

The basic definition of the Challenging White Supremacy Workshop says: "White Supremacy is an historically based, institutionally perpetuated system of exploitation and oppression of continents, nations, and peoples of color by white peoples and nations of the European continent, for the purpose of maintaining and defending a system of wealth, power, and privilege."

photo top: Orin Langelle

RACE

What Does It Mean to Say White Supremacy is a System?

The most common mistake people make when talking about racism (white supremacy) is to think of it as a problem of personal prejudices and individual acts of discrimination. They do not see that it is a system, a web of interlocking, reinforcing institutions: political, economic, social, cultural, legal, military, educational, all our institutions. As a system, racism affects every aspect of life.

By not understanding that racism is systemic, we guarantee it will continue. For example, racist police behavior is often reduced to "a few bad apples" who need to be removed, instead of seeing that it can be found in police departments everywhere. It reflects and sustains the existing power relations throughout society. This mistake has real consequences: by refusing to see police brutality as part of a system, and that the system must be changed, we guarantee such brutality will continue.

The need to recognize racism as being systemic is one reason the term *white supremacy* is more useful than the term *racism*. They refer to the same problem but:

A. The purpose of racism is much clearer when we call it "white supremacy." The word *supremacy* means a power relationship exists.

B. Although racism is a social reality, it has no biological or other scientific basis. Race is an unscientific term for differences between people; there is a single human race.

C. The term *racism* often leads to dead-end debates about whether a particular remark or action by an individual white person was really racist or not. We will achieve a clearer understanding of racism if we analyze how a certain action relates to the system of white supremacy. The term *white supremacy* gives white people a clear choice of opposing an inhuman system—or not.

What Does It Mean to Say that White Supremacy Is Historically Based?

Every country has a creation or origin myth, which is the story people are taught of how their country came into being. Ours says the United States began with Columbus's so-called "discovery" of "America," continued with settlement by brave pilgrims, won its independence from England with the American Revolution, survived a civil war, and expanded westward until it became the enormous, rich country you see today.

That is the origin myth we are all taught. It omits three giant facts about the emergence of the United States as a nation. Those facts demonstrate that white supremacy is fundamental to its existence:

Cancun, Mexico, September 2003.

A. The United States is a nation-state created by military conquest in several stages. The first stage was the European seizure of the lands inhabited by indigenous peoples, which they called Turtle Island. Before the European invasion, between 9 and 18 million indigenous people lived in what became North America. By the end of the so-called Indian Wars, about 250,000 remained in what is now the United States, and about 123,000 in what is now Canada.[1] That process created the land base of this country. The seizure of Indian land and elimination of indigenous peoples was the first, essential condition for the creation of what became the United States. The first step, then, was military conquest land genocide.

B. The United States could not have developed economically as a nation without enslaved African labor. When agriculture and industry began growing in the colonial period, a tremendous labor shortage existed. Not enough white workers came from Europe and the European invaders could not put the

RACE

remaining indigenous peoples to work in sufficient numbers. Enslaved Africans provided the labor force that made the growth of the United States possible.

That growth peaked from about 1800–1860, the period called the Market Revolution. During this time, the United States changed from being an agricultural/commercial economy to an industrial corporate economy. The development of banks, expansion of the credit system, protective tariffs, and new transportation systems all helped make this possible. The key to the Market Revolution was the export of cotton, and this was made possible by slave labor. So the second, vital step in the creation of the United States was slavery.

C. The third major step in the formation of the United States as a nation was the seizure of almost half of Mexico by war—today's Southwest—in 1846. A few years later, in 1853, the United States acquired a final chunk of Arizona from Mexico by threatening to renew the war. This expansion enabled the United States to reach the Pacific and thus open up valuable trade with Asia that included markets for export and goods to import and sell in the United States. It also opened to the United States vast mineral wealth in Arizona, agricultural wealth in California, and new sources of cheap labor to build railroads and develop the economy. Thus, the third step in the formation of this nation was military expansion.

This completed the territorial boundaries of what is now the United States. Those were the three foundation stones in the creation of the United States as a nation. Then, in 1898, the U.S. takeover of the Philippines, Puerto Rico, Guam, and Cuba by means of war against Spain extended the United States to become an empire. All but Cuba have remained U.S. colonies or neocolonies, providing new sources of wealth and military power for the United States. The colonization and incorporation of Hawaii completed the empire.

Many people in the United States hate to recognize the truth of the three steps. They do not like to call the United States an empire. They prefer the established origin myth, with its idea of the United States as a democracy from its early days. They and the institutions that uphold that myth could be called the Premise Keepers.

RACE

David Hanks

Border activists put up Alto a Guardian *(Stop Guardian) on the U.S.–Mexico border fence where it meets the Pacific Ocean against the "Guardian" militarization of the border, 2000.*

What Does It Mean to Say that White Supremacy Is a System of Exploitation?

The roots of U.S. racism or white supremacy lie in economic exploitation by the theft of resources and human labor. That exploitation has been justified by a racist ideology affirming the inferiority of its victims. The first application of white supremacy or racism by Euroamericans was against indigenous peoples, whose land was stolen; then Blacks, originally as slaves and later as exploited waged labor; followed by Mexicans when they lost their land holdings and also became wage-slaves. Chinese, Filipino, Japanese, and other Asian/Pacific peoples also became low-wage workers here, subject to racism.

In short, white supremacy and economic power were born together. The United States is the first nation in the world to be born racist and also the first to be born capitalist. That is not a coincidence. In this country, as history shows, capitalism and racism go hand in hand.

Andrew Stern / www.andrewstern.net

Anger erupts from the crowd after the suicide of Lee Kyung Hae during demonstrations against the WTO. Cancun, Mexico, September 2003.

How Does White Supremacy Maintain and Defend a System of Wealth, Power, and Privilege?

Racist power relations are sustained by the institutions of this society together with the ideology of whiteness that developed during western colonization. The first European settlers called themselves English, Irish, German, French, Dutch, and so forth—not white. Over half of those who came in the early colonial period were white servants. With so many enslaved Africans brought to the colonies, the planters who formed an elite class in the southern colonies were soon outnumbered by nonwhites. In the Carolinas, 25,000 whites faced 40,000 Black slaves and 60,000 indigenous peoples in the area.

Class lines hardened as the distinctions between rich and poor became sharper. The problem of control loomed large and fear of revolt from below grew among the elite. There had been revolts by white servants and Black slaves from the early years. Elite whites feared most of all that discontented whites—servants, tenant farmers, the urban poor, the propertyless, soldiers, and sailors—would join Black slaves to overthrow the existing order. As early as 1663, indentured white servants and Black slaves in Virginia had formed a conspiracy to rebel and gain their freedom.

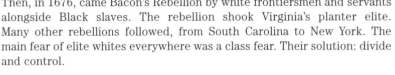

Then, in 1676, came Bacon's Rebellion by white frontiersmen and servants alongside Black slaves. The rebellion shook Virginia's planter elite. Many other rebellions followed, from South Carolina to New York. The main fear of elite whites everywhere was a class fear. Their solution: divide and control.

On one hand, the Slave Codes were enacted that legalized chattel slavery and severely restricted the rights of free Africans. The codes equated the terms *Negro* and *slave*. At the same time, rules were set for "servants." Their bonds were loosened; they were granted certain privileges such as the right to acquire land, join militias, and receive bounties for slaves they caught.

With these privileges they were legally declared white on the basis of skin color and continental origin. That made them "superior" to Blacks (and Indians). Thus whiteness was born as a racist notion to prevent lower-class whites from joining people of color, especially Blacks, against their common class enemies. The concept of whiteness became a source of unity and strength for the vastly outnumbered Euroamericans—as in South Africa, another settler nation—and key to defending white supremacy against class unity across color lines.

Manifest Destiny and White Supremacy

Since the time of Jefferson, the United States had its eye on expanding to the Pacific Ocean and establishing trade with Asia. Others in the ruling class came to want more slave states, for reasons of political power, and this also required westward expansion. Both goals pointed to taking over Mexico. The first step was Texas, which was acquired for the United States by filling the territory with Anglo settlers who then declared their independence from Mexico in 1836. After failing to purchase more Mexican territory, President James Polk created a pretext for starting a war with the declared goal of expansion. The notoriously brutal, two-year war was justified in the name of Manifest Destiny.

The doctrine of Manifest Destiny, born at a time of aggressive western expansion, said that the United States was destined by God to take over other peoples and lands. The term was first used in 1845 by the editor of a popular journal, who affirmed "the right of our manifest destiny to overspread and to possess the whole continent which providence has given us for the development of the great experiment of liberty and federated self-government."

The concept of Manifest Destiny and racism are profoundly linked. Even those who opposed expansion did so for racist reasons. For example,

RACE

major opposition to gobbling up Mexico came from politicians saying "the degraded Mexican-Spanish" were unfit to become part of the United States; they were "a wretched people . . . mongrels."

In a similar way, some influential whites who opposed slavery in those years said Blacks should be removed from U.S. soil, to avoid "contamination" by an inferior people.[2] Earlier, Native Americans had been the target of white supremacist beliefs that said they were dirty, heathen "savages" and also fundamentally inferior in their values. For example, they did not see land as profitable real estate but as Our Mother. Such people had to be forcefully isolated on reservations or, in limited cases, forcefully assimilated by being removed from their own culture.

The doctrine of Manifest Destiny established white supremacy more firmly than ever as central to the U.S. definition of itself. The arrogance of asserting that God gave white people (primarily men) the right to dominate everything around them still haunts our society and sustains its racist oppression. Today we call it the arrogance of power and it can be seen in all U.S. relations with other countries.

The material effects of white supremacy on peoples of color are all too clear in terms of economic, social, political, and cultural inequity. Even that ultimate affirmation of dominion, racist murder, or lynching still occurs to remind us that age-old power relations remain unaltered. That is not to deny the positive effects of long years of struggle to change those power relations, but to recognize that white supremacy remains intact systemically, as seen in the constant harm it does to the daily lives and aspirations of peoples of color.

Less understood than the material are the psychological and spiritual effects of white supremacy. Few whites understand what internalized racism does to people of color, who do not discuss those effects easily themselves. The self-hatred, desire to be like whites or even to be white, and assumption of inevitable failure are the dreadful legacy of white supremacy's teaching those lies by every means at its disposal. Maintaining control over any community has always required not only physical domination but also the ideological domination that says: things are as they should be. As you inferior creatures deserve them to be.

White Supremacy and Globalization

Racism has never stood still or remained unchanged in history. Today we see new forms emerging from the rapid growth of globalization. We can see that white supremacy has become more global than ever and millions of people of color have become globalized.

David Hanks

Global economic integration is not new in itself; we have seen the world capitalist economy in operation since the fifteenth century if not earlier. But today it is an extremely powerful set of interrelated policies and practices with a huge field of operations. It includes the "global assembly line" for production, with parts made in different countries; the whole world defined as the potential market for a commodity; and technological advances that facilitate economic integration more than ever before in human history. With corporate globalization has come a neo-liberalism that means privatization, deregulation, the decline of social services, and other policies.

The main victims are nations of color (politely called "developing" instead of impoverished) and peoples of color, as shown by the vast increase in migrant labor. The vast majority of immigrants to the United States today are the globalized: women and men, mostly of color, driven from home by dire personal poverty to find survival, usually in the global capitals. New eruptions of white supremacy often confront them.

It's been said that militarism is racism in action. We could also say that globalization is white supremacy in action as never before. Manifest Destiny now rages across not only Las Américas, but the whole world.

This essay was originally written as a presentation for the "Challenging White Supremacy Workshop" founded by Sharon Martinas in San Francisco in 1993. Entitled "What Is White Supremacy?" it was intended to offer a very basic, introductory understanding of racism to a mostly white audience. Slightly edited and updated here, the essay has always been seen as a practical tool, not an academic study, to begin opening minds that the society has kept closed for centuries.

RACE

Notes

[1] See M. Annette Jaimes, ed., *The State of Native America* (Cambridge Mass.: South End Press, 1992).

[2] See Anders Stephanson's *Manifest Destiny* (New York: Hill and Wang, 1995).

The New Enclosures: Planetary Class Struggle

By Midnight Notes Collective

Midnight Notes is a collective, which for more than a decade has directed its political intervention and theoretical work to the antinuclear, antiwar, and anticapitalist movements. (Midnight Notes, P.O. Box 204, Jamaica Plain, MA 02130. www.midnightnotes.org.)

Preface by George Caffentzis and Monty Neill

"Introduction to The New Enclosures" was written between 1989 and 1990, and was first printed in 1990 in Midnight Notes No. 10.[1] In this preface, two of us from Midnight Notes present the context in which it was originally written and explain why we think it has relevance to current struggles. The preface is followed by an edited version of the essay.

Midnight Notes was formed in the late 1970s, with one of its intentions to make the importance of work, wages (and wagelessness), and class struggle evident to the antinuclear movement of that time. We believed

photo top: Jutta Meier-Wiedenbach

CLASS

that the analysis of capitalism and the struggle against it that had developed in the extraparliamentary Left in Italy, in the international wages-for-housework movement, and in certain branches of the U.S. Left, could inform that and other movements. The first issues of *Midnight Notes* (*Strange Victories*) sketched out an analysis of energy and work that aimed to help the antinuclear movement make sense to the working class in the United States. In much of our ensuing work we examined energy, particularly oil, as a terrain of class struggle.

Throughout the 1980s we continued to insist on our peculiar brand of "vulgar marxism" that saw the face of struggle in the profits/wages numbers, though we understood the wage struggle as including, for example, the struggle of women with children to obtain welfare (wages for housework) or that of students for expanded financial aid (wages for students). But then new experiences and events broadened our conceptual horizon. We began to perceive—in the struggles for land in Africa, India, and the Americas; in the efforts in Mexico City to construct "civil society" after a devastating earthquake; in the water wars in Palestine; in the squatters' occupations in Zurich, Amsterdam, and Berlin; in the campaign to preserve the collective gardens of New York—a deeper structure to the wage struggle. This deeper structure had two sides.

On the one side, there would not be a wage struggle unless there were waged workers. But waged workers are not natural beings, they have to be created. If one has access to plentiful subsistence and powerful community, one is not likely to go out looking for a miserable wage. Wage workers were created by being driven out of subsistence. This was simple logic, engraved in the basic texts of the anticapitalist tradition. But we could see that this process was far from over. Indeed, in Africa it was being reintroduced as if it had never ravaged the continent hundreds of years before.

On the other side, wage workers have not been content to remain waged workers. They have continually tried to create environments where they are not totally dependent on the wage. In fact, they have tried to create ways of subsistence and access to wealth that are not mediated at all by the wage. These efforts, when successful, give waged workers more power to refuse work and to shape a life that is beyond capital.

These two sides express the contemporary reality, but the first points back to the beginning of capital, while the second points to its end. For this reason, capital (in all its embodiments) is always anxious to exterminate the subsistence existence and is continually carrying out search-and-destroy efforts to do so. Similarly, capital is ever watchful to enclose any new commons that might be constituted by workers. For example, the structural adjustment plans imposed by the World Bank and International Monetary Fund (IMF) are substantially designed to eliminate all forms of shared subsistence, from the right to the land, to food subsidies, to public schooling and health care.

Oakley Myers

In order to find a way to express this deeper structure of the struggle, we needed an appropriate language. For "The New Enclosures," we found the vocabulary of commons and enclosures most evocative and historically rich, since it speaks of a place where Marxism, ecology, indigenous, and antislavery struggles meet. We wanted to explore the ways in which the struggle for a commons defines modern capitalist reality and the efforts—which we continue to see as essentially the class struggle—to supersede it.

In the first *intifada*, the land war aspect of the struggle was made plain for the world to see: Palestinian youths were throwing stones at and being killed by Israeli tanks that were occupying their physical space in order to enclose Palestinians' means of subsistence (access to water being the most important). These youths were refusing to have a foreign state apparatus (either Israeli or Palestinian) negotiate the place where they lived and sustained their life. They wanted to fight for their common space with their own hands. In light of this experience, we began to speak of a "global intifada": we could see that in many sites around the world the direct defense of the commons was increasingly a feature of the struggle, though it took many different forms, and capital itself was intensifying the attack on old and new areas of common subsistence, ranging from the *ejidos* of Mexico to the pensions of western European workers.

That is why in the subsequent years Midnight Notes devoted so much attention to the Zapatista revolt and to the emerging antiglobalization movement.[2] They embodied the struggle not so much for a better wage deal with capital, but for a refusal of the neoliberal world that aimed to commodify and enclose all aspects of life, at whatever the wage level. Slogans like the Zapatistas' "Everything for everybody, nothing for ourselves" and the antiglobalization movement's "This world is not for

sale" succinctly express the struggle for the commons and against enclosure on a planetary level.

These struggles do not negate the wage struggle, but they do remind us that all struggle is based on the endurance of a precapitalist natural and social commons (from land to history and language) and the construction of new postcapitalist commons (from cyberspace to Social Security benefits).

We think, therefore, that the issues raised and the approach taken in "The New Enclosures" still have value more than a decade later. If the broad, cantankerous, contradictory, and evolving global working class is to overcome capitalism, it must construct a commons of space and social relations. In part, the construction of the new space evolves out of defense of the existing commons, of the rejection of enclosures old and new.

The New Enclosures

> ...the historical movement which changes the producers into waged workers, appears on the one hand as their emancipation from serfdom and from the fetters of the guilds, and this side alone exists for our bourgeois historians. But on the other hand these new freedmen became sellers of themselves only after they had been robbed of all their own means of production and all the guarantees of existence offered by the old feudal arrangements. And the history of this, their expropriation, is written in the annals of mankind in letters of blood and fire. —Karl Marx, *Capital, vol. 1*

> The docile Sambo could and did become the revolutionary Nat Turner overnight. The slaves, under the leadership of those from the more complex African societies, fought and ran away, stole and feigned innocence, malingered on the job while seeming to work as hard as possible. And they lived to fight another day. —George Rawick, *From Sundown to Sunup*

The last decade has seen the largest enclosure of the worldly commons in history; however, this corrosive secret is hidden behind the gleaming idols of globalism, the end of the blocs, and Gaian ecological consciousness. Glasnost, the end of the cold war, a united Europe, We Are the World, Save the Amazon Rain Forest, these are the phrases of the day. They suggest an age of historic openness, globalism, and the breakdown of political and economic barriers. In the midst of this expansiveness, however, Midnight Notes poses the issue of the "new enclosures," and in this essay we will

attempt to explain the meaning and importance of enclosures, both old and new, in the planetary class struggle.

The old enclosures were a counterrevolutionary process whereby, beginning in the late 1400s, farmers in England were expropriated from their land and commons by state officials and landlords. They were turned into paupers, vagabonds, and beggars, and later into waged workers, while the land was put to work to feed the incipient international market for agricultural commodities.

According to Marx, the enclosures were the starting point of capitalist society. They were the basic device of "original accumulation" that created a population of workers "free" from any means of production and thus compelled (in time) to work for a wage.

Enclosures, however, are not a one-time process exhausted at the dawn of capitalism. They are a regular feature on the path of capitalist accumulation and a structural component of class struggle. Any gain in working-class power demands a capitalist response—both the expanded appropriation of new resources and new labor power and the extension of capitalist relations—or else capitalism is threatened with extinction. Thus, enclosure is a process that unites the working class throughout capital's history, for despite our differences we all have entered capitalism through the same door: the loss of our land and of the rights attached to it.

The Apocalypse of the Trinity of Deals

Today, once again, the enclosures are the common denominator of working-class experience around the globe. In the biggest diaspora of the century, on every continent millions are being uprooted from their land, their jobs, and their homes and scattered to the corners of the globe by wars, famines, plagues, and the IMF-ordered devaluations (the four horsemen of the modern apocalypse).

In Nigeria, for example, people are being thrown off communally owned land by troops to make way for plantations owned and managed by the World Bank. The reason? The government points to the "debt crisis" and the IMF-dicated "Structural Adjustment Program" (SAP) allegedly devised for its solution. The SAP for Nigeria is similar to SAP's being implemented throughout Asia, Africa, and Latin America. They invariably include the commercialization of agriculture and massive devaluations that reduce the value of money and wages. The result is the destruction of village communities, emigration to nearby cities and then, for the desperate, clever, or lucky, a chance to work in New York or Naples.

CLASS

In the United States, millions are homeless and on the move. The immediate reasons are highly publicized: the farm crisis, the steep rise of rental and mortgage payments relative to wages, gentrification, the collapse of the social safety net, union busting. Behind these reasons, however, is a little-discussed fact: the decline, since 1973, of real wages for the majority of workers. The post–World War II interclass deal that had guaranteed real wage increases had ended, and the homeless are the shock(ed) troops of this reality.

In China, the transition to a "free-market economy" has led to the displacement of 100 million people from their communally operated lands. Their urban counterparts are facing the loss of guaranteed jobs in factories and offices and the prospect of emigrating from one city to another in search of a wage, and a similar scenario is developing in the Soviet Union and eastern Europe.

The "debt crisis," "homelessness," and "the collapse of socialism" are frequently treated as distinct phenomena by both the mainstream media and leftist journals. For us they are clearly aspects of a single process: the new enclosures, which must operate throughout the planet in differing, divisive guises while in reality being totally interdependent.

For every factory in a free-trade zone in China privatized and sold to a New York commercial bank, or for every acre enclosed by a World Bank development project in Africa or Asia as part of a "debt for equity" swap, a corresponding enclosure must occur in the United States and western Europe. Thus, when communal land in Nigeria is expropriated or when the policy of free housing for workers is abolished in China, there must be a matching expropriation in the United States, be it the end of a "good paying" factory job in Youngstown, the destruction of a working-class community in Maine, or the imposition of martial law in New York City's parks. With each contraction of "communal rights" in the Third World or of "socialist rights" in the Soviet Union and China, comes a subtraction of our seemingly sacred "social rights" in the United States.

This mutual contraction of the "right to subsist" in the Third World, the socialist countries, and in the United States is no accident. In no way could capital have won in any place if it had not operated in every place. Only if the Filipinos thrown off the land could be used in "free enterprise zones" in Manila or as immigrant workers in Italy could capital reduce real wages in the United States or sustain chronically high unemployment rates in Europe.

Capital's current attack with the new enclosures is a direct response to working-class attempts to claim space in the 1960s and 1970s. After World

War II, capital (in its Western and Eastern modes) had offered a variety of slogans to the world's working class: from "collective bargaining" and "racial integration" in the United States to the family "social wage" in the USSR to "colonial emancipation" in Asia and Africa. An enormous struggle to determine the content of these slogans ensued, but working-class initiatives transcended the limits of capital's possibilities. From the Watts riot to the Prague Spring to Italy's "hot autumn" to the last U.S. helicopter escaping from the fall of Saigon, the international profit picture was turning sour and capital confronted a life-and-death crisis. Consequently, all deals were off and capital went on the attack everywhere.

Now, at the end of the 1980s, capital seems to have achieved the nullification of these various social contracts. For example, the U.S. Left currently looks at "collective bargaining" and "racial integration" as nostalgic utopias, while Soviet workers anxiously watch as their "social wage" recedes into the past. Indeed, "colonial emancipation" is a phrase that, if any one has the bad taste to bring it up, can only cause derision. How have these "inalienable rights" been so rapidly alienated? Through the new enclosures which attempt to eliminate any relationship between members of the working class themselves and between them and the richness of the natural world or of their past.

These new enclosures, therefore, name a process that has been under way since the mid-1970s. The main objective of this process has been to uproot workers from the terrain upon which their organizational power has been built, so that, like the African slaves transplanted to the Americas, they are forced to work and fight in a strange environment where the forms of resistance possible at home are no longer available to them. Thus, once again, as at the dawn of capitalism, the face of the world working class is that of the pauper, the vagabond, the criminal, the panhandler, the street peddler, the refugee sweatshop worker, the merce-nary, the rioter.

The Pentagon of Enclosures

How have the new enclosures been implemented? First and foremost, the new enclosures operate exactly as the old enclosures did: by ending communal control of the means of subsistence. There are very few groups today who can still provide directly for their own needs with their land and their work. Even the last "aboriginals" from Indonesia to the Amazon are being violently enclosed in governmental reservations. Most commonly, the so-called "peasant" in the Third World today is a person who survives thanks to remittances from a brother or sister who has emigrated to New York or Madrid; or by growing, in the most dangerous work conditions,

CLASS

poppies or coca leaves for export; or by prostituting him/herself; or by migrating to the cities to join the swelling ranks of day laborers, street peddlers, or "free enterprise zone" workers, where conditions are often more dangerous than in the poppy fields back home.

The second major method of the new enclosures is again similar to the old: seizing land for debt. Just as the Tudor court sold off huge tracts of monastery and communal land to their creditors, so too modern African and Asian governments agree to capitalize and "rationalize" agricultural land in order to satisfy IMF auditors who will only "forgive" foreign loans under those conditions. Just as heads of clans in the Scottish Highlands of the eighteenth century connived with local merchants and bankers to whom they were indebted in order to "clear the land" of their own clansmen and women, so too local chiefs in Africa and Asia exchange communal land rights for unredeemed loans. The result now as then is enclosure: the internal and external destruction of traditional rights to subsistence. This is the secret hidden in the noise of the "debt crisis."

Third, the new enclosures make mobile and migrant labor the dominant form of labor. We are now the most geographically mobile labor force since the advent of capitalism. Capital keeps us constantly on the move, separating us from our countries, farms, gardens, homes, and workplaces because this guarantees cheap wages, communal disorganization, and maximum vulnerability to police and courts of law.

Fourth, the new enclosures require the collapse of socialism, from the USSR to Poland to China. The aim of enclosure could not be realized unless there was a dramatic increase in the international competition of workers and the resulting expansion of the world labor market. One-third of the world's working class could no longer be kept out of competition.

The anticolonial revolutions of the 1960s and the commodities boom of the 1970s gave socialism some breathing space, but by the 1980s the game was up. The reasons for socialism's collapse are, in retrospect at least, rather obvious. Socialism is another name for a class "deal" that normally exchanges a guaranteed job at a lower level of exploitation for lower wages. "Lower," of course, is a relative term and it presupposes a comparison with a capitalist standard. The deal works as long as the guarantees, the exploitation, and the wages are in sync.

By the 1980s, socialist wages had become too low on an international scale for the socialist working class to tolerate, the exploitation rate was simultaneously too high, and socialism's guarantees were looking less and less promising. With the computer-based technological leap, the expansion

Pantelho, Chiapas, Mexico.

of production into the low-waged Third World, and the fall of energy prices, the value of socialist work on the world market collapsed. The "deal" fell apart at the seams and the piecemeal attempts to patch it only worsened the tear. For example, the loans taken out by eastern European countries in the 1970s (similar to the Third World loans of the time) to allow them to take part in the technological leap has required an enormous increase in exploitation of workers and decrease in wages. The result: rebellion, disgruntlement, and emigration.

The fifth aspect of the new enclosures' operation is in its attack on our evolution: making us mutants as well as migrants! The disappearance of the rain forest, the hole in the ozone layer, the pollution of air, sea, and beach, along with the obvious shrinking of our living spaces, are all a part of the destruction of the earthly commons. Even the high seas have been enclosed in the 1980s with the dramatic extension of the traditional territorial limits. You need not be a science fiction freak to feel that we are guinea pigs in a capitalist experiment in nonevolutionary species change. Human workers are not alone in this speedup and shrink-down: animals, from protozoa to cows, are being engineered and patented to eat oil spills, produce more eggs per hour, secrete more hormones. Increasingly, land is valued not for how much food it can grow or what kind of buildings it can support but for how much radioactive waste it can "safely" store. Thus, a tired earthly commons, the gift of billions of years of transformation, meets tired human bodies.

CLASS

Capital has long dreamed of sending us to work in space, where nothing would be left to us except our rarefied and repressive work relations. But the fact is that the earth is becoming a space station and millions are already living in space-colony conditions: no good air to breathe, limited social/physical contact, a desexualized life, difficulty of communication, lack of sun and green . . . even the voices of the migrating birds are missing.

The bodily and personal common is also being enclosed for all to see. Appearance and attitude are aspects of work in the so-called "service industries," from restaurants to hospitals. In the past, how a worker looked or what s/he felt on the assembly line, farm, or in the mine was immaterial to the wage relation. This has definitively changed. Those who "work with the public" are now continually monitored from their urine to their sweat glands to their back brains. Capital now treats us as did the inquisitors of old, looking for the devil's marks of class struggle on our bodies. The most extreme case of this enclosure is in the increasing recourse to reconstructive surgery by members of the working class. It's not only "beauty queens" and "male leads" who must buy and re-buy their bodies piece-by-piece, reconstructive surgery is now seen as a must for many jobs in the "service economy."

These five aspects of capital's response to class struggle have been successful at least partially due to their ability to recapitulate working-class desires. After all, even during the period of the old enclosures many were attracted to the possibilities of consumption offered by urban life and did not wait for the state thugs' arrival on the village green to head for the city. A similar point can be made about present-day socialism, since the socialist workers' own desire to participate in the global exchange of labor has been a crucial factor in the fall of the walls of socialism. Indeed, the allure of the world market lies not in its evident exploitative consequences but rather in the potential it unleashes for travel, communication, and wealth appropriation.

The Spiral of Struggle

Although the new enclosures have been able to entice and divide, they have been fiercely fought and have brought about, unintentionally, an increased working-class knowledge and autonomy. Most obviously, the planet has rung and reverberated with anti-IMF demonstrations, riots, and rebellions. In 1989 alone, the streets and campuses of Venezuela, Burma, Zaire, Nigeria, and Argentina have seen confrontations between armed troops and students and workers who chant "Death to the IMF," loot foreign commodities markets, excarcerate prisoners, and burn banks. Though access to universal wealth is desired, the institutional forms of the world market that are using

the "debt crisis" to create the new enclosures are physically under a conscious attack throughout Africa, Latin America, and Asia.

Not only is the marketplace form of the new enclosures being resisted, there has also been a worldwide land war taking place in the 1980s. From South America up the Andes into Central America and Mexico there has been a desperate and chronic armed struggle over the control of land (frequently referred to in the United States as an aspect of the "drug wars"). In West Africa there is a micro-level of armed struggle against land seizures by the state and development banks (frequently discussed as anachronistic "tribal wars"). In southern Africa, the battle over land and its control, both in town and country, is classed as an aspect of "the struggle against apartheid," while in East Africa it's considered a "problem of nationalities." Land war is, of course, what the "Palestinian issue" is about, while from Afghanistan through India to Sri Lanka, the Philippines and Indonesia, the working class has taken up arms against the new enclosures in a wide variety of forms. But this land war has not been limited to a rural, Third World struggle. From West Berlin to Zurich to Amsterdam to London to New York, squatters, street people, and the homeless have battled against police, arsonists in the pay of real estate developers, and other agents of "spatial deconcentration," not simply for housing but for land and all that it means.

These direct, violent, and frequently armed confrontations have certainly limited the pace and scope of the new enclosures but there have also been other, often unintended, consequences of the new enclosures that will perhaps prove even more central to their universal leveling. First, the new enclosures have led to an enormous increase and intensification of working-class knowledge of the international class composition. Second, the new enclosures have forced an internationalism of working-class action, since the working class has never been so compelled to overcome its regionalism and nationalism, as people are losing not just their plot of land but their stake in their countries. Third, the very extremities of the conditions created by the new enclosures has compelled workers to develop their autonomy by imposing the task of creating a system of production and reproduction outside of the standard operating procedures of capitalist society.

The Last Jubilee?

But what of the postmodern antirevolutionary malaise? This malaise is strange indeed, for with the definitive collapse of the era's three basic deals, a moment of classic revolutionary crisis opens. Yet capital's fetishistic charm still seems potent. While all around us unprecedented

revolutionary events unfold, post-ists hail the end of revolution, the end of class struggle, or, implicitly and conversely, the total triumph of capital.

It is now time for other words and spells. In this essay we have reintroduced some old terms, "enclosure" and "commons." As we end let us recall another: "jubilee." We might at first be thought slightly mad. After all, as our comrades are being hunted down, blown up, imprisoned, and tortured around the globe, the very utterance of "jubilee" seems incongruous or even obscene. Is this the time for jubilation? But every struggle against enclosure and for the commons inevitably becomes a call of jubilee.

The term itself comes from the Old Testament but was revived in two central spots in the capitalist period. *Jubilee*, in general, meant the abolition of slavery, the cancellation of all debt, and a return of all lands to the common. It did occur periodically among ancient Mesopotamian peoples, including the Hebrews, but in the late eighteenth century the term was used in the English countryside to demand an end to enclosures, while across the Atlantic African slaves used "jubilee" to demand liberation from slavery. This word thus linked the poles of transatlantic struggle against capital in the pre-Marxian era. Can it do so again? Perhaps not, but the secret energies within the demand for jubilee are far from spent. On the contrary, at this moment when the roof has been blown off all the covenants between classes, the demand to re-begin the story of humankind in common is the force that capital itself must depend upon to create a true world market.

Down with the New Enclosures,

Time for the Last Jubilee . . .

Notes

[1] Midnight Notes in 1990 consisted of Michaela Brennan, George Caffentzis, Steven Colatrella, Dan Coughlin, Silvia Federici, Peter Linebaugh, Monty Neill, p.m., David Riker, John Roose, and John Wilshire-Carerra. The entire text of "The New Enclosures" can be found in *Midnight Oil: Work Energy War 1973–1992* (New York: Autonomedia, 1992).

[2] Compare with *Auroras of the Zapatistas: Local and Global Struggles in the Fourth World War* (New York: Autonomedia, 2001).

Try This At Home

By Jane Anne Morris

Jane Anne Morris is a corporate anthropologist and longtime activist and teacher, and has worked with the Program on Corporations, Law, and Democracy (POCLAD www.poclad.org) since 1995. She is author of Not In My Back Yard: The Handbook.

The Ambassador

It was Colombian Independence Day, so I suppose I should have expected to bump into the U.S. ambassador in the mummy room of the National Museum in Bogotá. What better way for the ambassador to demonstrate her deep concern for the people of Colombia and bone up on Colombian history? Like the fact that the National Museum building was originally designed to be the perfect prison—an application of the principles of Utilitarian Jeremy Bentham's 1787 Panopticon. From a single vantage point, one unseen overseer could monitor all activities of all prisoners, 24/7. Significantly, Bentham noted that the plan would work just as well for factories, schools, poorhouses, and hospitals.

photo top: Jason Justice

CORPORATE POWER

From 1905 until after World War II, "El Panoptico" was Colombia's most fearsome prison. The central surveillance point was a round guard tower (now an airy rotunda sponsored by the Siemens Corporation) with lines of sight radiating out toward eyelid-shaped windows on three floors of tiny prison cells. The Panopticon—like the junior high school intercom left on when the teacher is out, like the invisible "cookie" behind your computer screen—is about hierarchy and control. The system requires fewer overseers with whips, because inmates do the heavy mental lifting. Shrouded in a wraparound one-way mirror, the prisoner (student, teacher, consumer, citizen) is shaped more by the possibility of sanction than by its actual presence. Physical force stands down and waits on-call for special occasions, while self-censorship takes over daily operations. Because it derives its power from the inmates' internalization of the work of the watcher, the Panopticon succeeds whether or not there's anyone in the guard tower.

In Colombia, almost-daily massacres and assassinations are necessary to maintain corporate power, but in the United States the Panopticon is functioning quite well—it is most often the little man in one's own head that makes people into enthusiastic foot soldiers in the war against themselves. We live in a corporate-controlled Democracy Theme Park. Popular rides include the Regulatory Agency Roller Coaster and the Voluntary Code of Conduct Mule Train. The Reform Gallery features Welfare Reform and Campaign Finance Reform. In the Constitutional Rights Hall of Fame, people can take part in regular reenactments of famous battles. The democracy theme park even has its own museum, where other corporate power grabs are reinterpreted as "peoples' victories".

Ambassador Patterson has a role to play in the U.S. democracy theme park. So on Independence Day, the ambassador goes not to inspect helicopters used in the "War on Drugs," but through downtown Bogotá with its "Plan Colombia = guerra" graffiti to the national museum to check out the props for the "War on Democracy." When not mummy-gazing, Anne Patterson, the U.S. ambassador, is the on-site point person for stage-managing the Colombia campaign, a critical testing ground for global corporatization. Her job is to transform a corporate resource-grab of mind-boggling proportions and unsurpassed brutality into a fairy tale with a "War on Drugs" theme song. There will be lots of heroic action against giant mutant coca plants and cartoonlike bad guy "drug lords." Patterson has lots to do. She has to deny that U.S. aid supports right-wing paramilitary death squads. She has to deny that U.S.-sponsored "coca fumigations" are killing subsistence crops, domestic animals, and people. She has to deny a U.S. role in the provision of a Colombian army escort for a U.S. corporation's illegal drilling on indigenous lands. She has to deny U.S. complicity in the methodical assassination of Colombian labor leaders by U.S. soft drink corporation thugs. She also has to advertise and promote numerous U.S.-backed social, health, and educational programs whose primary existence is on billboards. And she has to read and sometimes respond to letters, faxes, and e-mails from pesky activists in the United States.

The Activist

Patterson is no busier than Sally, from Anytown, U.S.A. Sally—she's "one of us"— keeps a diary of her activism. Here is the last week's worth:

On Monday, she stuffs envelopes for Save the Dolphins campaign, and goes to a neighborhood meeting to discuss organic, sustainable food.

On Tuesday, she does research for her regulatory agency testimony to fight a local corporation's pollution permit; she leaflets at a demonstration to support boycotting a brand of gasoline.

By Wednesday it's time to work on Voluntary Code of Conduct provisions for corporations, then have a meeting to decide which "socially responsible" investments to recommend. (Here there's a note that the meeting broke up after an argument between two factions. One favored the corporation that hires people of color and women to build nuclear power plants; the other favored the corporation that's famous for union-busting but builds fuel-efficient cars).

Come Thursday, she sits down to write letters to state legislators, urging broader disclosure laws for chemicals. Then there's that fax to Colombia urging the U.S. ambassador to begin an investigation of the latest government-assisted civilian massacre. In the evening she "persons" a literature table at a panel discussion of unions and globalization.

On Friday there's a strategy meeting on helping the Community Health Clinic stay open two days per week. After that her group tries to decide what to do about sweatshops and deregulation.

Saturday is money day. In the morning there's a bake sale to pay lawyers to pursue regulatory agency and court appeals. In the afternoon there's a 5K Run fund-raiser to pay fees, fines, and lawyers to bail out banner-hangers from their last demonstration.

It's Sunday as she looks over her diary, the day that she must set priorities for the next week. She can't possibly contribute to all the causes that she cares about. Should she skip the dolphins and add social security? Should she forget Colombia and switch to Nigeria or East Timor? Should she work

on radioactive waste storage and worker safety instead of campaign finance reform and groundwater contamination? Should she skip the demos so she can spend more time in the library reading about others going to demos? Should she dress up as a mutant to publicize pesticide use in public schools?

By this time it's late Sunday night. Sally drifts off to sleep, and has a dream:

At a company picnic, two teams are playing a soccer game. Sally's on a team made up of people from the neighborhood, activists, and other concerned citizens; the other team is sponsored by something called MegaCorporation. Sally's team was getting close to scoring, but then Mega tilted the field so that the others had to run uphill. Then Mega disqualified some of Sally's teammates and declared that certain plays couldn't be used. But Sally and her friends kept playing harder and almost scored again. This time Mega stopped play and decreed that Sally's team would have to play blindfolded. Then they bought off the referees. Sally's team finally scored anyway but the referees said the goal didn't count.

The next morning over coffee, Sally remembers her dream and proceeds to interpret it:

The soccer game is how we're always fighting against Mega Corporation. When they tilt the field, that means that they have a built-in advantage with more resources to use against us, and tax-deductible expenses. Disqualifying our players is like when they sue us for writing letters to the editor, or tell us that we don't have standing. Banning certain plays is like when they say we aren't allowed to bring up certain topics or issues at hearings, or when our testimony is limited to two minutes. By withholding information— like about what chemicals they're using—corporations force us to play blindfolded. Buying off the referees is like when they grant favors to politicians, make campaign contributions, and use their political power to influence regulatory agencies and courts. When we score a goal but it doesn't count, that's like when suddenly a corporation is granted exemptions and variances from existing law. Or when a federal court throws out as unconstitutional a local law that we've worked for years to pass.

The Corporations

There is quite obviously a fundamental asymmetry between activist strategy and corporate strategy. We activists dress up as corporate executives to get into meetings and buildings, and as animals to get media coverage. When was the last time a corporate executive dressed up as an Earth First! member or a turtle or an U'wa to get attention for themselves? While we are stuffing envelopes, writing letters to our "representatives," and talking to twelve people at a time in living rooms, corporate executives are writing laws and buying television stations.

While the community response is to play harder—to try for bigger demonstrations at the Capitol, more letters to elected officials, more experts at the hearings—the corporate response is to simply *change the ground rules*. With increasingly unfair ground rules, no matter how hard we play, we won't ever score, or we won't score enough to matter. And corporate ground rules are not intended so much to affect a particular issue—though they do that—as to frustrate and dilute people's efforts over a broad range of issues.

People's efforts usually apply to only one issue at a time. Even if we share common values and care about many of the same issues, we are inevitably rivals structurally. Like Sally, we find that if we have spent our efforts trying to save the dolphins or promote sustainable agriculture, we have fewer resources and less time left to work on toxic cleanups or prisoners' rights. This same fragmentation is evident at conferences, where after an opening keynote speech, attendees fan off into an almost endless array of particularized workshops and panel discussions. How to stop one corporation from using one chemical. How to get communities to recycle one type of container. How to get one framed political prisoner out of jail. This isn't what corporate strategy looks like.

Corporate strategy is to change the ground rules for all—labor organizers, human rights workers, toxics campaigners, everybody. A corporation doesn't have a separate team of lawyers, experts, lobbyists, and public relations persons for each of the thousands of chemicals dumped into the environment. Or for each separate labor law violation. Or for each state, or each voluntary code of conduct, or each chamber of commerce. Most of what corporate strategists do works across the board: it helps the particular corporation in many areas, and, it makes corporations in general more powerful. This is what working on ground rules does for you.

As a result of this difference in strategy, where people's efforts are subtractive and divisive, corporation efforts are cumulative and synergistic. A score or victory for one corporation helps all corporations, but our work on one issue or campaign takes resources from others. In the soccer game analogy, we're exhausting ourselves struggling uphill trying to score a goal, and they're tilting the field. What we have termed ground

CORPORATE POWER

rules amounts to no less than the political process, the assumptions and understandings that in a democracy are supposed to result in self-governance by the people. The democracy theme park has obscured both the current ground rules and "who" is using and writing them. This "who" is not "The Corporation" because the corporation is not a who at all. People say "Monsanto did this" and "Philip Morris did that" with the casualness and familiarity you'd expect when describing an errant uncle with a hip flask. The more accurate term for the abstract legal fiction is Monsanto Corporation or Philip Morris Corporation. But corporations don't really *do* anything. The things that get done in the name of the corporation are done by people. Corporate executives make corporate policy, award each other golden parachutes, and hire lawyers to manage lawsuits and regulatory agency matters. They extract wealth from the work of others, call this the corporation's wealth, then use it to externalize costs onto society and the earth while funneling profits to a tiny group.

Business corporations in their current form—as vehicles for the concentration of wealth and power in the hands of an elite—are incompatible with democracy. That's why they are so popular with an elite whose status depends on ensuring that democratic processes don't happen. A corporation is the most recent and most successful effort to do all the things that elites hoped the Panopticon would do: preserve elite power. Corporate executives make decisions and manage the money, while workers follow orders (on pain of losing their livelihoods) and add value. The "corporation" is a legal fiction to hold money and power for a few; it gives them access to "corporate" resources and shields them from responsibility for their actions. But, finally, a corporation is not a sentient being, not a conscious actor, not a target, not a "citizen." It cannot be "punished" or negotiated with. It can't be "socially responsible," or have an opinion on global warming. It can't have "rights." If people believe it can do any of these things, then the corporation succeeds as a decoy to confuse issues and take the flak for an elite. But the corporation can still be deconstructed, and not a moment too soon.

Deconstructing "Reform"

In a world where "corporations" can break laws, they can also get permits. Most corporate harms to democracy (like other corporate harms—to human rights, the environment, and so on) are perfectly legal, because corporations have "permits" to conceal, oppress, and pollute, all courtesy of our supposedly democratic government. This is because many corporate powers, privileges, and even "rights" rode into town as drivers and stowaways on the "reform" bandwagon. Often, the "reform" is just another chip off the block of people's sovereignty.

CORPORATE POWER

Eric Wagner

Antiwar activists lock down at Lockheed Martin corporate headquarters, Sunnyvale, California, April 2003.

For instance, the biggest boost corporate campaign contributions ever got came from the so-called campaign reform bills of the post-Nixon era, which invented and legalized political action committees (PACs). This legalization of corporate interference with democracy replaced laws like this 1905 Wisconsin law:

> No corporation doing business in this state shall pay or contribute, or offer, consent or agree to pay or contribute, directly or indirectly, any money, property, free service of its officers or employees or thing of value to any political party, organization, committee or individual for any political purpose whatsoever, or for the purpose of influencing legislation of any kind, or to promote or defeat the candidacy of any person for nomination, appointment or election to any political office.

State legislators in Wisconsin, under constant pressure from corporate lawyers, weakened this law, and then national legislators preempted it by legalizing PACs. Yet, when in the 1970s legislators tossed this shovelful of sovereignty onto the corporate slag heap, the event was commemorated in the democracy theme park's "Reform" gallery.

Regulatory agencies have always been part of the corporate elite's "War on Democracy," masquerading as reform. State legislatures were never

CORPORATE POWER

models for direct democracy, but for a long time they remembered that corporations were only their creations, to remain subordinate and follow precise operating instructions. If corporate officers disobeyed, state legislatures simply voted to eject the corporation (if it was from another state) or dismantle it and take over the assets (if it was from the home state). Historically, regulatory agencies were designed by corporate lawyers to protect large corporations against public uproar, upstart competitors, and too-democratic state legislatures. They still do all that, plus provide years of character-building experience for those entrapped in their procedural mazes. After more than a century of failing to "rein in" corporations, they are still among the biggest attractions in the democracy theme park.

Antitrust laws provide another example of the "reforms" that shelved indirect democratic control of corporations and replaced it with feeble regulations. Until the 1880s, all states prohibited "corporations" from owning stock in other corporations. Most discussions of antitrust are superfluous and unnecessary when such prohibitions are in place. Under pressure from powerful corporate executives, state legislators removed these laws from the books, so that by the early twentieth century none remained.

Demanding transparency from government and its agencies is basic to self-governing. If you don't know what your government is doing, you don't live in a democracy. Current law requires corporate officers to reveal very little about their operations to the public, despite the fact that corporations are brought into existence through corporate charters granted by state legislatures. Disclosure laws that fall short of transparency are not "reforms," they are obfuscations. From its first year of statehood, Wisconsin required that all vaults, books, safes, books, and documents that pertained to a corporation's affairs and condition be open for inspection by the state that created it. Laws like this were typical and stayed on the books well into the twentieth century when people started believing that the abstract legal fiction of the corporation had "rights." Today, no proposed "reform" comes even close to the degree of disclosure once taken for granted.

The idea that a corporation can be "bad" leads quickly to the "reform" idea that it must be "punished." The mirage that corporations can be punished works against democracy by deflecting sanctions away from a controlling elite. The recent tobacco settlement is a case in point. For decades tobacco corporation executives and their predecessors made billions of dollars in profits by knowingly marketing an addictive carcinogen as a fashion accessory. Not a penny of the over $200 billion in fines will be paid by corporate executives, the decisionmakers of the corporation. Instead, that money will come from the usual places: workers (through lower wages and benefits), stockholders (lower dividends and stock prices), the general public (through health care and other externalized costs) and consumers—people still purchasing "nicotine delivery systems." Tobacco corporations even got legal immunity from some future liability in the agreement. The executives admitted no wrongdoing. Taking the product off the market is nowhere in sight. Life is good for corporation executives. They got a little bad publicity for a while, but nothing that a few name changes, some shifting of assets among corporate parents and subsidiaries, and slick advertisements can't fix.

The Corporate Social Responsibility (CSR) concept was invented by corporate executives in the 1930s to offer up as a "reform" to head off calls for democratic control. It has enabled corporate executives to frame the public debate around a few voluntary, temporary pacification measures instead of fundamental democratic change. The recent Enron Corporation collapse and subsequent high-profile accounting scandals inspired many prominent CEOs to go on tour ululating over the joys of "corporate citizenship." Even the CEO of CEOs, President G.W. Bush, stood in front of "Corporate Responsibility" wallpaper and positively swooned about corporate ethics. Democratic control of corporations is not mentioned in these performances. Voluntary codes of conduct—a subset of CSR—mirror the Panopticon system, with citizens in the cell blocks. Corporate executives who have persistently failed to follow mandatory codes of conduct (i.e., laws) promise to try to follow voluntary standards. Shielded by the guard tower (the legal fiction of the corporation), their actions are disclosed only when they choose. Voluntary codes of conduct are like laws, but without enforceable disclosure, monitoring, or performance provisions. As with other CSR measures, any corporate costs are tax deductible, either as business expenses or as donations.

While reducing the corporation's tax bill (if there is one) and the government's tax revenues, CSR bypasses the public process that in a democracy would determine how taxes are spent. CSR gives "the corporation" a good reputation, garners praise from communities, reduces corporate taxes, depletes the government's resources, bypasses the democratic process, and puts a handful of corporate executives in the position of making what are essentially policy decisions for the general public. After every labor struggle, depression, and social upheaval (like the "chain store wars" of the 1930s), there's an injection of "corporate social responsibility." At the end of the twentieth century, the brouhaha surrounding the World Trade Organization (WTO) precipitated another round of CSR pronouncements. Each of these "reforms" made society less democratic and moved the locus of control further away from the people.

CORPORATE POWER

Orin Langelle

Street actions against the Agribusiness Ministerial in Sacramento, California, June 2003.

Corporate lawyers working on behalf of the legal fiction of The Corporation use human constitutional rights to frustrate the people's will and further degrade our democracy. In a nutshell, the fruits of people's struggles are used by corporate lawyers to protect corporations against the will of the people. What better staging area from which to direct a "War on Democracy" than the hallowed grounds of the U.S. Constitution? Just as the "War on Drugs" camouflages the corporate resource grab in Colombia, the rhetoric of "rights" masks the corporate takeover of the Constitution. Abolitionists struggled to end slavery and pass the Fourteenth Amendment, including the equal protection clause. But since 1886, corporate lawyers have successfully claimed—through "corporate personhood"—that laws that "discriminate" against their corporations are unconstitutional under this clause. Laws specifically intended to discriminate against harms (toxic garbage, sweatshop-made clothing) are routinely declared unconstitutional. Historically, the equal protection clause has mostly been used to protect corporations against laws, not to protect human beings against discrimination. At best, African Americans and women have benefited from equal protection "lite," while corporations continue to reap the benefits of the full-strength version.

Corporate lawyers use the due process clause of the Fourteenth Amendment on behalf of "corporate persons" to support numerous appeals of laws and regulations. Claiming that a corporation's due process rights have been abridged, they demand appeals and rehearings and other procedures that were intended to protect the human and civil rights of human beings. Fourteenth Amendment "personhood" has functioned as a constitutional gateway for the granting of other "rights" to corporate persons. The Civil Rights Act of 1964, passed after much struggle and loss of life, was used by a transnational telecommunications corporation to sue a local government for monetary damages after it denied the corporation a desired cell tower site. Corporate lawyers argued that government action had violated the corporation's civil rights. Yet instances of racial profiling, police brutality, DWB ("Driving While Black") and other forms of discrimination provide daily reminders that civil rights for human beings are far from guaranteed.

The First Amendment doesn't work so well for human beings wanting to exercise free speech rights to talk about unions at their workplaces, or leaflet at a shopping mall. But it has worked very well for corporations seeking to escape product labeling laws (like the Vermont rBGH case) and evade already weak campaign finance laws. Fourth Amendment protections against unreasonable searches and seizures often fail to keep the authorities out of your apartment, your car, or your personal records. But corporate lawyers have used that same Fourth Amendment on behalf of corporate "persons" to keep OSHA (the Occupational Safety and Health Administration) and the EPA (the Environmental Protection Agency) from making meaningful inspections of corporate facilities, and to prevent other government agencies from seeing corporate records. This betrayal of centuries of people's struggles is woven deep in the fabric of U.S. law. It constitutes the ground rules.

In the corporate view, to ban chain stores is to deny corporate rights to equal protection before the law. To hold corporations to legislative standards is to deny them due process. To require labels on food is to violate corporate First Amendment rights. Meaningful inspection of factories is a violation of corporate Fourth Amendment rights. If all this is really unconstitutional, then we need to take another look at the Constitution. If it's judges bending over backwards to justify procorporate decisions, then we need to see about the judges. But either way, if it's unquestioned, it will continue to run the underground machinery behind the democracy theme park, while people outside wait in line for the rides. We don't hear much about any of this, in these terms, because news media corporations report it as "reform" and "defense of constitutional rights." Then it fits effortlessly into the democracy theme park. Every minute we don't challenge it, we reinforce it.

CORPORATE POWER

Try This at Home

I would like to invite Ambassador Patterson out from among the mummies in the renovated Panopticon to the rolling hills of Pennsylvania. We should invite Sally, too. In Pennsylvania, people decided to fight against the "War on Democracy" on their own turf by doing the most basic thing a self-governing people can do: protect their communities against poisons and assassins. People in a number of townships decided that corporate hog farms are a threat to their well-being and passed laws banning them. Working with Tom Linzey of CELDF (Community Environmental Legal Defense Fund), they passed a series of ordinances that is driving corporate lawyers hog-wild.

Walk into a roomful of lawyers and say you want to pass a law banning corporate hog farms, and before you draw your next breath they will have ticked off half a dozen reasons why that would be "unconstitutional." Current corporate ground rules, if followed, frustrate efforts at democratic local control. But instead of backing down when corporate lawyers say their laws are "unconstitutional," the Pennsylvanians are insisting on their democratic rights. They're basing their resistance on the earthshaking notion that they are a self-governing people, that corporations don't have the constitutional "right" to force them to allow their communities to be destroyed. By not backing down, by this seemingly simple act—passing a local law that addresses a community concern—these Pennsylvanians are challenging the whole pantheon of corporate law that the ground rules are based on. Any straightforward, commonsensical measure will have the same effect. Ban chain stores. Ban radioactive waste shipments. Require that all waste be recycled. Ban genetically modified organisms. All set up challenges to the same handful of ground rules that keep us from controlling the most basic aspects of our daily lives.

The sameness of these ground rules presents an opportunity. Once we get past the parts-per-million or cents-per-hour of our particular issues, we're up against the same lame corporate ground rules. If Sally fights the ground rules that she comes up against on her issues, and the Pennsylvanians fight the ground rules that corporate lawyers throw at them—sooner or later it becomes apparent that, while each is working on local issues and corporations, we're all organizing to oppose the same half a dozen or so ground rules. Even without going to meetings, our efforts will be cumulative and synergistic. Ambassador Patterson's job description would change, too. Right now, our states are chartering the corporations that are pillaging Colombia. U.S. consumers are buying products that come from Colombia. U.S. taxpayers are paying for the military occupation of Colombia. The roots of corporate power outside of the United States, and

David Hanks

the U.S. government's massive and often violent support of it, lie in the lack of direct local democracy at home. If we end the "War on Democracy" here in the United States, we won't be exporting it to our neighbors.

The Berlin Wall was taken down in 1989 by ordinary people, not by a specialized task force. It did not come down because of fancy legal arguments or because people were yelling at it. It came down because no one at any position in the hierarchy on either side of the wall could take it seriously. It was the last ride in a theme park that no one believed in any more. It was taken apart with joy, by people who were suddenly asking themselves, why did we wait this long? When we feel that way about the democracy theme park and corporate power, and can all cackle together at the silliness of a "corporation" having constitutional rights, they will come down too.

In current U.S. law, the term "corporation" encompasses municipal corporations, for-profit corporations, and many kinds of nonprofit corporations (including trade industry groups and educational and religious corporations). A century and a half ago in the United States, the form that the "business corporation" took would be nearly unrecognizable today. In some cases, for example, stockholders did not have "limited liability" as we know it today.

CORPORATE POWER

Despite the high-minded rhetoric generated by some of the early colonists and "founders," the European occupation of North America has never had a "golden age," either of sustainability or of democracy. Still, there are many amazing examples (most from before the Civil War when a few privileged white males ran the show) where it is clear that "corporations" were regarded as subordinate entities clearly subservient to the government of the time.

I am not advocating going "back" to a nonexistent time when we supposedly had a democracy in the United States. But some of the laws passed by corrupt state legislatures, especially before the late nineteenth century, are downright bold and wildly democratic in comparison to what passes as "reform" today in the early-twenty-first century.

10

Behind Enemy Lines: Inside the World Economic Forum

By Van Jones

Van Jones founded the Bay Area Police Watch, which has been key in organizing effective challenges to police brutality. He is the national executive director of the Ella Baker Center for Human Rights and an organizer with Books Not Bars.

Have you ever heard someone declare that the entire world is run by a small handful of people? You probably dismissed that person as a lunatic, right? Well, I have some disturbing news for you: "Yes, Virginia, there is a Global Ruling Class."

I saw it myself, up close and personal, with my own eyes—on the rich folks' side of the police barricades that surrounded the Waldorf-Astoria hotel during the World Economic Forum's (WEF) "Davos" gathering in New York City in February 2002.

Having spent a few days in their company, I have two observations about the global elite. First: it is a remarkably self-confident class—absolutely

image top: Seth Tobacman

RULING CLASS

assured of both the correctness of its "free market" course *and* its ability to carry forward that program on a world scale. In person, the global rulers maintain an easy confidence and grace, despite a global economic downturn. Despite the threat of terrorist violence from right-wing Islamic fundamentalists. Despite rising protests from anticapitalists on the Left. Despite the political and economic meltdown in Argentina. Despite corporate implosions like Enron. Despite various shocks to the system, the global rulers remain absolutely self-confident, genial, self-assured. One gets the impression that they are just a few hundred old chums, playing a fun and leisurely game of golf—with the entire earth as their green.

Second, the global rulers are *not* wed to any of the present institutions of global governance (WTO, IMF, World Bank) that we "antiglobalizers" have targeted. They are committed to one thing and one thing only: the continued success and long-term stability of capitalism as a world system. In fact, leading intellectual elites and business leaders were freely debating at the forum how to reform or abolish all of those institutions— but for reasons that would horrify most people of conscience.

How I Got In

Before I elaborate on these themes, let me explain how I gained access to one of the most exclusive gatherings in the world. Every year, the heads of the top 1,000 global corporations, members of parliament from dozens of nations, heads of state from several countries, and celebrities and notables from around the world gather in Davos, Switzerland, to mix and mingle over the course of an extended weekend. There are parties, galas, workshops, and speeches. And every year, the WEF selects 100 people (under the age of thirty-six) from around the world, declares them "Global Leaders for Tomorrow" (GLTs) and then invites them to attend.

As someone who inhaled tear gas in Seattle and got hit by a police car protesting the World Bank in Washington, D.C., I was shocked to be one of the few U.S. citizens to get the WEF's award in 2002. I did not seek out the honor, nor did I apply for it. (I don't think I'd even heard of the WEF before it sent me the award letter.) My only "claim to fame" is that I earned a law degree from Yale University in 1993 and then helped to found a human rights organization opposing U.S. police abuse and prison expansion. But most of the other GLTs were successful business leaders or elected officials in their own countries.

The selection process is highly secretive, so I don't know why they picked me. My best guess: The selection committee wanted to add some token

Street theater pageant about the global elite. School of the Americas, November 2001.

Linda Panetta

"social justice" flavor to the mix—and then picked my name off a list of people who have won other prestigious national or international awards.

To Accept or Not to Accept?

Whatever the rationale, I wound up with a coveted invitation to the ruling elites' biggest schmooze-fest. Of course, given what the "World Exploiters' Forum" stands for, it is not obvious that a Left activist like me should accept one of its awards. Many smart, hardworking progressives would "just say no" to any honors from the global rulers. And I fully respect everyone who feels that way.

But I took a different view. I looked at the award as a series of golden opportunities: to get on the other side of the barricades, to steal a first-hand look behind the ruling class's curtains, and possibly to use the WEF's own platform against it. Most activists have some degree of "privilege," which we use as best we can to help build the movement. I saw the award as a special privilege that I could put to good use.

Plain and simple: I knew that, in the eyes of the media, someone being honored by the WEF would have the perfect standing to criticize it.

RULING CLASS

Some of my colleagues worried that the WEF would try to "pimp" the fact that it was honoring someone from the "protest" community, to bolster its stodgy image. But the WEF never sent out one press release (or did anything else) to single me out from the other ninety-nine awardees (most of whom were mainstream political and business elites from around the world). Therefore, I was free and clear to go to New York and single myself out—by loudly challenging corporate-led globalization, from *inside* the WEF.

Media Coup

In that regard, my colleagues at the Ella Baker Center and I succeeded beyond our wildest expectations. My EBC colleagues worked overtime to get the media to spotlight my dissent at the super-elite gathering. Thanks to their efforts, literally millions of people around the world heard a searing critique of the WEF's elitism and exploitative agenda—from someone whom the WEF itself was honoring. Our little "media coup" has earned us a tidal wave of positive feedback from all over the country, as well as from Europe and Africa.

I got spots on CNN, NPR, and national Pacifica radio. I got to call the WEF "corporate cabal of economic royalists" on National Public Radio's *Marketplace*. And I sang the praises of the progressive World Social Forum in Brazil on CNN's *Business Unusual*—which reaches an international audience of several million people. (A friend got a call from his wife in Ghana, who says she saw me on TV in the motherland!) And for my "acceptance speech," I challenged the delegation with a hard-hitting poem that compared cops to "cavemen" and opposed the mass incarceration of youth. I did everything I could to forward the cause against corporate-led globalization, from the inside.

Massive Security Lockdown, Inside and Out

With practically the entire global ruling class in one building, security was tighter at the Waldorf-Astoria than anything I've ever seen or heard of. There were 4,000 police actively engaged in security for the event. To get into the Waldorf-Astoria, you had to have a special photo ID badge, with a computer chip embedded in it. After showing your badge at numerous police checkpoints just to get to the building and then into the foyer, you then had to press your badge against a translucent white panel. Your photograph and all your personal information would then somehow pop up on a computer screen that security guards would scrutinize. Only then would they wave you through the metal detectors and into the forum itself.

Seth Tobacman

Inside, I noticed that every one of the hotel security guards looked very formidable—and that each one had the same small, red emblems on their lapels. "Hey," I said, pointing to the starlike pin on one guard's suit jacket. "What's the name of your security firm?" He gave me a sly smile. "Secret service."

Men in suits with bomb-sniffing dogs would come sweeping through the corridors of the ultra-posh hotel at random intervals. Once, a swarm of Israeli secret service came rushing through the huge lobby, instantly parting the scores of people casually assembled there like the Red Sea. In the center of the swarm: Shimon Perez.

The massive security presence had a huge psychological effect on any would-be dissidents (like me) inside. For instance, at a big breakfast meeting, I wanted to publicly challenge former U.S. President Bill Clinton for doubling the U.S. prison population during his tenure. But the session ended before the moderator called on me. And—finding myself essentially alone in a strange place that was filled with hundreds of secret service agents, patrolled by dozens of police dogs and surrounded by 4,000 cops— I was too chicken-shit to just stand up and start yelling at him. Having been tear gassed in Seattle 1999 and hit by a police car at the year 2000 anti-World Bank protests in D.C., I like to think of myself as a fearless protester—a true "bad ass." But inside the locked-down Waldorf, I found myself acting as polite and cooperative as a choirboy.

Comic Relief

Of course, I saw all kinds of other famous people, the whole while. Bono. Bill Gates. Bishop Desmond Tutu. George Soros. Lauryn Hill. And— unforgettably—acting legends Sidney Poitier and Ossie Davis walking through the main lobby, arm in arm, like two shining Black Gods in a sea of pale faces.

And there are certain bizarre and laughable scenes that will be forever etched in my mind. For instance, I saw Bill Clinton bending all the way over at the waist to hug a small child. I was touched. But then I realized he wasn't embracing a kid. He was hugging sex expert Dr. Ruth. (No comment.)

And, one time, I was standing at a urinal, between two older white guys. I looked to my right and recognized one of the guys as GOP Senator Orrin Hatch. The guy to my left: failed GOP presidential hopeful Steve Forbes. I couldn't decide which one to turn to and salute first. So both of them escaped, high and dry.

Mona Caron

Political Observations

As surprising as I found some of the sights inside the Waldorf-Astoria, the things that I heard during the innumerable workshops, panels, and discussions were even more surprising.

First of all, the ruling class more or less understands itself to be a ruling class. Behind the closed doors, there is no pretense to democracy or humility. Countless sessions and workshops started with a discussion leader standing before a room of thirty to fifty power players and casually stating: "Okay, so we're here to make the world run better. Right now we've got in this room together everybody who can make a difference on (issue X). So let's get started." The idea that a few dozen CEOs and government officials should get together in a posh hotel and solve every problem from trade to AIDS did not seem to strike anyone as odd or undemocratic.

Second, everyone loved the protesters. In fact, most attendees took the demonstrations—and the huge police response—as an affirmation of their own self-importance. It was almost as if a bunch of really nerdy kids were chanting and marching around outside the coolest frat house on campus.

RULING CLASS

All the frat guys and gals inside would occasionally peek out the window and chuckle. But mainly they just kept their own party going.

While most attendees dismissed the demonstrations as "festive irrelevance," they did feel some need to speak occasionally to key issues raised by our movement. Clinton himself said with a wry smile about the demonstrations: "I'll bet most of you sitting in here actually agree with about 80 percent of what the protesters out there are saying." I looked around and saw dozens of heads bobbing in vigorous agreement. "Well, unlike them, you have a real opportunity to do something about it. So what are you going to do?" That was the attitude among a lot of the power elite.

So it quickly became a cliché for a speaker to say, "You know, I must say that the protesters have gotten a few things right. (Dramatic pause.) For instance, we have to do better on the issue of (hunger, the environment, whatever). But the way to do that is through *more* free trade, not less." In other words, we are enough of a factor that the global elite cannot ignore us. But we are too small and marginal still to make them really bite their nails and worry about us. So they give us just enough attention to dismiss us.

Third, I was surprised to hear repeated and very candid discussions of the problems with the World Bank, IMF, WTO, and other institutions. A number of workshops began with one dignitary or another saying. "Well, clearly, the institutions of global governance are not working properly. How do we fix them, or what do we replace them with?" I had to remind myself that these were the people who created these institutions in the first place. To us, organizations like the WTO are huge monsters that terrorize the globe. But they are house pets to the global elite. And they could easily imagine themselves trading them in for "something better," just like they do with their luxury cars and spouses.

But, lastly, I was horrified to learn the reason that the global rulers may seek real reforms of their institutions—bringing in civil society and labor unions, creating more transparency in their dealings, better incorporating human rights and environmental standards. It is not because of a concern for justice, ecological sustainability, or anything else admirable. It is because the present system is too unstable for them to plan well and earn their profits. It turns out that "instability" (their code word for everything from stock market crashes to terrorist attacks) is bad for business.

One greatly respected Harvard professor summed it up: "We can no longer export our capital to important parts of the Third World. But the Third World can still export terrorism and disease to us. Therefore, for our own

safety and security, we must take serious steps to reduce hunger and poverty in the global south." (Truly heartwarming stuff, I know.)

So be forewarned: we are not the only people saying "fix it or nix it" about the WTO and other institutions. Sections of the global elite are saying the same thing. But for very different reasons. Remember that when they come offering us the peace pipe and a smile.

MAINSTREAM MEDIA, RADICAL MESSAGE

My mission, as I saw it, was not to play politics on the inside. I wanted to use the platform to get a subversive message out to as many people as possible on the outside. And I did my best.

On CNN's *Business Unusual* (worldwide broadcast), I said: "If I were not invited on the inside, I would be on the outside [protesting] . . . . We are really I think at a point in history, we are going to look back and say, this was a point of a global crisis in democracy. The World Economic Forum, 3,000 people with more decisionmaking power than 6 billion people on the planet. That's not democracy. . . ."

And I added: "[The] mothers around the world who are trying to figure out ways to raise their children have as much wisdom or more than any CEO, but they are not being included in this process at the World Trade Organization, or the World Economic Forum. Our point is, include everybody. We need the wisdom of the whole human family to solve these problems. And that's the point we're making on the outside and the inside."

On National Public Radio's *Weekend Edition*, I said: "This is a tiny, elite gathering of global, economic royalists. Three thousand CEOs sipping martinis do not have more wisdom than the working people and the mothers around the world who are solving real problems every day with very few resources. That's the wisdom that we need to solve these problems. And these CEOs need to take their place at the table with the rest of us."

On Pacifica Radio's *Democracy Now* show with Amy Goodman, I said: "We have one, small, green soap bubble called planet earth. All of the life support systems are failing us. And we have 6 billion people who are locked out. We absolutely must speak truth to power. And we must build

RULING CLASS

power to combat this global elite that is dominating decisionmaking for the rest of us."

And I added: "The World Economic Forum is a symptom of a global crisis in democracy. And the World Social Forum is the antidote. And I think that there are certainly some honest people at the World Economic Forum. But the reality is that until the basic power relations have changed so that workers and ordinary people have the power to solve their problems at the grassroots level, the World Economic Forum is going to continue to be a corporate cabal, trying to run the planet, hoarding power at the top. And no amount of passing out awards and cookies and PR snow jobs is going to cover that up."

Oil, Globalization, and Islamic Fundamentalism

By George Caffentzis

George Caffentzis is a member of the Midnight Notes Collective. He is the coauthor, with Midnight Notes, of Auroras of the Zapatistas *and* Midnight Oil.

The destruction of the World Trade Center towers is a mass murder mystery, for the basic murder detective's questions—How? Who? and Why?—remain unanswered more than a year after the crime. Or, I should say, unanswered in the mind of those people like myself who have not accepted either the Bush administration's or the conspiracy theorists' narrative. I don't know how many people like me there are, but if the Gallup polls are correct, then most people in the United States accept the Bush Administration's story, while my guess is that most well-informed people in Europe and the Islamic world think that some combination of the CIA and the Mossad (Israel's intelligence agency) were-involved in stage-managing the attacks.

I propose that we detectives of 9/11 take another more radical approach. Let us assume that the hijackers and the organization(s) that supported

photo top: Linda Panetta

them did have some autonomy and were not completely the puppets of the Mossad and the CIA. What kind of motivation might have led them to perpetrate such a crime? Perhaps we can take as our guide in our investigation Wilkie Collins's, *The Moonstone* and many of the Sherlock Holmes adventures. For those late-nineteenth-century fictional detectives knew that murder was indivisible and that murder in London reflected and recapitulated murder in imperial outer lands.

What follows is an effort to apply this unorthodox method.

Oil, Globalization, and Islamic Fundamentalism

On a broad level, the events of September 11, 2001, can be traced back to the economic, social, and cultural crisis that has developed in North Africa, the Middle East, and West Asia in the aftermath of the Gulf War and, prior to it, the accelerating process of globalization, starting in the late 1970s. The first aspect of this crisis has been the impoverishment of urban workers and agriculturists in this area, due to Structural Adjustment Programs (SAPs) and import liberalization, dating back to Egypt's "open door" policy that cost the life of Anwar Sadat and saw the emergence of Islamic fundamentalism as a new political force.

From Cairo's "bread riots" of 1976 to the uprisings in Morocco and Algeria of 1988, both crushed in bloodbaths, to the more recent anti-IMF riots in Jordan and Indonesia, the difficulties of merely staying alive for workers has become more and more dramatic, causing major splits within the capitalist classes from Morocco to Indonesia as to how to deal with this rebellion from below (Midnight Notes 1992, Walton and Seedon 1994). A further element of crisis has been the situation in Palestine. This too was made more intense by the Gulf War expulsion of Palestinians from Kuwait and Israel's response to Palestinian demands with more settlements, the attempted usurpation of Jerusalem, and escalating repression. Regardless of their actual disposition toward the Palestinians, this situation has become a cause of great embarrassment for these ruling classes, revealing, as it does, their duplicity and the shallowness of their commitment to Arab and/or Islamic solidarity.

The most important factor of crisis has been the hegemonic role of the United States in the region, as exemplified by the devastation of Iraq, the U.S. government's proprietary relationship to the management of oil resources in the Middle East, and the building of U.S. bases in Saudi Arabia, Islam's most sacred land. On all these counts, deep divisions have developed within these ruling classes pitting pro-American governments— often consisting of royal dynasties in the Arabian Peninsula—against a

Mourning Mothers at Bechtel antiwar action, San Francisco.

David Hanks

SEPTEMBER 11

new generation of dissidents within their own ranks who, in the name of the Koran, have accused them of being corrupt, of squandering the region's resources, of selling out to the United States, of having betrayed Islam, all the while offering an alternative "social contract" to the working classes of North Africa, the Middle East, and West Asia and using their wealth to create a multinational network of groups stretching through every continent and often taking on a life of their own. For we must remember that every capitalist ruling class, however draconian in rhetoric, comes to power with a divisive "deal" for some part of the working class. Even the Nazis offered guaranteed employment and ultimately free lebensraum to the "Aryan" workers, if they joined in the oppression of their fellow workers. The Islamic fundamentalist ruling classes in waiting are no exception.

As a social program, Islamic fundamentalism has distinguished itself, in addition to its unmitigated bolstering of patriarchal rule, for its attempt to win over the urban populations through the provision of some basic necessities such as schooling, health care, and a minimum of social assistance. These initiatives were often undertaken in response to the ending of government subsidies and programs in areas that were dictated by the SAPs designed by the neoliberals in the World Bank and IMF. Thus, for example, it is the Islamic fundamentalist networks that organize health care and education in the Palestinian "territories," almost functioning as an alternative government to the PLO at the grassroots level (Nusse 1998).

As an economic program, Islamic fundamentalism has transformed an important geological and geographical fact into a political and theological one. For approximately 70 percent of the approximately 1 trillion barrels of oil of "estimated proved reserves" (according to 1995 estimates) lie under the sovereign territory of "Islamic" countries," where the majority of the population is at least nominally Muslim. This "gift of Allah" has formed the material basis of the notion of a "new caliphate" (comprising the bulk of Islamic countries from Senegal to Indonesia) that would have the power to take control of the bulk of the planet's oil resources. The ruling classes (supported by the mullahs) of this "new caliphate" could then

paradoxically use the surplus generated on the world oil market to finance a separation from the global consumer commodity market.

Over the last decade, as the crisis created by globalization in the Middle East and internationally has intensified, so has the antagonism of the Islamic fundamentalist networks against the United States and its domestic supporters in Islamic countries.

But this conflict has been stalemated in key countries. In Algeria, for example, the Islamic Salvation Front, which grew rapidly after the anti-SAP riots of 1988 and almost took state power electorally in 1991, was stopped by a military coup. For the last decade, through a horrendous civil war where between 60,000 to 70,000 were killed, the Algerian Islamic fundamentalists have been decisively weakened by attrition and military repression. In Egypt, the Mubarak regime has used direct repression as in Algeria, as well as a system of microscopic social surveillance to defeat the fundamentalist "tide."

The blockage of fundamentalist revival in the most important Islamic state, Saudi Arabia, was a less bloody affair, since it was backed by a huge treasury and the direct presence of U.S. troops. But it has been even more effective than the rocky equilibrium found in Algeria and Egypt. By 1996, the Saudi leadership was able to isolate, exile, or silence the most radical Islamists.

These setbacks have not been dramatically reversed by fundamentalists seizing state power in Sudan and Afghanistan, for in both countries they inherited, and were not able to end, long-standing civil wars. These wars eventually led to the end of these most open fundamentalist regimes.

The lingering civil war in Afghanistan led to the demise of the fundamentalist regime there, of course, once the United States and the local powers (Russia, Iran, and Pakistan) agreed on its termination and supplied the opposition with tanks (Russia) and air-support (the United States). After all, Russian-supplied tanks driven by Northern Alliance fighters, supported by U.S. bombs, conquered Kabul in November 2001.

The Bashir regime in Sudan, unable to defeat the southern Sudanese resistance, has been forced to curtail its fundamentalist experiment. In 1999, President Bashir declared a state of emergency and dissolved the parliament in a move against the National Congress, led by Sudanese fundamentalist theorist Dr. Hassan al-Turabi. Turabi was arrested in early 2001, and after September 11 the Bashir government openly sided with

Linda Panetta

Iraqi families threatened with eviction from their squatted home (in the wreckage of a former training center for Saddam Hussein's security forces) demonstrate at the entrance of U.S. Occupation Authorities, 2004.

the U.S. attack on its former ally, the Taliban regime in Afghanistan, and has since cooperated with Washington in its "terrorism" investigations.

It is important to note that Bashir's split with the Islamic fundamentalist party that had originally inspired and supported his regime came when Sudan finally became an exporter of petroleum in 1999, with the completion of a pipeline from the southern oil field to Port Sudan on the Red Sea. The pipeline was financed by Chinese, Malaysian, Argentine, Canadian, and British companies and has given the Bashir regime a way to access the international market.

This stalemate in Islamic fundamentalism's drive to power described above does not mean defeat, and there is no doubt that it continues to have an attraction within the ruling circles of the wealthiest Islamic nations. This internal contradiction has created a tangled net of consequences that are now embarrassing and endangering many people in the U.S. government and in the governments of the Middle East. For they have financed and trained the very generation of dissidents who are now so violently turning against them. On the one side, a portion of Middle Eastern oil revenues has been used to finance assaults on symbols of the New World Order, because of the divided loyalties of the Middle Eastern ruling classes; on the other, the U.S. government has financed and trained many members of this dissident branch of the Middle Eastern ruling classes in its effort to destabilize the Soviet Union in Afghanistan.

The governmental and informal financial and military support of armed Islamic fundamentalists did not end with the Soviet pullout from Afghanistan in 1989. These militants played important economic, military, and ideological roles that forwarded U.S. policy against Yugoslavia (in Bosnia and Kosovo) and against Russia (in Chechnya, Dagestan, and Uzbekistan) up until September 10, 2001 (compare with Kosovo [Bodansky 2001: 298–299, 396–400]). The deal apparently was: do the dirty work of fighting and destabilizing secular Communist, socialist, and nationalist regimes in eastern Europe, Caucasia, and Central Asia, and you will be rewarded.

This complicity and deal making is why, perhaps, the Bush administration is so hesitant to do what would be natural after such a massive intelligence and security failure attested to by the September 11 crimes: get rid of the incompetents. That would be difficult, for many of those who have been brought back in power into George W. Bush's administration were the ones who were responsible, during his father's presidency, for the training and financing of the very organizations they now hunt under the banner of "terrorism." Therefore, the executive dynasties in both the United States and Saudi Arabia must both be worried about "family members" who have been compromised by their past connections to the networks they now claim are responsible for the events of September 11.

The crude and desperate attempts by ideologists of the Bush administration to somehow connect, in ever more arcane ways, the antiglobalization movement with the Islamic fundamentalists is fueled by a desire to distract public attention and hide an anxiety that is summed up in the question: When will the long list of *real* connections between the "terrorist network" the Bush administration is hunting and its own personnel be revealed?

Why 9/11/01 and Why So Desperate?

These generalized facts concerning the hidden civil war within the oil-producing countries from Algeria to Iran serve to describe the context of the attacks on the World Trade Center and the Pentagon. I am assuming that the immediate perpetrators of the attacks were committed to some branch of Islamic fundamentalism. But these facts do not help us understand why the attacks took place in September 2001 and why the resistance to the United States took such a desperate form. For these attacks are symptoms of desperation, not of power, as they resulted in a devastating U.S. military response with predictable results: the destruction of thousands of Islamic fundamentalist militants along with a tremendous collateral damage on the people of Afghanistan and many other countries in North Africa, the Middle East, and West Asia. Who on the ground can survive such a maelstrom? Indeed, the actual perpetrators and their accomplices, whoever they are, must have been desperate to take such a risk with their own network and the lives of millions of people of the region. It is also probable that many (perhaps most) people, even in the most militant Islamic fundamentalist circles, objected to the bombings in New York and Washington, D.C., if not for moral, then simply for strategic reasons, knowing full well that their hard-fought-for achievements might all go up in smoke as a result of these actions.

Clearly something very important was in process that the perpetrators of September 11 felt needed desperate and inherently uncertain measures to thwart. What was it? The clue is in the national composition of the hijackers. If the U.S. Justice Department is to be believed, they were all citizens of Arab nations. Fifteen were Saudi citizens, two were from the United Arab Emirates, one was from Egypt, and one from Lebanon (*Associated Press Online*, 11/23/2001). Even though there is a paucity of information about them, they were clearly not the "wretched of the earth." They were mostly from professional or well-to-do families in the center of the Arab world. But they were involved in a life-and-death politics that

SEPTEMBER 11

they totally identified with. Although they did not leave a detailed manifesto behind, these facts lead me to conclude that if they were desperate, they were desperate about the politics not of Afghanistan, Chechnya, or Pakistan, but of their own countries.

David Hanks

If my hypothesis is right, then, the source of this desperation are events at the geographical center of Islam, Saudi Arabia, which echoed throughout the Islamic world.

My view is that the political factors motivating the mass murder and suicides of September 11 involved the oil industry and structural adjustment in the Arabian Peninsula. Here is the story:

Beginning in 1998 (after the collapse of oil prices due to the Asian financial crisis), the Saudi monarchy decided, for "strategic reasons," to globalize its economy and society, beginning with the oil sector. The oil industry had been nationalized since 1975, which meant that foreign investors were allowed to participate only in "downstream" operations like refining. But in September 1998 Crown Prince Abdullah met in Washington with senior executives from several oil companies. According to Gawdat Bahget, "The Crown Prince asked the oil companies' executives to submit directly to him recommendations and suggestions about the role their companies could play in the exploration and development of both existing and new oil and gas fields" (Bahget 2001: 5). These "recommendations and suggestions" were then submitted to a Supreme Council for Petroleum and Mineral Affairs in early 2000 (after being vetted by the Crown Prince), and, by mid-2000, the Saudi government began to cautiously respond to them by ratifying a new foreign investment law. Under the new law, "tax holidays are abolished in favor of sweeping reductions in tax on profits payable by foreign entities, bringing them nearer to levels that apply to local companies. Wholly owned foreign businesses *will have the right to own land*, sponsor their own employees and benefit from concessionary loans previously available only to Saudi companies" (Bahgat 2001: 6, my emphasis). [Nota bene: it is obvious why "the right to own land" would be a red flag for anyone committed to the sacred character of the Arabian Peninsula.] The Middle Eastern financial experts were literally falling over themselves in their effort to highlight the new investment regulation. One described it in the following words, "Keep your fingers crossed, but it looks as if Saudi Arabia is abandoning almost seventy years of restrictive, even unfriendly policy toward foreign investment" (MacKinnon 2000). This law constituted, in effect, a NAFTA-like agreement between the Saudi monarchy and the U.S. and European oil companies.

At the same time as this law was being discussed, a ministerial committee announced that up to $500 billion of new investments would be deployed over the next decade to change the form of the Saudi national economy. One hundred billion dollars of this investment was already promised by foreign oil companies.

In May 2001 the first concrete step in this stepped-up globalization process was concluded when Exxon/Mobil and Royal Dutch/Shell Group led eight other foreign companies (including Conoco and Enron from the United States) on a proposal for a $25 billion natural gas development project in Saudi Arabia. The financial press noted that the deal would not be very lucrative in itself, but that "It's part of a long-term ploy of the oil companies, [which] want ultimately to get access again to Saudi crude" (*LA Times*, 5/19/2001).

Thus, by the summer of 2001, the Saudi monarchy had cast the die and then legally, socially, and economically entered the Rubicon of globalization (but with its "fingers crossed," undoubtedly). It "globalized" not because the Saudi Arabian debt, though large, was unmanageable (as was the case with most other countries which bent to the globalizing dictates of the IMF) but because, faced with a intensifying opposition, the king and his circle realized that only with the full backing of the United States and European Union could they hope to preserve their rule in the coming years. In other words, confronted with significant social problems and an insurrectional element within its own class that could not be defeated by open confrontation, since it took on the garb of Islam too, the Saudi Arabian government decided that a rehaul of its economy would defeat its dangerous opposition through attrition and would further solidify its alliance with U.S. and European capital. This "home-grown globalization" strategy was aimed at reducing the large and growing unemployment rate among its young citizens, its dependence on oil exports, and its huge foreign labor. Inevitably, this initiative would impact the economic policies of the other oil-producing governments in the region, especially the Gulf Cooperation Council states—Oman, Qatar, United Arab Emirates, Bahrain, and Kuwait.

If it works, this "home-grown" globalization strategy would deal a decisive blow to the Islamicist opposition, undermining its ability to recruit

SEPTEMBER 11

David Hanks

Bay Area Direct Action Secret Society (BADASS) Affinity Group wearing photos of Iraqi civilians. San Francisco, 2003.

converts who would be employed in the upper echelons of a "globalized economy and society" instead of being driven to despair by political powerlessness and long periods of unemployment. But the introduction of foreign ownership of land and natural resources, backed up by large investments, and the hiring of more expatriates from Europe and the United States would force a major social change. The cat-and-mouse game that the Saudi monarchy had played with the fundamentalist dissidents (by which the king and his dynasty claimed to be even more fundamentalist than them) would end. Whatever hopes the Islamic opposition in the ruling classes of the Arabian Peninsula had ever harbored of getting their governments to send American troops packing and turning their oil revenues into the economic engine of a resurgent Islam were facing a historic crisis in the summer of 2001. Without a major reversal, the Islamic fundamentalist opposition would have to face the prospect of a total civil war in their own countries or face extinction. Certain elements of this opposition decided that only a spectacular action like the September 11 hijackings and destruction of thousands of people in New York and Washington could turn back the tide. Perhaps they hoped that if enough turmoil and uncertainty could be generated by the attacks in the United States, they would precipitate a strategic U.S. retreat from the Arabian Peninsula just as the bombing in Lebanon in 1983 lead to the U.S. pullout there.

After 9/11 in Saudi Arabia

The Saudi monarchy immediately responded to September 11 with a desperation of its own, by picking up the pace of globalization in a number of vital areas. Prince Abdullah, the chairman of the Saudi Arabian General Investment Authority, said on November 6 that "We must not let terrorism, acts of violence and conflict distract us from doing our daily work and planning for the future. We are on the brink of becoming one of the most exciting markets as restructuring gathers pace. . . . We want to allow the whole economy to be plugged into what is happening in the rest of the world" (*Middle East Economic Digest*, 11/16/2001). A few days later the formation of a new regulatory body for the power sector was announced which would explicitly be concerned with the protection of potential foreign investors. These are not abstract beings, for the very international oil companies that are investing in the natural gas initiatives mentioned before, like Exxon/Mobil and Royal Dutch/Shell Group, are planning to invest heavily in new power stations (*Middle East Economic Digest*, 11/16/2001). Along with this news came further details concerning the new Water Ministry, which will be in charge of "liberalization of the water sector and the introduction of foreign investment in desalination" (*Middle East Economic Digest*, 11/09/2001). Thus, one of the most important impacts of September 11 has been the Saudi monarchy's hurry to pass control over their country's power and water to the hands of international investors, especially international oil companies.

This approach began to change at the beginning of 2002, however, to be replaced by a falling out of old accomplices. On the one side, certain elements in the Bush administration saw 9/11 as the opportunity to rewrite the rules of the world oil industry. They had been profoundly unhappy with these rules since the nationalization period of the early 1970s, and had been trying to recolonize the oil fields since the Gulf War of 1991, but thus far they have been only successful in changing the class composition of the oil-producing proletariat and not the relations of ownership (*Midnight Oil* 1992: 39–57). The year 2001 was a moment of crisis of neoliberalism (given the worldwide recession), and the leadership of the Bush administration wanted to strike at a major bottleneck in its development: the oil and gas industry.

One can understand why. Oil and natural gas are basic commodities for the running of the world's industrial apparatus (from plastics to chemicals to pharmaceuticals to fertilizers to energy for cars and electric power plants). Who controls the commodity and its price controls the capitalist system. Yet oil is an unusual commodity. It is exempt from the rules of neoliberalism. The trading rules of the WTO do not apply to oil and the Organization of Petroleum Exporting Countries (OPEC); a self-proclaimed, if not completely successful, oligopoly is tolerated in a period when the "free market" ought to be determining the price of all commodities, especially basic ones. How could it be that even though OPEC now controls about 80 percent of the "proven oil reserves" it operates in contradiction to the larger rules of the neoliberal game? No wonder neoliberalism is in crisis!

This peculiar singularity is intensified by realizing who the main political figures in OPEC are now: in Iran there are the desperate Islamic clerics, in Saudi Arabia there is a ruling class that is divided between globalization and Islamic fundamentalism, in Venezuela there is the populist government of Chavez, in Ecuador there is a government that was nearly seized in a rebellion by the indigenous, in Libya there is Khadafy (need more be said?), in Algeria there is a government that just narrowly repressed an Islamist revolution, in Nigeria and Indonesia there are "democratic" governments with questionable legitimacy that could collapse at any moment. This list constitutes a "rogues' gallery" from the point of view of the thousands of capitalists who send a tremendous portion of "their" surplus to OPEC governments via their purchases of oil and gas. With such a crew of governments, OPEC is hardly an institution to energize a neoliberal world.

But the Saudi Arabia monarchy is the heart of OPEC and since 9/11 it has been openly denigrated by many in the Bush administration and the "permanent government" in Washington. This unprecedented attack climaxed in a briefing given by Laurent Murawiec, a staffer at RAND, to the Defense Policy Board—a collection of former senior officials and intellectuals who advise the Pentagon, such as Richard Pearle, Harold Brown, Newt Gingrich and Henry Kissinger—on the war on terrorism in July 2002. Murawiec concluded that Saudi Arabia is "the kernel of evil, the prime mover, the most dangerous opponent" of the United States in the Middle East (i.e., Bin Laden is truly a representative of parts of the Saudi ruling class) and that it "supports our enemies and attacks our allies" (*AP On Line* 8/06/2002). This means that the value produced by workers throughout the world (much of it in the United States) and transferred by the corporations to Saudi Arabia is directly feeding the very forces they are battling. The contents of the briefing were leaked to the press in early August and they quickly caused a scandal. The Saudi ruling circles responded by lamenting that they have been stalwart allies of the United States for more than half a century! But it was clear that the Bush administration was using the incident to demand an acceleration in the globalization of Saudi resources, or else.

The Saudis, however, did not capitulate and have fought back with the familiar "weapon of the weak": delay. The gas deal announced in May 2001 (which might have been the immediate trigger for 9/11) is a useful barometer for judging this struggle between the impatient neoliberals in the Bush regime and the Saudi monarchy divided between "home-grown globalization" supporters and Islamic fundamentalists. The turn in the story begins in January 2002:

> U.S. companies earlier this year had foreseen that delays in finalizing the contracts covering proposed projects were likely for several political and legal reasons. Diplomatic tensions between the two countries were frayed. In addition, the lucrative double-digit return on investment first offered by Saudi royals over a year ago was not consistent with that which oil company Saudi

Arabian Oil Co. later offered at the negotiating table [in January 2002]. (*Oil and Gas Journal,* March 11, 2002)

> The major stumbling block in the negotiations is reported to be an insistence by the oil companies for an average return of 15 percent. The Saudis want to allow a return of only 10 percent. The talks are also being hampered by divisions within the Saudi royal family, some prominent members of which are thought to be worried about the implications of giving Western oil companies direct access to the country's oil and gas reserves for the first time [*sic*]. (*Chemical Market Reporter,* May 13, 2002)

By the middle of July (with the release of the RAND report) the negotiations went into critical. It looked like the deal might even sink, even though much was riding on it. As the *Oil and Gas Journal* pointed out:

> Both sides are keenly aware that the success of the gas initiative has both political and economic implications for the country and the region. A new United Nations report by the Regional Bureau for Arab States notes that for Saudi Arabia and other Arab countries to realize their economic potential, trade barriers must be eased. (*Oil and Gas Journal,* July 15, 2002)

In fact, the Saudi monarchy gave Exxon-Mobil and Shell a July 31 deadline to agree on the basic negotiating points or else it would seek new bids for the projects. Then, in early September they restricted the number of fields that Exxon-Mobil, Shell, and the smaller bidders would be able to explore and exploit. Indeed, at the time of writing this essay (October 2002) the deal was still in limbo, clearly revealing the struggle within the Saudi monarchy and against a sector of the Bush administration that is demanding a total capitulation, which the monarchy cannot politically or economically afford.

This struggle over the control of the earth's oil and gas, which is now called "the war on terrorism," has quickly moved on since 9/11. The Bush administration gave it a new dimension by its decision to precipitate a war with the Iraqi government. Victory in such a war is widely seen as a way to definitively subvert the Saudi monarchy's and OPEC's economic power. Hence, 9/11 was just a moment in a much wider struggle for the determination of the great common of the planet lying beneath our feet.

On the basis of my investigation, then, the September 11 attacks on New York City and Washington, D.C., were the "collateral damage" of a struggle over the fate of oil politics in its heartland: the Arabian Peninsula.

Who then is the real killer? Not surprisingly, the usual suspect: capitalism.

SEPTEMBER 11

Bibliography

Anonymous. "Middle East and North Africa: 2000–2004." *Country Monitor* 8, no. 5, (2000): 5.

Bahgat, Gawdat. "Managing Dependence: American-Saudi Oil Relations." *Arab Studies Quarterly*, 23, no. 1, (2001): 1–14.

Bodansky, Yossef. *Bin Laden: The Man Who Declared War on America*, (Roseville, Calif.: Prima Publishing, 2001).

Bourland, Brad, "The Saudi Economy at Mid-2000: Highest Oil Revenues since 1981." *Middle East Executive Reports*, 23, no. 3 (March 2000).

Collins, Wilkie. *The Moonstone*, (Garden City, N.Y.: Garden City Publishers, 1948).

Cordesman, Anthony H.. *Saudi Arabia: Guarding the Desert Kingdom*, (Boulder, Colo.: Westview Press, 1997).

Doyle, Arthur Conan. *The Complete Sherlock Holmes, Vol. 1*, (Garden City, N.Y.: Doubleday & Co, 1930).

Faksh, Mahmud A.. *The Future of Islam in the Middle East: Fundamentalism in Egypt, Algeria, and Saudi Arabia*, (Westport, Conn.: Praeger, 1997).

MacKinnon, Colin, "Saudi Arabia: Major Change in Investment Climate." *Washington Report on Middle East Affairs*, 19, no. 6 (2000): 72–73.

Midnight Notes. *Midnight Oil: Work, Energy, War, 1973–1992*, (New York: Autonomedia, 1992).

Nusse, Andrea. *Muslim Palestine: The Ideology of Hamas*, (Amsterdam: Harwood Academic Publishers, 1998).

Walton, John and David Seddon. *Free Markets and Food Riots: The Politics of Global Adjustment*, (Oxford: Blackwell, 1994).

World Bank. *Claiming the Future: Choosing Prosperity in the Middle East and North Africa*, (Washington, D.C.: The World Bank, 1995).

Real War and Postmodern Illusions

By Chris Hables Gray

Chris Hables Gray is an author, academic, and anarchist-feminist.

Postmodern War at the End of War

War is not natural. Most people never fight in wars and some cultures never go to war. One of the main problems armies have is getting their soldiers to kill. But war is extremely complicated. It is not enough to be against it, we have to understand its origins and why it continues, if we are going to end it. Doing so will make it clear that certain psycho-cultural dynamics, such as patriarchy, nationalism, and religous fundamentalism are major causes of war. Some economic systems thrive on and foster war, especially authoritarian systems (fascism, state communism) and unbridled capitalism. And in particular, nation-states are the primary perpetuators of war today. To end war we will have to fundamentally change the dominant political, economic, and cultural institutions that have brought the human race to the brink of destroying itself. We know it is certainly possible to end war because war is a cultural invention that has

photo top: David Hanks

completely remade itself several times throughout its bloody history. We just have to do it soon because the new technologies of war mean that either war must end, or humanity will.

Theories certainly differ as to the origins of war. Some say it all started with "man-the-hunter" but I suspect that war's origins owe as much to man's role as the protector of the tribe, sacrificial prey as often as fighter, as Barbara Ehrenreich (1997) has eloquently argued. Once humans had pretty much triumphed over all of the predators but one, man himself, then it seems war was invented. It started as rite. Susan Mansfield (1982) has woven a compelling account of the psychological dynamics behind this. War still serves psychosocial needs as much as it now fulfills economic and political functions. The plasticity of war culturally, from almost bloodless ritual in tribal societies to the postmodern war we have now, gives us cause for hope.

The postmodern war system has been developing for over half a century. The paradoxes at its core have only deepened during this time because they cannot be solved technologically or even militarily. The continual proliferation of weapons of mass destruction, the invention of supposedly new types of conflict such as information war, and the rising importance of new military peacekeeping and peacemaking missions only illuminates the instability of postmodern war. It seems extremely likely that future conflict will be fundamentally different from ancient, modern, and postmodern war and it will be, in large part, either apocalyptic or utopian (peaceful), but certainly not both, but for now we have the strange system of postmodern war.

On January 20, 2000, Sergeant Major Philip Stoniger, the last member of the U.S. military mission to Haiti, was withdrawn. For six years, since the U.S. invasion in 1994 to restore the elected government of President Jean-Bertrand Aristide, there had been a continuous U.S. military presence in Haiti. With the departure of Stoniger that ended, although temporary humanitarian missions will continue. Sergeant Major Stoniger is a member of the elite army commando unit, the Green Berets. His speciality? political science (Perry, 2000).

Political science is a military speciality now? For sergeants? Indeed it is. Welcome to postmodern war where war is no longer an extension of politics; today it is politics that is an extension of war. But it is more complicated even than that. War is in the midst of a profound crisis. Only twice before has war changed so much. First, roughly 3,000 years ago, ancient war developed from ritual (primitive) war about the time civilizations arose. And 500 years ago, the process that led to modern war

A pile of spent artillery in a poor area of Baghdad. The shells are collected and then sold for their precious metal content. Sad'r City, Iraq, June 2003.

began with the rise of Renaissance rationality marked by Machiavelli's call for total political wars.

The quick and dirty story is that in both of these previous transitions war became more of a rational political instrument and much less of an irrational masculine ritual and slightly less of a naked grab for loot and power. Three thousand years ago a set of rituals became a way of life for some, an occupation for many, but in both cases conservative technologically and dominated by elites and their traditions. Five hundred years ago tradition began to be replaced by technological innovation and aristocracy gave way to meritocracy. Decisive battles became the goal and total war the norm. Up until World War II these trends continued until war became global, battle became continuous, and weapons became absolute. With atomic bombs as the first proof, it became clear that modern war's main assumption, of the political utility of total war, no longer held. Yet most of the modern war system remains in place: the military-industrial complex, the military mobilization of technoscience, and the assumption that war is still the most effective political tool available to policymakers. Hence, postmodern war.

The rise of modern war 500 years ago coincided with the invention of nation-states, the spread of European colonialism, and the triumph of

113

WAR

rationalism, especially as formalized in science and engineering. These developments were all related, so it should come as no surprise that the contemporary crisis of postmodern war is paralleled by the decline of the nation-state, the collapse of European colonialism, and a growing critique of reductionistic rationality.

So, unsurprisingly, contemporary war is very different than modern war. Many have noticed this in the resurgence of guerrilla war and its cousins (small war, dirty war, limited war, ethnic cleansing, terrorism) and there has also been much talk of a revolution in military affairs and a new world order and of the electronic and the automated battlefield and all the while we teeter on the edge of an apocalyptic conflict involving nuclear or biological weapons. Meanwhile, real peace struggles to be born. This transition period, these "interesting times," can best be described as postmodern, in my opinion. So what does this mean in terms of politics? The logical place to begin is with the problem of weapons of mass destruction.

Weapons of Mass Destruction

> By the fifteenth day, the tiny bruises on Ustinov's body had turned dark blue, and his skin was as thin as parchment. The blood pooling underneath began oozing through. It streamed from his nose, mouth, and genitals. Through a mechanism that is still poorly understood, the virus prevents normal coagulation: the platelets responsible for clotting blood are destroyed. As the virus spreads, the body's internal organs literally begin to melt away. (Alibek 1999, 131)

Nikolai Ustinov worked at a Siberian bioweapons lab called Vector. In 1988 he accidentally injected Marburg virus into his thumb. His horrible death makes him a good symbol for twenty-first-century weapons of mass destruction.

Biological warfare is not new. Poisoning wells with dead bodies was an ancient tactic and hundreds of years ago Native Americans were given the blankets of smallpox victims. During World War II the Japanese and the Germans experimented on humans with bioweapons and the British, Soviets, and Americans researched them as well. Many experts have been arguing that biological weapons are not so effective, and even repeated this during the anthrax attacks of the fall of 2001. But they didn't notice the fear that even ineffectual weapons can spread, and that while the death tolls were low, the potential was clear. This has been the case since World War II at least.

WAR

In 1942 the Japanese were already experimenting with anthrax on the Chinese in the camps of Unit 731. And anthrax is horrible, as the deaths in 2001 made clear. If it infects the lungs the victim can expect to first feel the symptoms of the flu or a cold. Then there is an "eclipse" period where the initial discomfort recedes. But the bacteria are merely proliferating. Suddenly they release a toxin that fills the lungs with liquid, turning the victim's skin "a faint bluish color." Choking and convulsions follow. "The disease is fatal in over 90 percent of untreated cases" (Alibek, 1999, 7–8).

But the infection need not be pulmonary. In 1979 technicians at Compound 19, a biowar plant in the Siberian city of Sverdlovsk, forgot to replace a clogged filter. Dry anthrax spores, of the military strain 836, were released on the city. Between 66 and 105 civilians died. The exact number is unknown, thanks to the skill of the cover-up, coordinated by the local Communist Party official, one Boris Yeltsin. While most of the initial victims died of pulmonary anthrax from inhaled pathogens, some were later infected through cuts on their skin by spores stirred up by disinfection procedures ordered by Yeltsin. The cultaneous infections produce black ulcerous swellings of the skin. If left untreated the bacteria soon produce toxins that bind to the cells of the body, especially white blood cells, killing them and then the host (Alibek 1999, 76–77).

Why make such a terrible weapon whose main target would clearly be civilians? The history of strategic bomb-ing offers an answer. As with the concept of bio-logical weapons, the idea of bombing cities originally provoked great horror among most civilians and military men. But now it is accepted, not only as a key weapon for war, but as a major tool for peacemaking, as U.S. bombings in Iraq and Serbia showed. Even though fascists bombed Guernica, and Japanese royalists bombed Shanghai, airmen from the great democracies, the United States and the U.K, bombed Hamburg, Dresden, and Tokyo in such a way as to create artificial weather systems called firestorms that consumed tens of thousands of workers (old men and women) and children. In the 1930s, even while the government of the United States was denouncing the bombing of civilians at Barcelona, Guernica, and Shanghai, the U.S. Army Air Force was perfecting the B-17 super bomber (Gray 1997, 134–7). And Western scientists, along with exiled anti-fascist Germans and Italians, built the atomic bombs.

In his brilliant history of U.S. strategic bombing, *The Rise of American Air Power: The Creation of Armageddon*, Michael Sherry argues that the political fanaticism of the Axis powers was matched by the technological fanaticism of the Allies. For the Germans, Italians, and Japanese, nationalistic/racist politics justified the exterminations (of Gypsies, Jews,

More than 1,000 Iraqis have made a home in Al Huda, the bombed wreckage of a former training center for Saddam Hussein's security forces. Here they protest their threatened eviction by the U.S. Occupation Authorities, 2004.

Slavs, Chinese, Koreans) and war on civilians. For the Allies, the existence of the technologies of strategic bombing and atomic weapons justified the extermination of cities. Sherry explains it was the product

> . . . of two distinct but related phenomena: one—the will to destroy—ancient and recurrent, the other—the technical means of destruction—modern. Their convergence resulted in the evil of American bombing. But it was a sin of a peculiarly modern kind because it seemed so inadvertent, seemed to involve so little choice. Illusions about modern technology had made aerial holocaust seem unthinkable before it occurred and simply imperative once it began. It was the product of a slow accretion of large fears, thoughtless assumptions, and at best discrete decisions. (1987, 137)

The system that produced strategic bombing and other aspects of total war is the same system that has produced nuclear and biological weapons. Biological and chemical weapons have often not been used because of their ineffectiveness. Difficult dispersal and slow infection rates have made them, so far, inferior weapons. Recent advances in biology and weapons platforms mean that this is changing. Soon biological warfare will be very effective. In particular, genetic engineering means that bioweapons that have heightened effects, limited targets (even racially

determined), and that are resistant to treatment can be created by altering existing pathogens and through combining different organisms. Missile, aerosol, and explosive technologies have improved so much that the delivery of these weapons is no longer the problem it has been in the past.

Improvements in technology also explain the return of chemical weapons. Hardly used since World War I, at the end of the twentieth century Iraq deployed them against rebellious Kurdish villages and it seems likely they will see more action. Biological and chemical weapons are often called the "poor man's nukes" and there is much truth to this. However, it disguises the fact that biological weapons in particular have more potential than nuclear weapons both for proliferation, since their production is becoming easier all the time, and for destructiveness. A single biological weapon could potentially kill hundreds of millions of people.

Even the most powerful nuclear weapon could not be expected to kill so many. Still, nuclear weapons have the advantage of having been used already in war and they are an acceptable part of international relations. This is why they have continued to proliferate. The fundamental hypocrisy of the nuclear powers—we have nukes and you don't and you can't—has meant that the Non-Proliferation Treaty is ineffectual. It is the technical and domestic political problems that have slowed proliferation, but hardly stopped it. Now that India and Pakistan have entered the nuclear "club" it is inevitable that more Muslim and Asian countries will acquire nuclear weapons if the international system remains the same.

The availability of nuclear material from the collapse of the Soviet Union, the proliferation of nuclear weapons, and the growing improvements in biological and genetic engineering mean that nonstate actors will eventually acquire weapons of mass destruction. When nonstates do what states do it is often labeled terrorism when, in actuality, nation-states have been the primary terrorists over the last few hundred years, as the regimes of Hitler, Stalin, and Pol Pot demonstrated. Still, the spread of weapons of mass destruction to groups besides nation-states is not good news. Walter Laqueur has made his career as an expert in terrorism, arguing that its threat was overrated. Recently he has changed his position completely,

> The ready availability of weapons of mass destruction has now come to pass, and much of what has been thought about terrorism, including some of our most basic assumptions, must be reconsidered. The character of terrorism is changing, any restraints that existed are disappearing, and above all, the threat to human life has become infinitely greater than it was in the past. (Laqueur 1999, 7)

It is a real danger, but perhaps not as great as the policy changes of the United States at the start of the twenty-first century that not only advocate the preemptive use of nuclear weapons but establish unilateral preemptive war as a key part of the U.S. strategic plan.

The Plan

The Plan is for the U.S. to rule the world.—(David Armstrong 2002, 76)

A series of official reports by the Secretaries of Defense Cheney (1992, 1993) and Donald Rumsfeld (2002) and key staff (Paul Wolfowitz and Colin Powell) lay out the current U.S. grand strategy. It is for the United States to be the "biggest bully on the block" in Powell's phrase (Armstrong, 78). It involves developing new technologies (nuclear bunker busters and other computerized weapons), new doctrines such as preemptive war, and dominance of space under the pretense of ballistic missile defense. The conquest of Iraq in 2003 was the proof by implementation of the idea of preemptive (aggressive) war (Chomsky 2003); the continued push for a missile defense is the continuation of the drive to control space.

The limitations of ballistic missile defense in general render the whole idea of an Intercontinental Ballistic Missile (ICBM) defense nonsensical. It isn't just that it costs the defender 10 to 100 times more to counter a deception by the attacker. That a small state or nongovernmental organization would choose to deliver weapons of mass destruction by rocket, instead of ship, toy plane, truck, or drug shipment is insane.

If the Star Wars system was really meant as a defensive system only (which is impossible in actual military terms, but let us pretend) then it would be trying to use an impossible technology to solve a horrible problem that was bought into being by technology in the first place. But, since the actual goal of the current plans is just to make the next step in the militarization of space a reality, we have a political goal being met by an impossible technology. The political goal is to make space the point from which the rest of the world can be dominated by various weapons, including those of mass destruction.

The militarization of space and its domination by the United States has been an explicit goal of parts of the U.S. military since the mid-1940s. Now there is a consensus at the Pentagon and it is shared by the executive branch and much of the national legislature. A Unified Space Command is in place and there are plans for the Space Force, a new military branch, to join the air force, navy, and army.

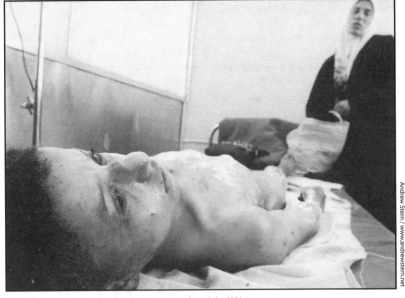

Iraq war burn victim, 2004.

Andrew Stern / www.andrewstern.net

General Joseph Ashy said in 1996 that

> It's politically sensitive, but it's going to happen. Some people
> don't want to hear this, and it sure isn't in vogue, but—
> absolutely—we're going to fight in space, We're going to fight
> *from* space and we're gong to fight *into* space. (Quoted in Scott,
> 1996, 51, original emphasis)

The Commission to Assess United States National Security Space
Management and Organization, chaired by the soon-to-be-appointed
secretary of defense, Donald Rumsfeld, reported (January 11, 2001) that,

> In the coming period the U.S. will conduct operations to, from, in
> and through space to support its national interests both on the
> earth and in space. . . . We know from history that every
> medium—air, land and sea—has seen conflict. Reality indicates
> that space will be no different. Given this virtual certainty, the
> U.S. must develop the means both to deter and to defend against
> hostile acts in and from space. This will require superior
> space capabilities.

Missile defense is just part of this major refocusing of military priorities for the
United States toward world dominance. To its supporters it seems inevitable.

WAR

It is our manifest destiny. You know we went from the East Coast to the West Coast of the United States of America settling the continent and they call that manifest destiny and the next continent if you will, the next frontier, is space and it goes on forever. —Sen. Bob Smith (R-NH), Senate Armed Services Committee

Meanwhile, defense intellectuals and established militaries have been flogging a new type of war, ostensibly based on information, and promising easy, maybe even bloodless, victories.

Two days before Christmas 1999, the BBC reported that the Revolutionary Armed Forces of Colombia (FARC), a Marxist guerrilla group, was Y2K compliant. Juan, FARC's systems manager, proudly announced that they had upgraded all of their complex databases, which chart kidnappings, among other things, to Windows 2000. Thanks to satellite telephones and laptops FARC maintains "Internet access even in the most remote jungle camps" (McDermott 1999).

FARC's wired status shows why it cannot be denied that computerization is changing war. But does this mean that a whole new type of war, information or net or cyber, has been created? No. Infowar comes out of two interrelated crisis. First there is today's crisis of information; the incredible increase in the power of information technologies in contemporary culture is causing numerous economic and political dislocations. Second, there is the current crisis of war itself. This ancient institution has reached its reductio ad absurdum in postmodern war as a direct result of the so-called information revolution which has made weapons of mass destruction (nuclear, biological, chemical) not only possible but accessible to many states and smaller institutions.

Ironically enough, it was globalization that triggered the deluge of information war theories. In the 1990s two RAND researchers, John Arquilla and David Ronfeldt, noticed that the Zapatista movement in Mexico was using the Internet to effectively mobilize international support. They stitched together a set of theories that took certain aspects of postmodern war—the centrality of information, the world communications system, the claim that politics (domestic and international) is now war by other means, the proliferation of undeclared wars and conflicts, the spread of war to every possible battlefield—and made of them absolutes. For a while there was a veritable craze for info/net/cyber war pronouncements and, no coincidence, massive funding requests to prepare for these "new" types of war. But now that the hysteria has worn off and the funding is in place, information war approaches are

being integrated into contemporary war practices and the idea of war fought totally in cyberspace has been abandoned.

U.S. confusion about the real uses of information war can be traced, in part, to the shift public attention can bring in conflicts. It actually demilitarizes them to some extent, but the problem is that it limits the usefulness of military means. The worldwide media attention the Zapatistas and their groups focused on Chiapas, along with the influx of rights activists to the area, sharply limited the Mexican government's ability to respond violently. What in other times would have been a bloody insurgency turned out to be a largely nonviolent conflict (Mathews, 1997, 54). José Angel Gurría, Mexico's foreign minister, concluded, "The shots lasted ten days and ever since the war has been . . . a war on the Internet" (quoted in Mathews, 1997, 54).

In the United States, the Unified Space Command has been put in charge of information war operations, a fitting choice since in many ways control of cyberspace is very similar to the control of outer space in its relationship to traditional battle. Cyberspace is just another operational front. In fact, the Pentagon very recently admitted as much. Air force general Richard Meyers, the new vice-chairman of the Joint Chiefs of Staff, said that cyber tactics were just "going to be one more arrow in the quiver" of military commanders (Kwong 2000). And it often won't even be a very important weapon.

For example, during the fall 1999 bombing war against Yugoslavia, the United States used offensive "cyber-war" weapons. While army general Henry H. Shelton, the chairman of the Joint Chiefs of Staff, didn't say what they were, one can assume various viruses were used to try and disrupt and disable Yugoslavian command and control and air defense systems (Associated Press, 1999). The mixed results of the Serbian operations show just how limited infowar operations can be, because information itself will always be imperfect. The 2003 Iraq War made the same point, with significant civilian casualties and friendly fire deaths even though the Iraqi military put up only minimal resistance.

Information Myths and Real War

Information theory is in its infancy but we do know that perfect information is impossible and that formal information systems are inevitably flawed with either paradoxes, limitations, or both. Hans Godel showed this applied to mathematics by turning the famous Cretan Liar paradox (if you meet someone who always lies and they tell you "I am a liar" what do you believe?) into an equation. Alan Turing and Alonzo

121

Church showed that the same principle applied to an infinite computer. From physics we learn that the observer effects the system (Heisenberg's Uncertainly Principle) and that sometimes to know one thing means you cannot know another (as with the behavior of electrons). From cybernetic theory it is clear that a subsystem cannot fully describe the larger system it is part of because a map is not the territory.

There have also been some insights of a more constructive vein. Complexity theory has shown that sometimes very small effects can change large systems (the butterfly effect), that sometimes overloaded systems transition into more complex systems, and that certain patterns repeat throughout systems at many different levels. What this means for the prediction and control of systems is that we now know many complex systems are "out of control" in that they cannot be controlled from outside. They have their own internal dynamics and achieve their own homeostasis, or now. Feedback loops, both positive and negative, are crucial for this.

War, as a very complex and volatile system, cannot be controlled, it cannot be managed, it cannot be predicted. This is as true of "real" bloody war as it is of virtual "cyberwar," as if any war that didn't damage and destroy bodies could really be called a war. So, while information war will not happen, "regular" wars will not happen either. As the first advocates of infowar point out, "Look around, no 'good old-fashioned war' is in sight" (Arquilla and Ronfeldt, 1997, 1). But what is in sight is a great deal of conflict. While some of it is incredibly horrible genocides and ethnic cleansings, and some of it is traditional struggles for resources or nation-state status, most war now is, in perfectly postmodern fashion, for peace. That irony should never be far from our minds. Elaine Scarry (1985, 62) reminds us that both torture and war depend on what is done to bodies.

> In each, the incontestable reality of the body—the body in pain, the body maimed, the body dead and hard to dispose of—is separated from its source and conferred on an ideology or issue or instance of political authority impatient of, or deserted by, benign sources of substantiation.

This "incontestable reality of the body" is still the fundamental ground of war even in these postmodern times. While the specific roles in wars that are played by bodies are proliferating wildly, their importance cannot be overstated. As Elaine Scarry and almost every soldiers' memoir ever written make clear, war is based on human bodies and what is done to them (wounding and killing), but the official doctrine now is that systems are what is important. Systems are mobilized and systems are targeted, not humans, nor machines alone. So when the U.S. and allied militaries target the sanitation systems and other infrastructures of a country like Iraq, leading directly to the death of hundreds and thousands of women and children, that is just a system effect. It isn't meant to be taken personally.

San Francisco antiwar march, 2003.

Of course, in many respects this is just a continuation of trends in late modern war that targeted civilians. The massive strategic bombing of World War II is a case in point. It was called "dehousing" because it ostensibly was aimed at knocking down or burning up workers' houses, even if this meant the killing of many these workers (women and old men) and their children. This is quite unlike the killing of civilians in ancient and colonial war, and by the Nazis and the Japanese in World War II, which was done consciously for terror, fun, and to clear conquered territory for settlement by the victors.

Meanwhile, the crisis of war has only deepened in the last decade. Weapons of mass destruction proliferate, unmanageable wars rage around the globe, and attempts to solve war's contradictions through technologies such as remote-controlled weapons or through reconceptualizations such as information war, or the privatization (to mercenaries and corporate security units) of security, continue to fail.

The Gulf War, only recently put forward as proof that war can still be an effective political instrument and relatively painless for the victors, is now seen in quite a different light, thanks to Gulf War Syndrome and the political resilience of Saddam Hussein as well as other factors (Vernon 2001; Bacevich 2001). That other great "victory," Afghanistan, has turned out to be less than decisive as well.

Still, the push for automating and informating war continues unabated, despite the continued decline of military force as an effective political instrument. For every instance where a political leader might be pressured into changing policy through military action, such as Sloban Milosevic was with the bombing of Serbia, there are many more cases of the utter failure

WAR

Jason Justice

Antiwar activists doing yoga direct action in the streets in front of Bechtel corporate office, San Francisco, March 19, 2004.

of military action to achieve political goals, even with an overwhelming force superiority. Somalia is a good example.

> From where he sat, Abokoi could see the mob descend on the Americans. Only one was still alive. He was shouting and waving his arms as the mob grabbed him by the legs and began pulling him away from the helicopter, tearing at his clothes. He saw his neighbors hack at the bodies of the Americans with knives and begin to pull at their limbs. Then he saw people running and parading with parts of the Americans' bodies. (Bowden 1999, 195)

This account of the downing of a U.S. helicopter in Mogadishu, as seen by a wounded (by helicopter fire) Somali, is in Mark Bowden's book *Black Hawk Down*. It shows that for some pilots war remains as visceral as ever.

Bowden's story also illuminates several other strange dynamics of contemporary war. When the Black Hawks were shot down incredible efforts were made to retrieve the bodies of the crew. In late modern and postmodern war a veritable fetish over the bodies of the dead soldiers has developed in the militaries of the industrial world. It seems eerily familiar to the homage paid to the dead that we see by primitive warriors who believed that the unhonored dead could not rest. In ancient war

defilement was still seen as horrible, as the *Iliad* makes clear with the dragging of Hector's corpse around the walls of Troy by Achilles, much as the Somalis dragged the dead American soldiers through the streets of Mogadishu horrified not just the world, but even many Somalis.

But such honor for dead bodies has not always been the practice. In fact, often during modern war's history the corpses of the dead were left to rot where they fell. After Waterloo English contractors collected the bones of the dead from both sides, ground them up, and sold them to fertilize English gardens (Ignatieff 1997, 113). Yet now there is an absolute mania to recover the dead, even to the extent of assuming that if their bodies cannot be found, then they are hidden away in some secret enemy camp. This is denial plain and simple: denial of what war does, denial of how horrible war is, denial of how fragile all our bodies are. The only way war can survive today, as an institution, is if we deny what it does to soldiers and just as much, what it might do to us all.

Seemingly far removed from massacred pilots and the heroic efforts to retrieve their bodies are stories about little portable computers, palm pilots, which the Associated Press (2001) tells us are sweeping through the U.S. military. The navy issues them to all graduates of Annapolis and most other officers. Palm pilots are now playing a major role in facilitating the incredible information flows that the contemporary U.S. Navy depends upon. From SEAL commandos to tank mechanics to stealth bomber pilots, all jobs in the military today integrally involve computers and other technologies in intimate integration with humans.

Despite tenacious resistance, this computerization continues and it seems like it will eventually remove most pilots from the sky and put them on the ground controlling vehicles from afar, and it will replace the majority of ships' crews with a few sea "pilots" who will practically "fly" large ships with the help of complex automated equipment (Gray 1997). The import of these changes cannot be trivialized, especially when you consider how pilots dominate the U.S. Air Force and Navy politically and how much they love to fly. But the pressure to minimize casualties through maximizing technology is irresistible, even if it hasn't really been proven militarily. Quite the reverse. Again and again close analysis shows that the highest technology can't win the simplest conflicts, such as the fighting in Somalia. In one revealing incident, during the raid that led to the destruction of the two Black Hawks, the rescue convoys were being controlled from the air. So instead of going straight to their objectives they were routed around and around through ambushes and back through them again because the big high-tech troop carriers couldn't fit down many streets and the

WAR

controlling observers, high above in helicopters, couldn't really see what was happening on the ground (Bowden 1999, 112).

For all the flash of high-tech cyborg (human-machine) systems on the ground or flying, war is still political and it always comes down to what is done to messy bodies. Consider this incident from the fighting in Mogadishu. An RPG is a rocket-propelled grenade.

> Then there was the woman in a blue turban, a powerful woman with thick arms and legs who came sprinting across the road carrying a heavy basket in both arms. She was wearing a bright blue-and-white dress that billowed behind her as she ran. Every Ranger at the intersection blasted her. Twombly, Nelson, Yurek, and Stebbins all opened up. Howe fired on her from further up the hill. First she stumbled, but kept on going. Then as more rounds hit her, she fell and RPGs spilled out of her basket onto the street. The shooting stopped. She had been hit by many rounds and lay in a heap in the dirt for a long moment, breathing heavily. Then the woman pulled herself up on all fours, grabbed an RPG round, and crawled. This time the massive Ranger volley literally tore her apart. A fat 203 round blew off one of her legs. She fell in a bloody lump for a few moments, then moved again. Another massive burst of rounds rained on her and her body came further apart. It was appalling, yet some of the Rangers laughed. To Nelson the woman no longer even looked like a human being, she'd been transformed into a monstrous bleeding hulk, like something from a horror movie. (Bowden 1999, 217–218)

Women have always participated in war, albeit at a lesser level then men. In ragged wars, such as the one in Somalia, women can be particularly important, and this women carrying ammunition was one of many killed by the U.S. troops out of necessity and otherwise. But in these types of conflicts, even when women are fighters, they are treated as exceptions that prove the rule: war is for men. But in today's high-tech military, because women are needed to fill so many skilled positions, their importance is actually leading to a redefinition of war's masculine nature.

> The real story of military policy in the 1990s was the transformation of the armed services from bastions of masculinity (an increasingly suspect quality) into institutions that were accommodating to women and "family friendly." . . . By decade's end, Americans took it as a matter of course that female fighter pilots were flying strike missions over Iraq, and that a terrorist attack on an American warship left female sailors among the dead and wounded. (Bacevich 2001, 86)

WAR

David Hanks

While war remains masculine there is now a real place for females since gender categorizations are increasingly rendered by rank (lower the rank, the more feminine) rather than genitalia. As Professor Bacevich's quotation above makes clear, most military specialities are now open to females, who today serve on most ships and in most cockpits. Only one area of war has been preserved for males among the high-tech militaries of the world: killing in close combat. It is an important exception but it doesn't change things much since more civilians are now targeted in war than soldiers are. War is about terror now after all, and there is even less space for peace in our lives.

Terror and Peace

The 2003 Iraq invasion has demonstrated just how problematical war is today. The United States carefully chose its opponent, a weak and unpopular dictatorship, and the timing (between 9-11 and the next election) and the war itself went relatively smoothly. But within days of victory tens of thousands of Iraqis were in the street demanding the United States leave and the dreaded weapons of mass destruction (WMD), the official reason for the invasion, were not to be found. While some chemical or biological weapon research equipment or weapons will probably be uncovered, it is clear that Iraqi WMD were not a real threat to the United

States or anyone else. Now the United States can expect growing resistance among Iraqis and others around the world to its military adventures, showing once again that as a political instrument (the central idea of modern war) war is almost useless now, no matter how great one's superiority is.

Despite the obvious dangers to humanity's future war is continuing. Colombia, Pakistan/India, China and Taiwan, Indonesia, Burma, Chechenya and the former USSR empire, and much of Africa are all sites of real and potential wars. According to UNICEF, in the ten years since the Convention on the Rights of the Child was adopted by the U.N. General Assembly (1990), 2 million children died in armed conflict (*Time*, 2000, 23). This shows that the current international system is failing disastrously.

On the bright side, few justifications remain for war and peace movements push for the end of ancient conflicts such as those in Northern Ireland and the Middle East. And nation-state sovereignty continues to decline despite spasms of nationalism. Nation-states aren't the only cause of war, certainly. Empires, tribes, and fundamentalist groups (religious or political) seem just as capable of violence. But our current international system is based on nation-states and their decline opens up a real opportunity, actually a necessity, to demilitarize politics.

Many international institutions, nongovernmental organizations, and individuals are working for this demilitarization which has become a major constraint on organized political violence, even if it hasn't stopped it. The unprededented worldwide mobilizations against the U.S. attack on Iraq demonstrated this conclusively. The United States may be the only nation-state superpower, but antiwar international civil society is another superpower, one which is waxing in strength as the mistakes and hubris of the U.S. government sap its power. Which helps us answer the single most important question about war: can it be abolished?

I would answer yes, but only if we all take part. For example, Professor Yamamoto and Charles Piller advocate not just international treaties to prevent the spread of bioweapons, but a ban on secret research, a ban on defensive research, and putting all genetic research in civilian control (1988, 235–236). The eminent physicist Sir Joseph Rotblat has called (1999) for all scientists and engineers to take the student Pugwash oath that pledges to "work for a better world" and not to "use my education for any purpose intended to harm human beings or the environment." Of course, the Hippocratic Oath did not keep many German and Japanese doctors from committing horrible crimes in World War II, but such oaths

are an important start. They are especially important for spreading the realization that what technoscience does is the responsibility of those who make it possible, not just political leaders.

There are many other examples: the rise of pacifist thinking in the last 200 years and of feminism in the last 100, the ending of the Vietnam War (the first time an imperial power has given up not because of defeat on the battlefield but rather in the hearts and minds of its citizens), thanks to protests around the world, the growing movement of veterans for abolishing war, the spread of cooperation between peoples, such as the European Union that has united the region that spawned the most horrific wars of the twentieth century. The movement against war has to happen everywhere, from the international level to the daily work we do.

The group Computer Professionals for Social Responsibility started during the debates about the Star Wars antimissile system. Today it continues, not just campaigning against baby Star Wars and other military illusions based on computerization, such as information war, but it also mobilizes computer professionals to empower workers and to safeguard privacy and other human rights threatened by new technologies. Just as postmodern militarization has seeped into every aspect of contemporary life, there must be a countermobilization against war. And it has to look at the underlying causes of war, and seek to address them, and not just focus in on the latest battle once it explodes on our TV screens.

Because war is certainly not natural. Most people never fight in war and most cultures are not at war most of the time. But aggression does seem to be a natural part of the human psyche and when combined with our current culture, with its compelling masculinist and nationalist stories, war becomes very powerful indeed. But it is too dangerous to allow. Even those who believe war is inevitable believe it must be ended.

One leading advocate of the "war is natural" school," Professor Marvin Harris of the University of Florida, concluded, after strenuously arguing that the few societies without war "shouldn't lead researchers into naively believing that they can abolish war" and deriding anthropologists for

believing that "if we can only talk to these people and convince them they will stop war" that: "we can and must abolish war if humanity is going to have any future at all" (McDonald 1999).

When even those who—mistakenly in my opinion—believe war is natural say it must be abolished it is clear that something must be, and can be, done. In 1994 a group of intellectuals posted a notice in the *New York Times*.

"IN MEMORIUM—Our commitments, principles, and moral values. Died: Bosnia, 1994 on the occasion of the 1,000 day of the siege of Sarajevo."

I wept for Sarajevo at that time, that brave, beautiful, attempt to keep tolerance and humanism alive in the face of insane ancient prejudices and postmodern weaponry. But it was too early to give up. Since then we have had massacres in a half-dozen more places, from Indonesia to Central Africa, and it is still too early to give up. We have nuclear escalation between India and Pakistan, the United States committing to aggressive war, war has become pure terror, and the spread of weapons of mass destruction continues around the globe and it is still too early to give up. Because we now have a worldwide movement against undemocratic globalization and aggressive war, we have a worldwide realization that our environment is in danger, and we have a worldwide understanding that human rights should be universal and that war is no longer an acceptable way of solving political differences. Now we just have to change the international political order. Of course, it won't be easy but as it is necessary, it is our only choice.

Bibliography

Alibek, Ken. *Biohazard*. (Random House, 1999).

Armstrong, David. "Dick Cheney's Song of America: Drafting a Plan for Global Dominance". *Harper's Magazine* (October 2002): 76-83.

Arquilla, John and David Ronfeldt. *In Athena's Camp: Preparing for Conflict in the Information Age*. (Santa Monica, Calif.: Rand, 1997).

Associated Press. "Handheld Computers Give Sailors a High-Tech Lifeline." *Great Falls Tribune*, February 25, 2001.

_____. "Campaign Against Yugoslavia Included Mysterious Cyber-Aspect." *Great Falls Tribune*, October 8, 1999: 4A.

Bacevich, Andrew J. "A Less than Splendid Little War." *WQ: The Wilson Quarterly* (winter 2001): 83–94.

Bowden, Mark. *Black Hawk Down: A Story of Modern War*. (Penguin, 1999).

Barbara Ehrenreich. *Blood Rites: Origins and History of the Passions of War*. (New York: Henry Holt, 1997).

Cheney, Dick. *Defense Planning Guidance for the 1994–1999 Fiscal Years*. (Washington, D.C.: Dept. of Defense, 1992).

_____. *Defense Strategy for the 1990s*. Washington, D.C.: Dept. of Defense, 1993.

Chomsky, Noam. "Interview by Michael Albert." ZNET (http//www.zmag.org/), April 13, 2003.

Gray, Chris Hables. *Postmodern War: The New Politics of Conflict*. (New York: Guilford; London: Routledge, 1997).

_____. "The Crisis of Infowar." in *Infowar,* ed. Gerfried Stocker and Christine Schopf. (NewYork: SpringerWien 130–136).

Ignatieff, Michael. *The Warrior's Honor: Ethnic War and the Modern Conscience*. (Owl Books), 1997.

Kwong, Arnold W. "Pentagon to Include Cyber Warfare as a Standard Tactic." Reuters, January 7, 2000. http://www.straitstimes.asial.com/cyb/cyb2_0107.html

Laqueur, Walter. *The New Terrorism: Fanaticism and the Arms of Mass Destruction*. (New York/Oxford: Oxford University Press, 1999).

Mansfield, Susan. *The Gestalt of War: An Inquiry into Its Origin and Meaning as a Social Institution*. (New York: Dial Press, 1982).

Mathews, Jessica T. "Power Shift." *Foreign Affairs*, 76, no. 1 (January/February, 1997): 50–66.

McDermott, Jeremy. "Columbia's Rebels Ready for Y2K." BBC World Service, December 23, 1999. (http://news.bbc.co.uk/hi/english/world/americas/newsaid_576000/576212.stm)

WAR

WAR

McDonald, Kim A. "Anthropologists Debate Whether, and How, War Can Be Wiped Out." *Chronicle of Higher Education* (December 3, 1999): A21.

Perry, Dan. "After Five Years, US Military Writes End to Mission in Haiti." *Boston Globe* (January 21, 2000): A4.

Rotblat, Joseph. "A Hippocratic Oath for Scientists." *Science*, 286, no. 5444, 1999.

Rumsfeld, Donald. "The Commission to Assess United States National Security Space Management and Organization Report." Washington, D.C.: US Congress, 2001.

_____. *Defense Planning Guidance for the 2004–2009 Fiscal Years.* Washington, D.C.: Dept. of Defense, 2002.

Scarry, Elaine. *The Body in Pain: The Making and Unmaking of the World.* (Oxford University Press, 1985).

Scott, William B. "USSC Prepares for Future Combat Missions in Space." *Aviation Week & Space Technology.* (August 5, 1996).

Sherry, Michael. *The Rise of American Air Power: The Creation of Armageddon.* (New Haven: Yale University Press, 1987).

Smith, Sen. Bob (R-NH). Senate Armed Services Committee ("Star Wars Returns" documentary, February 2000. http://www.envirovideo.com)

Time. "Notebook." (January 24, 2000): 18-23.

Vernon, Alex. "The Gulf War and Postmodern Memory." *WQ: The Wilson Quarterly* (winter, 2001): 68–82.

Yamamoto, Keith R., and Charles Piller. *Gene Wars: Military Control Over the New Genetic Technologies.* (Beech Tree Books/Morrow, 1988).

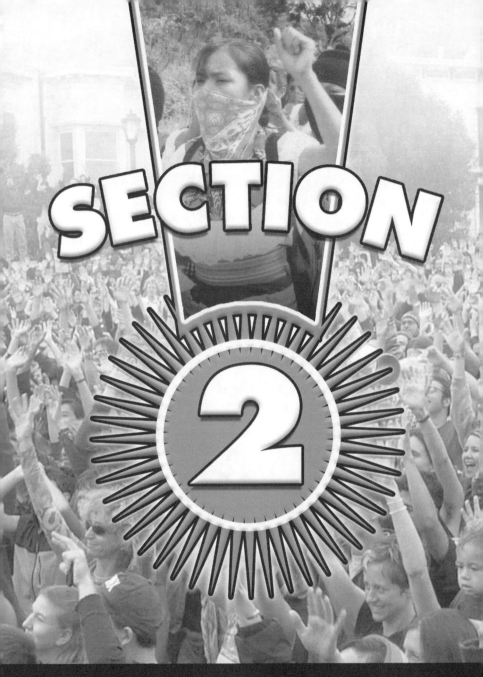

SECTION

2

HOW TO
CHANGE THINGS

photo top: Hilary Klein   background photo: David Hanks

Women protest militarization after Acteal massacre.
Photo: Mariana Mora

CHAPTER

13

Strategizing for a Living Revolution

By George Lakey

STRATEGY

First arrested in a civil rights campaign, George Lakey coauthored a basic handbook for the Civil Rights movement, A Manual for Direct Action, *and then five other books on social change. He currently works with Training for Change in Philadelphia (www.TrainingforChange.org). In forty-five years of activism he has led workshops for London anarchists, New York Act Up, West Virginia coal miners, Mohawks in Canada, African National Congress in Johannesburg, lesbians and gays in Russia, revolutionary student soldiers in a guerrilla encampment inside Burma, and many other movements and groups. He has published widely including the* Nation, First of the Month, *and* Clamor Magazine, *and is included in recent books including* Race, Class, and Gender *edited by Margaret L. Andersen and Patricia Hill Collins, and* The Battle of Seattle *edited by Eddie Yuen, George Katsiaficas, and Daniel Burton Rose.*

Otpor ("Resistance" in Serbian) began as hundreds, then thousands, then tens of thousands of young people took to the streets to rid their country of the dictator Slobodan Milosevic. Impatient with the cautious ways of many of their prodemocracy elders, the youths organized in coffee bars

Nicolas Pousthomis

Anti-government graffiti during Argentine uprising, December 19-20, 2001.

and schools, posted graffiti almost everywhere, and used street actions to embarrass the regime.

From the moment Otpor began, it had a strategy. They were immensely creative in their tactics and at the same time realized that no struggle is ever won simply by a series of actions. Otpor activists knew they could only succeed by creating a strategy that guided a largely decentralized network of groups.

Cynical outsiders were skeptical when Otpor activists claimed to have no leader, when they said that they were all leaders and shared the responsibility for their actions. What the skeptics overlooked was the power of strategy as a unifying force, taking its place beside the rebel energy and the lessons of recent history that these young people shared. Otpor activists didn't need an underground commander giving them their marching orders because they shared a strategy they believed in; they were happy to improvise creatively within that strategic framework.

Bojän Zarkovic, one of the Otpor trainers, told an audience at the A-Space (an anarchist coffeehouse) in Philadelphia about the boundless creativity of the young activists. They would virtually fill a wall of newsprint with their tactical ideas, he said, and then they would choose, in light of their strategy and also their preference for humor and pranks. The result was that Milosevic's attempt to portray them as a group of terrorists in the state-controlled media lost credibility. True, they wore black jeans, black leather jackets, and black T-shirts with a clenched fist silk-screened on the front, but their actions had humor and connected with the people. Passersby who saw them (and spread the word) debunked the media portrayal: "They're just our kids having fun and, you know, they're right about Milosevic!"

In October 2000, joined by hundreds of thousands of workers and professionals, the young people threw Milosevic out. By that time, his party was in disarray, his police in confusion, his army was split.

Late nineties Serbia was different in many ways from the situation facing activists in the United States or other countries now, but even so, Otpor's experience can stimulate our thinking. Given how many activists are tired

STRATEGY

of an endless round of protests that don't seem to add up to anything, Otpor activists' biggest gift to us might be their choice to unite around a strategy, to get creative about tactics, and let the strategy guide which tactics make sense and which don't.[1]

An Alternative View of Power

The young people who started Otpor had a clear conception of how domination works. They saw their society as a pyramid, with Milosevic and his cronies at the top, in alliance with business owners, party leaders, and generals. The direction of power was typically top-down, and included both obvious repression (the army, police, secret police) and subtle repression like a monopoly of the media and control over school curricula. Here's where Otpor activists diverged from conventional wisdom about power. Rather than buy into the top-down version of power that Milosevic wanted them to believe, they decided instead to picture Serbian society as organized into pillars of support holding up the dictator. If the pillars gave way, Otpor believed that Milosevic would fall. Since the top power-holders depend on the compliance of those beneath them to stay on top, Otpor's strategy was to weaken the compliance and finally to break it.

Here's just one example of how it worked in Serbia. One pillar of support for Milosevic was his police. Otpor systematically undermined that pillar. The young activists knew that fighting the police would strengthen police loyalty to Milosevic (and also support the mass media claim that the young people were hoodlums and terrorists). So they trained themselves to make nonviolent responses to police violence during protests. One of the slogans they learned during their trainings was: "It only hurts if you're scared." They took photos of their wounded. They enlarged the photos, put them on signs, and carried the signs in front of the houses of the police who hurt them. They talked to the cop's neighbors about it, took the signs to the schools of the police officers' children and talked with the children about it. After a year of this, police were plainly reluctant to beat Otpor activists even when ordered to do so, because they didn't want the negative reactions of their family, friends, or neighbors.

The young people joked with the plainclothes police assigned to infiltrate them and reminded the cops that everyone would get their chance to act for democracy. Through the assertive outreach of the activists, relationships were built with the police, even into the higher ranks. When the movement ripened into a full-fledged insurgency in Belgrade, many police were sent out of the city by their commanders while other police simply watched the crowds take over the Parliament building.

It wasn't easy, as one of my Otpur friends who had been beaten repeatedly told me. It was, however, simple; the strategy guided the young activists to develop creative tactics that took away one of the key pillars of the dictator's support.

Can This Work in Other Places?

One reason why the Otpor activists worked so efficiently at undermining the various pillars of Milosevic's support was because many knew that their bottom-up approach to power had already worked in other places. Consider what had happened within the lifetime of Otpor teenagers: the Philippine dictator Marcos had been overthrown by what was called "people power" in 1986; Communist dictatorships had been overthrown by people power in East Germany, Czechoslovakia, Hungary, and Poland in 1989; commanders in the KGB, the Soviet Army, and the Communist Party were prevented by people power from establishing a coup in Russia in 1991; a mass nonviolent uprising in Thailand prevented a top military general from consolidating his power in 1993; the South African whites' monopoly on political rule was broken in 1994 after a decade of peoples' struggle. In all these places the power-holders found their power slipping away because those they depended on refused any longer to follow the script.

When I was trying as a young man to puzzle out this alternative view of power, so different from what is usually taught in school, I encountered Bernard Lafayette, who was then a Student Nonviolent Coordinating Committee (SNCC) staffer from the deep South. He explained it to me with a metaphor. Bernard said that a society is like a house. The foundation is the cooperation or compliance of the people. The roof is the state and its repressive apparatus. He asked me what happens to the house if the foundation gives way. He went on to ask: "How will it change what happens if more weapons are put on the roof, bigger tanks, more fancy technology? What will happen to the house then, if the foundation gives way?"

Of course, the power-holders want us to believe that power is top-down, that we must be passive, that violence is the most powerful force. What power-holders would want us to know that the power is, in fact, in our hands? That instead of being intimidated by police, military, corporate leaders, media tycoons, and politicians, if the people were to find out that we give away our power through compliance, we could take it back again through noncooperation?

The use of nonviolent tactics to force change has a deep track record which is reaching critical mass. For example, hundreds of thousands of

people of color have used nonviolent direct action in campaigns for over a century in the United States alone. (In 1876 in St. Louis, African Americans were staging freedom rides against discrimination on trolley cars, to take one of thousands of examples.) In any given week there are community-based organizations all across the United States. engaged in nonviolent action: marches, sit-ins, street blockades, boycotts, civil disobedience, and the like. Books could be written just about the unions of people of color, like the hospital workers, hotel workers, and janitors, who go out on strike as well as use other tactics. Whites in the United States., especially working-class whites, also have a long track record of using nonviolent tactics to struggle for their goals. The challenge is not so much encouraging diverse peoples to engage in nonviolent struggle when they are up against it; the challenge is to link short-run struggles to more far-ranging goals.[2]

Strategy = Power

My friends in Otpor would be the first to admit that a mass insurgency that brings down a dictator is not enough—not enough to establish full democracy, respect for diversity, economic institutions in harmony with the earth, or other parts of their vision. It's one thing to open up a power vacuum through noncooperation (and that is a great and honorable achievement). It's another thing to firmly establish the democratic community we deserve.

For that, the strategy must go deeper. We need to create a strategy that builds at the same time as it destroys. We need a strategy that validates alternatives, supports the experience of freedom, and expands the skills of cooperation. We need a political strategy that is at the same time a community strategy, one that says "yes" to creative innovation in the here and now and links today's creativity to the new society that lies beyond a power shift.

With the help and feedback of many activists from a number of countries I've created a strategic framework that aims to support today's activists, something like the way Otpor activists were supported by their strategy. I call it strategy for a living revolution.[3]

The strategy not only encourages creating new tactics and more boldness in using the best of the old, but it also helps activists sort out which tactics will be most effective. Finally, the strategy brings in the dimension of time. It suggests that some tactics that are ineffective at one moment will be just right at another. It offers an organic, developmental framework of stages over time.

STRATEGY

An understanding of our place in the trajectory of history adds to our power. Activists from other countries have been heard to laugh at U.S. activists because we notoriously lack a sense of history. This strategy framework supports us to overcome our cultural limitation and learn to think like the historical beings that we actually are.[4]

The strategy framework has five stages: cultural preparation; organization-building; confrontation; mass political and economic noncooperation; and parallel institutions. The stages are in sequence, with lots of overlap. Like any model, this one is oversimplified in order to be more easily learned and worked with. One way to make the model more complex is to picture society as a cluster of subsocieties that respond to these stages at different rates, which means that activists might go through the first several stages over and over, so in reality we may end up more in cyclical motion than in any sort of linear progression. But for purposes of clarity in this essay, I'll present the five stages in a linear way and be glad if readers get from it a sense of movement over time.

STAGE ONE — Cultural Preparation

Some people call this politicization or consciousness-raising. I put it first because for revolutionary change we need new culture. We can't get rid of hierarchies of domination "out there" if we are still playing domination games in our own heads.[5] As Gandhi said, we need to be the change we want to see, and that's not just an individual process, it's a collective and cultural shift.

In this stage, cultural workers of all kinds get to challenge and support us all-out as together we build a culture of resistance. It's a great time for support groups that assist us to unlearn racism, sexism, religious bigotry, and the like. Oppressed groups work to discard the internalized messages that limit them.

One of the ways that many U.S. activists are particularly limited is in the understanding of class. Classism is one of the most unexamined oppressions in the United States, and is therefore an area of cluelessness among many activists. Many times I've heard activists who would never use slurs in referring to transsexuals or Puerto Ricans joke about "rednecks" and "white trash"! Classism goes well beyond language, however; some activists' unconscious replication of the mainstream's oppression of poor and working-class people influences everything from tactics to communication style to the difficulty in forming coalitions or even meeting people on the street. Getting a grip on unconscious classism will make a huge difference in the ability of U.S. activists to work for justice.[6]

The juice in this stage is vision. The primary task of every revolutionary movement is to create a vision of what activists want instead of the status quo. Vision inspires people to join us because they can contrast it with the consumerist hat tricks that the power-holders use to distract them from planetary crisis. Vision inspires us, because it not only clarifies what we want but reminds us why we want it. Vision reduces cooptation, because its integrity is a rebuke against meaningless compromise. Vision builds unity, because tactical disagreements and personality clashes are smaller when seen against the perspective of our goals.

The container in this stage is strategy. Without a container, it's very hard to hold the juice—if I have no strategy for making a difference, why even bother with vision? Strategy is therefore linked to vision. The more we study and participate in large-scale people power, the bigger our strategy will become and the more we will notice many of its aspects already alive in the body politic. Strategy counters despair and fosters vision. Vision informs strategy. We need the juice and the container.

STAGE TWO — *Organization-Building*

Organization is essential for a movement, because only through organization is it possible to generate enough force to make a difference. Spontaneous moments of resistance can no more accomplish substantial change than can occasional rioting—each can be appreciated in symbolic terms but structures aren't changed.

The United States poses an amazing contradiction when it comes to organizing. On the one hand, the United States is famous in the world for its "civil society," the voluntary groups that show up on all levels. In my urban neighborhood alone we have different groups working on the schools, the park, safety, cultural festivals, protesting gentrification, and literally dozens of other good causes. People from other countries who come to my neighborhood for activist training are sometimes amazed by how mainstream it is in the United States to roll up our sleeves and create groups to achieve goals.

On the other hand, radical activists can find it tough to build organizations—our very idealism can be an obstacle. We want our groups to reflect visionary values rather than the domination games that often plague mainstream organizations. What's tough is figuring out how to both be visionary and get the job done.

Some organizational forms seem to me to be especially promising in this stage: alternative institutions, ongoing affinity groups, transformational networks, and radical caucuses.

STRATEGY

Alternative institutions provide a great laboratory for putting vision to work. Food co-ops, presses, worker-owned enterprises, the list is large. As we consciously practice joining—both inside the alternative and outside, reaching out to the neighbors or to adjoining social circles—the alternatives can grow. We then learn to innovate systems that are both strong and democratic, highly productive and supportive of individual workers. We can support the organizational geniuses among us who, even if they aren't always warm and fuzzy, can figure out the complex connections that enable cooperation of scale and distance.

Ongoing affinity groups provide a support base for individuals to participate in a range of activities, from protesting to digging the community garden to jumping into a conflict as a human shield to protect people from getting hurt.[7] An affinity group can choose to work on one issue or campaign for a period, adding its energy and expertise to the struggle and performing an educational role, or it can be more mobile in the interest of building human links to prepare eventual coalition-building.

Transformational networks help groups to learn from each other and give mutual aid. Movement activists have come a long way in recent decades in learning how to share critical information rapidly.[8]

Radical caucuses based on identity or politics continue to be key. I've been fortunate to be in gay caucuses and working-class caucuses where we supported each other to reduce internalized oppression at the same time as we supported each other to change the larger organization we were part of. I've also been blessed as a white person to be part of a national organization where the people of color caucus worked so effectively that it became the agenda-setter for the organizational development.

In order to work optimally, the caucus must be visible to the wider group rather than trying to work covertly. It's hard to think of any organizational style that undermines movements as effectively as covertness; movements can even move ahead more easily with steep hierarchies than they can with invisible elements within.

Adopting a discipline of secrecy may at some times and places be useful, but it is a choice that needs careful thought, especially when we consider that it is often not necessary even in police states.[9] The most recent manifestation of covertness as an organizational style in the U.S. has been, among global justice activists, "security culture." Security culture hurts the movement in several ways.

One result of security culture is withholding trust. To win, movements need to expand. To expand, activists need to trust—themselves, each other, and the people they reach out to. When trustlessness is institutionalized, the movement can't recruit well outside its own circle. Who might be an agent, who might betray us, who cannot be relied on? The wariness is toxic because activists feed each other's fear.

Security culture also reduces the ability of direct actionists to develop and sustain alliances. Successful direct action movements learn to attract allies. The role of an ally is different from the role of a campaigner. The job of campaigners is to take the initiative and get the ball rolling; the job of allies is to come in and help push once the ball's rolling. In most U.S. cities and towns we find a lot of activists who simultaneously are campaigning on one issue and are allies to other campaigns. This flexibility works well, and helps to generate a climate that stays open to radical perspectives.

However, because security culture generates trustlessness, protesters have a hard time trusting allies. They sometimes enter a confrontation with authority politically isolated, having failed to reach out and open up the communication channels with people working on other projects. Where all this comes crashing down is at the moment of state repression, which is when allies are often most needed.

If security culture reduces the internal morale of the movement, reduces its growth potential, and hurts relationships with allies, what's the point? For one thing, secrecy makes possible certain direct-action tactics that rely on surprise, and we may be reluctant to give up those tactics. Secrecy and stealth may also appear in our movement because they strengthen the boundary between Insider and Outsider, they exaggerate differentiation.[10] This is perhaps a gratuitous and unhealthy impulse and should be examined honestly.

Unfortunately, the power-holders' security agencies also understand the negative impact of secrecy on the movement, and they use it to their own advantage.[11] They have abundant resources to invest in spies and electronic surveillance, and the more covert we are, the more resources they can demand (thereby increasing the already obscene size of the security state). Not only does this increase the power and affluence of their apparatus, but it also justifies their putting more people in our ranks, infiltrators who help make decisions and sometimes exercise leadership. And the more aware we are of this, the more scared we become and the less we trust each other, which is wonderful from the state's point of view.

STRATEGY

STRATEGY

Nicolas Pousthomis

Occupation, part of the popular rebellion in Argentina.

Fortunately, we can make other choices. We can draw inspiration from the choice of the Student Nonviolent Coordinating Committee (SNCC) in 1963–1964 to organize openly in Mississippi, perhaps the most violently racist state in the United States at the time. The dangers they faced were enormous: black SNCC workers dealt with men who were police by day and KKK by night; SNCC members often lived in Freedom Houses that were unprotected in the countryside; they had no guns and everyone knew it; the federal agents refused to protect them; the Mississippi media were against them as were most clergy. SNCC knew they would be hurt, jailed, tortured, and some would die, but they were not naive in choosing their attitude toward repression.

At the very beginning of 1964's Freedom Summer, three SNCC workers were murdered in an attempt to scare away other volunteers. SNCC refused to go underground, and that choice expanded the movement dramatically, both in Mississippi and nationally, won them powerful allies, and broke the political stranglehold of racism in that state. I would challenge anyone in today's movement to study that example and then explain why our movement should practice security culture. The more powerful choice is openness.

STAGE THREE — Confrontation

Cultural preparation and organization building are periods of some revolutionary movement expansion, but those two stages are not yet about mass action with revolutionary content. The mass protests that do occur from time to time usually contain little vision of a fundamentally new society; their keynote is saying "no" to, for example, the World Trade Organization, with a lot of vagueness about the big picture.

Stage three is a giant and prolonged drama. The audience is composed of the as-yet uncommitted public. The actors are the "good guys" (us) versus the "bad guys" (police, military, corporate chiefs, vigilantes). The movement's previous outreach to the public becomes more vivid now because it is fueled by open conflict. The public is more motivated to pay attention, chew over the issues, decide whether and how to commit.

The purpose of the third stage is rapid growth of the revolutionary movement itself, to the point where enough people become involved so that it's possible to enter stage four and seriously weaken the power-holders' pillars of support.

Although there has not yet been a social movement that has moved itself through these five stages in a fully conscious way, there are plenty of examples of movements that have used a smaller-scale confrontation stage to move into mass noncooperation.[12] Otpor, for instance knew that the mass media was controlled by the forces they were against and so they organized their confrontations with that in mind. Instead of concentrating on a few large-scale protests at symbolic places, they staged countless small and brief protests. They specialized in lighthearted, mischievous actions, which usually made fun of the regime, and they held them where a maximum number of passersby would see them. The passersby would also see the police beat up the youngsters, and by the next day the word-of-mouth communication had spread far and wide. Over and over Otpor made the same point: We are not terrorists; it's the police who are violent; we want democracy. Even in a city as large as Belgrade the combination of creativity and nonviolence motivated eyewitnesses to spread the word, and as the public began to swing over to Otpor's side the grafitti and posters reinforced the shift.

The confrontation stage is tricky—many movements have lost the game in this stage. We can learn from both failures and successes of movements in the United States and around the world. The following lessons can save us a lot of grief:

STRATEGY

Create "Dilemma Demonstrations."

The idea here is to create direct action that puts the power-holders in a dilemma: if they allow us to go ahead and do what we intend to do, we accomplish something worthwhile related to our issue. If they repress us, they put themselves in a bad light, and the public is educated about our message.

Many examples can inspire our creativity. Some campaigns to save old-growth trees have set up these dilemmas. If, for example, the protesters are allowed to sit in the trees, the trees are saved. If the protesters are stopped violently, the public is educated and new allies can be won.

African-American students in the South were very creative with such tactics, for example sitting at the lunch counter asking for coffee. If they were served, racism took a hit. If they were either attacked by civilians or arrested, racism also took a hit. The students didn't even need the signs they brought in order to make their point. The power-holders were repeatedly put in a dilemma: whatever they did resulted in lost ground for the status quo.[13]

Decide specifically whom we're trying to influence.

Using a term like "the public" is too simple a way to think about strategy. "The public" includes many subgroups, some of whom are very important to the success of a campaign, some less important, and some unimportant in the short run. If we create a map of the political territory and decide whom we most need to influence in what ways, we will create tactics that more frequently have the force that's needed.

For example, a small group in the Movement for a New Society once threw a monkey wrench into a U.S. foreign policy objective by correctly figuring out whom to influence through direct action. The United States was supporting, as it often does, a military dictatorship that was killing thousands of people. In fact, in Pakistan, dictator Yayah Khan was killing *hundreds of thousands* of people in East Bengal who wanted independence. The U.S. government lied about its support, but the activists learned that Pakistani ships were on their way to U.S. ports to pick up military supplies for the continuing massacre. The group also realized that if longshoremen refused to load the ships, the U.S. government would be foiled.

The problem was, the East Coast longshoremen were, if anything, politically inclined to support the government, and wanted to feed their families. The activists repeatedly tried to persuade the longshoremen to act in solidarity with the East Bengalis, without success. It was time for direct action. The group announced a blockade of the port, and began

practicing "naval maneuvers" with sailboats, rowboats, and the rest of its motley fleet. The media gave ongoing coverage, and longshoremen witnessed on television as well as in person the strange antics of protesters who seemed to believe they could stop a big freighter with tiny boats. The tactic raised the longshoremen's motivation to listen and discuss, and they agreed that, if the activists created a picket line, the longshoremen would refuse to cross it.

When the campaign succeeded in that city, the activists took it to other port cities and finally the International Longshoremen's union agreed that their workers would not load Pakistan-bound weapons anywhere in the United States. The blockade, initiated by a small group, succeeded because the group crafted direct action tactics specifically geared not toward the general public and certainly not toward the U.S. government, but toward the part of the public that most needed to be influenced to meet the strategic objective.[14]

As we design campaigns focused on the World Trade Organization or capital punishment or the sex trade we need to create a political/cultural/economic map of "the public" and decide whom we want to influence in what ways. Part of our power is in making such strategic choices.

Use campaigns more often, to become proactive rather than reactive.
Sometimes a strong reaction to a move of the power-holders can be very powerful, as it was in Seattle. By mobilizing around the WTO meeting and disrupting it, tremendous gains were made. The negative side of globalization was put on the public agenda for the first time, something that all of the organizing against the North American Free Trade Agreement had failed to do. New ongoing alliances became tantalizing possibilities. The very unleashing of rebel energy was itself positive.

While reacting occasionally is one thing, remaining in a posture of reaction is something else. A synonym for continuous reaction is "disempowerment." Gandhi's first principle of strategy was to stay on the offensive. Having our action agenda dictated by where and when the power-holders decide to have their meetings is not staying on the offensive.

Campaigns put us on the offensive. A campaign is a focused mobilization of energy with a clear objective, often in the form of a demand. Successful campaigns focus on their target over time—nine months, two years, even more if they have the people resources—with a specific demand that seems achievable.

STRATEGY

The United Students Against Sweatshops movement has worked mostly through campaigns, which is one reason why it has met with so much success. When these students choose their objective and identify the power-holder whose position needs to change, things become clear. Who is going to oppose them most strongly? And who are their greatest potential allies? In the early part of the campaign they can open communication with allies and have them already on board by the time the campaigners start direct action.

This is not a new idea. The victories of the Civil Rights movement that are now part of our activist lore were won through campaigns—the Montgomery bus boycott, for example, or the Birmingham struggle of 1963, in which a major industrial city was disrupted in order to force the federal government to pass an equal accommodations bill.[15] I sometimes think that, if it weren't for racism and the discrediting of the sixties, today's young activists would be studying all available books and videos to benefit from the brilliance of SNCC, CORE (the Congress of Racial Equality), and the Southern Christian Leadership Conference.

The victories of the grassroots antinuclear struggle waged in the United States during the 1970s and 1980s have also been all but erased from memory by a collusion of media and the educational system. That largely successful fight against nuclear power was directed against an amazing array of power: the federal government (both civilian and military), the banks which were making major profits from loans to utilities, the utilities themselves, the huge companies like General Electric and Westinghouse which made the nuclear plants, the construction companies, and the trade unions. The struggle also had to be waged against "conventional wisdom" in the United States, which believed, in the beginning of the 1970s, that nuclear energy was safe and cheap.

There isn't room here to describe the struggle, which often used mass direct action, from testifying at official hearings to civil disobedience. The movement remained decentralized, yet each local area expanded by designing and implementing campaigns. It's well worth the study for anarchists and others who don't want centralized leadership to run social movements.[16]

Heighten the contrast between protesters and police behavior.
The power of the confrontation stage is in the drama. Drama in the streets is, however, different from an off-Broadway play. A sophisticated theater audience might prefer characters to be multifaceted, without a clearly defined "good guy" or "bad guy." The drama of the streets cannot be so subtle: it really does come down emotionally to "the goodies" versus "the

baddies"—in our case, those who stand with oppressed people versus those who stand with greed, privilege, and domination.

The fence-sitters in the mainstream watching the drama in the streets are surprisingly open-minded about who are the goodies and who are the baddies. In their eyes maybe the goodies will turn out to be the protesters, and then again, maybe the police will be the goodies.

The protests at the 2000 Republican National Convention in Philadelphia provide a clear example. Some widely publicized police violence prior to the convention had damaged the image of the Philadelphia police force, while the activist organizers had done effective media outreach in the week leading up to the convention, receiving highly favorable publicity from the media. The result was that going into the first demonstrations the burden of proof was on the police to reestablish their credentials as responsible and controlled, and the protesters occupied the moral high ground. A succession of three clearly peaceful marches in three days sustained this balance, and when the group organizing the third march, the Kensington Welfare Rights Organization, was threatened with arrest, they took care not to be politically isolated and brought allies out in support. The police felt they had to back off the arrest threat, lest they confirm the fence-sitters, suspicion that the police really were "the baddies."

The second phase of the convention actions, however, reversed the roles. In the context of public fears and expectations, the police only needed to show restraint, flexibility, and control. This they did, avoiding tear gas, major pepper spray, rubber bullets, charges with or without horses. Protesters were caught without a style that would put them in stark contrast with the public behavior of the police. The blockading protesters looked . . . well . . . disruptive, and the police were helping the public by getting traffic moving again. The police chief, who had been on the defensive the week before, became a folk hero and the Philly mainstream could breathed a sigh of relief that "Our hometown police are much better than those out-of-control Seattle police, and where did these protesters come from, anyway?"

The great lesson to be learned here is that the drama of the streets cannot carry a complex analysis that requires long dissection and persuasion. The drama in street confrontations needs the simplicity of contrast between the protesters' behavior and that of the police.

The symbols used to heighten contrast depend on the situation. Black students who sat in at lunch counters in the South remained calmly seated

STRATEGY

149

at the counters while hysterical white racists hit and screamed at them. Gandhi designed a raid on a salt works in which demonstrators calmly walked across the boundary where they were beaten down by soldiers.[17] Vietnamese monks sat in meditative positions in the streets of Hue, in front of tanks, to help bring down the dictatorship in 1963.

A few years before the young Serb activists started Otpor, some of them had tangled with the state by launching student protests. That earlier wave of activity died out, and one reason was that young cops adopted student dress and joined the protests in order to smash windows and fight uniformed police. These police provocateurs were highly effective in changing the public focus from the dictatorship to the "student violence." Learning from that experience, Otpor decided from the beginning, as a matter of policy, that anyone who looked like an Otpor member but was caught fighting the police would be assumed to be a police spy and would no longer be considered an Otpor member. Otpor felt the stakes were so high (both success in overthrowing Milosevic and the safety of their members) that the group needed to draw a line.

Again, our power lies in our choices. We can choose to design our confrontations using appropriate symbols so that the portion of the public we most want to influence will see us as the people standing up for justice.[18]

Take an empowered attitude toward the prospect of state repression. Obviously, the purpose of repression is to induce fear, so that people will give up on fighting injustice. The power-holders have a range of tactics up their sleeves: one example is setting a huge bail for protesters charged only with misdemeanors. Power-holders are counting on our fear to change our behavior so as to make us less effective.

That's why one of the most fundamental choices any social movement makes is what kind of attitude to have toward repression.[19] It's natural for us to fear punishment, deprivation of liberty, losing our jobs. What we may not realize is that movements can make choices about how to handle threats from the state. Some movements notice that power-holders invite them to play the "Fear Game," and those movements that see through the game choose a different strategy.

For example, during the Montgomery bus boycott the power-holders decided to play the Fear Game by leaking the word that they had a list of black leaders who were going to be arrested. The leaders decided to take a powerful, proactive attitude; they went to City Hall as a group and demanded to be arrested at once. They carefully expanded their numbers

so that, more than likely, some individuals would not be on the list and could indignantly demand to be arrested rather than be insulted by not being considered a leader! More recently, labor unions in Decatur, Illinois, made a similar move: hundreds of workers filled City Hall and refused to leave until the intended arrests were actually made.

Consider the difficulty this puts the power-holders in. If the people refuse to fear them, the power-holders have lost one of their most potent weapons! Gandhi used to say that the British were not ruling India because the British were stronger, but rather because the Indians feared them. As soon as the Indians gave up their fear, he said, British rule would crumble. And it was so.

STAGE FOUR — Mass Political and Economic Noncooperation

As I write this in the spring of 2002, Argentina is in the throes of mass noncooperation—strikes, boycotts, civil disobedience of many kinds.[20] Popular assemblies in the barrios not only mobilize the demonstrations but also take on local issues and concerns, for example, preventing authorities from closing down a baker who couldn't afford to pay his rent. Local assemblies urge people who own their homes not to pay property taxes but instead to turn the revenue over to hospitals in their area that need medical supplies. Poorly paid workers have been striking for months, often blockading bridges and highways as well. In February they temporarily shut down the city's oil supply by blockading the entrance to the local refinery.

The steep decline of the Argentine economy—another "triumph" of neo-liberalism and the IMF—has precipitated this particular insurgency, and therefore Argentina has limits as a model. Ideally, we don't want to wait until poverty stares most people in the face (and the environment is thoroughly degraded) before mass noncooperation can be organized. All the more reason to be pursuing the first three preparatory stages as coherently and consistently as we can in order to arrive at the place where confrontation will grow into mass noncooperation.

During the confrontation stage the movement needs to grow, which is easier to do when the power-holders are busy discrediting themselves by responding violently to movement campaigns. But the period of fastest growth for the organizations will most likely occur during in the period of mass noncooperation. An atmosphere of turbulence encourages mainstream as well as radical people to seek alternative ways of getting things done. In Argentina, for example, workers are taking over some factories and operating them. "Of everything we sell," a ceramics factory

STRATEGY

worker said, "we divide the profits equally among all the people who work here."[21]

Neighborhood assemblies in Argentina have been formed and they typically meet weekly to agree on a list of demands and proposals for change, then bring the proposals to interneighborhood assemblies for agreement. Markets for barter have sprung up, where people trade everything from old video games to food to skilled services. No government money is allowed in these markets and credit slips are used as a kind of microcurrency. And of course there's been an explosion of Indymedia to supply the need for reliable information.[22]

Clearly, the purpose of mass noncooperation (dissolving the pillars of support) is to bring down the regime. There may be property destruction involved (in Argentina, middle-class people in suits have been breaking the windows of banks), although in some contexts it is strategically unwise. (Otpor used grafitti and defaced property by changing Milosevic billboards, but decided that smashing things would play into Milosevic's hands.[23])

Since mass noncooperation can open a power vacuum, why plan a fifth stage? The heartbreaking story of the Burmese students gives an answer. When I was smuggled across the border into the jungle encampment of the Burmese prodemocracy troops in 1990, I had a chance to learn from the students who participated in the 1988 uprising. They had an amazing story to tell, one that had been largely kept from activists around the world because of the extreme isolation policy of the Burmese dictator Ne Win.[24] The students had staged a series of small-scale nonviolent protests in 1987, getting beaten up, arrested, and some were killed. The movement grew and the grapevine carried the message: "Rise up on 8/8/88!" The date came, and with it a social volcano erupted; hundreds of thousands and then millions took to the streets. Students occupied government offices; peasants joined workers in striking, boycotting, occupying buildings and factories. The pillars of support for Ne Win tottered and the repression failed to stop the movement. One student tactic was, when confronting soldiers with guns pointed at them, for the bravest to step in front, tear off his shirt, and demand, "If you're going to shoot, shoot me first!" The soldiers could resist only so much courage like that.

With his army beginning to sympathize with the students, Ne Win made a very clever move. He pulled his army and senior ministers out of the capitol city, and to the immense surprise of the students, Rangoon (and Mandalay and other cities) were suddenly "theirs." Jubilation was mixed with confusion: What now? To add to the confusion, Ne Win had left

STRATEGY

marcha - mayo 2000   Flor, MTD Anibal Veron

military intelligence in plainclothes in the cities with orders to foment disorder, and he also unlocked the prisons to let everyone out.

Disorder grew in Rangoon until finally came the announcement: The government had "gotten the message from the people" and would agree to free elections; in the meantime it would come back into the cities with a reformed heart, a new name, and a new mission: to restore law and order. The dictatorship returned (killing thousands of students along the way) and refilled the power vacuum.

When I told the Burmese student soldiers about the five-stage model they immediately understood where their mistake lay: Because they had not done stage one (no vision of a democratic Burma) or stage two (creating alternative institutions and cohesive organization that could move into the power vacuum opened by stage four), they were shoved aside by the regime. They learned in the hardest possible way that insurrection is not enough.

STAGE FIVE — Parallel Institutions

After working through the overlapping stages of cultural preparation, organization-building, confrontation, and noncooperation, people with shared vision have the chance to root new institutions and values firmly in the soil of the new society. The institutions will have sprung from the seeds of the organizing stage: the alternative institutions, the networks, radical caucuses, and affinity groups.

In the fifth stage these organizations come fully into their own, as they become part of the infrastructure of the new society. In contrast to the old Leninist model in which the party seizes the state and then re-organizes society from the top down, this strategic model proposes a bottom-up restructuring, supported by the radicals who all along have been innovating organizational forms that reflect a radically democratic vision.

Picture this: the power-holders, whose legitimacy has already been eroding because of their inability or unwillingness to deal with the crises of ecology, poverty, injustice, and war, are now finding that their pillars of support are wobbly. They try to restore their power through a combination of cooptation and violence but it's too late for that now. Massive noncooperation leaves them with no option but to cede power.

This is the moment of opportunity for the visionary movement with its infrastructure of experienced organizers and facilitators to step into the vacuum and create, step by step, a new society, one that supports freedom and democracy rather than domination.

The new society is cocreated with mainstream people who have realized that the old way is no longer tenable. The radicals are not strangers to the mainstream folks, because the mainstream has seen them in caucuses within their unions and professions, alternative institutions in their neighborhoods, and affinity groups that serve as well as protest.

The affinity groups will have been growing in number and playing major roles in the noncooperation stage, and they will have gained valuable "battlefield" experience that enables them to make decisions quickly when conditions change in stage five. Because of their training and solidarity, the affinity groups could take on many of the more dangerous tasks of this final stage. With the discipline and courage they've gained, they could play a lightning-rod role regarding reactionary groups, confronting right-wing militias and others. They could help the radical caucuses occupy difficult sites, and could themselves occupy government offices of a repressive nature like the FBI and the military.

Many interventionary tactics in this stage can be carried out by matching alternative institutions to the previously existing ones. An occupation might be a temporary measure leading to the orderly dismantling of the institution itself—an intertribal revolutionary league of Native Americans would probably want to dissolve the U.S. Bureau of Indian Affairs, for example—and in other cases the occupiers would immediately start to work in the new way they had planned for.

STRATEGY

While it's true that this strategic model avoids the top-down controlling function so dear to the hearts of the Leninists, it does not throw out the need for coordination. Essential services must be provided, communication must be maintained, and judgments made about the best use of limited resources in a turbulent situation. Unity requires shared information and negotiated agreements among the forces for change.

In the advanced stages of struggle, coordinating councils will be needed on local, regional, national, and transnational levels. The transformational networks, which will have been developing their technologies all along, will come into their own in this last stage. If they do their work creatively, these councils will grow organically from the struggle, as have the spokescouncils in the antiglobalization confrontations where many affinity groups come together. The job of those who sustain transformational networks will be to retain the lessons learned from these experiments, put attention to cultural differences in communication style, and assist the newly formed councils to do their job.

The councils are the bodies that form, in the last stage, the parallel "governments." (I put "government" in quotes because these bodies may not look at all like the governments we've known thus far.) In this fifth stage the people pay their taxes to the councils instead of to the governments of the oppressive order. The councils organize essential services such as traffic regulation, garbage collection, and the like. In my personal vision, the national council works with the other councils to dismantle the national government by distributing its legitimate functions to local, regional, and transnational levels. The councils can also work with the workers' caucuses, cooperatives, and affinity groups to dismantle those corporations that are worth decentralizing.

Transformation Takes Time

Even on my most optimistic days, I know that fundamental change will take time. Shifting the power from those whose greed would destroy the planet to those whose humanity would heal it gives us the chance to create anew; the power shift doesn't itself make it happen.

The power shift will at least give us a chance to support the growth and well-being of both people and planet. A movement using the strategic framework proposed here will, however, have an additional advantage: It will bring to the task hundreds of thousands of skilled people with years of practical experience in better ways of providing for the commonweal. This strategy means that a movement won't be asking the fence-sitters to gamble on a bunch of hopes and half-baked ideas. It will get the credibility

it deserves through its courage, its creativity, and its ability to be in dialogue with the people.

The young activists in Otpor, when developing their strategy, agreed to frame the choice quite simply. "The dictatorship is about death," they said. "Otpor is about life." The simple truth of our message will be just as clear.

Notes

[1] My information about Otpor is mostly from interviews with Otpor activists during my training work in the Balkans. More Otpor lesssons are available in my *Clamor* magazine article "Diversity of Tactics and Democracy," available on the Web: www.TrainingforChange.org. A very useful video documentary (although it has a pro-U.S. bias) is *Bringing Down a Dictator* shown by PBS in 2002, available from Video Finders, 4401 Sunset Blvd, Los Angeles, CA 90027.

[2] For more information about the stronger inclination of people of color and of working-class people to use nonviolent action, as compared with whites and middle-upper-class people, see my pamphlet *The Sword that Heals: Challenging Ward Churchill's "Pacifism as Pathology,"* (2001) available through Training for Change and on its Website: www.TrainingforChange.org.

[3] I first described this model in the book *Strategy for a Living Revolution* (New York: Grossman, 1973, and in paper by W. H. Freeman, 1973). The revision of that book became *Powerful Peacemaking* (Gabriola Island, B.C.: New Society Publishers, 1987), which is now out of print. This article updates the argument and responds to some current movement controversies.

[4] I frequently call this five-stage model a "strategic framework" because it's not as specific as strategies are to be maximally useful. When I share the model with specific movement groups in various countries I find that they have the specific knowledge about their situation to "fill in the blanks" and turn the model into something more concrete for their own use.

[5] One source of clarity on this is the work of activist, writer, and witch Starhawk. Her classic book *Dreaming the Dark: Magic, Sex and Politics* (Boston: Beacon Press, 1988) is a good place to start. Among other things she distinguishes between power-over (domination), power-from-within, and power-with.

[6] A clear and inspiring book by a woman who built a grassroots organization by facing honestly the class and race divisions in our society is by Linda Stout, *Bridging the Class Divide* (Boston: Beacon Press, 1996).

[7] The value of human shields, also called protective accompaniment, came to widespread notice in spring 2002 with International Solidarity Network and others going to Palestine to reduce the killing on the West Bank. As an ongoing organized activity, accompaniment is only about twenty years old. For more on third-party intervention contrasted with other kinds of activism, see my *ZNet* article, "Pushing Our Thinking about People Power," reprinted on the Web: www.TrainingforChange.org. To learn about a major organization that does this work in various countries including Colombia, see the Web site: www.peacebrigades.org

[8] The Movement for a New Society (1971–1989) was organized specifically to be a transformational network, and even worked internationally to spur groups to learn rapidly from each other and do mutual aid. MNS activists joined campaigns, built alternative institutions, led trainings, and created New Society Publishers.

[9] An example comes from Poland, where after many years of Communist dictatorship a radical group of workers and intellectuals decided to break with their security culture and create an open, aboveground organization for human rights. The move was a breakthrough that supported the growth of the mass Solidarity movement, resulting by the end of the 1980s in the nonviolent overthrow of the dictatorship. This is one of a long list of dictatorships that have been overthrown by nonviolent "people power," despite the state's using military repression to defend itself. Just in the past few decades mass nonviolent action has played a decisive role in ousting one-party states and dictatorships in Bolivia, Haiti, Argentina, East Germany, Czechoslovakia, Hungary, Poland, the Philippines, the Baltic States, Mali, Malawi, Madagascar, and Benin, and prevented military-backed coups in Thailand and Russia. See Stephen Zunes, Lester R. Kurtz, and Sarah Beth Asher, eds., *Nonviolent Social Movements: A Geographical Perspective* (Malden, Mass.: Blackwell Publishers, 1999).

[10] Fortunately, we can create many, many tactics that do not rely on surprise. One resource to jump-start our creativity is Gene Sharp's book *The Politics of Nonviolent Action*, where he describes 198 tactics that have been used historically (Boston: Porter Sargent, 1973).

STRATEGY

STRATEGY

[11] During the movement against the Vietnam War FBI documents included a discussion of the importance of making activists believe there was "an F.B.I. man behind every mailbox." During a spokescouncil meeting preparing for the protests at the Republican National Convention, an activist took a break to call an anarchist house in west Philadelphia and learned from activists there that, when they randomly took their phone off the hook, they heard the spokescouncil meeting!

[12] In *Why We Can't Wait*, Martin Luther King Jr. shares a good deal of strategy thinking in the successful Birmingham campaign. He realized that, to induce Birmingham's black community to boycott the big downtown department stores (mass noncooperation), the campaign first had to create the drama of protest marches against dogs and fire hoses (confrontation). This worked so well that the store owners, fearful of losing profits from the big upcoming Easter shopping season, swung to the side of meeting the Civil Rights movement's demands.

[13] A new and powerful documentary look at black student strategy is in *A Force More Powerful*, which was shown by PBS in 2000; see the Web site, www.films.com.

[14] This campaign, which has more to teach us about direct action than there's room to go into here, is described blow-by-blow by Richard K. Taylor, *Blockade* (Maryknoll, N.Y.: Orbis, 1977). This campaign in solidarity with Bangladesh happened in 1971–72.

[15] *Why We Can't Wait* gives the behind-the scenes story of Birmingham and Dr. King describes the Montgomery campaign initiated by Rosa Parks in *Stride Toward Freedom* (books available in various editions). Readers interested in strategy will salivate while reading Taylor Branch's Pulitzer Prize–winning book *Parting the Waters: America in the King Years, 1954–63* (New York: Simon and Schuster, 1988). Some useful coverage of SNCC is in the documentary *Eyes on the Prize*, available in many local libraries.

[16] Behind-the-scenes strategy insights on that movement are revealed by a key participant, the late activist Bill Moyer, in his book *Doing Democracy* (Gabriola Island, B.C.: New Society Publishers, 2002). In his book Bill also shares his campaign design methodology, which has assisted a variety of movements.

[17] The historically accurate version in the film *Gandhi* is worth watching repeatedly.

[18] Police are sometimes sophisticated enough to be quite intentional in reducing the contrast. The Albany, Georgia, police chief defeated the African-American 1962 civil rights campaign led by the Student Nonviolent Coordinating Committee (SNCC) and Martin Luther King by carefully restraining his police and reducing the contrast. He astutely used his police to prevent Ku Klux Klan and other forces from beating up demonstrators, again to hinder black people from gaining the moral high ground. Dr. King applied the learning from this lesson in the following year's Birmingham, Alabama, campaign, and SNCC's most dramatic use of this lesson was in 1964 in Mississippi.

[19] To read about one choice, called security culture, go to the Web site: security.tao.ca *or* nocompromise.org. The article "Security Culture" states its basic assumption at the beginning: "To minimize the destructiveness of this government harassment, it is imperative that we create a 'security culture' within our movement." Some movements, operating in much more dangerous situations than the United States, Canada, or western Europe, have found that security culture maximizes rather than minimizes the destructiveness of government harassment.

[20] The information about Argentina in this and following paragraphs comes from reportage in *Z Magazine*, the issues of April and May 2002: "The Argentine Rebellion" by Roger Burbach and "Rebellion in Argentina" by Ana Nogueira, Josh Breitbart, and Chris Strohm.

[21] Ana Nogueira, Josh Breitbart, and Chris Strohm, "Rebellion in Argentina," *Z Magazine* (May 2002): 19.

[22] Ibid., 19-20.

[23] Larger-scale property destruction may accompany stage four and even violence against people, even though the movement chose a nonviolent strategy. In the turbulence and chaos that brings new elements of the population into play, a nonviolent movement can only do the best it can. For example, on October 6, when huge crowds surrounded Parliament, Otpor couldn't prevent right-wing soccer fans from torching the government building even though Otpor thought the right-wingers' tactics were as senseless as their politics.

[24] Even though it's a Hollywood film, *Beyond Rangoon* has an amazing degree of accuracy in depicting the uprising and the courage of Aung San Suu Kyi, the brilliant young woman who became the hero of the rebellion and won a Nobel Peace Prize. She has spent most of the time

STRATEGY

since the collapse of the insurrection under house arrest. A detailed account of the 1988 uprising is by the journalist Bertil Lintner, *Outrage: Burma's Struggle for Democracy* (White Lotus, 1990).

Decolonizing The Revolutionary Imagination: Values Crisis, the Politics of Reality, and Why There's Going to Be a Common-Sense Revolution in This Generation

By Patrick Reinsborough

Patrick Reinsborough is a writer, grassroots organizer, and popular educator who has worked on a wide range of issues including forest protection, nuclear power, police brutality, urban sprawl, peace in northern Ireland, indigenous rights, and numerous local and global environmental justice struggles. He is the cofounder of the smartMeme Strategy and Training Project and the Wake Up America campaign.

If you expect to see the final results of your work, you simply have not asked a big enough question. — I.F. Stone

Introduction: Post-Issue Activism

Our planet is heading into an unprecedented global crisis. The blatancy of the corporate power grab and the accelerating ecological meltdown is evidence that we do not live in an era where we can afford the luxury of fighting merely the symptoms of the problem. As is often noted, crisis

provides both danger and opportunity. The extent to which these two opposing qualities define our era will be largely based on the appeal and breadth of the social movements that arise to address the crisis.

This essay is part of my own struggle to explore a politics that is commensurate with the scale of the global crisis. In part it was inspired by a profound strategy insight I received while watching a circling bird of prey. The raptor seemed to spend hours calmly drifting on the breezes, waiting and watching, then suddenly made a lightning quick dive to seize its prey. Had I only witnessed the raptor's final plunge, I might not have realized that it took hours of patient surveillance for the raptor to be in the right place to make a seemingly effortless kill. I was struck by what a clear metaphor the raptor's circling time is for what our movements need to do in order to be successful. Social change is not just the bird of prey's sudden plunge—the flurry of direct confrontation—but rather the whole process of circling, preparing, and strategizing.

Analysis is the most import tool in the social change toolbox. It is this process of analysis—the work to find the points of intervention and leverage in the system we're working to transform—that suggests why, where, and how to use the other tools. Many of us are impatient in our desire for change, and those of us from privileged backgrounds are oftentimes unschooled in the realities of long-term struggle.

I often recall the Buddhist saying, "The task before us is very urgent, so we must slow down." This essay is my effort to "slow down" a bit and explore some new analytical tools. My hope is that it will incite deeper conversations about strategies for building movements with the inclusiveness, creativity, and depth of vision necessary to move us toward a more just and sane world.

Let's begin by asking why aren't more global North movements coming forward with systemic critiques? Why, despite the increasingly obvious nature of the crisis, isn't there more visible resistance to the corporate takeover of the global political system, economy, and culture?

The answer to this question lies in our exploration of how pathological values have shaped not only the global system but also our ability to imagine true change. The system we are fighting is not merely structural, it's also inside us, through the internalization of oppressive cultural norms that define our worldview. Our minds have been colonized to normalize deeply pathological assumptions. Thus, oftentimes our own sense of self-defeatism becomes complicit with the anesthetic qualities of a cynical mass media to make fundamental social change seem unimaginable.

As a result, activists frequently ghettoize themselves by self-identifying with protest, and fail to think of themselves as building movements that could actually change power relations. All too often we project our own sense of power-lessness by mistaking militancy for radicalism and mobilization for move-ment building. It seems highly unlikely to me

FTAA demonstrations, Quito, Ecuador. November, 2002.

that capitalism will be smashed one window at a time. Likewise, getting tens of thousands of people to take joint action is not an end in itself, rather only the first step in catalyzing deeper shifts in the dominant culture. Our revolution(s) will really start rolling when the logic of our actions and the appeal of our disobedience are so clear that they can easily replicate and spread far beyond the limiting definition of "protester" or "activist."

To do so, our movements for justice, ecology, and democracy must deepen their message by more effectively articulating the values crisis underlying the corporate system. We must lay claim to life-affirming, common-sense values and expose one of the most blatant revolutionary truths of the modern era: The corporate-rule system is rooted in sacrificing human dignity and planetary health for elite profit, and it is out of alignment with human values.

This is the domain of post-issue activism—the recognition that the roots of the emerging crisis lie in the fundamental flaws of the modern order and that our movements for change need to talk about redesigning the entire global system—now. Post-issue activism is a dramatic divergence from the slow progression of single-issue politics, narrow constituencies, and Band-Aid solutions. Traditional single-issue politics, despite noble and pragmatic goals, is not just a strategic and gradualist path to the same goal of global transformation. Too often the framework of issue-based struggle needs to affirm the existing system in order to win concessions, and thus fails to nurture the evolution of movements for more systemic change. Much of our social change energy is spent campaigning against the smoke rather than clearly alerting people to the fact that their house is on fire. Post-issue activism will not replace single-issue politics—the people and

POST-ISSUE ACTIVISM

ecosystems closest to the smoke need relief now—but rather, it will strengthen ongoing struggles by providing a larger social-change context. Post-issue activism is the struggle to address the holistic nature of the crisis, and it demands new frameworks, new alliances, and new strategies. We must find ways to articulate the connections between all the "issues" by revealing the pathological nature of the system. To do so we must rise to the challenge of going beyond (rather than abandoning) single-issue politics. We have to learn to talk about values, deepen our analysis, and direct more resources into creating political space for a truly transformative arena of social change.

To think about decolonizing the revolutionary imagination, we must reference the history of colonization. Through colonization, Western civilization ("a disease historically spread by sharp swords"[1]) has been violently imposed upon the entire world. Colonialism is not just the process of establishing physical control over territory, it is the process of establishing the ideologies and the identities—colonies in the mind —that perpetuate control. Central to this process has been the manufacture of attitudes of racism, nationalism, patriarchal manhood, and the division of society into economic classes. If we are to take seriously the prospect of decolonizing the revolutionary imagination then we must examine how these attitudes shape the way we conceive of social change. Likewise, we must remember that analysis is shaped by experience, and that those who suffer directly as targets of these oppressive attitudes often live the experiences that create clear analysis. Let us not forget that effective revolutions are based on listening.

In facing the global crisis, the most powerful weapon that we have is our imagination. But first we must liberate ourselves from the conceptual limitations we place on social change. As we expand the realm of the possible we shape the direction of the probable. This means directly confronting the myths and assumptions that make a better world seem unattainable. To that end, this essay endeavors to explore some tools to help us unshackle our imaginations and increase the momentum of the global justice movements' process of creating a political space to fundamentally redesign the global system.

On a final note of introduction I wish to clarify that most of the ideas presented in this essay are neither new nor truly my own. Ideas by their nature quickly cross-pollinate and grow beyond any individual's role in their articulation. All activists owe a great debt to shared experience. I personally am indebted to many seasoned activists and theorists from across numerous movements who have shared their thoughts and helped me deepen my analysis. Likewise, all of these ideas are a work-in-progress.

They are intended as tools to spark discussion and encourage debate, and it is my sincerest hope that they will generate more questions than they answer. Questions are always more radical than answers.

The Doomsday Economy

We live in a dangerous time, an urgent time, a time of profound crisis. Ecologically speaking it is an apocalyptic time defined by the sixth mass extinction of the earth's species,[2] the destruction of the last wilderness areas, and the forced assimilation of the planet's few remaining earth-centered cultures. Every ecosystem, every traditional culture, and every subsistence economy is on the chopping block as the global corporatizers force their consumer monoculture "development" model (read antidevelopment) upon the entire world. Corporate capitalism's drive toward global domination has literally pushed the life support systems of the planet to the point of collapse.

More and more people are recognizing that we are at a turning point. The corporate takeover—the latest offensive in the 500-plus-year conquest of the planet by Western culture—is being met with massive resistance around the world. However, the elite planners and architects of the global economy seem incapable of hearing their multitude of critics and are continuing to push toward total commodification, assimilation, and a global corporate state.

Over the last few years, as corporate power has begun to undermine the economic self-determination and political sovereignty of even the over-consumers of the global North, resistance has grown more visible in the heart of it all—the United States. Unprecedented coalitions have formed, and different movements have been uniting in creative mass protest to slow the pace of corporate globalization. But slowing things down is one thing, replacing the doomsday economy with a democratic, just, and ecologically sane world is another.

The global system is mutating. Although it remains deeply rooted in its history of colonial genocide, corporate power grabs, and ecological devastation, the structure has changed dramatically over the past generation. The biggest shift has been the rise of the speculative economy. As the world financial sector has been deregulated, with many countries forced to drop limits on investment, there has been a dramatic transition in economic priorities from the production of real goods to a global casino economy based on high-risk, short-term speculation.

POST-ISSUE ACTIVISM

In 1986 the world's foreign exchange markets were handling nearly $200 billion a day. By 1998 this figure had grown eightfold to $1.5 trillion dollars every day![3] Since the entirety of world trade is estimated to be worth about US $6.5 trillion a year,[4] that means that five days of currency transactions surpasses the value of an entire year of world trade. But the most important aspect of this so-called "financial revolution" is that the massive numbers represent growth in the speculative sector of the economy. Financial speculation has accelerated to the point that by the year 2000, for every $1 of international investment facilitating trade in real goods, $9 were being spent on short-term speculation.[5]

An understanding of the rise of the speculative economy is key to debunking the neoliberal myth of growing prosperity. The reality is that none of the money circulating in the speculative economy feeds anyone, clothes anyone, nor does it provide anyone with meaningful jobs. Rather, the speculative economy is mostly just a way for rich people—through their corporate institutional proxies—to use the money they already have to make more. Moreover, this massive speculative economy is a powerful destabilizing force that threatens local economies and ecosystems, since speculation is the opposite of sustainability and encourages a deeper disconnect between ecological realities (limits, natural cycles of production, etc.) and the arbitrary mechanics of financial manipulation.

Since 1980 the total value of the planet's financial assets (money in stocks, bonds, bank deposits, and cash) has increased sevenfold, from $12 trillion in 1980 to $80 trillion in 2000.[6] These statistics are supposed to represent the "rising tide that lifts all boats" and the "miracle of economic growth" that is the basis for the politicians' promise of prosperity. But anyone (especially those not brainwashed by the arcane logic of conventional economics) can see that surely seven more earths haven't been created over the last two decades—so where did all this new "wealth" come from?

Once we cut through the numbers games and semantics we recognize that what economists call economic growth is really the liquidation of the natural wealth of the planet. Almost literally, they are destroying the natural economy of living forests to make an economy of disposable paper on which they print money to tell themselves how rich they are. It is a true doomsday economy, incapable of seeing the natural systems that sustain life as anything other than resources to be extracted. The flawed accounting of the speculative economy hides the horrible truth that what the corporate globalizers call "progress" is really the earth's going-out-of-business sale.

Our strategies must be informed by the fact that we're not fighting that colloquialism once called in activist parlance "The Man"—these days we're

fighting "The Machine." This machine is the culmination of the pathological worldview that has hard-wired patriarchy, white supremacy, capitalist domination, and ecological illiteracy into the global operating system. The rich, white (self-congratulatory) men who have always benefited from global domination continue to do so, but ultimately they have created a runaway machine that is beyond even their own control.

Naming the System (Global Pathology)

In this era of escalating global crisis one of the most important roles radicals can play is to help build a common analysis of the system's flawed design. Not by imposing some kind of dogmatic vanguardism of a single analysis, but rather by creating the political space for a critical mass of people to define the problems they face in their own lives in a systematic way that allows the

> **A Few Notable Characteristics of the Doomsday Economy**
>
> - Corporatization and increasingly centralized control
> - Reliance on coercion (both physical and ideological) to maintain control
> - Drive to commodify all aspects of life
> - Community fragmentation/cultural decay (replacement of lived experience with representation—image-based mass culture, television addiction, increasing alienation)
> - Elevation of consumerism to the center of public life
> - Increased mechanization and blind faith in technology
> - Fetishization of speculative/financial wealth
> - Distorted accounting that masks the liquidation of ecological and social capital
> - Pathological values/flawed assumptions
> - Undermining of planetary life support systems, accelerating ecological collapse

imagining of fundamental change. We don't have to convince people that something is wrong—as corporate control becomes more blatant and the ecological crisis worsens, the system is doing much of the work to discredit itself. We must, however, help people to imagine alternatives that go beyond tinkering with the symptoms to actually dismantling and redesigning the global system.

Radicals have always struggled to build oppositional power by naming the system. If only it were as easy as putting "Capitalism" or "Corporate Rule" or "Algae Bloom Civilization/Insane World" on a banner, we'd have won the

POST-ISSUE ACTIVISM

Jason Justice

Crying Mother Earth holds victims of war and globalization.
Puppet by Arts in Action.

battle by now. But naming the system isn't merely a semantic or intellectual exercise. Rather, it is the revolutionary process through which a critical mass of people recognize the deadly design flaws of the current social order. The process of "naming" is our way of revealing the hypocrisy, brutality, and idiocy of the corporate-controlled world in order to build the popular consciousness necessary to inspire transformative action.

One of the beauties of the recent global uprisings has been their ability to look beyond tactical, cultural, and ideological differences to see a unifying commitment to structural change. The better we articulate the fundamental flaws of the current world order the more we will see links between the many types of resistance that are springing up to confront the doomsday economy.

A useful description of our current system can be found in the science of pathology, the branch of medical study that examines the nature of disease. The modern system is pathological on many levels, but the disease that most closely corresponds to the global crisis is the quintessential modern pathology—cancer. Cancer is not merely a metaphor but a literal diagnosis of the doomsday economy.[7]

Cancer is a perversion in the biological systems of the human body—our internal ecosystem—when a cell goes haywire and forgets its own boundaries and its own mortality. The infected cell lives forever, dividing and replicating itself without limits until it finally overwhelms the entire biological system of which it is a part. This disease, now so common at the cellular level, is a chillingly apt description of what is happening at the macrolevel—the emergence of a pathological world system.

Corporate power is a cancer in the body politic. Corporations are the institutional embodiment of the perverted values system of modern capitalism—shaped through the historic lens of white male supremacy to be antidemocratic, exploitative, and incapable of respecting ecological

limits. The corporation is a machine that blindly focuses on one function: the maximization of profits. As the elites attempt to institute de facto global corporate rule with their neoliberal free trade agenda, the cancer is metastasizing throughout the host—planet earth.

We can use this analogy to learn about the pathological nature of the corporate takeover by examining four ways in which cancer operates in our physical bodies.

1. *Cancer is a perversion by definition.* Cancer usurps the function of the cell away from the collective interest of the organism and into an illusory self-interest separate from the host. Corporations are the manifestation of a similar perversion in modern culture—alienation from nature and the failure to recognize that our collective self-interest is tied to the overall health of the biosphere. The corporate paradigm is incapable of seeing the ecological reality, the interdependence between humans and ecosystems that define the real limits of the economic sphere. It defines itself around unlimited growth and exists through its desire to expand, consolidate power, and subvert any limits placed upon its ability to maximize profits. Like the cancer cell, it forgets that it is part of and dependent upon a larger biological system

2. *Cancer rewrites the rules.* Cancer infects the cell's genetic instructions to make the cell operate separately from the rest of the organism. This is exactly what corporate elites have done, first in America and then around the world: rewritten the laws to limit democratic tendencies and to consolidate power. Since 1886, when corporations achieved legal "personhood" in the United States through judicial fiat, the corporate form has become the preferred method for elites to organize their wealth and rationalize their seizure of public property and assets.[8] Corporations continue to undermine the regulatory framework and to subvert democratic decisionmaking with campaign finance corruption, influence peddling, and public relations campaigns. Freed from its historic limits, the corporation has risen to become the defining institution of the modern world. The ideology of privatization has facilitated the corporatization of every aspect of life. International trade, health care, schools, prisons, even the building blocks of life itself—our genetic material—are all being gobbled up as corporations become the de facto tool of governance. Corporate pathology has become so ingrained that the Bretton Woods Institutions (World Bank, IMF, WTO) now overtly force rule changes to favor corporations over the public interest. The essence of the doomsday economy is that the same corporations who profit from destroying the planet are being allowed to write the rules of the global economy.

169

Structural adjustment is the macroeconomic equivalent of cancer reprogramming a cell.

3. *Cancer masquerades as the host.* Since cancer is not an outside invader but instead a perversion within the body's existing cells, our immune system fails to recognize it as a threat. The body's defenses fail to attack the cancer because the cancer masquerades as part of the body. This is probably cancer's most important quality for informing our strategies because it is central to understanding how the corporate takeover has managed to become so advanced without triggering a stronger backlash. Corporate rule masquerades as democracy. The elites use the symbols, trappings, and language of democracy to justify control while corporations hijack the democratic form without the democratic function. This process conceals the deepening values perversion—ecological illiteracy masquerades as "market forces," monopoly capitalism masquerades as "free trade," and doomsday economics masquerade as "economic growth."

4. *Cancer kills the host.* Cancer's suicidal destiny is a product of its initial perversion. If not confronted, cancer inevitably metastasizes, spreading throughout the body and killing the host. This is exactly what the corporate pathology is doing to the biosphere. Spread across the planet by waves of colonizers, from the conquistadors to the resource extraction corporations to the International Monetary Fund, the corporate system is on the brink of killing the host—the biological and cultural diversity of life on the planet. People's ability to govern their own lives is sacrificed along the way since corporate rule is antithetical to real democracy. By definition, corporate decisionmaking must operate within the narrow, short-term interests of their shareholders. Corporations are not wealth-generating machines as the American mythology would have us believe, but rather wealth-consolidating machines. Corporations extract the biological wealth of the planet, liquidating our collective natural heritage in order to enrich a tiny minority. The corporate drive to shorten the planning horizon, externalize costs, and accelerate growth has pushed the life support systems of the planet to the brink of collapse.

The Control Mythology: Consume or Die

At the center of the ever-growing doomsday economy is a perverse division of resources that slowly starves the many while normalizing overconsumption for the few. Maintaining control in a system that creates such blatant global injustice relies on the age-old tools of empire: repression, brutality, and terror. Multinational corporations have long since learned how to "constructively engage" with repressive regimes and put "strong central leadership" to work for their profit margins. Whether it's U.S.-approved military dictatorships or America's own ever-growing incarceration economy, the naked control that is used to criminalize, contain, and silence dissent among the have-nots is obvious.

But this brutality is just one side of the system of global control. Far less acknowledged is that in addition to the widespread use of the stick, the global system relies heavily on the selective use of the carrot. The entire debate around globalization has been framed to ensure that the tiny global minority that makes up the overconsuming class never connects their inflated standard of living with the impoverishment of the rest of the world.

IS THe ThReAT of WAR MAKING YOU SICK?

IF WAR BeGINS CALL IN SICK! DON'T GO TO WORK or SCHOOL HEAD DOWNTOWN

Hugh D'Andrade

Most people who live outside the small overconsumption class can't help but be aware of the system's failings. But for the majority of American (and more generally, global North) consumers the coercion that keeps them complicit with the doomsday economy is not physical; it is largely ideological, relying heavily on the mythology of America. It is this mythology that buys people's loyalty by presenting a story of the world that normalizes the global corporate takeover.

In this story, America is the freest country in the world and corporate capitalism is the same as democracy. The interests of corporations are represented as serving popular needs—jobs being the simplistic argument—and the goal of U.S. foreign policy is presented as a benevolent desire to spread democracy, promote equality, and increase standards of living. This control mythology prevents people from seeing how pathologized the global system has become. Much of this story is merely crude propaganda that relies on Americans' notorious ignorance about the world, but elements of the control mythology have become so deeply imbedded in our lives that they now define our culture.

Among the most deep-seated elements of the control mythology is the ethic of an unquestioned, unrestrained right to consume. Consumerism is the purest drug of the doomsday economy. It epitomizes the pathology—the commodification of life's staples and the human and cultural systems that have been created to sustain collective life.

Childrens' author Dr. Suess provides an eloquent critique of consumerism in his cautionary tale *The Lorax* when he describes how the forests get destroyed to make useless disposable objects appropriately called "thneeds." A slick businessman markets "thneeds" and maximizes production until the forest is entirely destroyed. This is the essence of consumerism—creating artificially high rates of consumption by getting people to believe they need excessive or useless things. Overconsumption (invented in America but now exported around the planet) is the engine that drives the doomsday economy. Bigger. Faster. Newer. More! More! More!

We live in a culture of information saturation that constantly redefines an increasingly insane world as normal. Media advocacy group, TV Free America estimates that the average American watches an equivalent of fifty-two days of TV per year.[9] As corporations have seized the right to manufacture and manipulate collective desire, advertising has grown into a nearly $200 billion-a-year industry and has become the dominant function of mass media. Feminist media critic Jean Kilbourne estimates that each day the average North American is bombarded by 3,000 print, radio, and television ads.[10] This media saturation plays heavily into the control mythology by overdigesting information, thereby shrinking our attention spans to the point where we can no longer reassemble the story of the global crisis.

The doomsday economy's elevation of consumerism to the center of public life is causing massive psychological damage to people around the world. Advertising works because it subtly assaults a customer's self esteem to get them to buy unnecessary stuff. This process is fundamentally dehumanizing. The culture-jamming magazine *Adbusters* has rehashed William S. Burroughs to give us the concept in a slogan: "The Product is You." The result is a pathologized global monoculture that fetishizes overconsumption, self-gratification, and narcissism. Although this may ensure ongoing profits for the corporations who manage the "culture industry," it also prevents people from recognizing the impacts of their overconsumption on communities and ecosystems around the world.

The control mythology masks the realities of the doomsday economy by narrowing the popular frame of reference to the point that it's impossible to see beyond the next up-grade of prepackaged lifestyle. The omnipresent commodification of all aspects of life turns freedom into

"image branding" and "product placement" while the distinction between citizen and consumer becomes more blurred. The army of one. Individual purchasing power. America open for business. How else could we get to the point where the United Nations estimates that nearly one in six people on the planet do not get their basic daily calorie needs met,[11] but in America shopping is still presented as entertainment?

In the corporatized world a person's rights are defined by their purchasing power—access to health care, education, a nutritious diet, mental stimulation, or nature are all a factor of how much money you have. The right to overconsume becomes the centerpiece of the new unspoken Bill of Rights of America, Inc. A country of the corporations, by the corporations, and for the corporations. The unification of Europe looks ready to follow a similar path towards a United States of Europe. The cancer spreads.

Consumerism is the manifestation of our pathological reprogramming to not ask questions about where all the "stuff" comes from. The American bootstrap mythology (as in, "pull yourself up by") relies on our ecological illiteracy to convince us that everyone could live the "American" overconsumption lifestyle if they only worked hard enough. Fully conditioned consumers think only in terms of themselves, acting as if there were no ecological limits in the world. The cancer cell operates as if it were not part of a larger organism.

The twisted logic of consumerism continues to function as a control mythology even as much of the affluence of working America has been siphoned off by corporate greed. A complex range of sophisticated anesthetics helps bolster the control mythology by keeping people distracted. Whether it's the digital opium den of 500-channel cable TV, the cornucopia of mood-altering prescription drugs, or now the terror-induced national obsession with unquestioned patriotism, there's little opportunity for people to break the spell of modern consumerism.

The mythology of prosperity still holds, even as the reality becomes more and more elusive. For now perhaps, but for how much longer? As author and media theorist James John Bell writes, "images of power crumble before empires fall."[12] There are many signs that the empty materialism of modern consumer life is leaving many ordinary people discontent and ripe for new types of political and cultural transformation.

Articulating the Values Crisis

To articulate the pathology of the corporate system we must avoid debating on the system's terms. As the classic organizer's tenet says, "We

have to organize people where they are at." In other words, if we tell people our truths in a way that that connects with their experience, they will understand it, and they will believe it.

I find that most people largely believe the stories that activists tell them about bad things happening in the world. Activists excel at packaging issues, explaining the problem, the solution, and the action that people can take. Activists break it all down into sixty-second raps with accompanying flyers, fact sheets, and talking points, and these tactics win important campaign victories. But where is our system-changing mass movement? Although many of our critics are so blinded by propaganda and ideology that they will always see us as naive, unpatriotic, or dangerous, there is already a critical mass of people who recognize that our society is facing severe problems.

This analysis is supported by the work of researcher and author Paul Rey, who has done extensive demographic research into the beliefs and values of the American public. Rey's work first received prominence through his discovery of the "cultural creatives" which he describes as the cultural by-product of the last forty years of social movements. The defining characteristics of this social grouping includes acceptance of the basic tenets of environmentalism and feminism, a rejection of traditional careerism, big business, and monetary definitions of "success," a concern with psychological and spiritual development, belief in communities, and a concern for the future. Perhaps most profound is the fact that since the mass media of America still reflects the modern technocratic consumerist worldview, cultural creatives tend to feel isolated and not recognize their true numbers. Most important, based on their 1995, data Rey and his coauthor Sherry Ruth Anderson conclude that there are 50 million cultural creatives in America and the numbers are growing.[13]

Rey has continued his work in *The New Political Compass,* in which he argues with statistical data that the Left/Right breakdown of politics is now largely irrelevant and proposes a new four-directional political compass. Rey's compass is a fascinating tool for illustrating the complexity of public opinion, mapping not only political beliefs but also cultural shifts. Rey contrasts the Left of New Deal liberalism and big government as "West" with the "East" of cultural conservatism and the religious right. Rey gives "North" on his compass to a grouping he calls the New Progressives, composed largely of cultural creatives and completely unrepresented in the current political system. He defines their major concerns as ecological sustainability, the corporate dominance, child welfare, health care, education, a desire for natural products and personal growth. He contrasts them with "South," who espouse the Big Business Paradigm of profits

POST-ISSUE ACTIVISM

Altered version of the control mythology's battle of the story.

before planet and people, economic growth, and globalization. Again, his statistical data has profound messages for all of us working to change the world. He estimates that whereas only 14 percent of the population supports the Big Business paradigm, 36 percent of Americans fall into the New Progressives category.[14]

To me the message is a simple affirmation of postissue activism. Our movements need to stop focusing on *only* the details and start getting the bigger picture of a holistic analysis out there. Unless the details articulate a broader vision, they are just more background noise in our information-saturated culture. The eighteenth-century political frameworks of left versus right no longer fully capture the political fault lines of our era. Perhaps a better description of the real debate is flat earth versus round earth. The corporate globalizers' program of ever-expanding industrial exploitation of the earth is in such deep denial of the ecological realities of the planet that it is akin to maintaining that the earth is flat. Fortunately, more and more people understand that the earth is in fact round and that we need to make some big changes to both the global system and the way we think of our relationship with the planet. What we need now are social movements with the vision and strategy to harness this consciousness into real momentum for shaping a better world.

The ability to choose your issue is a privilege. Most people involved in resistance are born into their community's struggle for survival. They

POST-ISSUE ACTIVISM

didn't choose their issue any more then they chose their skin color or their proximity to extractable resources. Activists from more privileged backgrounds have the luxury of choosing what they work on and have to be aware of the dynamics that privilege creates. To expand the base of struggle and support frontline resistance with systemic work we need to confront the silent (and frequently uninformed) consent of the comfortable.

Unfortunately, all too often we still speak in the language of single-issue campaigns and are thus competing with ourselves for overworked, overstimulated people's limited amount of time and compassion. The aware, concerned people who are not immersed in frontline struggle are constantly having to choose between issues. Do I work on global warming or labor rights? World Bank or deforestation? Health care or campaign finance reform? One result is that a lot of people fail to make the connection between a general sense of wrongness about modern society and their own interests and actions. Without an impetus to overcome the colonization of people's revolutionary imaginations it is often easier to retreat into self-centeredness, apathy, or cynicism.

One of the strengths of the emerging global justice movement has been to create a new framework that goes beyond the age of single-issue politics to present the corporate takeover as a unifying cause of many of the planet's ills. The problem has been the amount of information we've been packaging into the critique as we slowly try to work the public through the alphabet soup of corporate cronies, trade agreements, and arcane international finance institutions. I don't doubt people's ability to grapple with the mechanics of corporate globalization but I do doubt our movement's ability to win the amount of air time from the corporate media that we need to download endless facts.

Everything—including the corporate global system—is very complicated. But likewise everything is very simple. There is sick and healthy. Just and unjust. Right and wrong. Despite the obvious oversimplification of binary frameworks, the language of opposing values is a powerful tool to build holistic analysis and subvert the control mythology.

Ultimately, our society must shift collective priorities and engage in a values shift to overcome some of our deepest pathologies such as patriarchy, fear of "otherness," and alienation from nature. However, we must be very careful how we frame this concept. Picture yourself knocking on the country's front door and announcing that you have come to shift people's values. Slam! In fact, this is far too often the way that activists are perceived.

An alternative strategy for a first step is to articulate the values crisis. This means speaking to people in terms of their basic values and showing them that the global system that is engulfing them is out of alignment with those values. In other words we have a "values crisis," a disconnect between what kind of world people want to live in and the corporate world that is rapidly taking over.

David Hanks

Antiwar march and direct action, San Francisco, March 21, 2003.

POST-ISSUE ACTIVISM

Long-term activist and movement theorist Bill Moyer wrote about the concept within psychology of "confirmatory bias" or people's habit of screening information based on their own beliefs. In other words, people are much more likely to believe something that reinforces their existing opinions and values than to accept information that challenges their beliefs.[15]

Moyer's point is that social movements succeed when we position ourselves within widely held existing values. The emerging global justice movements are already laying claim to core values such as democracy, justice, diversity, and environmental sanity as part of an inclusive vision of a life-affirming future. Now our work is to expose the flawed values of the corporate takeover.

We can articulate the values crisis by showing people that corporate capitalism is no longer grounded in common-sense values. The corporate paradigm is a cancerous perversion that masquerades as being reflective of commonly held values while it writes the rules of the global economy to metastasize corporate control across the planet.

A simple dichotomy for articulating the crisis is the clash between a delusional value system that fetishizes money and a value system centered

around the biological realities of life's diversity[16] (*see sidebar*). We need to cast these opposing value systems as two very different paths for the future of our planet. The path shaped by life values leads toward many choices—decentralized, self-organizing, diversity of different cultures, political traditions, and local economies. In contrast, the money values path leads to fewer and fewer choices and finally to the homogeneity of global corporatization.

It is our job as activists to clarify the choice by revealing the nature of the system and articulating the alternatives. Will it be democracy or global corporate rule? Will we be subsumed into a fossil fuel-addicted global economy or will we build vibrant sustainable local economies? Which will win out, ecological sanity or pathological capitalism? Will it be the corporate globalization of economics and control or a people's globalization of ideas, creativity, and autonomy? Democracy versus corporate rule. Ecology versus pollution. Life versus the doomsday economy. Hope versus extinction.

Framing the Debate

One of the biggest pitfalls activists face to effectively articulate the values crisis is that the category of protester has been constructed to be highly marginal by the establishment. Within the pathological logic of corporate capitalism, dissent is delegitimized to be unpatriotic, impractical, naive, or even insane. Unfortunately, radicals are all too often complicit in our own marginalization by accepting this elite depiction of ourselves as the fringe.

The reality is that the elite policy writers and corporate executives who think the world can continue on with unlimited economic growth in a finite biological system are the wackos, not us. We are not the fringe. We can frame the debate. In fact, as Paul Rey's research has shown us, a sizable percentage of the population already shares our commitment to cultural transformation, and all we need to do is reach them.

The significance of the recent mass actions against corporate globalization has not been tactics. Movements aren't about tactics—take this street corner, blockade that corporate office—movements are about ideas. Movements are about changing the world. When we say a better world is possible, we mean it. We want a world that reflects basic life-centered values. We've got the vision and the other side doesn't. We've got biocentrism, organic food production, direct democracy, renewable energy, diversity, people's globalization, and justice. What have they got?

POST-ISSUE ACTIVISM

Money Values versus Life Values

exploitation / dignity

centralized control / democratic decisionmaking

commodification / sacredness

privatization / global commons

corporatization / collective responsibility

shareholders / stakeholders

output / throughput

disposable / renewable

mechanistic models / organic models

information / wisdom

productivity / prosperity

consumers / citizens

spectator / participant

global economy / local economies

extraction / restoration

monoculture / diversity

transferrable wealth / replenishable wealth

property / ecosystem

alienation from nature / earth-centered values

absentee landlordism / stewardship

ecological illiteracy / biocentrism

proxy decisionmaking / real democracy

short-term gain / sustainability

narrow economic indicators / full cost accounting

artificial scarcity / abundance

inequitable distribution / economic justice

corporate rule / global justice

empire / community

The System / systemic change

Styrofoam? Neoliberalism? Eating disorders? Designer jeans, manic depression, and global warming?

In a context where the elites hold so much power, almost all our actions are by necessity symbolic. Accepting this can be one of our greatest strengths and help us realize that the most important aspects of our actions are the messages they project into mass culture. We must exploit the power of narrative structure to weave our ideas and actions into compelling stories. Inevitably, our broadest consitituency will begin their interaction with new ideas as spectators. Thus, our campaigns and actions must tell inclusive, provocative stories that create space for people to see themselves in the story. We must tell the story of the values crisis. Our stories must make people take sides—are you part of the sickness or are you part of the healing? Are you part of the life-affirming future or are you part of the doomsday economy?

The first step is to separate dissent from the self-righteous tone that many people associate with protest. This tone can be particularly strong in activists from privileged backgrounds who are invested in visible "defection" as a way to validate their resistance. These politics of defection by their very nature create obstacles to communicating with the mainstream and frequently rely on symbols of dissent and rebellion that are already marginalized.

We need new symbols of inclusive resistance and transformation. We need a better understanding how to create effective memes[17]—self-replicating units of information and culture—to convey the values crisis. Memes are viral by nature, they move easily through our modern world of information networks and media saturation. We need to be training ourselves to become "meme warriors"[18] and to tell the story of values crisis in different ways for different audiences. We must get a better sense of who our audiences are, and target our messages to fit into their existing experiences.

We need to be media savvy and use the corporate propaganda machine. Not naively as an exclusive means of validating our movements, but as a tool of information self-defense to oppose the information war being waged against us. The corporate media is another tool we can use to name the system and undermine the grip of the dominant mythology. While we play at spin doctoring, we simultaneously need to promote media democracy and capitalize on the alternative and informal media and communication networks as a means to get our message out. Our movements must become the nervous systems of an emerging transformative culture.

Jason Justice

Street theater by the Ronald Reagan Home for the Criminally Insane — Bechtel, San Francisco

It's essential that we frame our ideas in such a way that as people wake up to the crisis they have the conceptual tools to understand the systemic roots of the problem. Over the next decade as the global crisis becomes more visible we won't have to do much to convince people about the problem. Rather, our job will be to discredit the elite's Band-Aid solutions and build popular understanding of the need for more systemic solutions.

Whether we are talking about biological contamination, financial collapse, or nuclear meltdowns, if we haven't framed the issue in advance, even the most dramatic breakdowns in the system can be "crisis-managed" away without alerting the public to the system's fundamental failings.. But if we do the work to challenge the control mythology and undermine the flawed assumptions, then people will know whom to blame. As we build a public awareness of the values crisis it helps shift the debate away from inadequate reforms and toward redesigning the global system.

This is the strategy of leap-frogging, or framing our issues in such a way that they force the public debate to "leap" over limiting definitions of the problem and elite quick-fixes to embrace systemic solutions. For example, instead of debating how many parts per million of pollution regulatory agencies should allow in our drinking water, we can challenge the right of industrial interests to poison us at all. An effective framing forces

— FRAMING THE CLIMATE CRISIS —

Global warming is an obvious example of an issue where leap-frogging is desperately needed. As global warming creates more visible eco-spasms it will soon become one of the macroissues that redefines politics as we know it.

Global warming, when expanded from the single-issue context of carbon dioxide pollution and redefined as a systemic issue of fossil fuel addiction, becomes a vehicle for exposing the global system's deep design flaws. Thus it can be used not only to show the moral and intellectual bankruptcy of a fossil fuel–based economy but also to indict the system that has created the fossil fuel chain of destruction. When framed properly, this story promotes not only environmentally friendly alternatives, but also democracy ("energy sovereignty"[19]) and the need to confront the racism and classism that has allowed the basic human rights of communities impacted by fossil fuel production to be ignored.

The global oil barons are among the most powerful interests on the planet and they have used their influence to block any realistic effort to transition away from fossil fuels. Despite the fact that it is scientifically inadequate to address the problem, the Kyoto Protocol—an international framework for reducing carbon emissions—has been stalled by the political influence of the fossil fuel industry. In response, many concerned American pressure groups have reduced their demands and lobbied for more minor concessions, like fuel efficiency standards, that they might be able to win without having to fundamentally challenge the corporate influence over politics.

But instead of reducing our expectations, when we face the limits of the existing political debate we need to expand our vision and have the courage to leap-frog the political logjams with the values crisis analysis. Strategically, the most significant aspect of the climate crisis is that we know it's going to get worse and more visible —so why settle for the limited concessions that can be "won" now?

Imagine, hypothetically, ten or fifteen years from now when superhurricanes displace 40 million in Florida, America's corn belt is withering under a mega-drought, and the eastern seaboard is spending $2 trillion building flood walls. The American public is going to want some answers. If possible, before it gets that bad it's important that people understand that we are not all equally culpable for the destabilization of the global climate. Sure, a lot of people drove SUVs and consumed way more than their share, but let's be clear who did more to destabilize the climate — the soccer moms or Exxon-Mobil?

It's up to activists to ensure that people understand that a small cartel of energy corporations and their financial backers knowingly destabilized our planet's climate for their own personal gain. This may turn out to be the most devastating crime ever perpetrated against humanity, the planet, and future generations.

How we frame the issue will help decide what actually happens when the problem becomes undeniable. Taking the time to frame the climate crisis systemically may not win concessions in the short term but it will pay off when people's outrage can be effectively channeled into fundamental change. Imagine two different scenarios: In the first, a decade of organizing and struggle belatedly convinces the oil barons to approve the Kyoto Protocol in its current inadequate form. As climate chaos accelerates, the oil industry plots how to maintain their monopoly during the transition to sustainable energy. In the other scenario, an empowered populace jails the oil executives, dissolves their illegitimate corporations, and uses their billions to fund the transition to clean energy. Which future would you rather live in?

questions to be asked about the upstream polluters—do we need their product? If so, how can we make it in a way that doesn't pollute? In order to successfully leap-frog colonized imaginations and entrenched power-holders, we must have the skill and courage to articulate real solutions that avoid concessions that dead-end in inadequate reforms.

It is essential that as the ecological crisis becomes self-evident we are building mass awareness of the system's design flaws. As we become more effective at leap-frogging the elite framing of problems, we can prepare people to accept the dramatic changes that will be necessary to make another world possible.

There are any number of macroissues that when framed correctly can help us name the system. Global warming, commodification of basic human needs from health care to water, the rate of technological change, systemic racism, the spread of genetic pollution, ongoing violence against women—these are just a few examples that can tell the story of the values crisis. The challenge is not what issue we work on but how we avoid becoming trapped in the limiting framework of single-issue politics.

Direct Action at the Point of Assumption

Direct action—actions that either symbolically or directly shift power relations—is an essential transformative tool. Direct action can be both a tactic within a broader strategy or a political ethic of fundamental change that defines all one's actions. Every direct action is part of the larger story we are retelling ourselves about the ability of collaborative power to overcome coercive power.

As we endeavor to link systemic change with tangible short-term goals we must seek out the *points of intervention* in the system. These are the places where when we apply our power—usually through revoking our obedience—we are able to leverage change.

Direct action at the *point of production* was one of the original insights of the labor movement. Labor radicals targeted the system where it was directly affecting them and where the system was most vulnerable. From wildcat strikes to sabotage, slowdowns, and factory occupations, point-of-production actions helped promote the dignity and rights of working people.

Modern frontline resistance movements often target the system at the *point of destruction*. We become the frontline resistance by placing our bodies in the way of the harm that is happening. Whether it's plugging the

POST-ISSUE ACTIVISM

Eric Wagner

Protest and nonviolent direct action at Bechtel, San Francisco.

effluent pipes that dump poison on a neighborhood, forest defenders sitting in trees marked for cutting, or indigenous peoples blocking road-building into their ancestral homelands, direct action at the point of destruction embodies values crisis. It polarizes the debate in an effort to attract the spotlight of public attention to a clear injustice. But, tragically, the point of destruction is oftentimes far from the public eye, and the values confrontation is made invisible by distance, imbedded patterns of bias, or popular ignorance. Frequently, the impacted communities have little political voice, so in order to provide support we must find other points of intervention.

Inspiring *point-of-consumption* campaigns have been used by many movements as a way to stand in solidarity with communities fighting at the point of destruction. This is the realm of consumer boycotts, attacks on corporate brand names, and other campaigns that target the commercial sector as a way to shut down the market for destructive products. Activists have confronted retailers selling sweatshop products and forced universities to cancel clothing contracts. Likewise, forest activists have forced major chains to stop selling old-growth forest products. Attacking the point of consumption expands the arena of struggle to mobilize consumers made complicit in the injustice of the globalized economy by making them more aware of their own purchasing decisions. These strategies can be based on a very accessible notion of "ethical shopping" or a more profound rejection of the consumer identity altogether.

The *point of decision* has always been a common and strategic venue for direct action. Whether it's taking over a slumlord's office, a corporate boardroom, or the state capital, many successful campaigns have used direct action to put pressure on the decisionmakers they are targeting. Much of the mass action organizing of the past few years has been largely aimed at redefining popular perceptions of the point of decision. The actions at WTO and World Bank meetings, G8 summits and free trade negotiating sessions have helped reveal the corporate takeover by showing

POST-ISSUE ACTIVISM

that it is these new institutions of corporate rule that have usurped decisionmaking power.

All of these points of intervention in the system are important, and the best strategies unite efforts across them. As the global financial sector has increasingly become the "operating system" for the planet, the pathological logic of doomsday economics has replaced specific points of decision in driving the corporate takeover. We aren't just fighting acts of injustice or destruction but rather we are fighting a *system* of injustice and destruction. In recognizing this we must expand our efforts to intervene in physical space, complementing them with similar initiatives in cultural and intellectual space. How can we sidestep the machine and challenge the mentality behind the machine? In other words, we need to figure out how to take direct action at the *point of assumption*.

Targeting assumptions—the framework of myths, lies, and flawed rationale that normalize the corporate takeover— requires some different approaches from actions at the other points of intervention. *Point-of-assumption* actions operate in the realm of ideas and the goal is to expose pathological logic, cast doubt, and undermine existing loyalties. Successful direct action at the point of assumption identifies, isolates, and confronts the big lies that maintain the status quo. A worthy goal for these types of actions is to encourage the most important act that a concerned citizen can take in an era defined by systematic propaganda—*questioning!*

Direct action at the point of assumption is a tool to decolonize people's revolutionary imaginations by linking analysis and action in ways that reframe issues and create new political space. Whether we're deconstructing consumer spectacles, exposing the system's propaganda, or birthing new rhetoric, we need actions that reveal the awful truth—that the intellectual underpinnings of the modern system are largely flawed assumptions. Direct action at the point of assumption is an effort to find the rumors that start revolutions and ask the questions that topple empires.

The first action of the radical ecology network Earth First! is a great example of direct action at the point of assumption. In 1981, at a time when many wilderness preservation groups were fighting the construction of new dams, Earth First! did a symbolic "cracking" of Glen Canyon Dam by unfurling a 300-foot-long plastic wedge from the top of the dam, creating an image of a fissure down the dam's face.[20] This simple symbol sent a powerful message that rather than just stopping new dams, wilderness advocates should be calling for the removal of big dams and the rewilding of dammed rivers. Within the industrial paradigm of dominating

POST-ISSUE ACTIVISM

POST-ISSUE ACTIVISM

A DJ spins CDs at a Reclaim the Streets party, February 14, 2004, Haight-Ashbury, San Francisco.

nature, the question of removing a megadam was an unthinkable thought—it was beyond the realm of imagination. The "cracking" action, however, challenged that assumption and created a new political space and a powerful image to forward that agenda. Two decades later, in the late nineties, the unthinkable thought had rippled right up to the power-holders and the U.S. government actually began removing dams.

Likewise, as the anticar movement has grown, groups like Reclaim the Streets have taken effective direct actions at the point of assumption to make the idea of car-free cities imaginable. Reclaim the Streets groups showed what a better world could look like with actions that occupy car-clogged streets and transform them into people-friendly spaces with music, festivity, comfy furniture, and in some cases even grass and plants. Similarly, activists around the world have taken creative "Buy Nothing Day" actions to attack the assumptions of consumerism by calling for a twenty-four-hour moratorium on consumer spending on the busiest shopping day of the year. This simple idea, often popularized using ridicule and humorous spectacle, has led to many successful efforts to define consumerism itself as an issue.

Direct action at the point of assumption has taken many forms—creating new symbols, embodying alternatives, or sounding the alarm. The

Zapatista ski mask is a well-known example of a symbol that functioned as direct action at the point of assumption. The ski masks worn by the Zapatista insurgents and particularly their spokesman Subcomandante Marcos, created a symbol for the invisibility of Mexico's indigenous peoples. Marcos has eloquently written of the irony that only with the ski masks on—the symbol of militant confrontation—was the government able to see the indigenous peoples it had ignored for so long.[21]

In Argentina the *cacerolazos*—the spontaneous mass banging on *cacerolas* (saucepans)—is a tactic that has helped topple several governments since the popular uprising began in December 2001. The simple, inclusive direct action of banging a saucepan has created a dramatic new space for people from many different backgrounds to unite in resisting neoliberalism and structural adjustment. It broke the assumption that people will simply accept the actions of a government that ignores them.[xxii]

Direct action at the point of assumption provides us with many new opportunities to expand the traditional political arenas because it is less reliant on specific physical space than other points of intervention. This gives us the opportunity to choose the terms and location of engagement. Effective point-of-assumption actions can transform the mundane into a radical conversation starter. For instance, putting a piece of duct tape across a prominent logo on your clothing can invite a conversation about corporate commodification.

Media activist James John Bell writes about "Image Events," events whether actions, images, or stories that "simultaneously destroy and construct [new] meaning." Image events either replace existing sets of symbols or redefine their meaning through the "disidentification" of humor or shock.[23] A simple application of this concept can be seen in what *Adbuster* magazine's founder Kalle Lasn has dubbed "culture jamming" to describe methods of subverting corporate propaganda by juxtaposing new images or coopting slogans.[24] For instance, when McDonald's hyperfamiliar golden arches are overlaid with images of starving children or Chevron's advertising slogan is rewritten to say "Do people kill for oil?" the power of corporate images are turned back upon themselves. This type of semiotic aikido exploits the omnipresence of corporate advertising to rewrite the meaning of familiar symbols and tell stories that challenge corporate power. These skills have been artfully applied in billboard liberations, guerrilla media campaigns, and creative actions, but unfortunately they often remain in a limited media realm. We need to expand guerrilla meme tactics to connect with long-term strategies to build grassroots power.

The reliance of many megacorporations on their branding has been widely acknowledged as an Achilles' heel of corporate power. Indeed, effective grassroots attacks on corporate logos and brand image have forced corporations to dump multimillion-dollar advertising campaigns and sometimes even concede to activists' demands. However, not only are there many powerful industries that do not depend on consumer approval but we no longer have time to go after the corporations one at a time. Our movements need to contest the corporate monopoly on meaning. We must create point of assumption actions that go beyond merely jamming the control mythology to actually substituting transformative, life-affirming stories. Culture jamming has largely been applied like a wrench to disable the brainwashing infrastructure of corporate consumerism. We must supplement the wrench with the seed by planting new, transformative stories that use the information-replicating networks of modern society to grow and spread. Our actions must create image events and launch designer memes with the power to supersede the controlling mythologies of consumer culture, the American empire, and pathological capitalism.[25]

Concerted direct action at the point of assumption in our society could be an effort to draw attention to the design errors of the modern era and encourage widespread disobedience to oppressive cultural norms. We need to plot open attacks on the symbolic order of antilife values. We need easily replicable actions, new symbols, and contagious memes that we can combine with grassroots organizing and alternative institution building to expand the transformative arena of struggle.

What would this look like? What are the big lies and controlling myths that hold corporate rule in place? Where are the points of assumption? How can we exploit the hypocrisy between the way we're told the world works and the way it actually works in order to name the system, articulate the values crisis, and begin decolonizing the collective imagination? These are all questions for our movements to explore together as we challenge ourselves to be pragmatic idealists, calculating provocateurs, and revolutionary dreamers.

Case Study: The San Francisco Uprising

The Bush administration's invasion of Iraq was met with massive resistance in the United States and around the world. In particular, the response in San Francisco was inspiring—20,000 people engaged in mass nonviolent direct action to shut down the financial district. Corporations invested in the mass destruction business (like Bechtel, Citibank, and the Carlyle Group) had their offices blockaded as did a military recruiting station, the British consulate, and a federal office building. Using tactics ranging from lockdowns to mobile blockades and critical mass bike rides, Bay Area residents transformed the usually car-clogged consumption zone into a living statement of hope and life-affirming resistance to Bush's war for empire. Over the course of the four business days after the invasion began, 2,600 people were arrested for engaging in acts of protest and resistance.

design: justicedesign.com

Illustration: Mona Caron

Although this uprising was decentralized and highly organic it grew out of a foundation of organizing laid by an affinity-group-based mobilization called Direct Action to Stop the War (DASW). For the preceding two months, DASW had organized the uprising's launching pad through a weekly spokescouncil, a Web site (www.actagainstwar.org), and the simple notion that a rational response to an illegal and unjust war

Direct Action to Stop the War's direct action manual used the day after the war on Iraq began to mobilize 20,000 activists to shut down San Francisco.

for empire would be a mass direct action shutting down the financial district.

The real success of the action came not only from the fact that several thousand people were preorganized into affinity groups, but that tens of thousands of people joined in on the day of the action. One of the reasons that so many people joined the action was that it was timed to harness a predictable mass psychic break—a point where the unfolding of events shatters people's illusions that the system reflects their values (such as justice, democracy, peace). A psychic break is a massive point of intervention in the system's assumption of obedience, when people are uniquely open to new actions. In an infamously progressive city like San Francisco there was a predictable antiwar majority but a common framework was needed to facilitate action and make opposition visible.

DASW's work to build this framework for popular resistance was aided by a strategy of telling the future. Telling the future (similar to the "scenario planning" used by the Pentagon and multinational corporations) is a method of manifesting a specific outcome by normalizing a possible scenario. Advertisers have long known that the best way to get people to

David Hanks

The Brass Liberation Orchestra plays as residents shut down the San Francisco Financial District, March 20, 2003.

do something (like buy their product) is to have them take action in their head first. Hence much of advertising is designed to help people imagine themselves buying a product—to normalize a specific commercial scenario. Strategies that tell the future can use some of the same principles to unify people around a common goal and vision to literally self-organize a specific future through building collective belief. DASW organizers challenged the mass media narrative of normalized passivity by promoting an alternative story where if Bush invaded Iraq, residents would rise up in a nonviolent insurrection and shut down the financial district.

The future uprising was foretold with a series of foreshadowing events ranging from a high-profile press conference to an open letter to city residents to preemptive actions in the financial district, including a shut down of the Pacific Stock Exchange in which eigthy people were arrested. All of this outreach, organizing, and media work was successful in the goal of promoting DASW's website and the action meeting spot, including getting it printed on the front page of newspapers and mentioned on major radio and television stations.

Likewise, in creating a public image of the action, DASW focused on a values-based critique that worked to mainstream the concepts of noncooperation and civil disobedience. The DASW Web site and kick-off press conference emphasized the diversity of participation by featuring endorsements from leaders of a cross-section of Bay Area communities— queer, labor, faith, people of color, veterans, seniors, even the former CEO of the Pacific Stock Exchange. Without sacrificing the opportunity to put out a systemic analysis, the organizing appealed to mainstream values— democracy, sense of security, justice, belief in international law, patriotism—and used them to leverage opposition to the invasion of Iraq. As a result the streets were flooded with people from different walks of life. The combination of effectively telling the future and articulating a values-based analysis had reached a cross-section of American society who had never engaged in direct action before.

POST-ISSUE ACTIVISM

190

David Hanks

Twenty thousand people shut down large parts of San Francisco using nonviolent direct action the day after the war on Iraq begins.

David Hanks

Global Intifada affinity group shuts down San Francisco Financial District's central artery—Market Street, March 20, 2003.

Eric Wagner

Outraged Bay Area residents stop commute traffic into Financial District.

Eric Wagner

Thousands join the San Francisco shutdown, transforming it from a planned mass action into a popular antiwar uprising.

This type of inclusive mass organizing may stretch the comfort zone of many radicals; however, it has great potential to exploit some of the growing fault lines in American society. Bush's naked imperial agenda is challenging a lot of Americans' sense of national identity as an international beacon of democracy and justice. Regardless of the fact that much of America's national story has always been a hypocritical mythology, there is an incredible opportunity for activists to lay claim to widely held values like security, democracy, and national pride and direct these energies into "imploding" empire. Let's ask ourselves how our resistance can galvanize antiwar sentiments into a deeper movement for fundamental change that articulates the values crisis—the disconnect between the values of empire and the values that ordinary Americans hold. In San Francisco the strategy worked well enough that 20,000 people took to the streets—with more refinement and widespread application, who knows what might be possible?

Beware the Professionalization of Social Change

The worst thing that can happen to our movements right now is to settle for too little.

But tragically that is exactly what is happening. We are largely failing to frame the ecological, social, and economic crisis as a symptom of a deeper values crisis and a pathological system. Thus, many of the modest visions of social change being put forward seem incapable of even keeping pace with the accelerating global crisis, let alone providing true alternatives to the doomsday economy.

Too many of our social change resources are getting bogged down in arenas of struggle that can't deliver the systemic shifts we need. Most of the conventional venues for political engagement—legislation, elections, courts, single-issue campaigns, labor fights—have been so coopted by elite rule that it's very difficult to imagine how to use them for strategies that name the system, undermine the control mythology, or articulate values crisis from within their limited parameters.

One of the most telling symptoms of our colonized imaginations has been the limited scope of social change institutions. Most social change resources get directed toward enforcing inadequate regulations, trying to pass watered-down legislation, working to elect mediocre candidates, or to win concessions that don't threaten the corporate order. One of the main reasons that so many social change resources get limited to the regulatory, electoral, and concessionary arenas is the fact that much of social change has become a professionalized industry.

The NGO—nongovernmental organization—a term made popular by the United Nations policy discussion process, has become the most familiar social change institution. These groups are frequently made up of hard-working, underpaid, dedicated people, and NGOs as a group do a great deal of important work. However, we must also acknowledge that generally the explosion of NGOs globally is a loose attempt to patch the holes that neoliberalism has punched in the social safety net. As government cedes its role in public welfare to corporations, even the unlucrative sectors have to be handed off to someone. A recent article in the *Economist* revealingly explains the growth of NGOs as " . . . not a matter of charity but of privatization."[26]

My intention is not to fall into the all-too-easy trap of lumping the thousands of different NGOs into one dismissable category but rather to label a disturbing trend, particularly among social-change NGOs. Just as service-oriented NGOs have been tapped to fill the voids left by the state or the market, so have social-change NGOs arisen to streamline the chaotic business of dissent. Let's call this trend NGOism, the belief—sometimes found among professional "campaigners"—that social change is a highly specialized profession best left to experienced strategists, negotiators, and policy wonks. NGOism is the conceit that intermediary organizations of paid staff, rather than communities organizing themselves into movements, will be enough to save the world.

This very dangerous trend ignores the historic reality that collective struggle and mass movements organized from the bottom up have always been the springboard for true progress and social change. The goal of radical institutions—whether well-funded NGOs or gritty grassroots groups—should be to help build movements to change the world. But NGOism institutionalizes the amnesia of the colonized imagination and presents a major obstacle to moving into the post-issue activism framework. After all, who needs a social movement when you've got a six-figure advertising budget and "access" to all the decisionmakers?

A professional NGO is structured exactly like a corporation, down to having an employee payroll and a board of directors. This is not an accident. Just like their for-profit cousins, this structure creates an institutional self-interest that can transform an organization from a catalyst for social change into a self-perpetuating entity. NGOism views change in reference to existing power relations by accepting a set of rules written by the powerful to ensure the status quo. These rules have already been stacked against social change. NGOism represents institutional confusion about the different types of power and encourages overdependence on strategies that speak exclusively to the existing

powers—funding sources, the media, decisionmakers. As a consequence, strategies often get locked into the regulatory and concessionary arenas—focused on "pressure"—and attempt to redirect existing power rather than focusing on confronting illegitimate authority, revealing systemic flaws, and building grassroots power.

The mythology of American politics as populist or democratic is rapidly being undermined by the blatant realities of corporate dominance. As people's confidence in the facades of popular rule (like voting, lobbying, and the regulatory framework) has waned, more and more campaigns are directly confronting destructive corporations. This is an essential strategy for revealing the decisionmaking power that corporations have usurped, but unfortunately most of these NGO-led efforts to confront individual destructive corporations are failing to articulate a holistic analysis of the system of corporate control.

This is an extremely dangerous failure because in pursuing concessions or attempting to redirect corporate resources we risk making multinational corporations the agents of solving the ecological crisis. This is a flawed strategy since by their very nature corporations are incapable of making the concessions necessary to address the global crisis. There is no decision-maker in the corporate hierarchy with the power to transform the nature of the corporate beast and confront its identity as a profit-making machine. The CEO who has an epiphany about the need to redefine her corporation as a democratic institution that looks beyond the limited fiduciary interests of shareholders will find herself on the wrong side of a century of corporate law. We need to avoid the temptation to accept concessions that legitimize corporate control and obscure the fundamental democracy issues underlying the global crisis.

Too often, political pragmatism is used as an excuse for a lack of vision. Pragmatism without vision is accepting the rules that are stacked against us while vision without pragmatism is fetishizing failure. The question shouldn't be what can we win in this funding cycle but rather how do we expand the debate to balance short- and long-term goals? Like a healthy ecosystem, our movements need a diversity of strategies. We need to think outside the box and see what new arenas of struggle we can explore.

This is not to say that corporate campaigns and winning concessions is merely "reformist" and therefore not important. The simplistic dichotomy of reform versus revolution often hides the privilege of "radicals" who have the luxury of refusing concessions when it's not their community or ecosystem that is on the chopping block.

POST-ISSUE ACTIVISM

Jason Justice

A more important distinction is which direction is the concession moving toward? Is it a concession that releases pressure on the system and thereby legitimizes illegitimate authority? Or is it a concession that teaches people a lesson about their collective power to make change and therefore brings us closer to systemic change?

NGOism creates ripe conditions for going beyond mere ineffectiveness and into outright complicity with the system. Time and time again we've seen social-change NGOs grow to become a part of the establishment and then be used as a tool to marginalize popular dissent by lending legitimacy to the system. Whether it's the World Wildlife Fund giving a green seal of approval to oil companies or the American Cancer Society's downplaying of environmental pollution's role in cancer,[27] it's clear that NGOs can become an obstacle to transformative change.

The professionalization of social change requires extensive resources, and it's obvious that NGO agendas can be shaped by their funding needs. Whether reliant on a membership base or institutional funders, NGOs are often forced to build a power base through self-promotion rather than self-analysis. Not only does this dilute their agendas to fit within the political comfort zone of those with resources, it disrupts the essential process of acknowledging mistakes and learning from them. This evolutionary process of collective learning is central to fundamental social change, and

Protests against police brutality and the war on Iraq following an April 7, 2003 police attack on demonstrators, longshore workers, and members of the media with rubber, wooden, and plastic bullets, concussion grenades, and motorcycles. The police attacked in response to a community picket to shut down SSA and APL corporations at the Oakland Docks, one of the major arteries for global capital's shipment of goods for the western United States. April 2003.

People from community, labor, and antiwar groups reclaim their right to picket and protest one month after the April 7 police attacks. The docks were again shut down, and this time the police backed down and did not interfere. May 12, 2003.

Eric Wagner

to have it derailed by professionalization threatens to limit the depth of the change that we can create.

When a system is fundamentally flawed there is no point in trying to fix it—we need to redesign it. That is the essence of the transformative arena— defining issues, reframing debates, thinking big. We must create the political space to harness the awareness of the increasingly obvious global crisis into a desire for real change toward a democratic, just, and ecologically sane world.

Our movements must evolve past mere mobilizing and into real transformative organizing. Transformative organizing is more than just making the protest louder and bigger. It's the nuts-and-bolts business of building alternatives on a grassroots level, and creating our own legitimacy to replace the illegitimate institutions of corporate society. Real transformative organizing gives people the skills and analysis they need to ground the struggle to reclaim our planet in both the individual and the structural arenas—the creation of new identities and the transformation of global systems.

It is essential that we don't waste all our energy just throwing ourselves at the machine. Resistance is only one piece of the social change equation. It must be complimented by creation. Movements need institutions that can be the hubs to help sustain our momentum for the long haul. There are definitely NGOs that play this role well, we just have to ensure that NGOism doesn't infect them with limiting definitions of specialization and professionalism.

We have to plant the seeds of the new society within the shell of the old. Exciting work is being done around the concept of *dual-power strategies*. These are strategies that not only confront illegitimate institutions, but simultaneously embody the alternatives, thereby giving people the opportunity to practice self-governance and envision new political realities. Examples of inspiring dual-power strategies are taking place across the world, particularly in Latin America. From indigenous autonomist communities in Mexico to the landless movement in Brazil to Argentina's *autoconvocados* (literally, "the self-convened ones"), peoples' movements are resisting the corporate takeover of their lives by defiantly living the alternatives.[27]

198

In the creation of these alternatives—the holistic actions of community transformation that go far beyond any of the limiting boundaries of professionalized social change—we see a vision of direct action at the point of assumption, actions that reveal new possibilities, challenge the assumptions of the corporate monoculture and create infectious, new political spaces.

We can fight the doomsday economy by devoking the apocalypse with visions of a life-affirming future. In doing so we lay claim to a radical's best ally—hope. But our hope must not be based on the naïveté of denial. Rather, our hope must be a signpost, a reminder of the potential of our struggles. We must not position hope as some mythic endpoint of struggle but rather, learn to carry it with us as a blueprint for our daily efforts.

Toward a Politics of Reality

Reality is that which is.

The English word "real" stems from a word which meant regal, of or pertaining to the king.

"Real" in Spanish means royal.

Real property is that which is proper to the king.

Real estate is the estate of the king.

*Reality is that which pertains to the one in power,
Is that over which he has power, is his domain, his
Estate, is proper to him.*

*The ideal king reigns over everything as far as the
Eye can see. His eye. What he cannot see is not
Royal, not real.*

He sees what is proper to him.

To be real is to be visible to the king.

The king is in his counting house.

—Marilyn Frye, "The Politics of Reality"

Feminist author Marilyn Frye writes about reality from the perspective of a lesbian fighting to "exist" within an oppressive heterosexist culture for which the idea of a woman who is not sexually dependant upon men is unimaginable. Her poem reminds us that reality is constructed, and that those in power get to decide who or what is "real." Or, in the words of the

Education, Living Wages & Healthcare – Not Warfare!

REAL DEMOCRACY NOT EMPIRE!

Direct Action to Stop the War
www.ActAgainstWar.org

PROTEST & NONVIOLENT DIRECT ACTION

7am
March 19
Embarcadero BART
San Francisco

Get Involved! Action Planning Spokescouncil:
Sunday March 14, 4pm & Thursday March 18, 6pm
St. Boniface, 133 Golden Gate, SF (Civic Center BART)

1980s band disco-industrial My Life with the Thrill Kill Kult: "'Reality' is the only word in the English language that should always be used in quotes."

Frye's poem uses the etymology of the word *reality* to expose the flawed assumptions that shape the dominant cultural lens. The king's counting house is the origin of today's corporate-driven doomsday economy. A "reality" that has colonized our minds to normalize alienation from nature, conquest, and patriarchal hierarchies. A "reality" based on the censorship of our history of collective struggle that makes us think rugged individualism is the only tactic for resistance.

"Reality" is the lens through which we see the world. If we want to create a different world we're going to need to create some new lenses. We can begin by understanding that the values that currently underlie the global system didn't win out because they are time-tested, democratically supported, or even effective. This "reality" is a product of the naked brutality of European colonization and the systematic destruction of the cultural and economic alternatives to our current pathological system.

The struggle to create political space for a truly transformative arena of social change is the fight to build a new collective reality. Our last (or is it first?) line of defense to the spreading consumer monoculture is the struggle to decolonize our minds and magnify the multitude of different "realities" embedded in the planet's sweeping diversity of cultures, ecosystems, and interdependant life forms.

At the center of these efforts must be the understanding that the ecological operating systems of the biosphere represent an overarching *politics of reality*. If we want to talk about reality in the singular, outside of its conceptual quotation marks, then we must talk about ecological reality—the reality of interdependence, diversity, limits, cycles, and dynamic balance. A politics of reality recognizes that ecology is not merely another single issue to lump onto our list of demands; rather, ecology is the larger context within which all our struggles takes place. A politics of reality is grounded in the understanding that the ecological collapse is the central and most visible contradiction in the global system. It is an implicit

On the one-year anniversary of the shutdown of San Francisco's financial district, DASW kicks off its Empire versus Democracy (beyond voting) campaign with a protest and nonviolent direct action on March 19, 2004, in conjunction with the global day of action against war on March 20, 2004.

The Infernal Noise Brigade comes to town for antiwar protests on March 19–20, 2004, San Francisco.

NO to AMERICAN TERRORISM

NO to OCCUPATION

On the day before the anniversary of the U.S.-led invasion of Iraq, a demonstration took place in Baghdad in tandem with protests around the world against the violence of the occupation on March 19, 2004.

acknowledgment that the central political project of our era is the rethinking of what it means to be human on planet earth.

Infernal Noise Brigade, March 19, 2004, San Francisco.

We have to confront the cancer and pull the dooms-day economy out of its suicidal nosedive. The move toward a politics of reality is the essence of a fight for the future itself. Indian writer and activist Vandana Shiva said it eloquently in her speech at the World Summit on Sustainable Development countersummit in August 2002: "There is only one struggle left, and that is the struggle for survival."

Jason Justice

Ecology must be a key ingredient in the future of pan-movement politics. But to achieve this, we must ensure that earth-centered values don't get appropriated by white, middle-class messengers and become artificially separated from a comprehensive critique of all forms of oppression. A global ecology movement is already being led by the communities and cultures most impacted by the doomsday economy, from international campesino movements to urban communities resisting toxic poisoning to the last indigenous homelands. Those of us dreaming of more global North counterparts to these earth-centered movements have much to learn from listening to the voices of frontline resistance.

The Western Shoshone people—the most bombed nation on earth who have survived half a century of U.S. nuclear colonialism on their ancestral lands in what is now called Nevada—have mobilized under the banner, "Healing Global Wounds." This inspiring slogan reminds us that despite the horrors of brutality, empire, and ecological catastrophe the strongest resistance lies in the ability to think big.

In facing the global crisis, the most powerful weapon that we have is our imagination. As we work to escape the oppressive cultural norms and flawed assumptions of the corporate system we must liberate our imagination and articulate our dreams for a life-affirming future. Our actions must embody these new "realities" because even though people might realize they are on the *Titanic* and the iceberg is just ahead, they still need to see the lifeboat in order to jump ship. It is by presenting alternatives that we can help catalyze mass defections from the pathological norms of modern consumer culture.[29]

POST-ISSUE ACTIVISM

Our job is to confront the sickness while articulating the alternatives, both ancient and new. Our true strength lies in the diversity of options presented by earth-centered values, whether we find the alternatives in the wisdom of traditional cultures, local economies, spiritual/community renewal, or ecological redesign. As we decolonize our own revolutionary imagination we will find new political frameworks that name the system and articulate the values crisis. We can base our work in an honest assessment of our own privilege, and a commitment to healing historic wounds. We can imagine a culture defined by diversity that promotes revolutionary optimism over nihilism and embraces collective empowerment over individual coercion. Not only can redefine what is possible, but we must!

We are already winning. Life is stronger than greed. Hope is more powerful than fear. The values crisis is in full swing, and more and more people are turning their back on the pathological values of the doomsday economy. The global immune system is kicking in and giving momentum to our movements for change. Call it an Enlightenment. Call it a Renaissance. Call it a common-sense revolution. The underlying concepts are obvious. As the saying goes—for a person standing on the edge of a cliff, progress must be defined as a step backward.

Imagination conjures change. First we dream it, then we speak it, then we struggle to build it. But without the dreams, without our decolonized imaginations, our efforts to name and transform the system will not succeed in time.

I take inspiration from a slogan spray-painted on the walls of Paris during the springtime uprising of 1968: "Be realistic. Demand the Impossible!" The slogan is more timely now than ever because the king can't stay in his counting house forever. And then it will be our turn. . . .

These ideas are works in progress. Feedback of all sorts (including scathing criticism) is welcome. Many of the concepts discussed in this essay have been translated into training and strategy tools through the work of the smartMeme Strategy and Training Project. Anyone interested in expanding upon or collaborating to implement some of these strategies are encouraged to contact the author at patrick@smartmeme.com or check out www.smartmeme.com. Join the fun! Start your own laboratory of resistance!

APPENDIX: a pragmatic dreamer's glossary

by the smartMeme Strategy and Training Project

The smartMeme Project is an emerging network of thinkers, trainers, writers, organizers, and earth-centered radicals who are exploring efforts to combine grassroots movement building with tools to inject new ideas into popular culture. To join in the fun and help expand and apply these concepts, check out the evolution at: www.smartmeme.com.

ABCNNBCBS — the increasingly blurred brand names for the same narrow stream of U.S. corporate-filtered mass media. This is the delivery system for the advertising product that giant media corporations sell to the general public. This process used to occur primarily through overt advertising. Increasingly, however, it has become a complex web of cross-marketing, branding, and self-promotion among different tentacles of the same media empires.

advertising — the manipulation of collective desire for commercial interests. Over the last twenty years as it has grown to nearly a $200 billion industry it has become the propaganda shell and dream life of modern consumer culture. (See control mythology)

articulating values crisis — a strategy in which radicals lay claim to common-sense values and expose the fact that the system is out of alignment with those values.

controlMeme — a meme used to marginalize, coopt, or limit the scale of social change ideas by institutionalizing a status-quo bias into popular perception of events. The type of memes that RAND Corporation analysts and Pentagon information warfare experts spend countless hours and millions of dollars designing.

control mythology — the web of stories, symbols, and ideas that defines the dominant culture's sense of normal, limits our ability to imagine social change, and makes people think the system is unchangeable.

confirmatory bias — psychological concept proven in studies which show that people are more likely to accept/believe new information if it sounds like something they already believe.

POST-ISSUE ACTIVISM

defector syndrome — the tendency of radicals to self-marginalize by exhibiting their dissent in such a way that it only speaks to those who already share their beliefs.

direct action at the point(s) of assumption — actions whose goal is to reframe issues and create new political space by targeting underlying assumptions.

earth-centered — a political perspective within which people define themselves and their actions in the context of the planet's ecological operating systems, biological/cultural diversity, and ongoing efforts to recenter human society within the earth's natural limits/cycles. An emerging term used to draw links and build alliances between ecological identity politics, land-based struggles, indigenous resistance, earth spirituality, agrarian folk wisdom, and visions of sustainable, ecologically sane societies both past and future. A politicized acceptance of the sacredness of living systems.

global crisis — the present time in the history of planet earth, characterized by the systematic undermining of the planet's life support systems through industrial extraction, unlimited growth, the commodification of all life, and emergence of global corporate rule. Symptoms include: accelerating loss of biological and cultural diversity, the deterioration of all ecosystems, the destabilization of global ecology (climate change, soil erosion, biocontamination, etc.), growing disparities between rich and poor, increased militarization, ongoing patterns of racism, classism, and sexism, and the spread of consumer monoculture. Part of the endgame of 200 years of industrial capitalism, 500 years of white supremacist colonization, and 10,000 years of patriarchal domination.

image event — an experience, event, or action that operates as a delivery system for smartMemes by creating new associations and meanings.

meme — (pronounced meem) a unit of self-replicating cultural transmission (i.e., ideas, slogans, melodies, symbols) that spreads virally from brain to brain. Word coined by evolutionary biologist Richard Dawkins in 1976 from a Greek root meaning "to imitate," to draw the analogy with "gene." "A contagious information pattern" — Glenn Grant.

movement — a critical mass of people who share ideas, take collective action, and build alternative institutions to create social change.

points of intervention — a place in a system, be it a physical system or a conceptual system (ideology, cultural assumption, etc.) where action can be taken to effectively interrupt the system. Examples include **point of production** (factory), **point of destruction** (logging road), **point of consumption** (chain store), **point of decision** (corporate HQ), **point of assumption** (culture/mythology), and **point of potential** (actions which make alternatives real).

political space — created by the ability of an oppositional idea or critique of the dominant order to manifest itself and open up new revolutionary possibilities. The extent to which our imaginations are colonized is the extent to which we lack political space and can't implement or even suggest new political ideas.

psychic break — the process or moment where people realize that the system is out of alignment with their values.

psycho-geography — the intersection of physical landscape with cultural and symbolic landscapes. A framework for finding targets for direct action at the point of assumption.

radical — a person committed to fundamental social change who believes we must address the roots of the problem rather than just the symptoms.

smartMeme — a designer meme that injects new infectious ideas into popular culture, contests established meaning (controlMemes), and facilitates popular rethinking of assumptions.

subverter — an effective radical who works within the logic of the dominant culture to foster dissent, mobilize resistance, and make fundamental social change imaginable.

tipping point — epidemiological term used to describe the point when a disease becomes an epidemic. Popularized by author Malcolm Gladwell to apply to the point where a new idea hits a critical mass of popular acceptance.

values — the social principles, goals, or standards held or accepted by an individual, group, or society. The moral codes that structure people's deepest held beliefs.

values crisis — the disconnect between common-sense values (justice, equality, democracy, ecological literacy) and the pathological values that underlie the global corporate system.

values shift — a recognition that the global crisis is the expression of pathological values that we need to change. An area of extreme difficulty to organize since people's values are very ingrained and the effective language to communicate in the values arena is often appropriated by powerful reactionary traditions and institutions (government, organized religion, patriarchal family, etc.).

Xerxes — ancient Persian emperor who, despite having the world's largest military force, overextended himself and was defeated by the unity and creativity of the Greeks, starting a long decline that led to the end of Persian dominance. A conceptual archetype for the fall of all empires. America take note.

Notes

[1] Merely, Michael, unpublished monograph "The Difficult Position of Being an Anti-Statist within the Context of Northern Ireland," 2002, available upon request from m.reinsborough@queens-belfast.ac.uk.

[2] The sixth mass extinction has become a widely accepted term within scientific circles to describe the current period of extinction. Dr. Niles Eldredge, the curator in chief of the permanent exhibition "Hall of Biodiversity" at the American Museum of Natural History, has an article "The Sixth Extinction" available at www.amnh.org, June 2001. Also see Harvard biologist E.O. Wilson's work.

[3] Data taken from BIS, 1999. *Central Bank Survey of Foreign Exchange and Derivatives Market Activity, 1998* (Basle: Bank for International Settlements). Thanks to Ricardo Bayon for his research into private capital flows for the Rainforest Action Network, "Citigroup and the Environment," February 2000.

[4] IMF, *World Economic Outlook* – October 1999. Washington, D.C.: International Monetary Fund, 1999.

[5] Ellwood, Wayne, *The No-Nonsense Guide to Globalization.* (New Internationalist Publications, 2001).

[6] Stats taken from *The Economist* (October 23, 1999) quoted in Ricardo Bayon's report for the Rainforest Action Network "Citigroup and the Environment," February 2000.

[7] Canadian philosopher John McMurtry has probably done the most to articulate this analysis in his (cumbersome but useful) book *The Cancer Stage of Capitalism* (Pluto Press 1999).

[8] Any analysis of the corporate takeover of the American legal system is indebted to the work of the Program on Corporations Law and Democracy. Info and materials can be found at www.poclad.org. Particularly noteworthy is their recent compilation, *Defying Corporations, Defining Democracy: A Book of History and Strategy,* edited by Dean Ritz and published by APEX 2001. Likewise, the 1993 pamphlet by Richard Grossman and Frank Adams, *Taking Care of Business: Citizenship and the Charter of Incorporation,* remains a classic. For a thorough discussion of the 1886 ruling and corporate personhood, see *Santa Clara Blues: Corporate Personhood versus Democracy* by William Meyers. The pamphlet can be ordered from www.iiipublishing.com.

[9] Facts cited in the *TV Free American* newsletter of the TV Turnoff Network, which has extensive facts and figures about television addiction. See www.tvturnoff.org

[10] The statistic comes from Jean Kilbourne's research into advertising and gender roles. Kilbourne is known for her award-winning documentaries *Killing Us Softly, Slim Hopes,* and *Pack of Lies.* Her latest book is *Can't Buy My Love: How Advertising Changes the Way We Think and Feel,* (Touchstone, 2000).

[11] Exact stat is over 800 million people living in hunger, 770 million in the global South or "developing world". Food Insecurity in the World 2001. Food and Agriculture Organization of the United Nations. Report is available at: http://www.fao.org/docrep/x8200e/x8200e00.htm.

[12] Bell, James John, *The Last Wizards Book of Green Shadows: The Destruction and Construction of Ideas in Popular Consciousness,* 2002. Out of Order Books, www.lastwizards.com.

[13] Rey, Paul, and Sherry Ruth Anderson, *The Cultural Creatives* (New York: Harmony Books, 2000): www.culturalcreatives.org.

[14] Rey, Paul, "The New Political Compass," prepublication manuscript, 2002.

[15] Moyer, Bill, *Doing Democracy: The MAP Model for Organizing Social Movements* (New Society Publishers, 2001). Bill—your

POST-ISSUE ACTIVISM

work inspired many and continues to nurture new generations of activists. R.I.P.

16 The contrast of money values versus life values is widely used. For a particularly eloquent articulation of it check out the books or lectures of Global Exchange cofounder Kevin Danaher. Most are available through www.globalexchange.org. Also useful is the work of David Korten, particularly *The Post-Corporate World: Life After Capitalism* (Kumarian Press, 1999).

17 Meme (pronounced meem) describes a building block of replicable meaning, a unit of cultural information with the ability to spread virally from brain to brain (such as ideas, slogans, melodies, symbols). Word coined by evolutionary biologist Richard Dawkins in analogy with "gene" from a Greek root meaning "to imitate." See *The Selfish Gene* (Oxford University Press, 1976). "A contagious information pattern" — Glenn Grant.

18 The term "meme warriors" was coined by Kalle Lasn in *Adbusters Magazine* and is expounded upon in his book *Culture Jam: How to Reverse America's Suicidal Consumer Binge and Why We Must* (New York: HarperCollins, 2000). Despite its miltiarist connotations, the term is not intended to be gender neutral.

20 The phrase "energy sovereignty" represents the simple but radical concept that local communities should have the right to decide how to meet their own energy needs. Thus "development" decisions around energy are placed in the context of local communities and ecosystems rather than the macroscale context of multinational corporations, privatized utilities, and global economic infrastructure. The term comes from Oilwatch, an international network of 120 ecological, human rights, religious organizations and local communities that support resistance against oil and gas activities from a southern countries perspective, (www.oilwatch.org.net.ec). Also see U.S.–based organizations Project Underground, (www.moles.org) and CorpWatch, (www.corpwatch.org).

20 Martha F. Lee, *Earth First! Environmental Apocalypse,* (Syracuse University Press, 1995).

21 The Zapatista uprising is one of the most documented revolutionary movements in recent history: there is no shortage of excellent coverage of their inspiring actions and important analysis. One of most the accessible and poetic of the compilations of Zapatista communiqués and the writings of Marcos is *Our Word Is Our Weapon,* edited by Juana Ponce de Leon (Seven Stories Press, 2000).

22 A spectacular account is recorded by John Jordan and Jennifer Whitney in their newsprint zine *"Que Se Vayan Todos : Argentina's Popular Uprising,"* May 2002. More info at www.weareeverywhere.org.

23 Bell, *The Last Wizard's Book.*

24 Lasn, *Culture Jam.*

25 Many of these strategies around "image events" and applying the elements of narrative structure to "telling the future" have been further developed by the smartMeme strategy and training project in their essays "The Battle of the Story" and "The Next Environmental Movement." These essays and an ongoing forum for activists to explore and apply these ideas is available at www.smartmeme.com.

26 Quoted in James Davis, "This Is What Bureaucracy Looks Like," in *The Battle of Seattle: The New Challenge to Capitalist Globalization,* ed. Eddie Yuen, George Katsiaficas, and Daniel Burton Rose (Soft Skull Press, 2002). The article is also a useful and relevant examination of NGOs.

27 The modern cancer epidemic has spawned a parasitic industry of drug companies that sell expensive treatment drugs, many of whom also produce carcinogenic chemicals. Connected to many of these hypocritical corporations are various high-profile, big-budget, nonprofit organizations that help keep public attention focused on expensive treatments (the mythic "cure") rather than the cause. For more information on the "Cancer Industry" see activist organizations like Breast Cancer Action (www.bcaction.org) and environmental justice resources like the Environmental Research Foundation (www.rachels.org).

28 For comprehensive writings, discussions, and organizing around the dual power concept, check out www.dualpower.net.

29 I am indebted to my conversations with Kevin Danaher for the lifeboat metaphor.

March against U.S. war on Afghanistan and post-9/11 racist attacks, 2002.

What Is Zapatismo? A Brief Definition for Activists

By Elizabeth (Betita) Martínez and Arnoldo García

Elizabeth (Betita) Martínez, a Chicana antiracist activist since 1960, is director of the Institute for MultiRacial Justice, a resource center for building alliances between peoples of color.

Arnoldo García is an editor of War Times *newspaper, works with the National Network for Immigrant and Refugee Rights, and is active with Zapatista solidarity, formerly with the National Commission for Democracy in Mexico.*

Zapatismo is NOT:

> Another armed struggle led by the people's vanguard
> A sudden all-out revolution by long-silent Indians
> A mysterious, masked leader who smokes a pipe

We need to set aside all those mass-media images and other distortions, and start realizing that zapatismo is a whole new concept of social

Seventy-seven Zapatista familes reoccupying their community of San Pedro, Nixtalucum, with 4,000 indigenous supporters after being violently driven out by police forces, Chiapas, Mexico, 1997.

ZAPATISMO

Jutta Meier-Wiedenbach

transformation. We need to move beyond our romanticized view of zapatismo to understand how much we can learn from it, to see it not as some exotic creature but as very relevant to resistance struggles around the world.

Rooted in the democratic, community-based culture of indigenous people, which includes a long history of resistance, zapatismo rejects the idea of a vanguard leading the people. Instead it is an affirmation of communal people's power, of grassroots autonomy. Zapatismo stands as a program for transforming society through a prolonged process of radicalizing democracy, and it represents an alternative model for national and global socioeconomic development.

Unlike previous groups in Latin America and other countries, the EZLN (Ejército Zapatista de Liberación Nacional/ Zapatista Army of National Liberation) submits itself to the mandates of the community. The Zapatistas are not a guerrilla force with a particular social base but rather, they are the social base itself, which has organized its own army. Its character is organic, determined by conditions facing the indigenous communities, above all poverty and oppression.

Jutta Meier-Wiedenbach

The Zapatistas say they are not proposing to take power but rather to contribute to a vast movement that would return power to civil society, using different forms of struggle. They seek to make a revolution that makes the revolution possible. The goal is not just to end the exploitation and oppression of indigenous peoples but democracy, freedom, and justice for all Mexico. In this spirit, they abide by the values expressed in their slogan: *For everyone, everything; for ourselves, nothing.*

The EZLN leadership consists of the Indigenous Revolutionary Clandestine Committee (Comité Clandestino Revolucionario Indígena, CCRI), federated by ethnic group and by community. Members hold their positions as long as they faithfully and effectively carry out the community's mandates. When the Zapatistas decided to rise up in Chiapas on January 1, 1994, the decision in one community was confirmed by twelve men, twenty-three women, and eight children; those who could sign did so, others stamped their fingerprints. This process expressed the ancestral indigenous practices of community democracy, using dialogue and discussion to arrive at shared solutions to communal problems. Indigenous people call it "allowing your true word to speak to my true word."

The Zapatistas recognize that building new communities requires conscious effort. Traditional community culture is necessary but not

215

sufficient; it has to be transformed in various ways. A major example is women winning a new place and leadership. Very shortly after the 1994 uprising, the Zapatistas issued a revolutionary law affirming the rights of indigenous women. Along with women in political and military leadership stand the women who have established and administer today's new co-ops. They speak to the transformation that continues to be necessary.

In this and other ways, zapatismo implies a profound process of social recomposition and the building of communities of masterless workers. Zapatismo has universal significance; not just for Chiapas or Mexico but for worldwide struggle against capitalist globalization. Zapatismo means that all traditions of resistance, cultures, and communities have to come together in a new way to win these changes. It says that above all, our struggles need to have roots and continuity.

With the Zapatista vision in hand, we can look with fresh eyes for ways to advance the global struggle for social justice.

1911 "The land belongs to the tiller"

Anti-neoliberal social movement

Zapatismo beyond Chiapas

By Manuel Callahan

Manuel Callahan currently teaches in the Ethnic Studies program at Humboldt State University. He is also a member of Acción Zapatista, a network of activists in Texas and California that support the EZLN while pursuing zapatismo locally.

This essay is a meditation on the political uses of Zapatismo in contexts outside of Chiapas, Mexico, especially the challenges involved in the attempt to put it into action in sites of privilege. The goal is to focus on key elements that constitute a political practice that is ethical, creative, and disciplined, as well as relevant in local and global contexts. Zapatismo may be an "intuition," as Subcomandante Marcos has suggested, but it also offers us a theoretical framework for political analysis, especially regarding encounter, dialogue, and difference, while establishing these concepts as explicit political practices and objectives.

The key elements of Zapatismo as a political and cultural practice that will be examined here include a politics of refusal, space, and listening, articulated in the statements *Ya Basta!* (enough); *dignidad y esperanza*

photo top: Mariana Mora

(dignity and hope); *mandar obedeciendo* (to lead by following); *nunca jamás un mundo sin nosotros* (never again a world without us); and *todo para todos y nada para nosotros* (everything for everyone and nothing for ourselves). The Zapatista intervention invites us to be clear about what we actually mean by these concepts, and to collectively arrive at an agreement of what they should look like in practice. We want to avoid approaches that rely on an authoritative, hierarchical apparatus or a uniquely "enlightened" system that directs, commands, or leads. We seek instead to arrive at a political practice that activates, a process that respects the agency, the voice, the creativity, and the engagement of an entire community. It is, as Marcos recently remarked, "an effort at *encuentro*," an encounter noted for a number of "tendencies" with the goal of "building common points of discussion." Thus, it is crucial that these tendencies be understood as something more than slogans.

The Zapatista intervention is not only a confrontation with the party-state or with the institutions of global capital and the cadres of intellectuals in their service, but it has generated controversy from within the Left. The Zapatistas' proposal of a "revolution to make a revolution possible" presents tendencies that stand in contrast with the strategies, organizations, and formations of the Left of past generations. Zapatismo does not seek to impose an ideology, an organization, or a party line, and in this sense, the Zapatistas have made it clear that the old language and methods no longer function. However, they are not proposing new dogmas to replace the worn-out language and ideologies of previous movements. They refuse to do battle within a framework that allows for endless political and academic debate, a process that fosters hierarchy, authoritarianism, and elitism. The Zapatistas do not claim to provide answers but, as they argue, "pose questions." "It is already known that our specialty is not in solving problems, but in creating them. 'Creating them?' No, that is too presumptuous, rather in proposing. Yes, our specialty is proposing problems."

While we have come to know the Zapatistas through their public interventions and direct actions, we are still unfamiliar with their specific internal processes of organization, especially the link between the military and civil formations. On the other hand, Zapatismo is available to us as a political and cultural practice we can discuss, analyze, interpret, and enact within the context of a globally networked mobilization against neoliberalism. For analytical purposes it is important to distinguish between the Zapatistas and Zapatismo. The EZLN (the Zapatista Army for National Liberation) is the army that serves the base communities. Zapatistas are comprised of the EZLN and their supporters. Zapatismo is a political strategy, an ethos, a set of commitments claimed by those who claim a political identity. Although the role of the EZLN as a catalyst has been critical, even Subcomandante Marcos has admitted, "the EZLN has reached a point where it has been overtaken by Zapatismo."

A Politics of Refusal

The EZLN has on several occasions, and with remarkable consistency and sensitivity, presented their views to the world in the form of declarations and communiqués. "As they say in these mountains, the Zapatistas have a very powerful and indestructible weapon: the word." Their word, offered to us in solidarity, brings with it an analysis of neoliberalism and an invitation to join in struggle.

Hilary Klein

Anniversary of Zapatista uprising, San Cristobal, Chiapas, January 1, 2003.

ZAPATISMO

The *Ya Basta!*, or "Enough!," of January 1, 1994, inaugurated the public phase of the EZLN's struggle and introduced the world to Zapatismo. Although initially the Zapatistas declared war against the Mexican government and threatened to march on the capital in the hope of serving as a catalyst for a general uprising, they quickly broadened their agenda and shifted their focus to creating and developing the political space necessary for radical democratic practice. *Ya Basta!* does more than declare an opposition to oppressive forces; it also represents a direct action with specific goals and strategies and invokes a long history of struggle. The 500-year legacy of resistance and the more recent history of revolutionary struggle in Mexico coalesced into a prolonged "No!" on January 1. "And so, with singular joy we dedicated ourselves to resisting, to saying 'no,' to transforming our poverty into a weapon. The weapon of resistance."

The Zapatistas' direct action declared *Ya Basta!* to the neoliberal project; the increased globalization of capital that is to be achieved by opening markets to trade, privatizing natural resources and state-run services, eliminating workers' rights, reducing the social wage and benefits, and homogenizing communities through consumerism, the commodification of everyday life, and the exaltation of private property and individualism.

219

The Zapatistas' first declaration was timed to coincide with the implementation of the North American Free Trade Agreement (NAFTA), and it outlined a list of grievances and demands that spoke to the structural violence the indigenous peoples of Chiapas have endured for generations. The immediate goals stated in the eleven demands they put forward—including work, land, housing, food, health care, education, independence, liberty, democracy, justice, and peace—articulated the needs and rights being denied to growing portions of Mexico's indigenous population, as well as all peoples made miserable by neoliberal policies throughout the world. NAFTA provided no alternatives, making it "a death sentence for the indigenous people." *Ya Basta!* is a statement of refusal, rebellion, and survival in the face of a future denied. The "No" can be shared, and as Gustavo Esteva has eloquently phrased it, transformed into "many yeses!'"

The challenge posed by the word spoken defiantly in resistance is to participate in a new political space (encounter), develop new political relationships or strategies of doing politics (dialogue), and collectively articulate a new political project (autonomy). The Zapatistas' commitment to creating political space and their selfless initiation of dialogue requires a response and participation by all parties. One response was heard in the *Ya Basta!* shouted by the "many-headed street movement" in Seattle and echoed in subsequent rumblings during the series of protests that followed.

A Politics of Space

Prior to Seattle, the Zapatistas hosted an astonished international Left in a series of *encuentros*, or encounters, which took place in the mountains of Chiapas. It has been through these gatherings, convened and hosted by the EZLN, that the Zapatistas have had the most profound impact. "The audacity of the Zapatistas," the Midnight Notes Collective reminds us, "was to open a clearing in the forest heavily patrolled by the Mexican Army and to allow others to come to speak to each other about capitalism and revolution." These gatherings established a crucial bridge between different worlds, and that bridge is manifest in a new "international"—not an international based on rigid party doctrines or the dogmas of competing organizations, but an "International of Hope," a web constituted by numerous autonomies, without a center or hierarchy, within which various coalitions of discontents can express themselves, in order to dismantle the forces and regimes oppressing all of them.

The Zapatistas have not organized beyond their own communities in Chiapas; rather they have animated and inspired countless numbers of

Zapatista communities mobilize to San Cristobal, Chiapas to celebrate anniversary of the uprising, 2003.

Anniversary of Zapatista uprising, San Cristobal, Chiapas. January 1, 2003.

ZAPATISMO

activists and intellectuals who experienced firsthand a rebel community enduring the siege of an arrogant power through dialogue, consensus, and direct action within their communities. The Zapatista model of *encuentro* does not rely on ideology, organizational affiliation, or even a fixed identity. And as the Zapatistas have made their very local struggle available to a national and international civil society, a global movement has arisen to articulate its own response to the processes of globalization, utilizing the strategies and tactics being shared so generously.

The new international is defined by *dignidad y esperanza*, "dignity and hope." "Dignity," the Zapatistas assert, "is that nation without nationality, that rainbow that is also a bridge, that murmur of the heart no matter what blood lives it, that rebel irreverence that mocks borders, customs, and wars." Specifically, the EZLN has, according to Enrique Dussel, presented a model of community "institutionalized through social means conducive to consensus, agreement, and decisionmaking." Dignity cannot be bestowed, rather, it is enacted as one actively participates in a community that acknowledges difference. "We define our goal by the way we choose the means of struggling for it." Dignity as a class concept, explains John Holloway, "is not in the first place a conflict between two groups of people: it is a conflict between creative social practice and its negation, or, in other words, between humanity and its negation, between the transcending of limits (creation) and the imposition of limits (definition)."

A Politics of Listening

Throughout the struggle, the Zapatistas have punctuated their statements, especially those circulated through the communiqués, with calls for democracy, liberty, and justice. These concepts, taken together, may be the most difficult, and the most crucial, to engage. In new political spaces all voices, all proposals must be responded to with respect. New political relationships must not be limited by institutions, organizations, or ideologies that seek to contain moments of resistance or rebellion. The new relationships must speak to the collectively defined obligations of a community in a dialogue based on respect. Political projects and proposals need to emerge organically, not be imposed by an individual or a cabal. The provocation suggested by this principle implies a reliance on our collective talents and abilities for self-governance that transcends systems of representative democracy. The Zapatistas have insisted that the marginalized, forgotten, and faceless are agents of history, and that they cannot be fully included simply by adding them in such a manner that does not alter the political relations that maintains their marginalization by elites. A "radical" or participatory democracy requires a system that seeks and respects the contribution of everyone, each sharing their own word.

Hilary Klein

"Perhaps," Subcomandante Marcos declares, "the new political morality is constructed in a new space that is not the taking or retention of power, but serves as the counterweight and opposition that contains it and obliges it to, for example, 'lead by obeying.'"

The Zapatistas demonstrated that it is possible to organize collective action based on a communitywide dialogue, consensus, and commitment. Given that in any local context there is not simply one single, homogenous community, how do we determine who leads and who obeys? *Mandar obedeciendo*, or "lead by obeying," suggests going beyond a system of hierarchy and rank where elites are conferred the duty and right to direct. The leadership of a community, the process from which it emerges and is articulated, requires clarification, such that *mandar obedeciendo* is not an excuse for a small coterie to direct, either out of cynicism or ambition. *Mandar obedeciendo* requires humility and a commitment to listening, neither of which can be taken for granted. It is an invitation to a profound transformation, collective and individual. Transformation is both necessary and integral to struggle as we provoke, incite, facilitate, inspire, listen, and work with one another with humility.

The emergence of the EZLN as a people's army is a narrative of transformation. The small group of urban revolutionaries who traveled to Chiapas expecting to become a revolutionary vanguard abandoned their conceptions of revolution once they were "contaminated by and

subordinated to the communities." In another move of transformation the community itself became armed. The Zapatistas emerged from a context of a variety of ethnic groups, political organizations, and economic interests. Early in the struggle, during the critical moment of the original EZLN's transformation from a vanguardist guerrilla to a community in arms, the Zapatistas reflected not one single indigenous identity, but the interests of Tzeltal, Tolojobal, Tzotzil, Chol, and Mam peoples, to name just a few.

The political imperatives of *mandar obedeciendo* also challenge many of the assumptions and previously unexamined strategies of organizing associated with "solidarity" efforts that often rely on a singular model, plan, or program fostering paternalism and elitism. Solidarity campaigns too often focus on a single issue, developing networks of short-lived and fragile coalitions that can be resistant to crucial modifications and slow to adapt to shifting contexts. More important, solidarity projects that represent, define, and speak for the struggle(s) of others presuppose the progress or development of those being aided and not the transformation of those providing the aid. Unfortunately, they are too ill-prepared to acknowledge the transformations already taking place in targeted communities.

In the effort to go beyond solidarity, *mandar obedeciendo* begins with the premise that communities made up of diverse constituencies are, to varying and complex degrees, already organized. Taking our cues from the EZLN, we can imagine, in place of solidarity work, a politics of refusal, listening, and community-building in which people become part of "the struggle" in their own way, at their own pace, and without being measured by any specific model of "conscientization" or a political program specified by "the organization." We must operate from the premise that a given community possesses the resources for its own transformation and has the collective genius to marshal those resources for political action. *Encuentro* as a model of political work presupposes individual and collective transformation that results from dialogue, and it allows for the possibility of individual and collective transformation into a community with purpose. Thus, the Zapatistas provide an important example of the possibilities for an unarmed guerrilla operating in sites of privilege, a resistance that makes direct action and disciplined formations central elements of their political practice without abandoning dialogue.

Todo para todos, nada para nosotros, "everything for everyone, nothing for ourselves," underscores the commitment to define struggle not by taking state power, but imagining a new world, "a world where many

Jutta Meier-Wiedenbach

worlds fit." Forsaking the desire to replace one elite with another, *todo para todos, nada para nosotros* invites us not to submit to individual needs but to elaborate collective ones. More important, it asserts that communities are driven by collectively articulated obligations, not by the competing interests of individual needs. Zapatista political proposals and strategy posit a "collective subject," demanding the fundamental rights that emerge from collective identities and communal needs.

Caminamos preguntando, or "we walk asking," challenges us to travel in dialogue with one another, always with a view of a shared horizon. We are often schooled to repress the fundamental impulse to question. A commitment to inquiry allows us to transcend the facade of ideology and the oppression of rigid institutions in favor of discovery. It contests a process in which we have been "educated" to accept being left out or rendered invisible to everyone, including ourselves. The violence of cultural homogenization produced through social fictions and the ideological maneuvers of a "democratic" system attempt to force us to deny ourselves as we deny the uniqueness and diversity of others. Processes of exclusion target specific communities, especially those groups who have chosen to resist, such as the communities who have taken up arms in Chiapas. Other groups, such as youth, women, communities of color, constituencies who craft diverse, often seemingly less obvious strategies of resistance, have also been marginalized as well and are threatened by relentless processes of homogenization.

Such exclusions could also be exerted in revolutionary movements, a history the Zapatistas have struggled not to repeat. Violence was not a means to dominate, or even convince others of the virtues of a Zapatista vision or program. Ideas asserted through the force of arms are always suspect, and as Marcos admits, "the task of an armed movement should be to present the problem, and then step aside." Able to pursue and develop a "model of peace," their change in strategy corresponds to Gandhi's often misunderstood explanation of nonviolence as being an appropriate strategy of the strong, not the weak. They have not abandoned the "model of war" altogether, but have held it in abeyance, the two possibilities working in conjunction to expand their political project for Mexico and beyond. Zapatista strength derives not only from their mobilizations but from the way in which people have rallied to their banner, confident in their commitment not to take state power and impose themselves as a revolutionary vanguard. "For us it would be a failure. What would be a success for the politico-military organizations of the sixties or seventies which emerged with the national liberation movements would be a fiasco for us," claims Marcos.

ZAPATISMO

Nunca jamás un mundo sin nosotros, "never again a world without us," seeks to reverse the history of marginalization in which communities have been systematically silenced. The *nunca jamás* is a declaration that recognizes that processes of marginalization and homogenization portend the extinction of a people, suggesting the necessity for action that must include cultural renewal. It proclaims the possibilities of a reimagined world, a world in which those in rebellion have responsibilities and obligations to one another. As a statement against elitism it reminds us that the struggle is not limited to the

Jeff Conant

Zapatistas or those in the South, but must be reimagined to include multiple struggles in numerous sites.

Zapatismo offers a strategy of struggle on a variety of fronts, including cultural ones. Fundamental to the Zapatistas' struggle to make themselves visible has been the claim that they narrate their own history and speak their own truths. The "not forgetting" reminds us to recover our past while we document our struggle. In asserting critical elements of a vibrant Mayan culture, the Zapatistas have successfully resisted market forces that seek to homogenize all people. Their struggle has been successful primarily because it has been rooted locally, a deliberate effort to maintain their commons by reclaiming their history, culture, and community.

We must also reclaim our histories and cultures as we reclaim our commons. In sites of privilege such as those found in the "the west," a consumer culture fosters values, attitudes, and practices peculiar to a disposable, individualistic, and competitive society. If we begin with a definition of community that stresses sharing knowledge of what works locally between generations and fulfilling collectively determined obligations with one another, then we must ask ourselves how do we

ZAPATISMO

collectively define obligations and acknowledge local wisdom in the face of cultural homegenization?

Notes in Conclusion

The Zapatistas' commitment to difference rather than identity, dialogue over command, and autonomy in opposition to state or market control has revealed a radical new practice, a commitment to theoretical reflection and direct action that does not subordinate local struggles (issues in particular contexts), prioritize actions (strategies of resistance), or alternative practices (strategies for living outside of state and market forces) to any specific political formation, program, or ideology. The Zapatistas have refused to do battle within a framework of old organizational structures. Thus, they have insisted that they will not fall back into the past that, as Marcos suggests, was defined by the battle over ideologies. During the March for Indigenous Dignity the Zapatistas made it clear they were not trying to turn back the clock to a bucolic past of native harmony. "No," proclaimed Marcos, "we Indian peoples have come in order to wind the clock and to thus ensure that the inclusive, tolerant, and plural tomorrow which is, incidentally, the only tomorrow possible, will arrive. In order to do that, in order for our march to make the clock of humanity march, we Indian peoples have resorted to the art of reading what has not yet been written. Because that is the dream which animates us as indigenous, as Mexicans and, above all, as human beings. With our struggle, we are reading the future which has already been sown yesterday, which is being cultivated today, and which can only be reaped if one fights, if, that is, one dreams."

ZAPATISMO

  228

Radical Politics: Assuming We Refuse, Let's Refuse to Assume

By Chris Carlsson

---

*Chris Carlsson played an important role in launching "Critical Mass,"
the monthly bicycle happening that has spread to 300 cities in the last
decade. He cofounded Processed World Magazine ("the underside of the
information age") and directs "Shaping San Francisco," an interactive
multimedia excavation of San Francisco's lost history. He can sometimes
be found with a group of drummers and friends called the Committee
for Full Enjoyment at actions against global capital.*

Preface

Radical anticapitalism has reemerged. Far from being over, history is
bending, wrinkling, and warping under myriad pressures from
globalization and its opposition, while savage capitalism's tendency to self-
destruct is on full display in the unfolding corporate scandals wracking
U.S. multinationals. While the banal barbarity of an expanding world
market continues to degrade and sometimes devour the people and
resources of the planet, social opposition is evolving too. Old slogans and

image top: Mona Caron

movements (descended from the confusingly labeled "sixties") have moved firmly into history, but the new shape of class conflict is still being discovered. And the anticapitalist movement that announced itself so loudly from the tear gas–filled streets of Seattle to the bloody byways of Genoa is far from a homogenous movement.

Our moment is one of equal parts hope and despair. From below it looks like the managers trying to keep a teetering world order under control are mostly succeeding, but that's in no small part because we get our news from their wholly owned propaganda machines. The percolating counter-sensibilities erupting from Argentina to Venezuela, South Korea to the Philippines, Nigeria to New York, are much harder to see and hear. This book is an important contribution to making new thinking more visible and accessible. For my part, I want to stop and rethink the assumptions that I've accepted—and allowed to shape my political behavior—since I started "doing politics" in the late 1970s.

Like everyone who was there, I was excited to be in Seattle for the anti-WTO protests in November 1999, and it far exceeded my expectations (and everyone else's!). It felt like a surprising breakthrough in radical politics. But was it? The anti–global capitalism demonstrations that began with Seattle and have continued since then constitute a more visible and successful form of protest than anything we saw in the preceding twenty years, but they haven't left me feeling particularly victorious or even that optimistic. The daunting tasks associated with an anticapitalist revolution are hard to face.

The current social movement against global capitalism has no concrete vision of an alternative to capitalism. The new anticapitalism has succeeded at mobilizing thousands to protest the big institutions, but not in defining the changes in daily life that may ensue from the transformation implied by the anticapitalist agenda. The World Social Forum has sought to bring together disparate movements and political forces to work together toward an affirmative agenda, and in the years since the various "1960s" movements were defeated or ran their course, people have learned an enormous amount about how to self-manage group processes, handle sexism and racism, and promote a culture of egalitarianism and participation. Antinuclear, peace, antipoverty, and identity politics movements have provided a rich training ground during the last quarter century. This has greatly strengthened our abilities to contest the global capitalist system within our daily lives. But neither at the WSF, nor anywhere else, has a coherent alternative to global capitalism emerged, even if important elements are taking shape.

This germinating culture of resistance must go beyond the exclusive and excluding culture of young radicals who like reclaiming streets, tree-sitting, or protesting multinational corporations. People who are usually dismissed as "average Americans" will also have to see an advantage for themselves in embracing an agenda of radical change. Those of us already committed to radical politics must develop enormous reservoirs of patience. It will take a sustained effort over the long haul to bring about change so deep that it recasts our whole conception of work, economy, and life itself.

I want to articulate a life worth living, one that inspires passionate commitment and engagement, and presents practical choices in daily life. After more than twenty years in and around radical political projects and movements, I want to stop and rethink. I want to get out of the familiar "box" in which our political efforts seem to remain stuck.

The walls of this box are made up in part of assumptions among anti-authoritarian grassroots movements and groups that I've been part of for years: unstated assumptions about power and leadership, organizational forms, and institutionalization. We believe in a radical vision that for the most part we cannot articulate, and we repeat self-defeating tactics out of habit and a misplaced urgency to "do something."

Dissatisfied with my own pat answers, I want at least to deepen our inquiry, even if I still don't solve the problems satisfactorily.

Utopia, or What Is It We Really Want?

The problem is that without a vision of Utopia there is no way to define that port to which we might want to sail. — David Harvey, *Spaces of Hope*

Most political activity is reactive and contrary, demanding a halt to this or that excess, perhaps sprinkled with rhetoric calling for an end to capitalism, all too often depending on a neo-Christian moral guilt over so-called "greed." A more fundamental critique of the system is lacking, and an articulated alternative is completely absent. It is common for radicals in our era to describe easily what they are against, but when it comes to what we are for, a painful silence descends. (A couple of notable exceptions are Ken Knabb's "The Joy of Revolution" in his collected skirmishes *Public Secrets*, and Michael Albert and Robin Hahnel's *Looking Forward*.) If anyone is ready to talk about a different way of life at all, it is in vague terms that defy ready application.

No one is ever going to get excited about radical social change if it doesn't promise to make their life much better in clearly demonstrable ways. Generally, advocates of an anticapitalist future have completely ignored this basic problem of . . . what shall we call it? . . . imaginative exploration . . . education . . . marketing? Most attempts to convince people to join oppositional political movements depend on moral outrage, shame, guilt, fear, and appeals to fairness. This is understandable, but it also underlines why radical politics attracts such a relatively small part of the population.

American society brags to itself through the mass media that it is the best of all possible worlds. People tend to go along with this, at least to the point of utter skepticism regarding suggestions that there could be a much better system. I think skepticism, reinforced daily by the mightiest propaganda machine in history, will only be overcome by an exciting, appealing, and credible alternative to the status quo. There are no compelling visions of this alternative in circulation. This is an era that rejects utopian thinking, either because it is by definition impossible, or because it is conflated with the totalitarian nightmares of the twentieth century. To dream of a more just, pleasurable, and well-organized life is somehow to believe in a totalizing system in which all aspects of human life that don't fit the new model are forcibly banished.

This is a poverty of imagination. Radical change can erupt from any number of sources and lead in unexpected directions. We have stopped imagining a better life. We limit our thoughts to tinkering with the more obvious inequities of the status quo.

The old opposition between "radical" and "reformer" finds its current incarnation among us in those who fight for a total transformation versus those who see the battle in terms of incremental change. To the radical, the minor changes achieved by reformers don't seem worth fighting for, or can even be seen as making things inadvertently worse. To the reformer, the sweeping change advocated by radicals seems naive or dogmatically prescriptive. In the face of this ready criticism, radicals are hesitant to declare for any particular set of proposals. This hesitance, in turn, leaves us politically weakened, incapable of going beyond a generalized yearning for an undefined "better," afraid of the authority established by any choice of specific institutional and material relations. But if we won't assert the authority of any specific alternative vision, the fundamental social question about "valid authority" is abdicated to moralistic nuts and neoliberal free marketeers.

The faith in the spontaneous creative powers of revolutionary action [has] disarmed the constructive political imagination

ANTI-CAPITALISM

The contagious pleasure of a movement like Critical Mass threatens the precariousness of today's world, which depends on cooperative participation by the majority of people as workers and consumers. San Francisco.

of the left . . . —Roberto Unger, "False Necessity: Anti-Necessitarian Social Theory in the Service of Radical Democracy," cited in David Harvey, *Spaces of Hope*

It boils down to accepting a type of social power. Any vision embraced, once adopted in the real world, precludes other visions. Any choice we make about how we'd like life to be arranged closes off other options. Instead of refusing to articulate anything, out of fear of imposing our visions (on helpless victims?), and thereby creating a new form of authority, let's accept the fact that stating our preferences and visions is a form of authority. Moreover, it is an acceptable form that enjoys only the power that it gains as other people embrace and share our vision. Of course, articulating such a vision is predicated on the notion that anyone could do the same, and that everyone should be encouraged to do so.

Ideally, I imagine a social upheaval that puts numerous well-spoken agitators before the public, addressing a range of issues, articulating a variety of goals, maybe even constituting together a utopian vision of a different way of life. If such a time arrives we can be sure it will not be tidy, it will not automatically find a consensus, and it will require a great deal of strenuous discussion and argument. This is something I look forward to eagerly. That said, I am also presently stymied by a problem of tactical imagination. What are the approaches, activities, and organizations that might overcome the dead-end of reforms that actually strengthen the status quo—but do it by articulating ideas and reaching goals that are genuine steps toward a life beyond capitalism? What are practical activities that make our lives better now and move us forward in terms of revolution, but avoid the boomerang of reformist cooptation?

I was in Seattle for the anti-WTO protests in November 1999. I also went to Washington, D.C., to protest the IMF and World Bank in April 2000. My associates and I (the Committee for Full Enjoyment) played drums and did support work in the streets for folks who were putting their bodies on the line in lockdowns. We also prepared printed materials in which we called for a more radical approach than the common demands of the protesters. In Seattle we distributed an antibusiness card called Life Not Trade, which went considerably beyond the liberal demand for "fair trade, not free trade." At the IMF/World Bank meetings, we handed out a different card called the Debt Wipe Card, a satirical anti–credit card calling for "Gifts Not Debts!" The two pieces varied from each other in certain respects but each featured these words in conclusion:

We are here in the spirit of a real alternative, maybe we should call it the Global Association of Gift Givers (GAGG). The passion for life is

the same passion that convinces us that together we can make life what we want it to be. In the streets we have re-created the public commons, at least temporarily. We reject trade, free or fair, for trade reinforces the pecuniary mentality that reduces human life to the arbitrary measurement of its products, to the Economy. As free people we can live better, work less (and enjoy the pleasure of the work we deem worthwhile) and provide an unprecedented level of material comfort to everyone on the planet. . . . When we abolish the Economy, we will see the world with new eyes, new energy, new possibilities. We make the world every day when we return to work for them. Why not make the world we want to live in instead?

These words resonated for many participants in the protest movement. They are important to me, too, because they go beyond the usual smorgasbord of tepid reforms and empty demands. But I must confess, they ring rather hollow as soon as you try to apply them to the real world, to imagine what actions we might take immediately to begin reaching for the world these words describe.

One of the self-imposed problems this kind of thinking has created is an inability to embrace any goals other than the most sweeping imaginable. But that position soon resembles a religious one that posits a complete simultaneous, spontaneous transformation of everyone everywhere. Those who take this position seek a change that is without historic precedent or any connection to real people living in the real world. They scorn intermediate goals as muddled reformism and liberal cooptation. Having participated for years in maintaining this impossible conundrum I am fed up with being stuck. This does not mean I want to turn to electoral politics or the tired ideas of the old or new Left or liberals. But it does mean I don't feel at ease with the constant rejection of every initiative that anyone tries in this culture on the grounds that it isn't the total transformation. Revolutions do happen, and social institutions can be radically altered—even abolished—in short periods of time. But to presuppose a total change as the definition of an acceptable political program, and to have no ideas of intermediate, achievable goals is, finally, a failure of practical imagination.

Institutionalization, or The Problem of Fighting for the Long Haul without Becoming Comfortably Dependent on the Way Things Are

How do we launch political opposition in entirely ad-hoc and short-term ways again and again without having to reinvent the wheel each time? Can

CRITICAL
MASS
SAN FRANCISCO

Jim Swanson

ANTI-CAPITALISM

we have ongoing, long-term political resistance that doesn't turn into a kind of alternative business? How do we pay for staff, offices, phones, and equipment, and keep a focused oppositional political movement alive if not through selling T-shirts and coffee mugs, bake sales, seeking support from foundations and large donors? Can we grow our political opposition without institutionalizing our organizational forms? Can we make sure practical knowledge is shared and spread without institutionalizing that process?

If we don't institutionalize ourselves, with organizations, resources (computers, printing presses, radio stations, video production facilities, meeting rooms, offices, homes, etc.), and the like, we have to reacquire access every time we begin organizing on a new project. On the other hand, as we seek greater permanence and reliability, we tend to duplicate resources and infrastructure, since our efforts tend to be highly localized and specific. If we share space and media equipment across issues, groups, time, and space, we can make much greater use of the limited resources we have.

Currently it is common to create small businesses and collectives to acquire productive resources, sell our skills and resources (to "movement" groups and on the open market), and maintain the necessary infrastructure that way. But that leaves it all tangled up in the structures of small business and profitability. For example, I've brought print jobs to small, collectively owned businesses, but they need to charge nearly the same as any business to do the work, and similarly, I do a lot of free design and typesetting work for interesting political projects, but I reserve the right to decide who has a right to my labor or my facilities. So where's the "movement" at that moment? The small business model, even collectively owned, is a poor solution to the problem of continuity and sustained resistance. (Granted, it is often a much better solution to the problems of personal survival than working for "The Man.")

In the 1970s—learning from the example of the anarchists of the Spanish Revolution of the 1930s—the antinuclear and peace movements organized into small affinity groups. This model has reemerged in the various summit protests of the past three years. This antiinstitutional, ad-hoc movement is based on small affinity groups that come together to organize specific actions as part of the larger demonstration. The affinity groups thus avoid being subsumed into the logic of small business. They also avoid the bureaucratization and salaried hierarchies of ongoing nonprofit organizations. There is no need to maintain structures of property, ongoing expenses for offices and equipment, etc. Being rooted in local small groups is one of the anticapitalist movement's greatest strengths, both depending on and reinforcing real communities and face-to-face networks of neighbors and friends.

A notable quality of the affinity group structure is its dependence on meetings and consensus, and this constitutes both a strength and a social liability. The tyranny of meetings, especially those run by consensus, can be extremely exhausting and often demoralizing. When it works, it can be a source of genuine collective euphoria. But it tends to burn people out and often leaves a trail of bitter feelings in its wake. This derives in part from questions of power, and our difficulties in facing and creatively handling the inevitable differentiation among people in any group.

There is also an implicit assumption that the affinity group is somehow a prefigurative formation of the kind of life we want to live in the future. In that respect it becomes an agent of subcultural exclusion. Not everyone is inclined to organize their lives through face-to-face meetings and consensus. It attracts some personalities and political ideologies, and repels many others. For those who are part of an affinity group, and have participated in the political movements of the past quarter century, it is hard to accept that for lots of people it is precisely the anonymity and lack of responsibility that daily life in the capitalist market provides that makes them feel "free." You get your money from your job and you spend it however you see fit, privately and anonymously. There is no accountability for the meaning of the work you do (if someone pays you, that's all that matters), nor for the invisible social costs of what you consume. There is a great freedom to the individual in this arrangement, and one that

ANTI-CAPITALISM

advocates of social revolution and human liberation must take into account when they propose an alternative life based on a high level of accountability and responsibility. The American ideological commitment to "freedom" usually deemed hypocritical by radical critics, may be less false than commonly thought. Freedom from accountability and responsibility is powerfully attractive to many people.

With this in mind, we might be better off describing our goals in other terms than "freedom," even if we believe that it is crucial to free ourselves from the logic of buying and selling. Our society is increasingly characterized by emptiness, isolation, alienation, and fragmentation. It is a society that craves "community" and human conviviality so much that cults and religions easily find new recruits in spite of their patently absurd belief systems. Seeking "community," many people urgently embraced the empty nationalism of flag-waving in the face of the September 11 attack, hoping perhaps to bolster a connection that few notice or feel in the course of normal daily life. Isn't the radical agenda more about creating lively communities of people who can count on each other and are therefore held accountable to shared standards of responsibility and participation?

As we seek a balance between our revolutionary impulses and our need to nurture and sustain a revolutionary movement—perhaps across generations—we cannot avoid grappling with the dialectic of personal freedom and social accountability. Accountability is always a form of authority, and a necessary part of a liberated future. Our yearning for community is at some point antithetical to the yearning for freedom. We seek recognition, appreciation, and accountability in community—precisely the qualities absent in our anonymous "freedom" as wage slaves and consumers.

As we think about institutionalization, we face our own mortality, our own issues about "settling down," building a home, and making commitments. The frenzied life we've adapted to under late capitalism is defined by a high degree of personal mobility and choice. Can we embrace stability and rootedness in a way that enhances our quality of life and doesn't seem like a retreat from personal freedom? Can we build new institutions that promote individuals freely committing to each other instead of being responsive to the impersonal dictatorship of economic efficiency? Can we build lasting institutions that transcend the need for charismatic individuals to hold them together? Can institutions promote revolution? What kind of institutions do we need to consolidate a new way of life as the old order begins to collapse under the weight of its own corruption, illegitimacy, and inability to meet human needs?

David Hanks

ANTI-CAPITALISM

The Tactical Cul-de-Sac, or the Problem of Identifying and Using Real Social Power

In November 1999 an exciting coalition manifested in Seattle. Direct-action anarchists, mainstream labor unionists, environmentalists and Third World solidarity activists united to protest the WTO. For a brief time it seemed that this new coalition had really changed the nature of social opposition. Seattle proved again the oldest lesson of revolution: that we are *much* stronger in our unity than any of us are alone. But by the time April 2000 rolled around and a similar effort was made to "shut down" the World Bank/IMF meetings in Washington, D.C., it was clear that the coalition had already returned to its original fragments, and was not unified in tactics or strategy, and certainly not unified in a shared vision. In the ensuing two years, much effort has been spent on trying to rebuild similar coalitions, but without much success.

The distinctive elements of the "Seattle coalition" are not revolutionary when taken alone. Their goals are partial and reformist (except some of the anarchists, but they are the same people who really need to help answer the questions raised in this article). The social power these groups wield is largely a matter of public perception or the lack thereof; in other words, the solidarity activists, ecologists, and labor activists all depend on

getting attention in the mass media as their primary lever of power. The surprisingly successful seizure of downtown Seattle during the WTO reintroduced us all to the occupation of public space as a form of social power. Even while it was under way, however, bitter fights broke out among the occupiers about the behavioral norms of the occupation, obliquely endorsing the propaganda counterattack that sought to invalidate the entire protest on the grounds that some protesters were "naughty." This latter technique is used during every "successful" protest or direct action (which become recorded as instances in which things "got out of control"). The use of force, however nonviolently, is always deemed a greater affront and violation than the blatantly violent behavior that passes as "normal business practices" in the world market.

The preparations of the authorities (who were delighted to radically increase their security budgets in the wake of Seattle) prevented similar achievements in later summits and political conventions where protesters gathered. Also, most trade unionists, solidarity activists, and mainstream environmentalists were dissuaded from participating, either because they were afraid of the violence (that the state would provide, even if the protesters didn't), or because they didn't want to be associated with what had become an "extremist" approach. European protesters took up the fight during the September 2000 IMF/World Bank meeting in Prague, Czech Republic, where again they succeeded in exercising the social power of occupying public space, as they did even more dramatically in Genoa, Italy, in July 2001.

Anyone who has been in a major urban riot and has walked the deserted streets behind the lines of confrontation has had a taste of liberated space. A similar sensation comes in the wake of earthquakes, floods, blackouts, so-called "natural" disasters. But the everyday liberation of social space requires not just a spasm of refusal and disobedience, or an unpredictable and occasional event, but a creative reinhabitation of the spaces in which we live as an everyday truth. What is most notably suspended during these brief tastes of liberated space is business as usual. People stay home from work and school. Strangers are suddenly your friends. It is common to extend a helping hand and to feel the connected euphoria of real human community. Seattle and the rest gave all their participants a major dose of this intensely seductive experience.

War: The Ultimate Answer of the State

The state learned from these gatherings, too. In Québec, Göteborg, Sweden, and Genoa, Italy, greater and greater force was employed, leading to shootings and finally death in Italy in the summer of 2001. The increasing militarization of the summits and their protests seemed to be heading towards a dead-end for both sides. As the rubble of Genoa was being cleaned up, no one could foresee the September 11 terrorist attacks in the United States. Leaving aside the many mysteries and unanswered questions about CIA complicity and government malfeasance, the attacks opened the door to a rapidly intensifying militarization of daily life. The attack on Afghanistan and concurrent expansion of the United States military into the crucial oil-rich Central Asian republics is one side. More important

David Hanks

for radicals is the use of war in derailing and decomposing social movements.

War is a uniquely powerful weapon of the ruling order against its enemies. Not only can it bomb and kill with impunity in far-off strategic regions of the world, but it can criminalize dissent and employ far stronger weapons against opponents at home. Just by declaring a "time of war" (which is mysteriously different than declaring war itself), the government awakens a significant number of people from its standard slumber of indifference. Suddenly thousands of previously sullen and silent citizens are openly and loudly patriotic, on the lookout for enemies, and aggressively hostile to any dissent, even silent refusals to endorse the new jingoism.

Inside of social movements, meanwhile, confusion is sown. After an attack on the national territory some people who had been in the opposition find it necessary to rally to the cause of national self-defense, regardless of the lack of factual information on the causes, motives, or even identities of the

ANTI-CAPITALISM

"enemy." Political agendas that attack symbols of national pride, that question the legitimacy or competence of political leaders, that oppose policies and behaviors that created the context in which the attacks took place are pushed aside. "This is not the time," say reasonable people, even if they still support the politics. Caution rules, strident opposition is muted, and political movements that were rolling toward an unknown climax are catastrophically derailed. Picking up the pieces in the wake of a wartime fragmentation can take as long as building the movement did in the first place.

If a military draft ensues, if the economy is put through a centralizing process of wartime command, people are uprooted, the communities that have slowly developed over generations are abruptly ripped apart, while work processes are restructured, factories and offices are moved, and workers with suspicious political ideas are fired without explanation. Attempts to carry on building any movement through this process are remarkably difficult. In the United States, the government used its entry into World War I in 1917 to shut down publications deemed "subversive," and to criminalize thousands of radical agitators, anarchists, and trade unionists, many of whom were ultimately deported in 1920 after the Palmer Raids. World War II saved capitalism in the United States after Roosevelt's New Deal was failing, needing the boost of wartime spending to lift the economy and relegitimize the American Way. Radical socialists and Communists who had been deeply involved in the burgeoning growth of trade unions during the 1930s saw their achievements suspended during the war, and themselves criminalized soon after the war. The cold war hysteria that still lingers in the United States was used to divide radical opposition from acceptable "mainstream" trade unionism, which ultimately contributed to the demise of labor as an important political force in U.S. politics.

George W. Bush took the presidency through the Florida fraud and ensuing Supreme Court coup. During his first months in office, he was a laughingstock, a bumbling fool without legitimacy or capability. September 11 was crucial to his ability to maintain his presidency. The social movements contesting the plans of global capitalists were forced to pause. Then, in the face of the so-called War on Terrorism, they have had to regroup while defending themselves from slanderous attacks by various right-wing commentators who quickly painted anyone not in lockstep with the ruling elite as a terrorist. Citizens who were beginning to hear the messages of the movement and see the protests in a sympathetic light had their frame of reference quickly and completely altered by the hysteria following September 11. The painfully slow process of reframing questions of development and globalization has suffered a major setback.

The New Shape of Class Conflict

Our mass-market culture channels desires for collective euphoria into spectator sports and religion. My goal as a revolutionary is to link the desire for shared experiences, community, and collective euphoria to more spaces in which we can live without "business as usual." The two major components of business as usual are working and shopping. Most of our assumptions about the "real world" are profoundly shaped by our experiences at work, the place where we reproduce ourselves, where we "pull our own weight" and make a contribution (we hope) to society's general well-being. And it is at work that most people are more fragmented, disconnected, and isolated than ever before. The redesign of work away from individual craftsmanship and an integrated knowledge of any particular line of endeavor is far advanced. In the past quarter century, the twin processes of exporting the dirtiest jobs to faraway countries and automating the ones that remain has turned a large portion of the workforce into temporary, contingent, semiskilled workers who shift from job to job, industry to industry, as the needs of business dictate. Most workers today have very limited knowledge of the purpose of their work, or how it fits into the larger processes that lead to real goods and services. The transience in workplaces has done a great deal to prevent attempts to build new kinds of workplace-based communities and organizations (unions being the most formal example).

Existing trade unions are usually part of the problem, however, not the solution. Most workplace organizing is inherently conservative insofar as people are motivated by a desire to protect their status as wage-workers, perhaps to gain a bit more in wages and benefits. And yet I still think workplace organizing is the key to any future successful revolt. But how can one get organized on the job, win over wavering coworkers who aren't sure they're ready to join up, gain a majority of folks as active allies, when your goal is to abolish the whole setup of daily life? It doesn't make much sense in the absence of a larger culture of revolt. It makes even less sense in the absence of a social vision of a life beyond the Economy, where human time is freely shared, production and distribution is freely organized by those who do the work, and so forth.

This is a very serious problem. Radical revolt depends on overthrowing the reproduction of everyday life, in large part at the point of production (and distribution). If people are organizing on the job, it is always to gain protection from arbitrary bosses, to improve wages and benefits, or to assert a right to control some aspect of the workplace. How does getting organized to defend oneself personally now (in a given historic moment of the capitalist division of labor) lead to an assertive collectivity that may

ANTI-CAPITALISM

eventually take over every- thing? In asking this question I paint myself into the corner. There is no room for radical steps between the first goal and the total change. In the worst case, this leads to a numbing paralysis or a disdainful, condescending participation in struggles that I already think are going in the wrong direction!

Moreover, it doesn't take into account the overwhelming transience that plagues the structure of work. Few people remain at the same job or workplace more than a few years. New workers are expected to be good, fast learners and multitalented, able to shift from task to task.

Jim Swanson

Work is so thoroughly structured in most places that the workers are easily replaced. Mounting any kind of ongoing, organized resistance at a given workplace depends on trust and familiarity between the workers. These are not qualities easily attained when you've only known each other for a few weeks or months, and then only through the strained "niceness" of corporate culture.

Opening spaces in this closed world of work—physical or virtual—where people can connect is a crucial step. Organizing on the job brings people together in a basic conspiracy. Workers together can alter the rhythms of work, open up free time for each other, and divert resources to other ends than that on which the company is focused. They can also force the company to take profits and plow them back into wages and benefits. In the best case, organizing on the job can create counterinstitutions at work that eventually become the framework for disempowering the managers and self-managing the job. Though this, in itself, leaves unchallenged what the company actually does, it sets the stage for a collective approach to deeper questions.

Although the site of work and production is crucial, people are finding new ways of connecting outside of work. A movement that has grown under the

radar during the past decade is that of bicyclists who gather in over 300 cities worldwide in a monthly event called Critical Mass. Starting in San Francisco in 1992, it has spread by word of mouth and by the internet, embraced by people who want to assert a countersensibility to a self-destructive life that passes as normal. Rather than tying political expression to a given workplace or political agenda, Critical Mass has provided a public arena for self-expression and a reclaiming of public space from the logic of the economy. Critical Mass underscores the primacy of transit as a contested arena. Bicyclists have withdrawn from the exploitative relations of car ownership and the degrading second-class citizenship (and waste of time) imposed by public transit. But this revolt is personal and invisible—until the creative eruption of Critical Mass proclaims these myriad isolated acts to the world as a shared act. It is a public declaration that suddenly reveals individual choices to be social, political, and collective responses to the insanity that passes as inevitable and normal. In creating a moving event, celebrating and being a real alternative, Critical Mass simultaneously opens up the field of transit to new political contestation, and pushes it to another level by pioneering swarming mobility as a new tactic. Taking place in downtown financial districts and consisting of dozens or hundreds of people who work in those same districts underscores the break with daily life expectations Critical Mass helps create. The contagious pleasure of a movement like Critical Mass threatens the precariousness of today's world, which depends on cooperative participation by the majority of people as workers and consumers. Critical Mass provides encouragement and reinforcement for desertion from the rat wheel of car ownership and its attendant investments. But even more subversively, it does so by gaining active participation in an event of unmediated human creation, outside of economic logic, and offering an exhilarating taste of a life practically forgotten—free, convivial, cooperative, connected, collective.

Doing Nothing Is Sometimes Something (or Slow Down the Speedup)

One of the most painful ironies of this era has to be the amazing overwork of radical activists. So many people drawn to political movements during this long, difficult period have found themselves overwhelmed by the amount of work needed to mount a demonstration, carry on an educational campaign, publish a 'zine or book, organize a union, fight a company. Time and again activists burn out over low or no wages, very long hours, bizarre interpersonal relationships with others who seem to have unresolved psychological problems, and a general anxiety that comes from being a tiny underdog in a world that goes to the victors.

ANTI-CAPITALISM

It's too common for those who are most capable and interested to get so pulled in that they sacrifice important aspects of their humanity. Many are attending meetings every day, going to important demonstrations and events, organizing their friends to the point where they only have friends who are part of their organizing efforts. The ready use of guilt and shame to keep people doing work for free or very little is routine. The guilt or pressure that drives people to overwork and overparticipate is itself a crippling quality.

By the mid-1970s, the overwork and psychological distress common to political activism pushed many people to define their lifestyle choices as a sufficient contribution to political change. Unfortunately, for too many, taking a political stand has come to mean shopping properly. The underbelly of this critique, however, is the implication that to be "truly" political we must "do something"—something more than just shop well. It's true that our effort to pursue a revolutionary agenda requires creative action and steady public participation. But the urge to "do something" often leads to demonstrations and political forms (in print and on the streets) that are utterly unimaginative, dogmatic, repetitive, and profoundly self-defeating. As someone who has marched in countless demonstrations, published scores of flyers, posters, and 'zines, and participated in dozens of street theater interventions, I admit to feeling depressed, less powerful and less effective after a demonstration.

The Seattle movement was launched by West Coast activists who led the way with colorful giant puppets and other new forms of creative protest. They have pioneered an exciting break with the visible style of leftist protest that dominated the past decades, and it has been exhilarating to be a part of it. Nevertheless, the urgency to attend rallies, create puppets, organize demonstrations and the like, itself reproduces the pattern of taking action without a clear idea of where we're going.

"The personal is political," an insight of the 1970s feminist movement, was an important reintroduction of subjective values and experience to the political landscape. In that sense it parallels the age-old concern for ensuring consistency between means and ends. Participants in a renewed radical movement must find ways to live well now—not based on sacrifice and guilt, nor defined by a deferred gratification that will come "after the revolution." "Living well is the best revenge," goes the saying. Resisting overwork and self-sacrifice is an important radical goal in itself. If we aren't enjoying our lives and finding fulfillment in human connections, our ability to sustain a long-term revolutionary effort is compromised. We need to take the time to develop our philosophical and political depth, study history, ecology, and technology, and practice imagining the world we want

ANTI-CAPITALISM

to live in. If we cannot trust each other to take the lead, create lasting institutions, articulate more clearly where we're trying to go, and create living examples (insofar as it's possible) of the way we want to live, we will have a hard time convincing others to join us. We have to make it clear that we're fighting for a world dramatically better than the insane world of today.

A longer version of this essay appeared in Processed World, *September, 2001.*

10 YEARS

CRITICAL·MASS

MASA CRITICA · КРИТИЧЕСКАЯ МАССА · クリティカル マス · KRITISKE MASSE

SAN FRANCISCO · FRIDAY SEPTEMBER 27th · 2002

Moving Through the Symbols

By Naomi Klein

Naomi Klein is a writer-participant in the global justice movement. She has written No Logo—Taking Aim at the Brand Bullies *and* Windows and Fences.

The first edition of the book *No Logo* ends with an image of activists speaking in hushed tones about their plan to build a global anticorporate movement. Then, when the book was at the printer's, something happened that changed everything: on November 30, 1999, the streets of Seattle exploded in protests against the World Trade Organization. Overnight, that hushed whisper turned into a shout, one heard around the world. This movement was no longer a secret, a rumor, a hunch. It was a fact.

Seattle took the political campaigns described in *No Logo* to a much more prominent place in the political discourse. As the mass demonstrations spread to Washington, D.C., Quebec City, New Delhi, Melbourne, Genoa, Buenos Aires, and elsewhere, debates raged in the press about police and protester violence, as well as what alternatives there are—if any—to what the French call "wild capitalism" (*capitalisme sauvage*). The issues

photo top: David Hanks

behind the protests changed too. In very short order, college-age activists who started off concerned with the unethical behavior of a single corporation began questioning the logic of capitalism itself and the effectiveness of trickle-down economics. Church groups who had previously demanded only the "forgiveness" of Third World debt were now talking about the failure of the "neoliberal economic model," which holds that capital must be freed of all encumbrances to facilitate future development. Instead of reform, many were calling for the outright abolition of the World Bank and the International Monetary Fund. And ad-busters were no longer satisfied with jamming a single billboard, but were busy creating new and exciting networks of participatory media like the Independent Media Centers, now in dozens of cities around the world.

Meanwhile, the institutions that have been the primary enforcers and defenders of global neoliberal policies have been going through their own metamorphoses. The World Bank, the IMF, the WTO, and the World Economic Forum have stopped denying that their model of globalization is failing to deliver the promised results, and have begun preoccupying themselves—at least in public statements—with the paradoxes of debt slavery, the AIDS pandemic, and the billions left out of the global market.

Like so many other activists and theorists in this field, ever since Seattle exploded onto the world stage I have been swept up in the unstoppable momentum of the globalization battles: speaking, debating, organizing, and traveling way too much. We've been doing, in other words, what movements should do—we've been moving. Often so fast that it has seemed impossible to keep up with the latest twists and turns, let alone to step back and reflect about where all this motion is leading us.

It was only after the September 11 attacks that, at least in North America, this context began to change. All of a sudden, everyone seemed to be talking about the gap between the global haves and have-nots, as well as the absence of democracy in so many parts of the world. But though the North American public was becoming more aware of the failings of the global economy—failures glossed over in the press during the euphoria of boom-time prosperity—it was suddenly much harder to transform that awareness into political action. Rather than pushing governments to change clearly faulty policies, a fearful population was instead handing their politicians stacks of blank checks, freeing them to barrel ahead with more of the same: new tax cuts for wealthy corporations, new trade deals, new privatization plans. To engage in dissent in this climate was cast as unpatriotic.

Thousands shut down the WTO in Seattle. November 30, 1999.

Tens of thousands take over a major U.S. city and transform it into a festival of resistance. Seattle, November 30, 1999.

There are other challenges that North American activists have faced since September 11. Activists began targeting corporations in the mid-nineties as a response to the fact that so much that is powerful today is virtual: currency trades, stock prices, intellectual property, brands, and arcane trade agreements. By latching onto symbols, whether a famous brand like Nike or a prominent meeting of world leaders, the intangible was made temporarily actual, the vastness of the global market more human-scale. Yet the dominant iconography of this movement—the culture-jammed logos, the guerrilla-warfare stylings, the choices of brand name and political targets—looks distinctly different to eyes changed by the horrors of September 11. Today, campaigns that rely even on a peaceful subversion of powerful capitalist symbols find themselves in an utterly transformed semiotic landscape.

This struck me recently, looking at a slide show I had been pulling together just before the attacks. It is about how anticorporate imagery is increasingly being absorbed by corporate marketing. One slide shows a group of activists spray-painting the window of a Gap outlet during the protests in Seattle. The next shows Gap's recent window displays featuring its own prefab graffiti—the word "Independence" sprayed in black. And the next is a frame from Sony PlayStation's State of Emergency game featuring cool-haired anarchists throwing rocks at sinister riot cops protecting the fictitious American Trade Organization. When I first looked at these images beside each other, I was amazed by the speed of corporate cooptation. But looking at them after September 11, the images had all been instantly overshadowed, blown away by the terrorist attacks like so many toy cars and action figures on a disaster movie set.

It could hardly have been other otherwise. The attacks on the World Trade Center and the Pentagon were acts of real and horrifying terror, but they were also acts of symbolic warfare, and instantly understood as such. As many commentators have put it, the towers were not just tall buildings; they were "symbols of American capitalism." Predictably, many political opponents of the anticorporate position have begun using the symbolism of the attacks to argue that these acts of terrorism represent an extreme expression of the ideas held by the protesters. Some have argued that the attacks were only the far end of a continuum of anti-American and anti-corporate violence: first the Starbucks window in Seattle, then the WTC.

Others have gone even further, arguing that free-market polices are the economic front of the war on terrorism. Supporting "free trade" has been rebranded, like shopping and baseball, as a patriotic duty. U.S. trade representative Robert Zoellick has explained that trade "promotes the values at the heart of this protracted struggle," so the United States, he says, needs a new campaign to "fight terror with trade." In an essay in the *New York Times Magazine*, Michael Lewis makes a similar conflation between freedom fighting and free trading when he explains that the traders who died were targeted as "not merely symbols but also practitioners of liberty. . . . They work hard, if unintentionally, to free others from constraints. This makes them, almost by default, the spiritual antithesis of the religious fundamentalist, whose business depends on a denial of personal liberty in the name of some putatively higher power."

David Hanks

San Francisco anti-FTAA march in conjunction with the Zapatista March on Mexico City, spring 2001.

The new battle lines have been drawn, crude as they are: to criticize the U.S. government is to be on the side of the terrorists, to stand in the way of market-driven globalization is to further the terrorists' evil goals.

There is, of course, a glaring problem with this logic: the idea that the market can, on its own, supply solutions to all of our social problems has been profoundly discredited by the experience of September 11 itself. From the privatized airport security officers who failed to detect the hijackers' weapons to the private charities that have so badly bungled aid to the victims to the corporate bailouts that have failed to stimulate the economy, market-driven policies are not helping to win the war on terrorism. They are liabilities. So while criticizing politicians may be temporarily out of favor, "People Before Profit," the street slogan from the globalization protests, has become a self-evident and viscerally felt truth for many more people in the United States since the attacks.

The most dramatic manifestation of this shift is the American public's changing relationship to its public sector. Many of the institutions and services that have been underfunded, vilified, deregulated, and privatized during the past two decades—airports, post offices, hospitals, mass transit systems, water and food inspection—were forced to take center stage after the attacks, and they weren't ready for their close-up. Americans found out fast what it meant to have a public health care system so overburdened it cannot handle a routine flu season, let alone an anthrax outbreak. There were severe drug shortages, and private labs failed to

FORWARD MOVEMENT

Orin Langelle

come up with enough anthrax vaccines for U.S. soldiers, let alone for civilians. Despite a decade of pledges to safeguard the U.S. water supply from bioterrorist attack, scandalously little had been done by the overburdened U.S. Environmental Protection Agency. The food supply proved to be even more vulnerable, with inspectors managing to check about 1 percent of food imports—hardly a safeguard against rising fears of "agroterrorism."

And most wrenchingly of all, it was the firefighters who rushed in to save the lives of the bond traders and other employees in the towers, demonstrating that there is indeed still a role for a public sector after all. So it seems fitting that on the streets of New York City the hottest-selling T-shirts and baseball hats are no longer the ones displaying contraband Nike and Prada logos, but the logo of the Fire Department of New York.

The importance of a strong public realm is not only being rediscovered in rich countries like the United States, but also in poor countries, where fundamentalism has been spreading so rapidly. It is in countries where the public infrastructure has been ravaged by debt and war that fanatical sugar daddies like Osama bin Laden are able to swoop in and start providing basic services that are usually in the public domain: roads, schools, health clinics, even basic sanitation. And the extreme Islamic seminaries in Pakistan that indoctrinated so many Taliban leaders thrive precisely because they fill a huge social welfare gap. In a country that spends 90 percent of its budget on its military and debt—and a pittance on

education—the *madrassas* offer not only free classrooms but also food and shelter for poor children.

In understanding the mechanics of terrorism—North and South—one theme is recurring: we pay a high price when we put the short-term demands of business (for lower taxes, less "red tape," more investment opportunities) ahead of the needs of people. Post–September 11, clinging to laissez-faire free-market solutions, despite overwhelming evidence of their failings, looks a lot like blind faith, as irrational as any belief system clung to by religious fanatics fighting a suicidal jihad.

For activists, there are many connections to be made between the September 11 attacks and the many other arenas in which human needs must take precedence over corporate profits, from AIDS treatment in Africa to homelessness in our own cities. There is also an important role to be played in arguing for more reciprocal international relations. Terrorism is indeed an international threat, and it did not begin with the attacks in the United States. As Bush invites the world to join America's war, sidelining the UN and the international courts, globalization activists need to become passionate defenders of true multilateralism, rejecting once and for all the label "antiglobalization." From the start, it was clear that President Bush's coalition did not represent a genuinely global response to terrorism but the internationalization of one country's foreign policy objectives—the trademark of U.S. conduct on the world stage, from the WTO negotiating table to the abandonment of the Kyoto Protocol on climate change. These arguments can be made not in a spirit of anti-Americanism, but in a spirit of true internationalism.

By far the most important role for those concerned with the explosion of corporate power is to act not only as voices of opposition but also as beacons—beacons of other ways to organize a society, ways that exist outside of the raging battles between "good" and "evil." In the current context, this is no small task. The attacks on the United States and the U.S. attacks on Afghanistan have ushered in an era of ideological polarization not seen since the cold war. On the one hand, there is George W. Bush claiming "You are either with us, or you are with the terrorists"; on the other, there is bin Laden, asserting that "These events have divided the world into two camps, the camp of the faithful and the camp of the infidels." Anticorporate and prodemocracy activists should demonstrate the absurdity of this duality and insist that there are more than two choices available. We can spread rumors about the existence of routes not taken, choices not made, alternatives not built. As Indian novelist and activist Arundhati Roy wrote after September 11, "the people of the world do not have to choose between the Taliban and the U.S. government. All

FORWARD MOVEMENT

the beauty of human civilization—our art, our music, our literature—lies beyond these two fundamentalist, ideological poles." Confronted with a deadly multiple-choice exam, the answer should be, "None of the above."

Well before September 11, there was a growing awareness in movement circles that attention needed to shift from "summit-hopping" to articulating and building these alternatives. For more than a year, the largely symbolic attacks on individual corporations and trade summits were being vocally challenged by many who feared that globalization battles—with their smashed McDonald's windows and running fights with police—were beginning to look like theater, cut off from the issues that affect people's day-to-day lives. And there is much that is unsatisfying about fighting a war of symbols: the glass shatters in the storefront, the meetings are driven to ever more remote locations—but so what? It's still only symbols, facades, representations.

In response, a new mood of impatience was already taking hold, an insistence on putting forward social and economic alternatives that address the roots of injustice, from land reform in the developing world to slavery reparations in the United States to participatory democracy at the municipal level in cities around the world. Rather than summit hopping, the focus was moving to forms of direct action that attempt to meet people's immediate needs for housing, food, water, life-saving drugs, and electricity. This is being expressed in countless unique ways around the world.

In India, it means defiantly producing generic AIDS drugs for the rest of the developing world. In Italy, it means taking over dozens of abandoned buildings and turning them into affordable housing and lively community centers. You can see the same spirit coursing through the actions of the Landless Peasants' Movement of Brazil, which seizes tracts of unused farmland and uses them for sustainable agriculture, markets, and schools under the slogan "Ocupar, Resistir, Producir" (Occupy, Resist, Produce).

It is in South Africa where this spirit of direct action may be spreading most rapidly. Since a sweeping privatization program was instituted in 1993, half a million jobs have been lost, wages for the poorest 40 percent have dropped by 21 percent, and poor areas have seen their water costs go up 55 percent and electricity as much as 400 percent. Many have resorted to drinking polluted water, leading to a cholera outbreak that infected 100,000 people. In Soweto, 20,000 homes have their electricity cut off each month. In the face of this system of "economic apartheid," as privatization is called by many South African activists, unemployed workers in Soweto have been reconnecting their neighbors' cut-off water and the Soweto Electricity Crisis Committee has illegally reconnected power in thousands of homes.

No matter where it takes place, the theory behind this defiant wave of direct action is the same: activism can no longer be about registering symbolic dissent. It must be about taking action to make people's lives better—where they live, right away.

Jeff Conant

The question now facing this movement is how to transform these small, often fleeting

Street theater at the World Social Forum in Mumbai/Bombai, India. January 2004.

initiatives into broader, more sustainable social structures. There are many attempts to answer this question but by far the most ambitious is the annual World Social Forum, launched in January 2001 in Pôrto Alegre, Brazil. The WSF's optimistic slogan is "Another World Is Possible" and it was conceived as an opportunity for an emerging movement to stop screaming about what it is against and start articulating what it is for. In its first year, more than 10,000 people attended a week of more than sixty speeches, dozens of concerts, and 450 workshops. The particular site was chosen because Brazil's Workers' Party (Partido dos Trabalhadores, the PT) is in power in the city of Pôrto Alegre, as well as in the state of Rio Grande do Sul, and has become known worldwide for its innovations in participatory democracy.

But the World Social Forum is not a political convention: there are no policy directives made, no official motions passed, no attempts to organize the parts of this movement into a political party, with subordinate cells and locals. And that fact, in a way, is what makes this wave of activism unlike anything that has come before it. Thanks to the internet, mobilizations are able to unfold with sparse bureaucracy and minimal hierarchy; forced consensus and labored manifestos are fading into the background, replaced instead by a culture of constant, loosely structured, and sometimes compulsive information-swapping. Although individual intellectuals and key organizers may help shape the ideas of the people on the streets, they most emphatically do not have the power or even the mechanisms to lead them in any one direction. It isn't even, if truth be told, a movement. It is thousands of movements, intricately linked to one

Pakistan Social Forum at the World Social Forum in Mumbai/Bombai, India. January 2004.

Dancers at the World Social Forum in Mumbai/Bombai, India, January 2004.

another, much as "hotlinks" connect their websites on the net. And while this network is wildly ambitious in its scope and reach, its goals are anything but imperial. This network unrelentingly challenges the most powerful institutions and individuals of our time, but does not seek to seize power for itself. Instead it seeks to disperse power, as widely and evenly as possible.

The best example of this new revolutionary thinking is the Zapatista uprising in Chiapas, Mexico. When the Zapatistas rose up against the Mexican military in January 1994, their goal was not to win control over the Mexican state but to seize and build autonomous spaces where "democracy, liberty, and justice" could thrive. For the Zapatistas, these free spaces, created from reclaimed land, communal agriculture, and resistance to privatization, are an attempt to create counterpowers to the state, not a bid to overthrow it and replace it with an alternate, centralized regime.

It's fitting that the figure that comes closest to a bona fide movement "leader" is Subcomandante Marcos, the Zapatista spokesperson who hides his real identity and covers his face with a mask. Marcos, the quintessential antileader, insists that his black mask is a mirror, so that "Marcos is gay in San Francisco, black in South Africa, an Asian in Europe, a Chicano in San Ysidro, an anarchist in Spain, a Palestinian in Israel, a Mayan Indian in the streets of San Cristobal, a Jew in Germany, a Gypsy in Poland, a Mohawk in Quebec, a pacifist in Bosnia, a single woman on the Metro at 10 P.M., a peasant without land, a gang member in the slums, an unemployed worker, an unhappy student, and, of course, a Zapatista in the mountains." In other words, he says, he is us: We are the leader we've been looking for.

Marcos's own story is of a man who came to his leadership not through swaggering certainty, but by coming to terms with political doubt, by learning to follow. The most repeated legend that clings to him goes like this: an urban Marxist intellectual and activist, Marcos was wanted by the state and was no longer safe in the cities. He fled to the mountains of Chiapas in southeast Mexico filled with revolutionary rhetoric and certainty, there to convert the poor indigenous masses to the cause of armed proletarian revolution against the bourgeoisie. He said the workers of the world must unite, and the Mayans just stared at him. They said they weren't workers but people, and, besides, land wasn't property but the heart of their communities. Having failed as a Marxist missionary, Marcos immersed himself in Mayan culture. The more he learned, the less he knew.

Orin Langelle

Chiapas, Mexico.

FORWARD MOVEMENT

Out of this process, a new kind of army emerged—the Zapatista Army for National Liberation (EZLN) is not controlled by an elite of guerrilla commanders but by the communities themselves, through clandestine councils and open assemblies. Marcos isn't a commander barking orders, but a subcomandante, a conduit for the will of the councils. His first words in his new persona were: "through me speaks the will of the Zapatista National Liberation Army."

The Zapatista struggle has become a powerful beacon for other movements around the world precisely because it is organized according to principles that are the mirror opposite of the way states, corporations, and religions tend to be organized. It responds to concentration with a maze of fragmentation, to centralization with localization, to power consolidation with radical power dispersal. The question is: could this be a microcosm for a global strategy to reclaim the commons from the forces of privatization?

Many of today's activists have already concluded that globalization is not simply a good idea that has been grabbed by the wrong hands. Nor do they believe that the situation could be righted if only international institutions like the WTO were made democratic and accountable. Rather, they are arguing that alienation from global institutions is only the symptom of a much broader crisis in representative democracy, one that has seen power and decisionmaking delegated to points further and further away from the places where the effects of those decisions are felt. As one-size-fits-all logic sets in, it leads at once to a homogenization of political and cultural choices, and to widespread civic paralysis and disengagement.

If centralization of power and distant decisionmaking are emerging as the common enemies, there is also an emerging consensus that participatory democracy at the local level—whether through unions, neighborhoods, city governments, farms, villages, or aboriginal self-government—is the place to start building alternatives to it. The common theme is an overarching commitment to self-determination and diversity: cultural diversity, ecological diversity, even political diversity. The Zapatistas speak of building a movement of "one 'no' and many 'yeses'," a description that defies the characterization that this is one movement at all, and challenges the assumption that it should be. What seems to be emerging organically is not a movement for a single global government but a vision for an increasingly connected international network of very local initiatives, each built on reclaimed public spaces, and, through participatory forms of democracy, made more accountable than either corporate or state institutions. If this movement has an ideology it is democracy, not only at the ballot box but woven into every aspect of our lives.

All of this makes it terribly ironic when critics attempt to make ideological links between anticorporate protesters and religious fundamentalists like bin Laden, as British secretary of state for international development Clare Short did in November 2001. "Since September 11, we haven't heard from the protesters," she observed. "I'm sure they are reflecting on what their demands were because their demands turned out to be very similar to those of bin Laden's network." She couldn't have been more mistaken. Bin Laden and his followers are driven not by a critique of centralized power but by a rage that more power is not centralized in their own hands. They are furious not at the homogenization of choices, but that the world is not organized according to their own homogenous and imperialist belief system.

In other words, this is a classic power struggle over which the great, all-knowing system will govern the day; where the battle lines were once communism versus capitalism, they are now the God of the Market squaring off against the God of Islam. For bin Laden and his followers, much of the allure of this battle is clearly the idea that they are living in mythic times, when men were godlike, battles were epic, and history was spelled with a capital H. "Screw you, Francis Fukuyama," they seem to be saying. "History hasn't ended yet. We are still making it."

It's an idea we've heard from both sides since September 11, a return of the great narrative: chosen men, evil empires, master plans, and great battles. All are ferociously back in style. This grand redemption narrative is our most persistent myth, and it has a dangerous flip side. When a few men decide to live their myths, to be larger than life, it can't help but have an impact on all the lives that unfold in regular sizes. People suddenly look insignificant by comparison, easy to sacrifice by the thousands in the name of some greater purpose.

Thankfully, anticorporate and prodemocracy activists are engaged in no such fire-and-brimstone crusades. They are instead challenging systems of centralized power on principle, as critical of left-wing, one-size-fits-all state solutions as of right-wing market ones. It is often said disparagingly that this movement lacks ideology, an overarching message, a master plan.

This is absolutely true, and we should be extraordinarily thankful. At the moment, the anticorporate street activists are ringed by would-be leaders, anxious for the opportunity to enlist them as foot soldiers. It is to this young movement's credit that it has as yet fended off all of these agendas and has rejected everyone's generously donated manifesto, holding out for an acceptably democratic, representative process to take its resistance to the next stage. Will it be a ten-point plan? A new political doctrine?

Perhaps it will be something altogether new. Not another ready-made ideology to do gladiatorial combat with free-market fundamentalism and Islamic fundamentalism, but a plan to protect the possibility and development of many worlds—a world, as the Zapatistas say, with many worlds in it. Maybe instead of meeting the proponents of neoliberalism head-on, this movement of movements will surround them from all directions.

This movement is not, as one newspaper headline recently claimed, "so yesterday." It is only changing, moving, yet again, to a deeper stage, one that is less focused on acts of symbolic resistance and theatrical protests and more on "living our alternatives into being," to borrow a phrase from a recent direct-action summit in New York City. Shortly after *No Logo* was published, I visited the University of Oregon to do a story on anti-sweatshop activism at the campus that is nicknamed Nike U. There I met student activist Sarah Jacobson. Nike, she told me, was not the target of her activism, but a tool, a way to access a vast and often amorphous economic system. "It's a gateway drug," she said cheerfully.

For years, we in this movement have fed off our opponents' symbols— their brands, their office towers, their photo-opportunity summits. We have used them as rallying cries, as focal points, as popular education tools. But these symbols were never the real targets; they were the levers, the handles. The symbols were only ever doorways. It's time to walk through them.

Weaving Imagination and Creation: The Future in the Present

By Marina Sitrin

Marina Sitrin is a New York City–based antiauthoritarian activist, writer, and dreamer. Marina is currently working on an oral history of the autonomous social movements in Argentina entitled Horizontalidad: Voices of Popular Power in Argentina.

"This is as far as I can take you," I was told by the bus driver from Mexico City as we arrived at the outskirts of Tepoztlán. He pointed and nodded in the direction of a hill to indicate which way to walk. Barricades of rocks and branches marked the intersection of the highway and the small road to town. I picked my way around the barricades and began the walk to the town center. All along the steep cobblestone streets I noticed wall after wall decorated with political graffiti, all containing messages about the need to stop the construction of a golf course, "*Fuera con el club de golf*" (golf course—get out) read many. People I passed along the way walked both tall and confident. I was greeted with smiles and nods. In the town center, the zócalo, the art-filled walls illustrated what had taken place. The first of a series of murals depicted what appeared to be politicians or businessmen, reptilian creatures in suits, attempting to build a golf course

image top: Florencia Vespignani

The citywide general assembly where smaller assemblies converge to vote on decisions affecting the entire city area, Buenos Aires, Argentina February 2002.

Andrew Stern / www.andrewstern.net

in the town. Water is scarce and key to survival in many Mexican towns, including this one, and the golf course threatened to devour the water the townspeople needed to survive. A group of murals also showed people coming together and resisting. One of the final groups of murals showed the corporate reptiles being forced to leave, and in their place was a town now run by the people. This in fact was true. Tepoztlán was being run in common by the townspeople, without police, politicians, or political parties.

I spent the next few days talking to people about their struggle. Community members explained their need and desire to resist, as well as the means they had chosen to use. They saw active participation in the decisionmaking process as key to their success and vision and thus they had facilitated constant conversations to achieve a directly democratic atmosphere. They explained that the mayor of the town had been approached by Mexican and international businessmen who wanted to "develop" the town by building a massive golf course and business "park." The people stated their opposition, and while the mayor said he would not allow it, he in fact made back-door agreements to give away and sell community land, as well as a large quantity of the town's water allotment. After a series of protests and struggles, the people of the town, now unified in struggle and vision, went into City Hall and nonviolently took it over, expelling the mayor. This was not a symbolic occupation of the town center, it was a new movement with no relationship to any political party, running the town in common. The movement called itself Frente Popular (Popular Front). People immediately organized nonviolent patrols to make sure all was safe and secure, as well as ensure that no police or military vehicles could enter the town and take it away from the occupants—hence the barricades. Neighborhood assemblies were held all around the town, as well as mass assemblies at night to collectively plan for the next day.

Every evening while I was there, community meetings were organized in the zócalo, near the volleyball net, and often after a match. These meetings took the form of presentations of what had occurred that day,

PREFIGURATIVE POLITICS

followed by open conversation, discussion, and planning. Themes for discussion were decided collectively and always open. There were facilitators and a microphone was passed around. People were more than simply active in their community, it *was* their community. Necessity caused creativity and a collective vision arose. It was a struggle without parties or imposed ideologies, from the grassroots from beginning to end.

Although I was in Tepoztlán ten years ago, the memory is very much alive for me today. I can still see the faces of people in the mass meetings as they discussed and debated the future of their town. I can hear the voice of a young adolescent explaining the history depicted in the murals to me, his voice so very proud. It continues to be an inspiring example of people creating as they resisted, by making their means the ends they desire: nonviolence, direct democracy, and mutual aid. The struggle was a process, and the process a part of the struggle. It is from examples like this that I garner my inspiration—my vision—that we can and will create a society in which all have a voice and work collectively for the whole. My vision, my utopian ideal, comes from my desires, as well as all of the very real experiences around me.

It is 2003, and I am now writing from Buenos Aires, Argentina. The social movements in Argentina, since the popular rebellion beginning in December 2001, are one of the most inspiring and creative articulations of the politics of creation and collective imagination that I have ever heard of or experienced. My eyes fill with tears as I try to express the beauty of what is being created. People feel that they are actors for the first time in their lives, finding dignity through collective action and mutual respect, meeting their basic needs through mutual aid, direct democracy and cooperation. Communities and workplaces coming together to not just think of a new way to organize socially and collectively, but doing it, every day. This is done through creating new relations and new territories, on street corners, in the street, in the neighborhoods, and the collective kitchens, as well as in occupied abandoned banks, transformed into social centers. I am not alone with my tears. People in the social movements also feel profoundly moved by what is being created. It is not just that people are organizing, but the way in which people are organizing. Importance is placed on the how, and not the what, on the construction of new social relationships. This is seen in many ways; for example, all in the movements have a voice and are autonomous, while seeing themselves as a part of a collective, that no one has power over another, and with the use of direct democracy and the politics of horizontalism. Through the use of these means of organizing ends are created. Many people now have food who did not before, schools, libraries, and microenterprises have been organized,

PREFIGURATIVE POLITICS

Florencia Vespignani

a tres meses - setiembre 2002   *Flor, MTD Anibal Veron*

and are being run collectively, using direct democracy and horizontalist politics. Argentina is articulating through experience a new politics of organization, vision, and creation. Horizontalism, a word and relationship that is translated from the Spanish *horizontalidad*, coined by the Argentine social movements, is now beginning to be used by antihierarchical and directly democratic groups around the world. The meaning is seen in the new social relationships developing in Argentina, the creation of new people, new relations, and a new society.

The forms of decisionmaking and internal relationships we use reflect ideologically what we want to create, as our parallel structures, from temporary medical collectives to occupied lots turned to gardens, actually create a vision of what we imagine to be possible. We need to be pragmatic, philosophical, and visionary simultaneously, while creating a space for the three to be separate. Bringing the vision into being is as much about creating the space to envision now as it is about creating a future visionary space. Some in our various movements are involved in decentralized networks as experiences in direct democracy and nonhierarchy, while for others the process is purely a useful means of achieving a desired goal. The thread through it all is vision, a creative, varied, and revolutionary imagination that weaves together the present with the future.

Importance of Vision

There are countless movements around the globe struggling to create a more just world, making the world in which we want to live every day with our various struggles of creation and resistance. "Another World Is Possible" has become the slogan of many in the international movement for global justice, reflecting a shift toward a more visionary and utopian theoretical framework. We share an ideal of a world where each can be free as individuals yet cooperative, where we are all free from want yet full of desire, where the environment is not exploited, where there is no oppression and difference is celebrated. As Leslie Wood of the Coalition for the Human Rights of Immigrants in New York City puts it, "Of course another world is possible, and [it is] necessary to say it because it triggers our thinking and imagination. I've always believed another world is possible, partially as a negative response—that this can't be as good as it gets, war, pollution, etc. You see it all the time, the possibility, in the relationships between people, the relationship and process in the creation of community gardens and other spaces where people can create these visions and use imagination. Where people are free to create and change and free to dissent." We can see the possibility of this world in our organizing. With our vision we push our organizing further toward creating that world; from alternative structures to internal relationships. Another world is not only possible; it is under construction. To actualize a vision, a strategy needs to exist, along with a high degree of organization. The forms these can take vary. I will address the issue of strategy only as it directly intersects with vision.

Role of Vision

The Zapatistas in Mexico, the assemblies, occupied factories, and movements of the unemployed in Argentina, the autonomous movements in South Africa, as well as countless others about which I still do not know, are all movements and struggles that provide inspiring examples of attempts at direct democracy and collective decisionmaking. They also reflect various forms of a vision of a society free from need, yet full of desire. The creativity of these struggles is one of the major reasons for their importance to us. They articulate a vision and work toward it while at the same time gathering inspiration from their activity. In imagining a new society, it is useful to look around the world as well as historically to see where, when, and how those who have come before us have envisioned a new society, and how they struggled to make it a daily reality. This is not only in order to say that, yes, people have collectively and democratically run their own societies, or to learn concrete strategy from historic

PREFIGURATIVE POLITICS

victories and failures, but most important, history is one of the places where we can see our various passions realized, even if only briefly. Our belief and feeling that we can and will create a just, equal, and more beautiful world becomes all the more grounded when we can glean from those that have come before us pieces of our vision realized. History is not to show us that we stand on the shoulders of giants in order to see far, but that we stand on the shoulders of regular people of various heights and they help us understand and feel where we are now.

For some people envisioning a better, more equitable society, means looking at the past, finding those things or moments that inspire us, and transposing them onto the present. For others, vision begins with inspiration drawn from everyday social relationships—seeing our current interactions as the creation of the future. For still others, the beginning point is the future place we know we can create, a place that is not rigid or based only on past examples, or in the little things we do in our daily lives to support and love one another, but on a combination of all past, present, and future interactions. "The most significant threat to the system and the most hopeful prospect is not our militant opposition, but our positive alternatives," as David Solnit of Art and Revolution so eloquently stated. "Unlike in society generally, we get a taste of what it would be like to participate democratically in decisions. This was seen quite powerfully in Seattle in the organization of the direct action: thousands of people got to taste thousands of people making decisions in an openly democratic way. Those experiences then translated into liberating the streets for a day. That taste of how things could be left a lot of people with a strong thirst for what they tasted."

Our society does not teach us to envision or imagine a different world from the one in which we live, one in which we make decisions, work collectively, or have even the capacity to do so. Quite the opposite. The American Dream (and its various international manifestations) has been, and continues to be, crucial in the maintenance of the current political and economic system, including the maintenance of cultural hegemony. Although the language is of imagination, it is a dream in a box, one that discourages vision. It is a dream of and for things, one where each individual or family unit strives to get something or somewhere, most often material. I believe many envision a different society, one where each can be an individual and also part of a greater whole, though the media and dominant culture counter that vision constantly with concepts of the impossible and the portrayal of the individual as completely atomized and self-interested. Due in large part to this cultural and political bombardment, most people have a vision, but it remains abstract or gets denied the space to breathe.

How many times has each person reading this had a conversation with someone about various alternative visions and utopias that closes with the likes of, "Yeah, but people are not like that" or "It can never happen." If we do not respond to these arguments with concrete examples of people who have actualized a vision, and with the reasons why a new society is not only possible but actually present here and now in a germinating stage, people will continue to see vision as a mere dream. As visionaries we have a responsibility to share our various visions with those around us. Sometimes it can feel like pointing out the obvious, but just as we naturally enjoy, and I believe need, to hear a loved one say they love us when we already know they do, we also need to point to all of the marvelous individual and collective acts of solidarity around us, the collective as well as the individual. If the lens provided by the dominant culture is indeed cracked and curved, we need to provide other possible lenses through which to see. If we look at those around us and those that have come before us all over the world, we can see and feel the possibility of another world as well as its creation and construction.

On any given day there are so many acts of solidarity and goodwill around us we sometimes neglect to see them. I am reminded of only the other day when taking the subway in New York City, a woman had a little girl by the hand and a stroller. As she approached a set of stairs more than one stranger asked if she needed help carrying the stroller up the stairs. This is a small example, but I have lived in New York for over a decade and have not once seen a person with a baby carriage have to wait more than a second before someone offered help. This is just something that people do, we help each other when we see the need. We are told that people do not do that, that people are selfish and only help themselves or cause damage. In looking at the events of September 11, the international media was filled with stories of terror, hatred, and people as a whole were portrayed as terrible. What was not discussed was the tremendous amount of human solidarity that occurred. Solidarity came from all over the world, and incredible solidarity existed among people in New York City. On the one-year anniversary of 9/11 the dominant culture was trying to erase our memory of the solidarity. The media reported again and again only on hatred, war, and death. We refuse to be erased. The days and months after 9/11 was one of the most inspiring experiences I have had, especially because of the context of destruction and death. Hundreds of thousands of people volunteered and helped each other all over the city. This help and solidarity ranged from thousands lining up to donate blood to EMTs and other professionals going to the site to see how they could be of use to people reaching out to their neighbors and strangers to see if they needed anything, even just to talk. People organized to provide food and child care in different neighborhoods, visited mosques and individuals who

might face a violent backlash and volunteered time to escort them around the city. People gathered to sing and hold each other. We created space in parks in which to have constant conversations about everything from our feelings to world politics. We created public art, with murals and statues for the dead and for the living. We resisted the hatred and insisted on creating space for vision. We were afraid for so many reasons, we were in such pain, and we came together in a way that was remarkable, but not surprising.

From Reaction to Revolutionary Vision

If we are not imagining and creating, we can get trapped in the historical error of resistance without vision. Resistance is key to change, but it will only be momentary if there is not also a simultaneous discussion of a vision and what we are creating, of getting at the roots of the problem while simultaneously creating the solutions. Revolution is not a thing to achieve or win, but an ongoing and continual transformation of all things. Revolution is now and has no end. "What I Believe is a process rather than a finality," said Emma Goldman, "Finalities are for gods and governments, not for the human intellect." Without vision our struggles are reactive, without struggle our vision is academic. What we do as individuals who want to transform society, as revolutionaries, is to help create space where humanity can flourish and at the same time imagine how much further we can go. We do not just organize a demonstration against something bad, but create a process in which everyone can have a voice. We create something good in and through our resistance, as did the people in Tepoztlán, as do the popular movements in Argentina and South Africa.

We create organizations and collective structures so as to protect ourselves and one another, with parallel structures such as squats, legal and medical collectives, and safe spaces. We demonstrate as well as imagine what the world will be like when we do not have to demonstrate and react. We keep the vision in our collective minds so that as we resist we create. When we stop creating and visioning a movement can die. According to Robin D. G. Kelly in *Freedom Dreams: The Black Radical Imagination*, "too often our standards for evaluating social movements pivot around whether or not they 'succeeded' in realizing their visions rather than on the merits or power of the visions themselves. By such a measure, virtually every radical movement failed because the basic power relations it sought to change remain pretty much intact. And yet it is precisely those alternative visions and dreams that inspire new generations to continue to struggle for change." What Kelly reminds us of, in other words, is that when we are not allowed to be individuals acting as a part of a group, the group cannot exist for long. It can seem complicated

PREFIGURATIVE POLITICS

Giant puppets honor the one-month commemoration of the government murder of Darío and Maxi, two young piquetero unemployed workers movement activists. Buenos Aires, Argentina, July 2002.

or multifocused to try to resist and create simultaneously, but it is only complicated when we forget to envision what we can create and work toward that larger goal. It is a lovely and complicated interconnected process.

The Future in the Present Creation as Seen in Parallel Institutions and Structures

The future is in the present creation, while the present is guided by our future utopia. Decisionmaking constitutes one area where this is seen. Most groups and individuals working together in the global justice movements strive toward various forms of consensus. Consensus is usually defined as a group attempt to reach a decision by working toward a synthesis of ideas, rather than by virtue of the strongest and most vocal opinion winning an argument. For consensus to be effective, all those participating must be actively involved in the discussion process. The goal is the autonomy of the individual while working collectively. How we interact and make decisions is key to moving forward together to maintain space for all people—while making decisions. While this may sound simple or obvious, participating with others when we cannot maintain a sense of self or we feel our ideas subjugated to the larger whole is not only disempowering, but prevents the creation of a society where all can be equal in our difference.

PREFIGURATIVE POLITICS

Argentina Indymedia

This goal of consensus in decisionmaking can also be used by larger bodies and networks. It can and has been used by groups internally and then in larger discussions and meetings where each smaller group has a voice through a representative of sorts and these voices speak to each other to again make decisions for all of the groups. The way this has worked most effectively in the global justice movements is through the spokes-council model. This is a model of decisionmaking originated in the United States with Native Americans and has been used by many other anti-authoritarian groups from the Spanish anarchists in the 1930s to certain groups in Paris in May 1968. A spokes-council generally looks like the spokes of a wheel, thus the name, where the center circle is comprised of the voices from each group's "spokespeople." As proposals and ideas arise, the group talks among itself and empowers the spokesperson to speak on the various issues. In this way each person has a voice in their group and each group a relationship to the others. In many of the convergences against international financial institutions, spokescouncils were held in the evenings preceding the activities to discuss and decide a number of strategic and tactical issues, representing at various times and in various cities anywhere from a few hundred to more than a thousand. Recently Independent Media Centers around the globe have had international virtual spokescouncils; the concept is the same as those that take place in physical locations, only each spokesperson sits at a computer monitor and the group sits around them, and rather than speaking they type. Although not all the decisions made in groups and in spokescouncils are, in and of themselves, visionary or revolutionary, the process is. Participating in decisions that will affect us directly in a way that is directly democratic is something we strive for, yet do not attain in our daily lives. In this way the structure and process is not only a reflection of what we desire, it is the living reality of our future desire. It is the future vision realized in the present.

In many respects the easiest way to conceptualize a theory or visualize a possibility is to see it in physical space. In real space and time, a theory or vision gets to play itself out. In thinking of creating a democratically run community garden, for example, one has to look at physical space, discuss and agree with others how best to use that space, what needs are involved, how things are to be prioritized, how decisions are made, by whom, and so on. It is in our collectively run spaces, our parallel institutions, that we can see tangible results of our theoretical visioning. Many in the directly democratic social movements in Argentina also see a new politic developed spatially. As Martin K., of the neighborhood assembly Colegiales explains, "The assembly is on the street corner and in the street. How does the new politics show itself, it does so with territory, with time and space. It materializes itself here in space, not with ideology, but with sensibility. It was as if all of us were balls rolling and floating at different velocities

and the assembly helped create a space for all of us, to slow down the various velocities and make a space for all. That is the new politics and the new territory."

In our many movements we function in a directly democratic manner. In working with and developing these institutions we become actors in our lives, making decisions over things that will directly affect us and others. Some examples of such institutions within the global justice movements are the Independent Media Centers, legal collectives, medical collectives, convergence spaces, and free kitchens, to name a few.

Many of these institutions were created out of needs in the global justice movements. The first Independent Media Center was formed in Seattle in 1999 for the anti-WTO protests; the need was the fact that the mainstream media do not cover news from the perspective of the people actually making history. The first global justice legal collective was formed to help prepare activists for potential legal repression as well as to facilitate discussions for a collective legal strategy that would help activists protect each other using forms of solidarity. Since Seattle, dozens of IMCs have been organized around the world through international cooperation as well as over a dozen legal and medical collectives in North America. These parallel institutions of mutual aid fill a need as well as set an example of a way of organizing institutions that is nonhierarchical and directly democratic. There is no coercion in the form of organizing or in the goals. All involved are volunteers and the reward in exchange for one's labor lies in being a part of community and filling a need; the value is the importance of the act recognized by the individual and the collective.

PREFIGURATIVE POLITICS

Means and Ends

The concept of means and ends are not only useful to discuss the global justice movement and the struggles in Argentina or South Africa, but are a part of our everyday interactions everywhere. One cannot compartmentalize struggle or creation. Creation and vision take place all over, from our community groups to the local school board to our work-place and school. Our means are our ends all the time and everywhere, the future is always the present in creation.

One personal example of a struggle for means and ends took place in a university in which I used to study, the New School. It is not on the level of assemblies in Argentina, direct action in South Africa, or the shutdown of the WTO, but is equally important in that it is a day-to-day struggle to make the means the ends of the struggle.

The U.S. labor movement in past decades has not been motivated by a vision of what is possible. Instead, the leadership has defined the movement in terms of past, and largely reactive practice. There are two exceptions to this that I want to point to; one is the graduate student organizing at Yale University, and the other is the organizing at the New School University. Both of these groups see the means of organizing as a part of what they are attempting to create. Both position formal legal recognition of the union as a secondary focus, the primary focus being the creation of a directly democratic and participatory organization able, as such, to secure such recognition. Both groups intend to create a new type of unionism.

Yale graduate students began organizing a union in the early 1990s. They have sought "voluntary" recognition from the university. What this means, essentially, is that the union forces the hand of the university administration through moral, economic, and political means. The goal has been to create a union, the vision is to have as much direct participation as possible, which is also the definition of the goal. In this case the vision and process cannot be separated. The result has been an amazing organizing process in which, although the union is not yet formally recognized, material gains have been won equal to and often more substantial than other universities with graduate student unions.

Union members speak of the organizing process as the attempt to create a constant conversation. An atmosphere exists in which students feel that the university is theirs, that the decisions they make have import, that they have more of an active role in their own lives and in one of the institutions that exercises control over them. This is key to any organizing, but exceptional considering the hierarchical structures that normally comprise union leaderships and organizations. The goal and means of creating a union through constant conversation is inspiring and something from which other movements can learn.

In the spring of 2002 graduate students at the New School University, previously the New School for Social Research, began the process of unionizing. Central to the organizing was and continues to be a vision of the way the institution could be, as well as its relationships within the university. Bread-and-butter issues are clearly important but as Erin Koch, a graduate student in anthropology stated, "The union is what we are creating day to day with our relationships, it is not an end goal that is achieved by a vote, but a process." Not only is a future vision key to the organizing efforts, but the way in which the struggle occurs is also central. The group strives for as much participation as possible, designing itself in a horizontal, nonhierarchical manner. This is not always easy and is

olla popular - julio 2000   Flor, MTD Anibal Veron

Florencia Vespignani

different from the organizational structure of most unions, but the group is dedicated to resisting old and bureaucratic ways of organizing.

Unfortunately, two national unions are currently attempting to take leadership of this unionizing process. Those who have been a part of creating the visionary organizations are resisting this attempt, and continue to organize a union that is made up of those who want to see a directly democratic organization based on, and rooted in, the people organizing and not the staff of these bureaucratic institutions. Those organizing hope to help to set an example for others who wish to organize themselves. The example they hope to set is that all organizing should begin with the vision of what they want first, and a process that reflects that vision. For these reasons, they believe that the best union is one organized with this vision from the inside, and not by national bureaucratic institutions that, by definition, cannot have such a local vision, much less directly democratic structures. Regardless of the outcome, the New School has placed itself on the map for visionary organizing and for resisting the money and bureaucracy of big labor. Although the future is not yet written, the groups are inspiring in their methods and vision of a different union.

It is not just about "winning" a struggle, but the process, which no matter how or where they take place forever transform people's ways of seeing

themselves and their relationship to others. Paula, an activist in Argentina, reflected on the experiences of the assemblies in this way. "The experiences have produced profound transformations in people, in the subjectivity of people, in people feeling themselves as actors for the first time in their lives. In the assemblies people from all different backgrounds, from different ages and social situations have come together to discuss and listen to each other, each person's opinion and voice not being valued as more or less than any others, this is extremely important, especially considering how the political parties work, which is the opposite. What is being constructed is a new way to do politics. People are the protagonists, the subjects. If the assemblies disappeared tomorrow, it would not be something so serious because something fundamental has changed in people. People will never again be passive in their lives."

Many other examples exist of people envisioning a future possibility and realizing the vision in the present practice, although these visions are not always articulated. One of the goals of this essay is to place conscious visioning at the center of all of our activity so as to be able to realize that vision in our everyday activity. As Subcomandante Marcos of the Zapatistas put it, "In sum, we are an army of dreamers, and therefore invincible. How can we fail to win, with this imagination overturning everything. Or rather, we do not deserve to lose."

PREFIGURATIVE POLITICS

Reclaim The Cities:
From Protest to Popular Power

By Cindy Milstein

Cindy Milstein writes for various antiauthoritarian periodicals. She designed and wrote for the booklet Bringing Democracy Home, *and is a contributor to* Confronting Capitalism *and* Anti-Capitalism: A Field Guide to the Global Justice Movement. *She is also on the board and a faculty member at the Institute for Social Ecology in Vermont, a board member of the Institute for Anarchist Studies, and coorganizer of the Renewing the Anarchist Tradition conference. In addition to studying and teaching political theory, she has long been active in community organizing, anarchist projects, and social movements.*

"Direct action gets the goods," proclaimed the Industrial Workers of the World nearly a century ago. And in the relatively short time since Seattle, this has certainly proven to be the case. Indeed, "the goods" reaped by the direct action movement here in North America have included creating doubt as to the scope and nature of globalization, shedding light on the nearly unknown workings of international trade and finance bodies, and making anarchism and anticapitalism almost household words. As if that

image top: Florencia Vespignani

weren't enough, we find ourselves on the streets of twenty-first-century metropolises demonstrating our power to resist in a way that models the good society we envision: a truly democratic one.

But is this really what democracy looks like?

The impulse to "reclaim the streets" is an understandable one. When industrial capitalism first started to emerge in the early nineteenth century, its machinations were relatively visible. Take, for instance, the enclosures. Pasturelands that had been used in common for centuries to provide villages with their very sustenance were systematically fenced off in order to graze sheep, whose wool was needed for the burgeoning textile industry. Communal life was briskly thrust aside in favor of privatization, forcing people into harsh factories and crowded cities.

Advanced capitalism, as it pushes past the fetters of even nation-states in its insatiable quest for growth, encloses life in a much more expansive yet generally invisible way: fences are replaced by consumer culture. We are raised in an almost totally commodified world where nothing comes for free, even futile attempts to remove oneself from the market economy. This commodification seeps into not only what we eat, wear, or do for fun but also into our language, relationships, and even our very biology and minds. We have lost not only our communities and public spaces but control over our own lives; we have lost the ability to define ourselves outside capitalism's grip, and thus genuine meaning itself begins to dissolve.

"Whose Streets? Our Streets!" then, is a legitimate emotional response to the feeling that even the most minimal of public, noncommodified spheres has been taken from us. Yet in the end, it is simply a frantic cry from our cage. We have become so confined, so thoroughly damaged, by capitalism as well as state control that crumbs appear to make a nourishing meal.

Temporarily closing off the streets during direct actions does provide momentary spaces in which to practice democratic process, and even offers a sense of empowerment, but such events leave power for power's sake, like the very pavement beneath our feet, unchanged. Only when the serial protest mode is escalated into a struggle for popular or horizontal power can we create cracks in the figurative concrete, thereby opening up ways to challenge capitalism, nation-states, and other systems of domination.

This is not to denigrate the direct action movement in the United States and elsewhere; just the opposite. Besides a long overdue and necessary critique of numerous institutions of command and obedience, the movement is quietly yet crucially supplying the outlines of a freer society. This prefigurative politics is, in fact, the very strength and vision of today's direct action, where the means themselves are understood to also be the ends. We're not putting off the good society until some distant future but attempting to carve out room for it in the here and now, however tentative and contorted under the given social order. In turn, this consistency of means and ends implies an ethical approach to politics. How we act now is how we want others to begin to act, too. We try to model a notion of goodness even as we fight for it.

This can implicitly be seen in the affinity group and spokescouncil structures for decisionmaking at direct actions. Both supply much needed spaces in which to school ourselves in direct democracy. Here, in the best of cases, we can proactively set the agenda, carefully deliberate together over questions, and come to decisions that strive to take everyone's needs and desires into account. Substantive discussion replaces checking boxes on a ballot; face-to-face participation replaces handing over our lives to so-called representatives; nuanced and reasoned solutions replace lesser-of-two- (or three-) evils thinking. The democratic process utilized during demonstrations decentralizes power even as it offers tangible solidarity; for example, affinity groups afford greater and more diverse numbers of people a real share in decisionmaking, while spokes-councils allow for intricate coordination—even on a global level. This is, as 1960s' activists put it, the power to create rather than destroy.

The beauty of this new movement, it could be said, is that it strives to take its own ideals to heart. In doing so, it has perhaps unwittingly created the demand for such directly democratic practices on a permanent basis. Yet the haunting question underlying episodic "street democracy" remains unaddressed: How can everyone come together to make decisions that affect society as a whole in participatory, mutualistic, and ethical ways? In other words, how can each and every one of us—not just a counterculture or this protest movement—really transform and ultimately control our lives and that of our communities?

This is, in essence, a question of power—who has it, how it is used, and to what ends. To varying degrees, we all know the answer in relation to current institutions and systems. We can generally explain what we are against. That is exactly why we are protesting, whether it is against capitalism and/or nation-states, or globalization in whole or part. What we have largely failed to articulate, however, is any sort of response in relation to liberatory institutions and systems. We often can't express, especially in any coherent and utopian manner, what we are for. Even as we prefigure a way of making power horizontal, equitable, and hence,

RECLAIM THE CITIES

hopefully an essential part of a free society, we ignore the reconstructive vision that a directly democratic process holds up right in front of our noses.

For all intents and purposes, our movement remains trapped. On the one hand, it reveals and confronts domination and exploitation. The political pressure exerted by such widespread agitation may even be able to influence current power structures to amend some of the worst excesses of their ways; the powers that be have to listen, and respond to some extent, when the voices become too numerous and too loud. Nevertheless, most people are still shut out of the decisionmaking process itself, and consequently, have little tangible power over their lives at all. Without this ability to self-govern, street actions translate into nothing more than a countercultural version of interest group lobbying, albeit far more radical than most and generally unpaid.

What the movement forgets is the promise implicit in its own structure: that power not only needs to be contested; it must also be constituted anew in liberatory and egalitarian forms. This entails taking the movement's directly democratic process seriously—not simply as a tactic to organize protests but as the very way we organize society, specifically the political realm. The issue then becomes: How do we begin to shift the strategy, structure, and values of our movement to the most grassroots level of public policymaking?

The most fundamental level of decisionmaking in a demonstration is the affinity group. Here, we come together as friends or because of a common identity, or a combination of the two. We share something in particular; indeed, this common identity is often reflected in the name we choose for our groups. We may not always agree with each other, but there is a fair amount of homogeneity precisely because we've consciously chosen to come together for a specific reason—most often having little to do with mere geography. This sense of a shared identity allows for the smooth functioning of a consensus decisionmaking process, since we start from a place of commonality. In an affinity group, almost by definition, our unity needs to take precedence over our diversity, or our supposed affinity breaks down altogether.

Compare this to what could be the most fundamental level of decision-making in a society: a neighborhood or town. Now, geography plays a much larger role. For historic, economic, cultural, religious, and other reasons, we may find ourselves living side by side with a wide range of individuals and their various identities. Most of these people are not our friends per se. Still, the very diversity we encounter is the life of a vibrant city. The accidents and/or personal decisions that have brought us together often

Andrew Stern / www.andrewstern.net

Argentines who had their money stolen by banks kick at their metal-protected windows.

create a fair amount of heterogeneity precisely because we haven't all chosen to come together for a specific reason. In this context, where we start from a place of difference, decisionmaking mechanisms need to be much more capable of allowing for dissent; that is, diversity needs to be clearly retained within any notions of unity. As such, majoritarian decisionmaking processes begin to make more sense.

Then, too, there is the question of scale. It is hard to imagine being friends with hundreds, or even thousands, of people, nor maintaining a single-issue identity with that many individuals; but we can share a feeling of community and a striving toward some common good that allows each of us to flourish. In turn, when greater numbers of people come together on a face-to-face basis to reshape their neighborhoods and towns, the issues as well as the viewpoints will multiply, and alliances will no doubt change depending on the specific topic under discussion. Thus the need for a place where we can meet as human beings at the most face-to-face level— that is, an assembly of active citizens—to share our many identities and interests in hopes of balancing both the individual and community in all we do.

Trust and accountability also function differently at the affinity group versus civic level. We generally reveal more of ourselves to friends; and such unwritten bonds of love and affection hold us more closely together, or at least give us added impetus to work things out. Underlying this is a

higher-than-average degree of trust, which serves to make us accountable to each other. On a communitywide level, the reverse is more often true: Accountability allows us to trust each other. Hopefully, we share bonds of solidarity and respect; yet since we can't know each other well, such bonds only make sense if we first determine them together, and then record them, write them down, for all to refer back to in the future, and even revisit if need be. Accountable, democratic structures of our own making, in short, provide the foundation for trust, since the power to decide is both transparent and ever amenable to scrutiny.

There are also issues of time and space. Affinity groups, in the scheme of things, are generally temporary configurations—they may last a few months, or a few years, but often not much longer. Once the particular reasons why we've come together have less of an immediate imperative, or as our friendships falter, such groups often fall by the wayside. And even during a group's life span, in the interim between direct actions, there is frequently no fixed place or face to decisionmaking, nor any regularity, nor much of a record of who decided what and how. Moreover, affinity groups are not open to everyone but only those who share a particular identity or attachment. As such, although an affinity group can certainly choose to shut down a street, there is ultimately something slightly authoritarian in small groups taking matters into their own hands, no matter what their political persuasion.

Deciding what to do with streets in general—say, how to organize transportation, encourage street life, provide green space, and so on—should be a matter open to everyone interested if it is to be truly participatory and nonhierarchical. This implies ongoing and open institutions of direct democracy, for everything from decisionmaking to conflict resolution. We need to be able to know when and where citizen assemblies are meeting; we need to meet regularly and make use of nonarbitrary procedures; we need to keep track of what decisions have been made. But more important, if we so choose, we all need to have access to the power to discuss, deliberate, and make decisions about matters that affect our communities and beyond.

Indeed, many decisions have a much wider impact than on just one city; transforming streets, for example, would probably entail coordination on a regional, continental, or even global level. Radicals have long understood such mutualistic self-reliance as a "commune of communes," or confederation. The spokescouncil model used during direct actions hints at such an alternative view of globalization. During a spokescouncil meeting, mandated delegates from our affinity groups gather for the

purpose of coordination, the sharing of resources and skills, the building of solidarity, and so forth, always returning to the grassroots level as the ultimate arbiter. If popular assemblies were our basic unit of decision-making, confederations of communities could serve as a way to both transcend parochialism and create interdependence where desirable. For instance, rather than global capitalism and international regulatory bodies, where trade is top-down and profit-oriented, confederations could coordinate distribution between regions in ecological and humane ways, while allowing policy in regard to production, say, to remain at the grassroots.

This more expansive understanding of a prefigurative politics would necessarily involve creating institutions that could potentially replace capitalism and nation-states. Such directly democratic institutions are compatible with, and could certainly grow out of, the ones we use during demonstrations, but they very likely won't be mirror images once we reach the level of society. This does not mean abandoning the principles and ideals undergirding the movement (such as freedom, cooperation, decentralism, solidarity, diversity, face-to-face participation, and the like); it merely means recognizing the limits of direct democracy as it is practiced in the context of an anticapitalist convergence.

The Zapatistas, along with other revolutionaries before them, have already shown that declarations of "democracy, freedom, justice" resonate. But they have proved as well that municipalities can strive to become autonomous from statecraft and capital, to put human and ecological concerns first, while retaining regional and global links of solidarity and mutual aid. Such is one form of dual power emanating from an antiauthoritarian vision of social transformation. There are now hints of others, still in their infancy: the European Social Consulta (ESC) and the neighborhood assemblies in Argentina. While the ESC is being intentionally organized by those who already consider themselves radical and the assemblies have been organically established by many who have never seen themselves as political before, both imply that all are capable of self-legislating, self-managing, and self-adjudicating the good society.

The ESC is doing this explicitly by attempting to create a common meeting space that connects local and regional groups and social movements in a "horizontal and decentralized fashion." As the ESC's proposed hallmarks insist, this requires "a call for critical reflection, debate, direct action and the development of alternatives to the current system as tools for social transformation." It entails the rejection of capitalism as well as "all forms and systems of domination and discrimination." Significantly, both in its

RECLAIM THE CITIES

en el gallinero - noviembre 2000   Flor, MTD Anibal Veron

Florencia Vespignani

RECLAIM THE CITIES

internal structure and how it hopes to engage society at large, the ESC affirms "direct and participatory democracy and the capacity of all human beings to create the world in which they want to live and to actively participate in the decisions that most affect them." Still in the formative stage, the ESC may fail to live up to its own aspirations, much less reach out beyond a small circle of radicals. In the meantime, though, it is an inspiring example of a prefigurative effort aimed at forging another possible world. For instance, one ESC proposal is to bring issues raised at local assemblies together at a European-level social consulta during the European elections of 2004, thereby dramatically contrasting direct with quasi-representative democracy and perhaps unleashing dual power institutions in the process.

Argentina's neighborhood assembly movement is already asserting itself as such. A spiraling sense of desperation and powerless have combined to force people not only out onto the streets to loudly demonstrate but into an empowering dialogue with their neighbors about what to do next—on

— HOW TO CHANGE THINGS —

the local, national, and global levels. Since late December 2001, some fifty neighborhoods in Buenos Aires have been holding weekly meetings and sending delegates every Sunday to an interneighborhood general coordinating gathering. The anarchist Argentine Libertarian Federation Local Council writes that the assemblies have been "formed by the unemployed, the underemployed, and people marginalized and excluded from capitalist society: including professionals, workers, small retailers, artists, craftspeople, all of them also neighbors." As the Libertarian Federation notes, "The meetings are open and anyone who wishes can participate," and common to all assemblies is the "non-delegation of power, self-management, [and a] horizontal structure." It is too early to say whether these assemblies will function as participatory paths to a reformed version of the same old governmental structures or supply Argentineans with a glimpse of their own ability to make public policy together,. But for the moment, the Libertarian Federation reports that "the fear in our society has turned into courage. . . . There is reason to hope that all Argentineans now know for certain who has been blocking our freedoms."

At worst, such fragile experiments will serve as reminders to future generations that directly democratic ways of making social, economic, political, and cultural decisions are a tangible alternative. At best, they will widen into dual powers that can contest and perhaps even replace not only old but also new forms of domination.

Any vision of a free society, if it is to be truly democratic, must of course be worked out by all of us—first in this movement, and later, in our communities and confederations. Even so, we will probably discover that newly defined understandings of citizenship are needed in place of affinity groups; majoritarian methods of decisionmaking that strive to retain diversity are preferable to simple consensus-seeking models; written compacts articulating rights and duties are crucial to fill out the unspoken culture of protests; and institutionalized spaces for policymaking are key to guaranteeing that our freedom to make decisions doesn't disappear with a line of riot police.

It is time to push beyond the oppositional character of our movement by infusing it with a reconstructive vision. That means beginning, right now, to translate our movement structure into institutions that embody the good society; in short, cultivating direct democracy in the places we call home. This will involve the harder work of reinvigorating or initiating civic gatherings, town meetings, neighborhood assemblies, citizen mediation boards, any and all forums where we can come together to decide our lives, even if only in extralegal institutions at first. Then, too, it will mean

RECLAIM THE CITIES

reclaiming globalization, not as a new phase of capitalism but as its replacement by confederated, directly democratic communities coordinated for mutual benefit.

It is time to move from protest to politics, from shutting down streets to opening up public space, from demanding scraps from those few in power to holding power firmly in all our hands. Ultimately, this means moving beyond the question of "Whose Streets?" We should ask instead "Whose Cities?" Then and only then will we be able to remake them as our own.

Organizing Communities: Building Neighborhood Movements for Radical Social Change

By Tom Knoche

Tom's experience with community organizing spans a twenty-seven-year period including four years in Baltimore, Maryland, and over twenty in Camden, New Jersey. He has primarily worked with very low-income people on a wide range of issues.

This essay is about community organizing from an anarchist perspective. In a nutshell, it is about how people can work together where they live to decentralize power, giving citizens and their organizations more control over their quality of life. It is about making politics and economics much more democratic. It is about sharing power; it is not about winning power over others. It is about transforming communities so they provide fuller and richer life individually and collectively (see Freire, 1968, 13). It acknowledges that no revolution will be meaningful unless many Americans are engaged in the process, and that we challenge traditional values that promote profit, self-interest, and hierarchical organization. The building blocks of any revolutionary movement—regional, national, or international—will be local organizations that embrace these ideals.

photo top: David Hanks

Many people probably cringe at the notion of any person or group being "organized" and believe that the very idea is manipulative. They can point to countless community organization leaders who ended up on government payrolls. They can't see how winning traffic lights and playgrounds does any more than help the system appear pluralistic and effective. Such skepticism makes sense. Community organizing has always been practiced in many different ways to accomplish many different things. In reviewing the history of neighborhood organizing, Robert Fisher summed it up this way:

> While neighborhood organizing is a political act, it is neither inherently reactionary, conservative, liberal or radical, nor is it inherently democratic and inclusive or authoritarian and parochial. It is above all a political method, an approach used by various segments of the population to achieve specific goals, serve certain interests, and advance clear or ill-defined political perspectives. (Fisher, 1984; 158).

If we look at some of the progressive strains of community organizing theory, we still face a lot of confusion about what it is and how it is used. Saul Alinsky, a key figure in the development of community organizing as we know it today, wrote:

> We are concerned about how to create mass organizations to seize power and give it to the people; to realize the democratic dream of equality, justice, peace, cooperation, equal and full opportunities for education, full and useful employment, health and the creation of those circumstances in which man can have the chance to live by the values that give meaning to life. We are talking about a mass power organization that will change the world. . . . (Alinsky, 1971; 3)

The Midwest Academy, a training institute for community organizers founded by some ex–civil rights and SDS leaders, asserts that:

> More and more people are finding that what is needed is a permanent, professionally staffed community membership organization which can not only win real improvements for its members, but which can actually alter the relations of power at the city and state level. . . . These groups [citizen groups] are keeping government open to the people and are keeping our democratic rights intact. (Max, 1977; 2)

A senior member of ACORN (Association of Communities Organized for Reform Now), a national association of mostly urban community

organizations, describes the goal of organizing as strengthening people's collective capacities to bring about social change (Staples, 1984; 1). ACORN organized local communities, then employed its constituency at the national level, attempting to move the Democratic Party to the left. Finally, a participant in a workshop on community organizing I conducted many years ago characterized community organizing as "manipulating people to do trivial things."

In this essay I will focus on how community organizing can be useful in advancing an anarchist vision of social change. Community organizations that build on an anarchist vision of social change are different from other community organizations because of the purposes they have, the criteria they have for success, the issues they work on, the way they operate, and the tactics they use.

The term "community organizing," as used in this essay, refers to social change efforts which are based in local geographically defined areas where people live. This is the key distinction between community organizing and other forms of organizing for social change that may be based in workplaces or universities, involving people where they work or study instead of where they live. Some issue-oriented organizations are considered community organizations if their constituency is local.

Local organizations in communities, workplaces, and schools are the building blocks of any radical transformation of our society. It is at the local level that people build day-to-day relationships. It is most likely how they will be politicized for the first time, working to improve conditions where they live, work, or study. Most people do not change their values and beliefs through some intellectual process. They do so as a result of interaction and shared experiences with people they care about and respect.

Goals of Anarchist Organizing

Anarchist community organizing must be dedicated to changing what we can in the immediate and to undoing the socialization process that has depoliticized so many of us. We can also use it to build an infrastructure that can respond and make greater advances when political and economic systems are in crisis and therefore vulnerable to change. The following goals illustrate this concept:

1. *Helping people experiment with decentralized, collective, and cooperative forms of organization.*

ORGANIZING COMMUNITIES

Youth of Laotian Organizing Project march against Chevron Texaco's toxic Richmond refinery on international day of action against the WTO. 2001

We have to build our American model of social change out of our own experience; we can't borrow revolutionary theory in total from that developed in another historical and/or cultural context. Community organizations can help people log that experience and analyze it. Because of our culture's grounding in defense of personal liberty and democracy, social change engineered by a vanguard or administered by a strong central state will not work here.

David Bouchier is on the right track when he says, "For citizen radicals, evolution is better than revolution because evolution works" (Bouchier, 1987; 139). We must learn new values and practice cooperation rather than competition. Community organizations can provide a vehicle for this "retooling." "This means that a cultural revolution, a revolution of ideas and values and understandings, is the essential prelude to any radical change in the power arrangement of modern society. The purpose of radical citizenship is to take the initiative in this process" (Bouchier, 1987, 148).

Any kind of alternative institution (see Ehrlich et al., 1979, 346) including cooperatives, worker-managed businesses, and so on, that offers a chance to learn and practice community control and self-management is important. We must experience together how institutions can be different and better. These alternative institutions should be nonprofit, controlled

David Hanks

and staffed by residents of the community they serve, and supported by the people who benefit from their existence. Most charities and social service agencies do not qualify as alternative institutions because they are staffed and controlled by people who usually are not part of the community they serve; they therefore foster dependence.

The recent proliferation of community land trusts in this country is an exciting example of community-based, cooperative, and decentralized organizations. Through these organizations people are taking land and housing off the private market and putting them into their collective control.

I was a board member of North Camden Land Trust (NCLT) in Camden, New Jersey, from its inception in 1984 until the early 1990s. The land trust now controls over 100 properties. All of the families who live in NCLT housing are of low income. All were previously tenants; they now collectively make decisions about the housing and property that is part of NCLT. The development of the land trust embodies many of the elements described in this essay—cooperative organization, skill development, collective decisionmaking, etc.—that constitute community organizing grounded in a social anarchist vision for society.

2. Increasing the control that people have over actions that affect them, and increasing local self-reliance.

This involves taking some measure of control away from large institutions like government, corporations, and social service conglomerates and giving it to the people most affected by their actions. David Bouchier describes this function as attaining "postive freedoms." Positive freedoms are rights of self-government that are not dependent on or limited by higher powers (Bouchier, 1987, 9).

In the neighborhood where I live and work, after about ten years of community organizing, residents started to demand control over land use decisions. They stopped the state and local governments' plan to build a second state prison on the waterfront in their neighborhood. Instead of stopping there, the residents, through a series of block meetings and a neighborhood coalition they established, developed a "Peoples' Plan" for that waterfront site. Between 1990 and 1993, people worked together to create a land use and development plan for the entire neighborhood (*The North Camden Plan*, 1993). Control of land use has traditionally rested with local government (and state and federal government to a much more limited extent), guided by professional planners and consultants. Neighborhood residents should control land use in their neighborhood, since they are the ones most directly affected by it.

ORGANIZING COMMUNITIES

3. *Building a counterculture that uses all forms of communication to resist illegitimate authority, racism, sexism, homophobia, and capitalism. In low-income neighborhoods, it is also important that this counterculture become an alternative to the dominant culture that has resulted from welfare and drugs.*

Every movement must use the media to advance its ideas and values. Educational events, film, community-based newspapers, and so forth are all important. The local community advocacy organization in North Camden has done a good job of combining fund-raising with the development of counterculture. They have sponsored alternative theater that has explored the issues of battered women, homelessness, and sexism. After each play, the theater group conducted an open discussion with the audience about these issues. These were powerful experiences for those who attended.

The question of confronting the dominant culture in very low-income neighborhoods is one of the greatest challenges facing community organizations. Many families have experienced welfare dependence for four generations. Now they are faced with extreme pressure to get off public assistance, facing a job market that does not pay wages and benefits adequate to support a family. Others have become involved in drug traffic as a response to economic hardship. The welfare system and illegal drug traffic have radically altered many peoples' value systems and lifestyles in a negative way. People worry about survival, and believe they are entitled to anything they can obtain in order to survive, regardless of the effect on others. Fear and grief are part of everyone's life. Many families have lost loved ones either to violence or the criminal justice system. These realities have not fostered a cooperative spirit. The response of low-income people to welfare and poverty is not irrational, but it is a serious obstacle to functioning in a system of decentralized, cooperative work and services.

One experience in this regard is relevant. A soup kitchen called Leavenhouse has operated in Camden for twenty years. During the first nine years of its existence, it was open to anyone. In 1990, the soup kitchen changed into a feeding cooperative on weekdays, with guests having to either volunteer a few hours in the kitchen or at two homeless day centers, or purchase a ticket for $5, good for the entire month. Daily average attendance dropped from 200 to about 30. The idea of cooperating to provide some of the resources necessary to sustain the service was outside the value system of many people who previously used the kitchen. They perceived the meals at Leavenhouse as a "gimme."

By 2002, the co-op had grown to about sixty people. The people who join each month generally appreciate the more tranquil eating environment and feel good about their role in it. The members now participate in decisions about the operation of the co-op. Friendships and information sharing (primarily about jobs) have been facilitated. Fewer people are being served, but more meaningful relationships and political objectives are now being realized.

4. *Strengthening the "social fabric" of neighborhood units—that network of informal associations, support services, and contacts that enables people to survive and hold on to their sanity in spite of, rather than because of, the influence of government and social service bureaucracies in their lives.*

John McKnight (1987) has done a good job of exposing the failure of traditional social service agencies and government in meeting people's needs for a support structure. They operate instead to control people. Informal associations ("community of associations"), on the other hand, operate on the basis of consent. They allow for creative solutions, quick response, interpersonal caring, and foster a broad base of participation.

A good example of fulfilling this purpose is the bartering network that some community organizations have developed. The organization simply prints a listing of people and services they need along with a parallel list of people and services they are willing to offer. This strengthens intra-neighborhood communication. In poor neighborhoods, this is especially effective because it allows people to get things done without money, and to get a return on their work that is not taxable.

Criteria for Success

Many community organizations measure success by "winning." The tangible result is all that matters. In fact, many organizations evaluate the issues they take on by whether or not they are "winnable." The real significance of what is won and how it is won are of less concern.

For organizations that embrace an anarchist vision, the process and the intangible results are at least as important as any tangible results. Increasing any one organization's size and influence is not a priority concern; stimulating many decentralized, politically active groups is. The success of community organizing can be measured by the extent to which the following mandates are realized:

ORGANIZING COMMUNITIES

1. People learn skills needed to analyze issues and confront those who exert control over their lives.

2. People learn to interact, make decisions, and get things done collectively—rotating tasks, sharing skills, confronting racism, sexism, homophobia, and hierarchy.

3. Community residents realize some direct benefit or some resolution of problems they personally face through the organizing work.

4. Existing institutions change their priorities or way of doing things so that the authority of government, corporations, and large institutions is replaced by extensions of decentralized, grassroots authority.

5. Community residents feel stronger and better about themselves because of their participation in the collective effort.

Picking Issues

Much of the literature about community organizing suggests that issues should be selected that are: 1) winnable; 2) involve advocacy, not service; and 3) build the organization's constituency, power, and resources. "Good issue campaigns should have the twin goals of winning a victory and producing organizational mileage while doing so" (Staples, 1984; 53).

These guidelines have always bothered me, and my experience suggests that they are off the mark. Issues should be picked primarily because the organization's members believe they are important, and because they are consistent with one or more of the purposes listed above. Let me offer a few guidelines that are a bit different:

1. Service and advocacy work must go hand-in-hand, especially in very needy communities.

People get involved with groups because they present an opportunity for them to gain something they want. It may be tangible or intangible, but the motivation to get involved comes with an expectation of relatively short-term gratification. The job of community organizations is to facilitate a process where groups of people with similar needs or problems work together for the benefit of all. Through this process, people learn: 1) to work cooperatively; and 2) that their informal association can usually solve problems more effectively and quickly than large bureaucracies and established institutions.

I will offer an example to illustrate this point. When Concerned Citizens of North Camden (CCNC) organized a squatter campaign in 1981, the folks who squatted and took all of the risks did so because they wanted a house and because they believed squatting was the best way to get one. Each one of the original 13 squatter families benefited because they eventually got title to their house. The advocacy purpose was served because a program resulted that allowed 150 other families to get a house and some funds to fix it up over the subsequent five years. And because CCNC stayed involved with each family and facilitated a support network with them over many years, most of the houses are still occupied by low-income families. The government bureaucracy tried to undermine this program on numerous occasions, but without success. Participants willingly rallied in each crisis because they benefited in a way they valued deeply. The squatter movement allowed them to win something that they knew they would never realistically be able to win through any traditional home-ownership programs. The squatters were poor, most had no credit histories, and most were Hispanic. But official discredit, for whatever reasons, was meaningless because people knew the effort had worked for them. The city reluctantly sanctioned the squatting initiative because of the strength and persistence of the movement.

2. *Issues that pit one segment of the community against another—for example, issues that favor homeowners over renters, blacks over Puerto Ricans, and so on—should be avoided.*

Most issues can be addressed in ways that unify neighborhood residents rather than divide them.

3. *Some issues address the distribution of power in critical areas more than others.*

Community organizing usually covers a broad range of issues—from better sanitation to affordable housing to bank lending practices. Some of these issues clearly are about gaining control over basic needs where lack of control has had profound negative effects. Organizing alternative institutions in these areas is especially important. For example, community land trusts take housing off the private market and give control over land and affordable housing. Credit unions make sure that a community's assets stay in the community. Control over some local media (neighborhood radio, newspapers, etc.) gives people information they wouldn't get elsewhere. Alternative institutions that control energy will

ORGANIZING COMMUNITIES

become more and more important. Decentralized control over solar and wind power, and block-level cogeneration, for example, will allow people to control an area of their lives where escalating costs may be devastating for most families.

Winning more local grassroots control over land, capital, energy, food supply, health care, the media, education, and housing is some of the most important—and revolutionary—work that community organizations can do.

4. An informal involvement in broad political issues should be maintained on a consistent basis.

Although I believe the decentralized associations at the local level (neighborhood, school, workplace, or citywide) are the foundation of any social change movement, people must also connect in some way with broader social change issues. Social change cannot just happen in isolated places; we must build a large and diverse movement.

We need to integrate actions against militarism, globalization, nuclear power, economic sanctions, and so on, with action on local issues. They often can and should be tied together. This requires getting people to regional and national political events from time to time, and supporting local activities that help people to connect with these broader issues.

Two issues that I recently worked on illustrate this point. Three years ago, various organizations in Camden came together to advocate living wage legislation. Welfare reform was forcing people to take jobs that could not support their family. Expanding the number of living-wage jobs was a reasonable response. Taking on that issue led to much broader discussions and political education about privatization, changes in the local economy as a result of corporate globalization and reduced trade barriers, and the federal minimum wage.

Many local groups in southern New Jersey came together to support residents in the Waterfront South neighborhood in Camden who were fighting the St. Lawrence Cement corporation and the New Jersey Department of Environmental Protection (NJDEP). In a blatant display of environmental racism, NJDEP granted St. Lawrence Cement a permit to emit sixty tons of small particulate matter into the air every year, even though the predominantly minority community adjacent to the plant was already surrounded by eleven major polluters, including two Superfund sites. Research revealed St. Lawrence Cement's international connections, its poor environmental record in other parts of the world, and NJDEP's pattern of

FIRST THEY IGNORE YOU

THEN THEY LAUGH AT YOU

THEN THEY ATTACK YOU

THEN YOU WIN

Morgan Fitzpatrick Andrews

ORGANIZING COMMUNITIES

discrimination in permitting plants such as St. Lawrence Cement in poor and minority neighborhoods all over the state.

In these examples, the local campaigns made the concept of globalization real and understandable. Within the United States, corporations set up operations wherever local communities and governments are least able to make them accountable in terms of the wages they pay, the environmental destruction they cause, and the resources they exploit. Their behavior is the same on a global scale; the larger scale just gives them more opportunities and choices.

5. Avoid the pitfalls of electoral politics.

This is a very controversial area of concern for community organizations. The organizations I have worked with in Camden have vacillated in their stance regarding electoral politics.

The danger of cooptation through involvement in this arena is severe. Whenever a group of people start getting things done and build a credible reputation in the community, politicians will try to use the organization or its members to their advantage.

I have yet to witness any candidate for public office who maintained any kind of issue integrity. Once in the limelight, people bend toward the interests that have the resources necessary to finance political campaigns. They want to win more than they want to advance any particular platform on the issues. We delude ourselves if we believe any politician will support the progressive agenda of a minority constituency when their political future depends on them abandoning it.

I have participated in organizing campaigns where politicians were exploited because of vulnerabilities they had, and where one politician was successfully played off against another. It is much easier for a community organization to use politicians to advance a cause if neither the organization nor its members are loyal to any officeholder. Regardless of who is in office, community-based organizations will have to organize and confront them to get what they want.

Operation

For organizations committed to the long-term process of radical social change, the way they operate is more important than any short-term victories that might be realized. The discipline, habits, and values that are developed and nurtured through an organization's day-to-day life are an important part of the revolutionary process. Some guidelines for operation follow.

1. Have a political analysis and provide political education.

> Lower-class and working-class neighborhood organizing must develop long-range goals which address imbalances in a class society, an alternative vision of what people are fighting for, and a context for all activity, whether pressuring for a stop sign or an eviction blockage. Otherwise, as has repeatedly happened, victories that win services or rewards will undermine the organization by "proving" that the existing system is responsive to poor and working people and, therefore, in no need of fundamental change (Fisher, 1984; 162).

Any organization that is serious about social change and committed to democratic control of neighborhoods and workplaces must devote

considerable energy in self-development—building individual skills and self-confidence and providing basic political education. The role of the state in maintaining inequality and destroying self-worth must be exposed.

This is particularly necessary in low-income and minority neighborhoods where people have been most consistently socialized to believe that they are inferior, that the problems they face are individual rather than systemic, and where low-quality education has left people without the basic skills necessary to respond to what goes on around them. Self-esteem is low, yet social change work requires people who are self-confident and assertive.

This dilemma is another of the major challenges in community organizing. The socialization process that strips people of their self-esteem is not easily or quickly reversed. This problem mandates that all tasks be performed in groups (for support and skill-sharing), and that training and preparation for all activities be thorough.

2. Be collectively and flexibly organized; decentralize as much as possible.

Radical organizations must always try to set an example of how organizations can be better than the institutions we criticize. All meetings and financial records should be open and leadership responsibilities rotated. Active men and women must work in all aspects of the organization—office work, fund-raising, decisionmaking, financial management, outreach, housekeeping, and so forth. The organization's diversity must mirror that of the community where it operates.

Teams of people should work on different projects, with coordination provided by an elected council. Pyramidal hierarchy with committees subordinate to and constrained by a strong central board should be avoided. The organization must remain flexible so that it can respond quickly to needs as they arise.

3. Maintain independence.

This is extremely important and extremely difficult. No organization committed to radical social change can allow itself to become financially dependent on the government or corporations. This does not mean that we can't use funds from government or private institutions, but we can't get ourselves in a position where we owe any allegiance to the funders.

ORGANIZING COMMUNITIES

In 1983, the Farm Labor Organizing Committee was involved in a march from Toledo, Ohio, to the Campbell's Soup headquarters in Camden, New Jersey. They were demanding three-party collective bargaining between Campbell, the farmers it buys from, and the farm laborers who pick for the farmers. A coalition of groups in Camden worked to coordinate the final leg of the march through Camden. Many community-based organizations in Camden, however, refused to participate because they were dependent on donations of food or money from Campbell's Soup.

The bankruptcy of such behavior was driven home a decade ago when Campbell closed its Camden plant and laid off 1,000 workers. They made no special effort to soften the impact on the workers or the community. All resources come at a price—even donations. We simply cannot accept funds from individuals or groups who condition their use in ways that constrain our work, or we must ignore the conditions and remain prepared to deal with the consequences later.

Alternative funding sources are providing a badly needed service in this regard. In Philadelphia, the Bread and Roses Community Fund raises money for distribution to social change organizations. In 1983, it spun off the Delaware Valley Community Reinvestment Fund (now known as the Reinvestment Fund), an alternative lending institution that provides credit for community-based housing and community development projects. Social change organizations in the Philadelphia/Camden area are extremely indebted to these two support organizations. They play a vital role in helping organizations to maintain their independence.

4. Reach out to avoid isolation, but keep the focus local.

Community-based organizations must maintain loose ties with other grassroots groups. Progressive groups should be able to easily coalesce when that makes sense. We can always benefit from ideas and constructive criticism from supportive people who are not wrapped up in the day-to-day activity of our own organization.

This is another way that left-wing "united way" groups like the Bread and Roses Community Fund in the Philadelphia area play an important role. They identify and bring together groups in the region with a similar political agenda. Through Bread and Roses, the community advocacy organization in North Camden (CCNC) for many years maintained a very loose but productive relationship with the Kensington Joint Action Council (KJAC) in Philadelphia. KJAC squatted first, and helped CCNC plan its squatter campaign. CCNC spun off a land trust first and assisted

Democractic National Convention, Los Angeles, July 2002.

KJAC in the development of their own land trust, Manos Unidas. Each has benefited from the other.

Statewide and national organizations try very hard to pull in active local organizations and get leaders involved in issues at the state level. Be wary of the drain this can place on the local work. (Cloward and Piven, in *Poor Peoples' Movements*, do a wonderful job of illustrating this danger in their discussion of welfare rights organizing.) Successes are won via direct action, not via formal organization.

5. Do not foster cross-class dependencies.

This applies especially to community organizing in low-income areas where the local resources are extremely scarce. Many well-to-do "do-gooder" organizations like to have a ghetto project. It makes them feel good. Community organizations do not exist to alleviate ruling class guilt. Dependency on upper-class skills and money is a problem. Poor and working people must wage their own struggle. There may be outsiders with a different class background who can be helpful, and who respect the autonomy and dignity of the people they assist. Unfortunately, they are not the norm.

An illustration of this is provided by the soup kitchen in North Camden. Suburban church folks, once they heard about Leavenhouse, were more than willing to send in volunteers each day to prepare and serve the meal. Leavenhouse discouraged them, except perhaps occasionally with one or two people at a time. This allows the soup kitchen to develop local ownership, and for neighborhood residents to feel good about taking care of each other. It avoids the traditional social service model where one group comes into the city and delivers a service to another group of people who lives there and takes it.

Leavenhouse does accept money and food donations from outside the neighborhood, but its basic operating costs are covered with the rent of the community members who actually live at Leavenhouse. The outside income is extra; without it Leavenhouse will not shut down.

6. Have a cultural and social dimension.

Cultural and social events not only help to build a counterculture, but they help people feel good about who they are and where they come from. This is an important dynamic in overcoming powerlessness. Political music, film, and theater are especially effective in building class unity and strength, and in providing basic political education.

7. Staff the organization, to the greatest extent possible, with local workers and volunteers.

This seems obvious, but many community organizations draw on outsiders to perform the bulk of their work.

In Camden, nonprofit community organizations that provide affordable housing do it in three different ways. One organization matches suburban church groups with vacant houses. The church groups then purchase materials and provide volunteer labor to do the rehabilitation work. Another group relies on contractors to perform the work, few of which are based in Camden. A third group has hired and trained neighborhood residents to do all rehabilitation work. The workers are paid a decent wage for what they do. The latter approach develops skills in the neighborhood, allows neighborhood residents to feel good about improving their community, and fosters cooperative work habits that the construction crew members will hopefully carry into other organizations in the community.

Since the crew employed by the third organization is paid a living wage, the first organization mentioned above rehabilitates more houses for less

money. Again, when the commitment is to social change, the short-term tangible results are not the most important measure of success.

Tactics

A considerable body of literature has been written about tactics in organizing and political work. I do not want to rehash all of that here, so I'll offer just a few guidelines about tactics that have consistently proven themselves. The discussion here is relevant to advocacy campaigns designed to take some measure of authority from government or private interests and put it in community control, or to force a reallocation of resources (public or private) in the interest of the community.

1. Be disruptive.

The tendency today is for community organizations to be less militant and confrontational, working through established community and political leaders to "engineer" the changes they want. The tactics of the 1960s are no longer in vogue. I can't tell how many times people have said to me, "the sixties are over." They are the same ones who are still waiting to see their community's demands realized.

No tendency could be more dangerous to the future of community organizing. The historical record and my experience says the opposite. We must be disruptive. No guideline is more important in the consideration of tactics. We can't change the system by testifying at hearings, negotiating at meetings, and lobbying elected officials. We must defy the rules of the system that fails to meet our needs. We must use guerrilla tactics that harass, confront, embarrass, and expose that system and its functionaries.

Frederick Douglass made this point most eloquently almost 100 years before the idea of community organizing as we know it took shape:

> Let me give you a word on the philosophy of reform. The whole history of the progress of human liberty shows that all concessions yet made to her august claims have been born of earnest struggle. . . . If there is no struggle, there is no progress. Those who profess to favor freedom and yet depreciate agitation are people who want crops without plowing up the ground, they want rain without thunder and lightning. (Foner, 1975, 437)

These words are often copied and quoted, but community organizations heed them inconsistently at best. One reason may be that "it takes an incredible amount of disregard and neglect to get ordinary people angry

ORGANIZING COMMUNITIES

enough to engage in confrontation" (Simmons, 1994, 123). In effective community organizations, people have gotten beyond their socialized inhibitions and idealism, and understand why confrontation is so important.

2. Decide on clear, precise and measurable demands; they are the cornerstone of any organizing campaign.

A group must know exactly what they want, before they begin to confront the opposition. Frederick Douglass understood this, too:

> Power concedes nothing without a demand. It never did and it never will. Find out just what any people will quietly submit to and you have found the exact measure of of injustice and wrong which will be imposed upon them, and these will continue until they are resisted with words, or blows, or with both. The limits of tyrants are prescribed by the endurance of those whom they oppress . . . (Foner, 1975, 437)

3. Gradually escalate the militancy of your tactics.

The tactics in a campaign should gradually escalate in militancy, so that people new to political struggle are not intimidated. Let the militancy of the tactics increase at the about the same pace as the intensity of their anger.

There are usually some activists involved in community organizing who want to escalate the tactics quickly. They are ready to do civil disobedience at the first demonstration. Be careful. Most poor and working folks are not in a position to do this. They have children; they live on an economic margin; they are taking care of sick family members. They do not have the luxury of worrying only about themselves, or risking the few assets they do have.

4. Address different targets simultaneously.

The tactics should be simultaneously directed at different parts of the system that are responsible for the injustice or grievance that needs to be resolved.

In the campaign to stop construction of a second state prison in their neighborhood, North Camden residents directed tactics at the commissioner of corrections, the private landowner who was willing to sell the waterfront land to the state for the prison, local politicians, the governor, and the two gubernatorial candidates.

ORGANIZING COMMUNITIES

★ ★ ★ ★

Globalization has complicated the question of targets immensely. Institutions that adversely affect local communities are more and more likely to be large, with tentacles extending nationally and globally. Mergers, acquisitions, and trade agreements mean that local institutions may engage in many different activities, in many different places. Local managers may not have much authority (see McKnight, 1995; 156). The board of directors may be inaccessible because they are based in a foreign country. The implications for local organizing are several.

Research has to be much more sophisticated. Connections with other organizations that have taken on your local nemesis in other places or on other issues are more important. New and more creative tactics will be needed that can impact a much larger and elusive target that is less vulnerable to local pressure.

I mentioned the St. Lawrence Cement case in the section on Picking Issues. It is relevant here as well. Research involved learning about its poor environmental record in Canada and Europe, as well as in the United States. South Camden Citizens in Action reached out to a group in the Hudson River Valley that was organizing against a new St. Lawrence plant there. They talked about joint demonstrations and press events in New York City, but the logistics and limited resources of the South Camden group precluded such regional tactics.

The campaign to get the U.S. military out of Vieques, Puerto Rico, further illustrates the complicated nature of targets we must confront. I spent a week camped on the navy's target area, and attended countless meetings in preparation for the morning in early May 1999 when federal marshals removed everyone from the civil disobedience camps. The range of organizations and people engaged in this campaign, and the multiple targets that were being addressed, was simply overwhelming.

This issue started at the local level, with residents on the island of Vieques demanding that the U.S. Navy stop using the island for military exercises. The navy is a formidable target for the 9,500 people on Vieques to take on, so they had to reach out to organizations all over the globe representing people that the U.S. Navy has maligned. They brought in religious leaders to confront the moral issue, environmentalists to confront the ecological degradation, health advocates to confront disease caused by the chemicals used in explosives, and peace activists who opposed the oppressive U.S. military presence in Puerto Rico. Other *countries* that paid the U.S. government to conduct military exercises became targets when the people of Vieques asked that they stop using the island. Other targets included the United Nations, federal judges, the governor of Puerto Rico, the

ORGANIZING COMMUNITIES

David Hanks

Environmental justice activists march against WTO and toxics at Chevron Texaco refinery in Richmond, CA. 2001.

ORGANIZING COMMUNITIES

president, Congress, the secretary of the navy, and so forth for a local issue directly affecting about 9,500 people.

5. Avoid legal tactics.

Legal challenges are difficult. They take a lot of energy and money; people who aren't trained in the law have a very difficult time understanding the process; and they are easy to lose. I have never experienced success with a legal challenge.

When North Camden residents opposed construction of the first state prison in their neighborhood, they sued the state on environmental and land use grounds because the state planned to use valuable waterfront land for the prison. After a year of preparation, the case was heard before an administrative law judge. He threw the case out on a technicality. Understand that he was appointed by a governor who had made a public commitment to construct 4,000 more prison beds during his term in office.

Five years ago, citizens in the Waterfront South neighborhood in Camden sued the local sewer authority (CCMUA) because the odor from the plant was choking the neighborhood. They won in court, and the authority was obligated to spend $7 million to get rid of the offensive odors resulting from its operation. Five years later, the CCMUA claims it has spent most of the money, but the odors persist. Must the residents go back into court to get the order enforced? What is the likelihood of success this time? If the lawyers had been engaged instead to manage an escrow account, and a mass organizing drive got residents to pay their sewer fees into an escrow account instead of to the CCMUA, the result might have been different.

Citizens would have strong financial leverage; they would not be beholden to the court system to do the right thing.

Our legal system is set up to protect the interests of private property. Using it to fight those interests is obviously problematic.

6. Use direct action.

Direct actions are those that take the shortest route toward realization of the ends desired, without depending on intermediaries. A simple example might help to clarify. If a group of tenants is having a problem with a landlord refusing to make needed repairs, they can respond in several ways. They could take the landlord to court. They could get the housing and health inspectors to issue violations and pressure the landlord to make repairs. Or they could withhold rent from the landlord and use the money withheld to pay for the repairs. Along the same vein, they might picket the landlord's nice suburban home and leaflet all of his neighbors with information about how he treats people. The first two options put responsibility for getting something done in the hands of a government agency or law enforcement official. The latter courses of action keep the tenants in control of what happens.

At a major state-funded construction project in Camden, residents wanted to make sure that city residents and minorities got construction jobs. Following the lead of some militant construction workers in New York City, they organized people who were ready to work, and blocked the gate to the job site at starting time. Their position was simple; they would move when local people were hired. The group got talked into negotiating and supporting an affirmative action program that would force the contractor to hire local people whenever the union hall couldn't provide a minority or city resident to fill an opening. The enforcement of that program was so mired in red tape that only a handful of local workers got hired. The group would have fared much better if they had stuck with their original tactic—the most direct one.

7. Have fun.

The tactics used should be fun for the participants. This isn't always possible, but often is. Street theater can often be used to change a routine action into a fun one. Let me provide a few examples.

When Concerned Citizens of North Camden (CCNC) ran its home-owner program (the program that resulted from the squatting in 1981), the city

ORGANIZING COMMUNITIES

tried various mechanisms to discredit it. On one occasion when they threatened to cut some of the public funds involved in it, CCNC conducted a funeral march with about 100 people and carried a coffin from North Camden to City Hall where a hearing was being held on the Community Development Block Grant funds. Right in the middle of the hearing, a squatter came out from inside the coffin and told the crowd how the people's movement could not be silenced and made a mockery of the hearing. The effect was spectacular, as was the press coverage the next day.

When trying to stop the second prison, residents circulated a special issue of the community newspaper that made fun of the land owner, the mayor, and the commissioner of corrections. The front page of the paper included photos of the three, captioned with the names of the Three Stooges (the resemblance was striking). The text on the front page made fun of each person's role in the project. We circulated the paper at a big public meeting, which all three of these officials attended. It helped give people courage and set the atmosphere for people to freely speak their minds. When people talk about the prison campaign, they laugh and remember "the three stooges."

Finally, when the homeless problem started to escalate in Camden (1983), we learned that people were being turned away from available shelters because there was not enough space. Leavenhouse, a local soup kitchen, then started to serve its meals on the steps of City Hall one day each week. This created a party-type atmosphere; a couple hundred people would gather to eat and hang out every Wednesday at noon. As the weather got colder, it became less fun, but the persistence was important. Three months after we started, in December, the city agreed to make a public building available as a shelter and agreed to adopt a policy that no homeless person would be denied shelter in Camden. The good aspect of this action was that homeless people were able to participate and help make it happen. It was a concrete way that they could have fun and feel good about helping to improve their own situation.

Concluding Comments

The kind of community organizing described here is not easy or straightforward. It can be extremely frustrating, with many pitfalls, temptations, and diversions pushing it off the track and allowing it to assume a more liberal posture. This essay described some of the main challenges—overcoming the welfare/drugs culture; maintaining independence; working with people with few skills and low self-esteem; taking on bigger and more complicated targets spread all over the globe.

Community organizing from an anarchist perspective acknowledges that successful revolution will depend on a strong grassroots foundation. This will require a history of work in cooperative, decentralized, revolutionary organizations in communities, workplaces, and schools. The task before us is to build and nurture these organizations wherever we can. There are no shortcuts.

Works Cited

Alinsky, Saul D. *Rules for Radicals*. (New York: Random House, 1971).

Bouchier, David. *Radical Citizenship*. (New York: Schocken Books, 1987).

Ehrlich, Howard, DeLeon and Morris, eds. *Reinventing Anarchy*. (Boston: Routledge and Kegan Paul, 1979).

Fisher, Robert. *Let the People Decide: Neighborhood Organizing In America*. (Boston: Twayne Publishers, 1984).

Foner, Philip S., ed. *The Life and Writings of Frederick Douglass*. (New York: International Publishers, 1975).

Freire, Paulo. *Pedagogy of the Oppressed*. (New York: Seabury Press, 1970).

Goodwyn, Lawrence. *Democratic Promise: The Populist Moment in America*. (New York: Oxford University Press, 1976).

_____. *The Populist Moment*. (New York: Oxford University Press, 1981).

Max, Steve, "Why Organize?" (Chicago: Steve Max and the Midwest Academy, 1977).

McKnight, John. *The Careless Society: Community and Its Counterfeits*. (New York: Basic Books, 1995).

_____. "Regenerating Community" *Social Policy*, winter 1987, 54–58.

Morris, David. "A Globe of Villages: Self Reliant Community Development," *Building Economic Alternatives*, Winter 1987.

Piven, Frances Fox, and Richard A. Cloward, *Poor People's Movements*. (New York: Vintage Books, 1979).

Simmons, Louise B. *Organizing in Hard Times*. (Philadelphia: Temple University Press, 1994).

Staples, Lee. *Roots to Power*. (New York: Praeger, 1984).

ORGANIZING COMMUNITIES

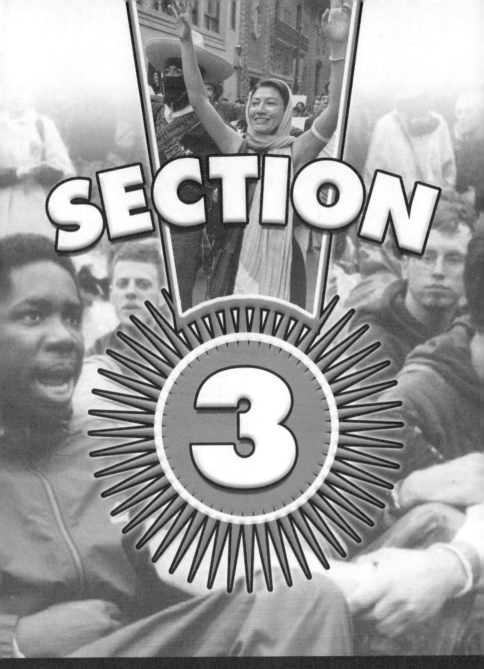

SECTION

3

IDEAS IN ACTION

photo top: Jutta Meier-Wiedenbach   background photo: Orin Langelle

Pageant of the Argentine uprising at School of the Americas, November, 2002.
Photo by Linda Panetta

Que Se Vayan Todos: *Argentina's Popular Rebellion*

PART I

By Jennifer Whitney and John Jordan

Jennifer Whitney is an activist, writer, and musician who works with the Black Cross Health Collective in Portland, Oregon, and drums with the Infernal Noise Brigade, a radical marching band based in Seattle.

John Jordan is an artist, activist, and writer; he worked with London Reclaim the Streets (1995–2001) and has given up the security of a teaching job to immerse himself in the popular rebellion in Argentina.

Both Jennifer and John are a part of the editorial collective Notes from Nowhere, which published the book We Are Everywhere: The Irresistible Rise of Global Anticapitalism.

Watch This Space

When we first landed in Buenos Aires on February 15, 2002, we were immediately searching for signs of the insurrection. Would this airport feel different from any other? Would the streets be clogged with traffic, or with

photo top: Nicolas Pousthomis

crowds? Was the garbage still being collected and the mail delivered? Never having been in a country in the midst of a mass social rebellion, we wondered what would appear different in everyday life.

Riding into the city, we got our first clue. The barren stretches of highway that link cities with airports, so similar all over the world, are always flanked by rows of large billboards, advertising the staples of international business—credit cards, mobile phones, hotels, airlines. This was true on this sterile strip of land as well, but something was different.

More than half of the billboards were bare, with huge white spaces where advertisements would have been. There was something beautiful about them as they stood enormous in their emptiness, drained of the poisonous images of consumption, yet seductive in their nothingness, freed from commerce and filled with possibility. They somehow stood for the space of change that this country is undergoing; they spoke of the pause, the blank sheet of paper waiting to be filled; they were the space from which a society could begin to imagine something different, the space from which people could begin to put dreams into action.

The Tin Pot Insurrection
February 2002

We've arrived on a Friday. Every Friday night since mid-December last year, there has been a massive *cacerolazo* in Buenos Aires, when the people converge in the political center of the city, the Plaza de Mayo, and create an enormous racket by banging on *cacerolas*, or saucepans. These huge *cacerolazos* developed spontaneously on December 19, 2001, the day when the uprising exploded after smoldering in the provinces for several years. It now involves just about every sector of Argentinean society.

December 19th was the turning point, the day when the Argentines said "Enough!" The stage had been set the day before, when people began looting shops and supermarkets to feed their families. The president, Fernando de la Rua, panicked and declared a state of emergency, suspending all constitutional rights and banning meetings of more than three people. That was the last straw. Not only did it bring back traumatic memories of the seven-year military dictatorship that killed over 30,000 people, but it also meant that the state was taking away the last shred of dignity from a hungry and desperate population —their freedom.

On the evening of the 19th, our friend Ezequiel was on the phone with his brother who lives on the other side of town. They were casually chatting,

314

when his brother suddenly said, "Hang on, can you hear that noise?" Ezequiel strained to hear a kind of clanging sound coming through the receiver. "Yes, I can hear something on your side of the city but nothing here." They continued talking, and then Ezequiel paused, and said, "Wait, now I can hear something in my neighborhood, the same sound . . ." He ran to the window.

Assembly Parque Lezama make decisions in an occupied bank building.

People were standing on their balconies banging saucepans and coming out onto the sidewalks banging pots; like a virus of hope, the *cacerolazo*, which began as a response to the state of emergency, had infected the entire city. Before the president's televised announcement of the state of emergency was over, people were in the streets disobeying it. Over a million people took part in Buenos Aires alone, banging their pots and pans and demanding an end to neoliberal policies and corrupt governments. That night the finance minister resigned, and over the next twenty-four hours of street protest, plainclothes policemen killed seven demonstrators in the city, while fifteen more were killed in the provinces. The president resigned shortly thereafter, and was evacuated from the presidential palace by helicopter.

Within a fortnight, four more governments were formed and collapsed. Argentina was now set on a major high-speed collision course, with the needs and desires of its people on one side, and the demands of the IMF, the inept government, and global capitalism on the other.

Rivers of Sound

Our friends tell us to meet them for tonight's *cacerolazo* in the café of the Popular University of the Mothers of the Plaza de Mayo. The place is an enormous social center, right opposite the national congress building, and is run by the well-known mothers of the disappeared, whose courageous actions alerted the world to the mass disappearances during the military dictatorship between 1976 and 1983.

Nicolas Pousthomis

Workers assemble to coordinate their work and make decisions in Zanon ceramic factory, one of South America's largest, which workers occupied and ran themselves after owners threatened to shut it down.

Night falls, and before long we begin to hear the repetitive rhythm of pot-and-pan banging drift across the square. A small crowd of around fifty people has congregated in the street—they are young, old, rich, poor, smartly dressed, scruffy—but all are armed with spoons, forks, and a whole variety of metal objects to bang on: cooking pots, lids, kettles, soda cans, car parts, cookie tins, iron bars, baking trays, car keys. The rhythm is high pitched and monotonous, and above it people sing catchy tunes instead of dull political chanting; often they include the key slogan of this movement: "*Que se vayan todos!*" literally, "They all must go," meaning that the *entire* political class goes, every politician from every party, the supreme court, the IMF, the multinational corporations, the banks—*everyone* out so the people can decide the fate of this economically crippled country themselves.

The Neighborhoods Rise

Every week people make this pilgrimage, from every corner of Buenos Aires, some of them coming as far as five miles. They walk with their *asambleas populares*, the neighborhood assemblies that have spontaneously sprouted up over the last few months in over 200 different neighborhoods in the city, and throughout the surrounding provinces. These assemblies are rapidly becoming autonomous centers of community

ARGENTINE REBELLION

Nicolas Pousthomis

Argentine uprising in Plaza de Mayo, government center in Buenos Aires, December 19, 2001.

participation. Most meet weekly (the more ambitious, twice a week), and all meet outside—in squares, parks, and even on street corners.

Every Sunday there is an assembly of assemblies, an interneighborhood plenary in a park, attended by over 4,000 people and often running for more than four hours. Spokespeople from rich, poor, and middle-class districts attend to report back on the work and proposals of their local assemblies, share ideas, and debate strategy for the following week's citywide mobilizations.

The local assemblies are open to almost anyone, although one assembly has banned bankers and party activists, and others have banned the media. Some assemblies have as many as 200 people participating, others are much smaller. One of the assemblies we attended had about 40 people present, ranging from two mothers sitting on the sidewalk while breast feeding to a lawyer in a suit to a skinny hippie in batik bell-bottoms to an elderly taxi driver to a dreadlocked bike messenger to a nursing student. It was a whole slice of Argentine society standing in a circle on a street corner under the orange glow of sodium lights, passing around a brand-new megaphone and discussing how to take back control of their lives. Every now and then a car would pass by and beep its horn in support, and this was all happening between 8 P.M. and midnight on a Wednesday evening!

ARGENTINE REBELLION

Nicolas Pousthomis

Que Se Vayan Todos *(Out With All of Them) the slogan of the Argentine uprising, Plaza de Mayo, Buenos Aires, December 19-20, 2001.*

It all seemed so normal, and yet it was perhaps the most extraordinarily radical political event we'd ever witnessed—ordinary people seriously discussing self-management, spontaneously understanding direct democracy, and beginning to put it into practice in their own neighborhoods. Multiply this by 200 in Buenos Aires alone, and you have the makings of a popular rebellion, a grassroots uprising that is rejecting centralized political power. As Roli, an accountant from the Almagro assembly said: "People reject the political parties. To get out of this crisis requires real politics. These meetings of common people on the street are the fundamental form of doing politics."

Outside of the weekly meetings, the assemblies meet in smaller committees, each one dedicated to a different local issue or problem. Committees of health are common—with many local hospital budgets slashed, there is an urgent need to develop alternatives to the collapsing public welfare system. Some are suggesting that people who own their own homes withhold their property tax, and instead give that money to the local hospitals. Many assemblies also have alternative media committees, as there is a widespread critique of the mainstream media's representation of the rebellion—it took a large *cacerolazo* outside their head offices to get them to cover the uprising more accurately. However, the spirit of distrust for any large corporate entity remains, and local assemblies are beginning to print their own news sheets, broadcast updates on local radio stations, and put up Web sites.

In addition to the innumerable meetings and the weekly *cacerolazo*, the assemblies also organize local street parties and actions. In one neighborhood, for example, the assembly organized a picket to prevent the authorities from closing down a baker who could not afford to pay his rent.

From Rebellion to Reconstruction

For the workers of the Zanón ceramics factory in Neuque, it is this spirit of optimism that has enabled them to occupy their factory, one of Latin America's largest ceramics producers, for the last six months, running it with astounding results. The company stopped production last year,

claiming that it was no longer profitable and that they could no longer pay the workers' salaries. Rather than join the growing ranks of Argentina's unemployed, the workers decided to occupy the factory and keep the production lines running themselves.

"We showed that with two days' worth of production, we were able to pay the wages of all the workers for that month," explained Godoy, one of the 326 workers involved in the occupation. The workers market the tiles at 60 percent of the previous prices and have organized a network of young vendors who sell them in the city. José Romero, a maintenance worker at the factory, adds, "This fight has opened our eyes to a lot of things."

Like so many in this movement, they are critical of hierarchical forms of organization. Godoy continues, "Now we have no full-time officials. The officials work eight hours like everyone else and we do our union activity after hours. The decisions are all made at general assemblies of workers, not behind closed doors." Photographs of the occupied factory show workers laughing and joking as they pull tiles out of the kilns.

Meanwhile, a mine in Río Turbío has been occupied, as well as a textile factory in Buenos Aires, which recently opened its doors for an International Women's Day festival. These worker-run endeavors are setting examples for Argentine factories everywhere. One manufacturer who was on the verge of bankruptcy called his workers together and told them that since he could no longer pay their salaries he would instead turn over the blankets produced in the factory, which the workers could either sell or take to the local barter markets, to exchange for other commodities. Perhaps he was worried by the example set at Zanón, or perhaps he was beginning to recognize the futility of continuing business as usual in such unusual times.

Popular Economics

The barter markets are another extraordinary example of necessity breeding ingenuity and enabling Argentines to survive the crisis. We visit the *Trueque La Estación*, the Station Exchange, that takes place twice a week in a four-story community center on the outskirts of the city, where we are shown around by Ana, a shy engineer wearing thick glasses. "The politicians have stolen everything from the people, they want to control everybody," she explains. "People come here because they don't want to be in the system."

The place is bustling; we can hardly move through the jovial throngs of people perusing the rows of tables offering goods and services. You can

Nicolas Pousthomis

Ahorristas *pound on the sheet metal-protected banks that took their savings when the IMF-controlled economy collapsed.*

buy anything here, or rather, you can exchange anything here, from eggs to bumper stickers, miniskirts to spices, cucumbers to crocheted toilet roll covers, as long as you use bartering currency—small, brightly colored notes that look a bit like Monopoly money.

The system is simple: people take their products to the market and sell them for barter credit. The vendor is then able to use this to purchase products they need in return. If you have nothing to exchange and want to participate, you must buy credits from a bank with cash. But most people have something to trade, if they are imaginative enough, and though these people are deeply lacking in cash, they have a surplus of imagination.

Piles of bric-a-brac cover some tables, while others have neat and ordered displays. A young woman sits behind a pile of underwear reading Nietzsche while a mother carrying her child in a sling does a swift trade in home-baked pies. On one table Frederick Forsyth novels jostle for space with fashion magazines and books about the Spanish civil war. Huddled beside the stairs, an indigenous Bolivian family chats over wooden boxes of fresh vegetables. On the top floor a doctor in a pristine white coat offers to take our blood pressure, while a dentist demonstrates some procedure using a lurid pair of false teeth. People are having their hair cut in one room while manicures and tarot readings are offered in another. There are classes in technical drawing as well as immigration advisement.

Occasionally the *trueque* radio station (which "broadcasts" through a crackly PA system) announces new services being offered.

These barter clubs began in 1995 when the recession began to be felt. Since then they have developed into a whole network and are now known as *nodos*, meaning nodes, or points of concentration. Currently there are several thousand *nodos* in existence throughout the country, with well over 2 million people taking part. For many of them it has become the only way of surviving the economic crisis.

Beware the Bourgeois Block

It's noon on a Monday, and we are on Florida Avenue, the main pedestrian shopping street of Buenos Aires, no different from London's Oxford Street, with its numerous McDonald's, Tower Records, and Benettons. This busy street, normally full of bankers and businesspeople making quick lunch-time purchases, runs along the edge of the financial district. But today something is not quite normal. The rustle of shopping bags is drowned out by a deafening racket.

A crowd of about 200 people are beating on the sheet metal that protects the entrance of a bank. They bang with hammers, ladles, monkey wrenches—one woman even removes her shoe to use as a tool. The entire facade of the building shudders under the fury of the vibration of the blows being rained upon it. The force of some of the tools manages to punch gaping holes straight through the metal; agile gloved hands prise the sheets apart. Suddenly the armor falls away and the crowd cheers.

A handful of people split off and invade a bank lobby across the street. Within a fraction of a second all six ATM machines are systematically smashed, shattered glass flies, and a woman sprays the word *chorros*, or crooks, in huge letters on the marble wall. Nervous bank employees watch the scene from behind a glass door; an egg sails through the air and breaks against it. The bankers flinch, then turn away.

The crowd repeats the accusatory chant, "*Ladrones, ladrones,*" or thieves, and then join in a longer chant, while jumping ecstatically up and down, waving portfolios and briefcases around. The chant translates loosely as "Whoever is not jumping is a banker, whoever is not jumping is a thief . . ." When this dies down, everyone casually exits the lobby and moves on to the next bank, less than fifty yards up the street.

These kinds of tactics have become archetypes of contemporary protest: the shattered glass and graffiti the same from London to Genoa, via

ARGENTINE REBELLION

Seattle, Prague, and Québec City. Here in Buenos Aires, however, things are very different.

For one thing, it was impossible to tell the demonstrators from the passersby. Men in suits and ties with briefcases in one hand and hammers in the other, women with gold bracelets, handbags, and high heels sharing cans of spray paint, anonymous suits on their lunch break joining the fracas and then melting back into the crowd. The scene was astonishing— not only was it impossible to tell who was who, but also, businesses remained open, leaving their doors and windows unprotected, fearless of looting or damage, as it was perfectly clear that the targets were the banks and nothing but the banks. Even McDonald's, usually having the honor of being the first to lose its windows, left their doors open.

Another difference is that this is not the black bloc. No one is masked, although one woman covers her face with a newspaper and large sunglasses, understandable if you've survived the disappearance of 30,000 of your fellow citizens. The spirit of "militant" (and often, macho) clandestinity is completely absent. It is broad daylight—while the bank is being trashed, shoppers are buying sneakers next door, and the handful of police, unable to do anything, stand idly, watching sheepishly. This is the most open, accountable, and disciplined property damage (one can hardly call it a riot when the police don't fight back) that we've ever witnessed. It's also probably the most surreal. If one must call these people a bloc, and why not, as they move and act as one, maybe "bourgeois bloc" would suit them best.

The *ahorristas*, or savers, hold their demonstrations three times a week. On the day we followed them, seventeen banks were "visited." Before meeting the *ahorristas*, it was difficult to imagine women with shopping bags and high heels kicking at corporate windows, huge lipstick grins spreading as they watched the glass shatter into thousands of pieces. That day they also surrounded every armored security van transporting cash from bank to bank that they came upon and covered each one in graffiti, while men in pin-striped suits proceeded to unscrew the wheel nuts and others pried open the hood, tearing out wires from the running engines. Soccer moms jumped up and down on top of the vans, smashing anything that could be broken—side mirrors, headlights, license plates, windshield wipers, and antennae. For three hours on a Monday afternoon, our understanding of the world was turned on its head, all our preconceptions and stereotypes melted away. "This could be my mom," we kept thinking.

The *ahorristas* are the upper- to lower-middle class who have had their life savings frozen by the government's shutdown of the banks. Dressed in shirts and ties, pumps and designer sunglasses, they just don't seem the

de la rua y cavallo - mayo 2001

Flor, MTD Anibal Veron

Florencia Vespignani

Florencia Vespignani

piquete - noviembre 2000   *Flor, MTD Anibal Veron*

sort who would be smashing up corporate property. They are architects, computer programmers, doctors, housewives, accountants, and even bank employees, one of whom explained, "It's not just the banks who are thieves, it's the government and the corporations. They confiscated the money we had in the bank. They stole it." She pauses, and then shakes her fist. "I am very angry!"

And yet the *ahorristas* are not simply the selfish petit bourgeoisie, worried only about their own money. Their struggle has broken out of the enclosure of self-interest, and has begun to encompass a critique of much of the social system. They have publicly allied themselves to the movement of the unemployed (who have become known as the *piqueteros*, literally, "those who picket") and many take part in the assemblies. "A lot more than just the government must change here," says Carlos, a computer programmer, who has painted slogans all over his suit. His words echo those of a *piquetero* we met at a blockade: "We, the *piqueteros*, and all the people who are fighting, are struggling for social change. We do not believe in the capitalist neoliberal system anymore."

A Postscript for the Global Anticapitalist Movement

The last decade saw the increasing delegitimization of the neoliberal model, as a movement of movements erupted up on every continent. By

identifying the underlying global problem as capitalism, and by developing extraordinary international networks of inspiration in very short amounts of time, it felt almost as if history were speeding up.

Then history did what it does best, surprising us all on September 11, and it seemed for a while that everything had changed, forcing a reappraisal among activists, particularly in the global North. It challenged us all to take a deep breath, put our rhetoric into practice, and think strategically, and fast. Then three months later, history seemed to resume its accelerated speed, when Argentina erupted, followed closely by the collapse of Enron. It seemed that despite the distraction of the "war on terror," neoliberalism was continuing to disintegrate.

Perhaps the biggest challenge that global movements face now is to realize that the first round is over, and that the slogan first sprayed on a building in Seattle and last seen on a burning police van in Genoa, "We Are Winning," may actually be true. The crisis of legitimacy faced by capitalism expands exponentially almost daily. But the next round will be the hardest. It will involve applying our critiques and principles to our everyday lives. This is exactly where Argentina can show us an inspiring way to move forward.

The situation in Argentina contains many elements of the anticapitalist movements: the practice of direct action, self-management, and direct democracy; the belief in the power of diversity, decentralization, and solidarity; the convergence of radically different social sectors; the rejection of the state, multinational corporations, and financial institutions. Yet what is most incredible is that the form of the uprising arose spontaneously—it was not imposed or suggested by activists, but rather, created by ordinary people from the ground up, resulting in a truly popular rebellion that is taking place every day, every week, and including every sort of person imaginable.

In this way, Argentina has become a living laboratory of struggle, a place where the popular politics of the future are being invented. In the face of poverty and economic meltdown, people have found enough hope to continue resisting, and have mustered sufficient creativity to begin building alternatives to the despair of capitalism. The global movements can learn much in this laboratory. In many ways it is comparable with the social revolutions of Spain in 1936, of France in May 1968, and more recently, in southern Mexico, with the 1994 uprising of the Zapatista Army for National Liberation (EZLN)—all rebellions that inspired, then and now, millions around the world.

ARGENTINE REBELLION

325

Nicolas Pousthomis

Unemployed piqeteros block roads, demanding a relief unemployment subsidy.

It was a spirit of innovative solidarity that sparked a transformation of the practice of politics, and led us into the first stage of this new evolution of people's movements. The Zapatistas sowed the seeds for creating "rebellions which listen" to local needs and demands, and which are therefore particular to each place, and activists from around the world responded, not only through traditional forms of international solidarity as practiced during the 1970s and 1980s, particularly by Central American solidarity groups, but also through applying the spirit of Zapatismo by "listening" at home.

This network of listening that has occurred between many different cultures has been a cornerstone for the first round of this global movement, as it wove together its multiple differences, forming a powerful fabric of struggle. The second round needs to maintain the networks that nurture the flow of mutual inspiration, because no revolution can succeed without hope. But the global anticapitalist movement also needs the reassurance of seeing its desires and aspirations being lived on a daily basis. The Zapatista autonomous municipalities in Chiapas are a kind of model, but are firmly rooted in indigenous culture, are small enclaves within a larger state, and are largely unexportable. Argentina, however, is an entire society undergoing transformation. It is a model that is much easier for the movements, especially those of the global North, to imagine implementing at home.

There is a joke currently circulating the Japanese banking community, that goes: "What's the difference between Japan and Argentina?" "About eighteen months." These bankers well know that the economic situation in Argentina will occur elsewhere, and that it is inevitable that the tug-of-war between people's desires for a better life and the demands of global capital will result in explosions across the planet. A recent report by the World Development Movement documents seventy-seven separate incidents of civil unrest in twenty-three countries, all relating to IMF protests, and all occurring in the year 2001. From Angola to Nepal to Colombia to Turkey, the same cracks are appearing in the neoliberal "logic," and people are resisting. A dozen countries are poised to be the "next Argentina," and some of them may be a lot closer to home than we ever imagined.

We need to be prepared, not only to resist but to find ways to rebuild our societies when the economic crisis hits. If the popular rebellion in Argentina succeeds, it could show the world that people are able to live through severe economic crisis and come out the other side, not merely having survived, but stronger and happier for struggling for new ways of living.

The economic crisis in Argentina continues to spiral out of control. Having succeeded in winning legal battles against the government (setting legal precedent that ricochets around the globe) and recovering their savings from banks, thousands of depositors are withdrawing their money from the banking system as fast as they can. In recent days a judge has sent a police contingent and a locksmith to a branch of HSBC to recover a claimant's savings, while the vault of a branch of Banco Provincia was opened with the aid of a blowtorch. With the banking system about to go belly up, the government decided to close all banks for an "indefinite holiday." When the IMF refused again to loan more money and the Argentinean Congress threw out a bill that proposed converting the frozen bank savings into IOU government bonds, the new minister of economy resigned. In an emergency press conference, President Duhalde declared, "Banks will have to open again and God knows what will happen then. Banks cannot be closed permanently. It would be absurd to think of a capitalist system without banks."

It may be absurd to think of a capitalist system without banks, but it is equally absurd to believe in the continuation of the present global system. Perhaps the most realistic thing to imagine at the beginning of this already war-torn century is a system free of capitalism, one without banks, without poverty, without despair, a system whose currency is creativity and hope, a system that rewards cooperation rather than competition, a system that values the will of the people over the rule of the market. One day we may look back at the absurdity of the present and remember how the people of Argentina inspired us to demand the impossible, and invited us to build new worlds which spread outward from our own neighborhoods.

PART 2

Returning to Rebellion — July 2002
by John Jordan

I arrived back in Argentina the day after the surprise announcement that early elections would be held in March of the following year. "I'm not going to vote, why condemn your candidate to hell? No one can govern this country," exclaims my friend Anabella on the way home from the airport.

Nicolas Pousthomis

The unemployed decide to block the circulation of goods on highways to make their demands.

It's true—no one in their right mind would want to take on the presidency of a country in such crisis. It's difficult for any politician to appear in public without being hounded by angry citizens, making campaigning a difficult task. General elections in most countries tend toward farce, George W. Bush's Florida coup being the most memorable recent example. But in a situation where the hatred for politicians is so endemic that the ex–finance minister, Domingo Cavallo, has employed a decoy in a mask, Argentina's elections are set to be pure burlesque.

Voting is compulsory in Argentina, unless you are 500 kilometers from your home on polling day. During the elections of 1999, an anticapitalist group took several hundred people 501 kilometers outside of Buenos Aires, to hold debates about direct democracy and register with an extremely perplexed local police force the fact that they weren't going to vote. In last October's congressional elections, a record 22 percent cast blank votes or abstained —many put pictures of Osama bin Laden in their voting envelopes. Recent polls have revealed that 63 percent of Argentineans don't believe in representative democracy. This time around many more will abstain. But breaking the law is commonplace now—even the middle classes, or what's left of them, are regularly refusing to pay taxes, or electricity bills.

There are three serious candidates who are struggling neck-and-neck in the polls. One of them, Luis Zamora, is a fascinating political paradox. Zamora is an ex-Trotskyite who has rejected his political past and has set up a social movement called "Self-determination and Freedom," which is influenced by Zapatismo and autonomist ideas.

His movement is using the public space opened up by the election process, mainstream media debates, and so on, to bring to light the rejection of representation and to highlight other forms of power such as the *asambleas* and the notion of direct democracy. When asked what he will do if he is elected, Zamora says he wouldn't last a day and that he doesn't want to be president anyway. "Go self-determine yourself," he says. "Take care of yourself, take it into your own hands. If you don't take it into your own hands, nothing is going to change."

He describes what is happening in Argentina as "a revolution in the heads of millions," a process where the entire country is rethinking representative politics, discovering horizontal ways of organizing, and beginning to realize a situation where "the population is doing politics" rather than the politicians. "The population is finding that it is facing itself," he explains, "Its culture is always to look above, this is the culture that we all have. This is why this moment is so passionate and beautiful, because it is rethinking this."

Killing Piqueteros

The *piquetero* movement has been growing across the country, and despite a media campaign of criminalization and warnings from the president that the government was no longer going to tolerate roadblocks, a large mobilization took place on the 26th of June, blockading some major arteries into Buenos Aires. After dispersing the crowd with tear gas, rubber, and real bullets, the police hunted *piqueteros* throughout the city, often firing from the back of cruising pickup trucks. What followed was the cold-blooded murder of two organizers, Darío Santillán and Maximiliano Kosteki, both in their early twenties and both from the most radical *piquetero* network. Darío was shot in the back at close range while he was helping Maxi, who had been shot in the chest. By the end of the day, 160 people had been arrested and over a hundred injured. It seems that the whole thing was set up as a stage-managed confrontation by the state, but it failed to break the movement and the response from every part of the popular rebellion was incredible. Thirty thousand took to the streets in support of the *piqueteros*, and within days, President Duhalde went on TV to apologize. The head of the secret service, the minister of justice, and

the chief of the Buenos Aires police force were all forced to resign, and the police officers involved in the operation were jailed. Days later, Duhalde announced the early elections, brought forward by nearly a year—a clear sign that he is hanging onto power by his fingertips, and that in Argentina it is people in the streets who are making politics.

Beneath the Masks

The bus drops us beside a dirt track dotted with perilous potholes filled with rubbish. The sulfurous smell of raw sewage rises from shallow channels of gray water that run alongside. We have arrived in Admiralte Brown, a huge sprawling neighborhood somewhere beyond the southern edges of Buenos Aires. It feels like a hybrid of shantytown, wasteland, and a crumbling soviet housing estate, a place where hope is in short supply and jobs are even fewer—unemployment runs at over 80 percent here. Yet this is a stronghold of one of the most radical groups of *piqueteros*, part of the Aníbal Verón network that was targeted on the 26th of June when Darío and Maxi were murdered. This network is itself is part of the larger Movimiento de Trabajadores Desocupados (MTD—Movement of Unemployed Workers).

A small, hand-painted sign marks the entrance to the MTD bakery. We pick our way through a pile of bicycles parked in the passageway leading to a courtyard where about twenty people sit in a circle taking part in a workshop. Most are in their early twenties—some a lot younger, a few a lot older. Despite the occasional barking dogs, the gusts of wind, crowing cocks, and small children running between the chairs, the participants seem intensely focused as Lola, the energetic young *piquetera* facilitator, hands out strips of paper. Stuck on the rough concrete wall in front of them is a large sheet of flip-chart paper divided into two columns, the left labeled "MTD," the right: "Capitalist System of Production."

The workshop is about to begin. As if on cue, a man bounces into the courtyard carrying a basket of warm doughnuts, which he passes around. Astor works in the collective bakery. Short and stocky, dressed in bright colors, and occasionally nicknamed Monkey, his wide face continuously beams a cheeky smile. He sits down munching a doughnut and joins the workshop.

"What's the difference between a bakery here and a bakery in the capitalist system?" asks Lola. "Who are we producing for here?"

Argentines topple their government on December 19-20, 2001, Buenos Aires..

"We produce for our neighbors," pipes up Yvette, a gray-haired woman in her fifties, her brown face furrowed like a deeply ploughed field, "and to teach ourselves to do new things, to learn to produce for ourselves."

"For whom do the bakers work in a capitalist system?" Lola continues.

"For the managers, for a corporation," replies María, who sports a silver ring in her nose.

"The people working in bakeries are people like us," says Astor, "but they have to work long hours, often up to 3 A.M. when the dough goes in the ovens. They work their bodies to the bone."

Miguel, slouched in the corner and wearing an Iron Maiden sweatshirt, butts in: "And yet the people who work hardest get the least reward; they work in subhuman conditions, earn nothing, and continue to work. But we produce so that everyone can live better." For a moment the group falls into contemplative silence.

Each strip of paper that Lola handed out has a statement written on it about either the collective MTD form of production or capitalist forms of production. The idea is that they attach their strip of paper on the appropriate column of the flip chart and explain why they think it should go there.

ARGENTINE REBELLION

Florencia Vespignani

en reunion - noviembre 2002   Flor, MTD Anibal Veron

A glum looking guy with long shaggy hair in a polyester black and red Nike tracksuit stands up first. He reads out his strip of paper. "The most important aim is to make profits." He shakes his head. "In the capitalist system, they don't care about peoples' health or nature. To them all that is interesting is making money. We produce for the needs of our neighbors . . . we need each other."

Yvette is next. "Only one person makes decisions." She slaps the strip onto the "capitalist" column. "We decide things together here, and the money we make we share among all of us."

One by one they all take turns, standing up, eloquently explaining the ways the different systems are organized and discussing each point at length. Suddenly two cats start to fight in the tree that overhangs the courtyard. Tania, a punky twenty-one-year-old who wears a chain and padlock around her neck and is in charge of the *piqeteros'* security, throws a stone at the screaming cats, who scamper across the rooftops.

The workshop winds down with a long discussion about the problems of working collectively. They discuss the issue of some people in the groups who didn't participate in the process of contributing part of their income

to the collective and how the *asamblea*, after much discussion, decided to expel them.

"Do these principles we have been talking about really happen in the MTD?" asks Lola, provocatively. Her extraordinary facilitation had meant everyone in the group had contributed to the debates.

"When we work together there are always some problems. Not everyone is used to common work," says Yvette.

"We are so used to a capitalist work system," exclaims María. "My father worked in a capitalist system, so did his father—we are all so used to being told what to do. For many people it's difficult to take any initiative, they just wait to be given orders. And you know what?" she continues, grinning. "We still have some authoritarians in our group! I'm not going to name names." Everyone bursts into laughter.

The Strength of Sharing

Martín is in his thirties, short, with dark piercing eyes and sharp features. He founded the Admiralte Brown *piquetero* group with Darío two and a half years ago by putting up a few posters. Today the group has two sections that meet in four different assemblies, with over 200 participants; the *piquetero* movement has become the key energy behind the popular rebellion spreading across Argentina, and Darío is dead, shot by the police three weeks ago.

Martín is the main person showing us around and introducing us to people here. His commitment to nonhierarchical organizing, like everyone's in the group, is total. He seems to have a leadership role that is not about coercion or command but about networking and storytelling. He displays a potent humility, yet has a charismatic confidence that enables him to make connections between people, and he has a great knack for telling inspiring tales.

As we walk through the sprawling district, he lists the different activities that they have self-organized: "We have a group building sewage systems and another that helps people who only have tin roofs on their houses to put proper roofs on. There is a press group to produce our own media and makes links with the outside media. We have the *Copa de Leche* (cup of milk), which provides a glass of milk to children every day. There's the bakery you just saw, and we're building vegetable gardens and a library. What we are about to see is the *ropero*, the common clothes store."

ARGENTINE REBELLION

333

Another wooden sign welcomes us to the MTD *ropero*. We walk into a small room where half a dozen women are sitting around a table. Behind them a set of shelves has a few articles of clothing folded on it. One woman is sewing by hand. They greet us warmly and sweet *mate* is handed around by Griselda, who shows us her red, swollen fingers: "We mend all the clothes by hand," she says, "It hurts my fingers so much, but we have no sewing machines."

She explains the function of the *ropero*, which distributes clothing to families who can't afford it. MTD people hand out explanatory leaflets, especially on the other side of the neighborhood, which is marginally better off but suffers just as much unemployment. People who have old clothes bring them here, where they are cleaned and mended. Then, twice a month, the *ropero* is open for people from the whole neighborhood to come and take clothes for free.

"How do you avoid people taking more than their fair share?" I ask.

"We have simple rules: no more than three items per person, and we have a book where we write down who has taken what," she says, showing us a neatly written ledger with a dedication to Maxi and Darío written on the inside page. "But the other day a mother came who has ten children, and we didn't have enough to give them all the clothes they needed," she sighs.

A collection of objects hangs on the walls of the room. There is a faded picture of Jesus wearing a crown of thorns, a gaudy plastic clock, and next to it a press cutting with the large headline *Autogestion*, a beautiful word that has no direct equivalent in English but means autonomous self-organizing, self-management. Beneath it is a hand-written sheet of paper that explains some of the principles of the movement. Listed under "Criteria for Work" are such things as: "Don't be a tourist in your groups, don't just sit and watch"; "Respect others"; "Give voluntary money to the common funds, especially if you get a Plan (unemployment subsidy)"; and "Go to the assemblies." Another column explains the criteria for assemblies, including "Give priority to those who don't speak"; "Don't be authoritarian"; "Don't speak for others"; and finally, "Criticize, don't complain." Griselda points out the back issues of the Admiralte Brown MTD photocopied newsletter also pinned to the wall, telling us that many of the women here cannot read and that every week when the newsletter comes out she reads it to them.

A woman at the end of the table holds up a pair of child's trousers she is working on, pointing to a large rip at the knees. "We don't have any material to make a patch, so we are cutting off the legs and turning them

ARGENTINE REBELLION

Florencia Vespignani

asamblea - mayo 2002   *Flor, MTD Anibal Veron*

into shorts," she explains. She then picks out a pair of Nike trousers from the shelf to show us what good condition some of the clothes that she mends are in. As she shows them to us, I wonder about the journey these trousers must have made, from the hands of a sweatshop worker in East Asia, via ships and shops, to Argentina, where they were bought, worn, donated, and then mended by another hand, finally to be given away as part of the project of an anticapitalist movement of unemployed workers.

Building Power

We are invited to have lunch with some of the people who work on the newsletter. They live on the other side of Admiralte Brown where small concrete houses give way to row after row of identical gray apartment blocks. Over lunch in a small flat that doubles as the newsletter office, we talk about global networks of resistance and swap stories of struggle and tactical tips. I tell them about the very different kind of roadblocks that I had been involved in with Reclaim the Streets in London. They tell me about the "Queen of the *Piquete*" fashion show that was put on by queer *piqueteros* during a roadblock. The extraordinary image of drag queens dancing through barricades of burning tires is a hard one to shake.

These kinds of apocalyptic images are the overriding public image of the *piqueteros*. Days before the murders of Darío and Maxi, the mainstream

ARGENTINE REBELLION

media manufactured stories of violence, including rumors that some *piqueteros* were preparing for armed uprisings inspired by leftist guerrillas. Minutes after the deaths, the media reported police statements that the deaths were the result of rivalry between different *piquetero* groups, something they had to retract when pictures of the police shooting directly at individuals at close range became public. Two enormous demonstrations of support with people from every social strata have taken place since then, and the *piquetero* movement is continuing to grow rapidly. "Since the 26th, links to the neighborhood assemblies movement have grown; they realize that we are not that different from them," explained Ana, one of the editors of the local MTD newsletter.

The murders and mass arrests of the 26th changed a lot for the Aníbal Verón network. "None of us are born an MTD activist—we have to become one. We are a new movement," María explained to me. "Since the deaths we have two priorities—to change the way we organize so as to dismantle the growing fear of repression, and to have food for everyone in the movement." A big debate is taking place about the tactic of using masks during actions, and it seems a decision has been made to stop wearing masks for the time being.

The challenge is to present the movement as unemployed workers first, *piqueteros* second. The *piquete* is just a tactic—though an amazingly successful one. They block the roads, demand a specific number of unemployment subsidies, and more often than not, get them from the local government. They have also used the tactic to back various demands, including getting food.

But it's the constructive aspects of the movement that they want to show the world: the self-organization, the direct democracy, and the numerous neighborhood projects such as the bakery, the *ropero*, and so on. As in many protest movements, it is these constructive elements which are so difficult to make visible. A powerful current runs deep in our culture that obscures constructive, creative situations with the spectacle of conflict and confrontation.

The murders were less than twenty days ago, and yet no one seems paralyzed by despair. "If another *compañero* had been killed, Darío would have kept up the struggle, in fact he would have worked even harder. . . . We have to continue to fight for food and projects—if we give up, we will have nothing," says Tania.

ARGENTINE REBELLION

Pillars of the Movement

After lunch we go to one of the two weekly MTD assemblies happening simultaneously in Admiralte Brown that afternoon. Next to piles of burnt plastic and a ruined wall with a circled A and the words *False Euphoria* graffitied onto it, a group of seventy or more people stand in a makeshift circle. Raising their voices against the cold biting wind, they openly discuss the problems of the past week, share information, and make plans for the following days.

A key event will be next week's commemoration of the June repression. Activists from the United States, part of Art and Revolution (one of the key groups involved in the Direct Action Network that shut down the WTO meeting in Seattle), have been working with the *piqueteros* over the last few days building giant puppets out of cardboard for the commemoration events. A young woman proudly presents her puppet, attached to a long stick that she holds high in the air.

It's mostly women who do the speaking at the assembly. Earlier, Ana had told me how women are the ones hit hardest by unemployment. When there is no food to put on the table, no clothes to dress the children, it is they who are at the sharp end of poverty. Often the men feel rejected and become paralyzed by the loss of identity that follows unemployment, and in many cases it's the women who have been the first to get out of the home into the streets to take part in *piquetes*. "Women's struggle is the pillar of the movement," she tells me.

Transforming the Fences

After the assembly, Martín takes us across a soccer field that has probably never seen grass and whose goals are so rusty that they seem to have been bent by the wind that blasts across this place. He shows us the *Copa de Leche*, the project that distributes milk to children.

Copa de Leche is housed in a squatted building next to an occupied plot of land. The fences that previously surrounded the land have been removed and all that remains of them are a few broken concrete posts. The rest have been cut up and used to build a brand-new oven for baking bread, a huge roaring outdoor oven standing on the edge of the deserted field and surrounded by newly dug vegetable plots. On the side of the oven one could just make out the words *Cambio Social* (social change) painted there the day before by young *piqueteros*, trying out their paint brushes during the puppet-making workshop.

Two huge men are stoking the fire and as we arrive we see them pull out a tray of freshly baked bread. Their faces beam with pleasure as they set eyes on the steaming loaves, the first batch ever to come out of the oven. They pass them to an elderly woman who takes them into the building, only to return a few seconds later scowling and handing them back, saying they haven't been cooked enough, that the dough inside is still raw. The men hang their heads with bruised pride and hastily stuff the tray back into the oven.

The image of fences being pulled down and the posts being turned into something practical is a beautiful metaphor for the transformation of the enclosures of capital into creative autonomous tools of social revolution—a transformation that involves people beginning to build the life that they want and preparing to defend it rather than simply protesting against what they don't want.

Whenever I asked people what had changed in their lives since they became involved in the MTD, they told me that the loneliness and isolation of unemployment and poverty had disappeared. Tania said to me, "The biggest change was the relationship with other people in the neighborhood, the development of friendship and the possibility of sharing. When you're on a roadblock and you have nothing to eat, the people next to you share their food. Now I feel I'm living in a large family, my neighbors are my family."

The fear and mistrust sown by the military dictatorship destroyed connections between people, and since then the dictatorship of the markets has built even more fences and separations. Now, the fences are being pulled down by the strength of sharing.

When I asked Tania whether she was aware of any past examples of self-management and autonomy—the Diggers, the Paris Commune, and so on, she replied: "No, I don't know these things. All I know is that I have lived here in the neighborhood all my life, and I see that people don't have proper homes, or food to put on their table, or streets that aren't muddy tracks—and I don't know what name to give to what we are doing here. All I can call it is 'social change.'"

Authors' note: Some names of individuals have been changed.

ARGENTINE REBELLION

Argentina's New Forms of Resistance

By Patricio McCabe

Patricio McCabe is active with Nuñez-Saavedra neighborhood assembly, is a writer, longtime activist, and teaches high school.

The southern cone of America is witness to a cruel paradox. There we find a country which, though it exports food for 330 million people annually, cannot feed its own 37 million inhabitants. That country is Argentina and, of course, it wasn't always like this.

In the context of Latin America, Argentina was considered exceptional for a good part of the twentieth century. Until the mid-seventies, it was enviable for its high levels of education, an unusually high amount of industrial development for the region, and above all for a social mobility that welcomed and absorbed an enormous quantity of immigrants from all over the world.

At the institutional level, however, there was a revolving door between civil governments and military coups. Whenever the workers made advances in gaining new rights, the military sector—with the complicity of the U.S. government—was called in to put a stop to those pretensions.

image top: Florencia Vespignani

During the first half of the seventies, under a popular government, the workers attained 48 percent of the gross national product. This was no concession of the capitalist class, but rather the fruit of the struggle of powerful labor and student organizations. In those years, the idea was growing that a social alternative to capitalism might be possible. Political prisoners were released, and some groups were turning to armed struggle. The capitalists were not able to conduct business as usual in such an atmosphere, and they decided to initiate a change of direction in order to be able to increase their profits. The first step was the destruction of the popular organizations, and once more they turned to the military and the wink of complicity from the U.S. embassy.

The year 1976 was a bloody milestone in the history of Argentina. On March 24 one of the most violent military coups in the already violent history of the continent took place. Some statistics will help to illustrate: 300 concentration camps, 30,000 detained-disappeared, and close to 300,000 exiled were the result of the "social surgery" performed on the body politic. The stated objective was to eradicate any glimmer of rebellion and to erase through terror the memory of any social change. And in this way, Argentina entered into its darkest years.

Atop this leveled landscape, the capitalists placed an IMF-sponsored economic shift. It was already clear that the attempt to extract profits from factories caused innumerable problems, so production was reoriented to livestock and agriculture, and to the financial speculation that was the order of the day. An economic model of this nature did not need factories, and these were closed one after the other.

The people were terrified, and for quite a while no collective projects or dissenting actions seemed possible. And so the first reaction to the dictatorial terror did not come from the sectors that previously had been active protagonists, but from a group of mothers of detained-disappeared. These mothers, defying death, opened the space for a new type of struggle that was to become known around the world. Seated in the plaza in front of the house of government (Plaza de Mayo), these housewives asked something impossible: the safe return of their sons and daughters who had been abducted by the military. The Mothers of the Plaza de Mayo were the first manifestation of a different way of doing politics. At a time when any action had seemed impossible, their resistance inspired the invention of new practices. The politics that the Mothers introduced was not reasonable, it did not emanate from the possibilities of the moment, but on the contrary, it was an attempt to introduce a new logic. Their message is that death must be defied in order to found a new life.

a tres meses - setiembre 2002   *Flor, MTD Anibal Veron*

Florencia Vespignani

By the time the military dictatorship came to an end, Argentina had been completely transformed. There were hardly any factories left in operation, the external debt had risen from $9 billion to $30 billion, and the new civil government found itself completely dependent on the mandates of the IMF. Over the next several years, the workers reinstated their struggle, but their stance was mostly reactive as they struggled to defend what they had from being taken away.

This was exemplified during the process of privatization. The "suggestion" of the international financial organizations was for Argentina to open up its economy to foreign capital and reduce the role of the state in public services, since in the view of the IMF this would ensure that the external debt could be repaid. Of course, the result was a major dependency upon foreign investment and the layoff of thousands of public employees. In order to create the "necessity" to privatize the state-owned companies, these had been intentionally "emptied," with the services they rendered becoming progressively worse until the mass media clamored for the modernization that could be brought about by privatization. The workers staged strikes in their own defense while the state bureaucrats who managed them worked to destroy them. Thus, the unions ended up associated with the defense of inefficient companies that offered substandard services, and the workers ended up struggling in isolation with no public support. The result was the defeat of this first round of struggles for the return of democracy.

Once the state companies were privatized and with most of the factories closed, the people began to face a new problem: unemployment. Unemployment rates soared to previously unknown levels: around 20 percent of the labor force with a similar percentage underemployed. A laid-off worker had little chance of reentering the workforce, and unemployment soon became synonymous with hunger for enormous sectors of the population. In the face of this threat, very few workers were willing to risk their jobs by striking, and so these actions ceased. The only resistance came from the students who saw threats to the system of free public education, and they worked on developing radical actions combined with direct democracy. In 1995, thousands of students created a human chain to prevent the delegates from entering Parliament to vote on a law that would open the door to the privatization of public education. That struggle was strongly criticized at the time by the mass media and the government who compared the students to the military for attacking democratic institutions. However, the student movement had brought up an idea that would grow in the years to follow: to eschew representative democracy and to seek direct democracy.

The Piquetero *Movement*

Two years later, a new form of struggle emerged from the unemployed workers in the provinces, which consisted of blocking roads to demand a subsidy for unemployment. This tactic has its origins in a factory-workers' practice known throughout the world: the picket (*piquete*) consists of blocking the entrance of a factory to prevent nonstriking workers from entering, in order to stop production. In this case, since they had already been banished from the site of production, the unemployed decided to block the circulation of goods in order to make their demands. Not only was this an original idea, but the way in which the actions were achieved was a breakthrough as well: direct democracy.

The first massive *piquete* took place in a province of southern Argentina, and in its coverage of the event the mass media pointed out that the government was having difficulty finding a leader to negotiate with. In response to the question of who was responsible for the direct action, the *piqueteros* simply responded: All of us! Those in charge of negotiating were in revolving positions that were revocable if they didn't represent the group's demands well. Without leaders to corrupt, the negotiations became quite complicated for the government; the *piquetero* movement was something they couldn't grasp, literally and figuratively.

The methods of the *piqueteros* signal a watershed in resistance history.

Previous forms of struggle had been hampered by the logic of representation—the unions, political parties, and the armed resistance organizations were and still are hierarchical structures with established leaders. Since this is a reflection of how the state is organized, the state knows exactly how to confront this logic. Direct democracy, however, is not easily assimilated by the state and it poses new problems.

An ahorrista *attacking a bank in protest of a government-imposed freeze of bank accounts, Buenos Aires, Argentina., February 2002.*

And so, along with the Berlin Wall, a way of understanding politics also fell. "Blocking the roads opens the way" is an expression that summarizes the gamble that the *piqueteros* took.

Previously, an unemployed worker would attempt to resolve his situation by approaching a local government functionary who, in exchange for his vote, would give him bags of food. As the bourgeois political system lost more and more credibility, the only way to become elected was to offer money and some food to the unemployed who, in this manner, "worked." As time passed and the country's situation worsened there wasn't much left to distribute, and in those crisis conditions the unemployed workers began to organize their demands collectively, rather than individually. In the face of a total indifference to their demands, the last resort was the decision to block the roads.

The blocking of roads to demand subsidies from the state is perhaps the only characteristic in common among the thousands of *piquetero* organizations that currently organize in Argentina. When they succeed, the government allocates an amount of subsidies to each organization; generally these don't exceed $50 per family, roughly one-third of the minimum income needed to survive. Many of the organizations distribute the subsidies individually by means of a point system: unemployed workers who have participated in the majority of marches and assemblies have a greater possibility of receiving the subsidy. Some of the organizations of greater Buenos Aires (where a third of the country's population lives) have a hierarchical structure with well-known leaders, and some have negotiated with the government to arrange partial road clearances so that traffic can move via alternate routes.

ARGENTINA'S NEW POLITICS

Andrew Stern / www.andrewstern.net

But there are other organizations—not the majority, but growing in number—with horizontal organizational structures that are more loyal to the original *piquetero* experience. These groups seek direct democracy and distribute the state subsidies in assemblies after a collective discussion. They remain autonomous from the state, from political parties, and from the unions. They hold education workshops where their members are schooled in basic movement practices, and others to address problems of health and nutrition. The potential of this movement is far from exhausted, and many are looking to the example of their actions.

The 19th and 20th of December, 2001

In December 2001, Argentina's financial crisis made front-page news in papers all over the world. The government's decision to close banks and freeze assets had worsened the situation for a broad majority of the population, and for many it had become intolerable. When thousands of Argentines began looting stores to obtain food and other life necessities, the government decreed a state of emergency that, among other things, suspended democratic liberties such as the right to gather and demonstrate. But on the day that the state issued its most restrictive orders, a huge, completely spontaneous demonstration broke out in Buenos Aires, and people poured into the streets, chanting a slogan that no one had heard before: "All of them must go! Every last one of them!"

At midnight on the 19th, a crowd of people headed for the Plaza de Mayo, banging on pots and pans and chanting. They stationed themselves in front of the government offices and remained there singing until dawn. This was not simply a reaction to the economic crisis, it was an antistate response to state repression. The people were shaking off the terror of the years of military dictatorship, and once again, there was no leader with whom the government could negotiate—this was another insurrection without author. There was a pitched battle at the plaza, with the crowd driving back the police time after time until they finally withdrew at dawn. The confrontations continued the next day and did not cease until the president resigned. A people's mobilization had managed to topple the government.

The pots and pans did not quiet down, however, and the demonstrations continued while four more presidents fell in succession. Meanwhile, the crisis appeared unsolvable.

344

The Popular Assemblies

As the months passed, neighbors who had joined in protests on the streets began to meet in assemblies. The spirit of those assemblies can be summarized in manifestos like the following transcript from a bulletin of the Nuñez-Saavedra assembly:

What is your dream?

Do you remember the 19th of December?

That night you said, enough of thieves.
Yes, you shouted it. . . . I heard you . . . we all heard you.
We also heard you when you said
I no longer want to be who I was.
I don't want them to decide anymore for me.
I don't believe in any politician anymore.
Nor in judges, nor in union leaders, nor in bankers.
Nor big businessmen, nor policemen.

I felt so much pride to see you and me

I did not expect so much of you . . . even less of me, you surprised me.
Because of that . . . because YOU pushed me. . . . I am walking to find a way.
. . . banging pots . . . thinking out loud in the assemblies, with my neighbors

Where are we going? you ask.

Well, we are trying to create with the neighbors a democratic assembly system from which our representatives can come forth. The majority express a firm refusal of existing political parties, there is no space for them in the assemblies. . . .

Assemblies sprouted like mushrooms in each neighborhood of the capital and extended out into the suburbs. There are now over 200 of them and the common thread is the rejection of all politicians, summed up in the slogan, "Everyone must go!" But just as in the *piquetero* movement, there are different political perspectives that coexist in the movement of the popular assemblies. One sector of the assemblies attempts to put pressure on the government by means of marches and demonstrations because they believe that without the resources of government, it won't be possible to

achieve any lasting change. Their objective is to seize power either by electoral means or direct action.

Another sector, however, believes that a different power must be created because nothing can be salvaged from what already exists. In general, they tend to operate by redefining public space, occupying coffee shops, banks, and fields with the objective of making cultural centers or organic gardens. There is not yet a theory to unify these practices, but that doesn't deter things, in fact, the occupation of spaces is a growing trend.

Similar things are happening in the workers' movement. With the economic crisis, many of the capitalists abandoned their factories and these are being appropriated by the workers who then self-manage them by forming cooperatives. It is calculated that around eighty factories are in this situation. Lately, there have been congresses of workers to discuss the best way of taking charge of production.

The refusal to delegate to others the solutions to the problems in our lives is creating experiences of self-determination previously unthinkable in this corner of the world. The process is completely open at this point, and its end result is uncertain. How long will the world's ruling class tolerate the experiments under way in Argentine society? Will the resistance be able to transform itself into an alternative to government? These questions remain without answers.

CHAPTER 24

Consciousness + Commitment = Change

By the Coalition of Immokalee Workers

The CIW is a community-based worker organization whose members are largely Latino, Haitian, and Mayan Indian immigrants working in low-wage jobs throughout the state of Florida.

The NAWS (National Agricultural Workers Survey) paints a very grim picture of conditions under which farmworkers live and work. Low wages, sub-poverty annual earnings, significant periods of un- and underemployment, and low utilization of safety net programs all add up to a labor force in significant economic distress.
— U.S. Department of Labor Report to Congress, January 2001

Taco Bell is a multi-national corporation with $5.2 billion in annual sales, and is part of Yum Brands, the world's largest restaurant system with $22 billion in annual receipts. Yet the tomatoes Taco Bell uses in their tacos and chalupas continue to be produced under sweatshop conditions. To a significant extent, Taco Bell's tremendous global revenues are based on cheap ingredients for the food they sell, including cheap tomatoes picked by farmworkers in Florida paid sub-

photo top: David Hanks

poverty wages. Well, we as farmworkers are tired of subsidizing Taco Bell's profits with our poverty. We are calling for this boycott today as a first step toward winning back what is rightfully ours—a fair wage and respect for the hard and dangerous work we do.
—Lucas Benitez, CIW, in Orlando, April 1, 2001, at protest announcing formal call for the national boycott of Taco Bell

The CIW is the strength of the poor worker.
—Diego Bautista Mateo, CIW member, January 1998, during thirty-day hunger strike by six CIW members

Immokalee, the heart of Florida's tomato and citrus industries, and the place where the Coalition of Immokalee Workers was born, is more a labor reserve than a town. It is an unincorporated place where the population nearly doubles (to somewhere between 20,000 and 30,000 people) during the nine months of the year from September to June that the agricultural industry needs workers. (From June through August, most farmworkers migrate north to states along the length of the East Coast for the shorter northern harvest season.)

The workforce is 85 to 90 percent male. The median age is twenty-four and falling (in fact, according to one local health official, the average age of Immokalee's farmworkers is closer to twenty-one). The vast majority of the young, single males living and working in Immokalee come from rural farming communities in Mexico, Guatemala, and Haiti, in that order. Most are very recent immigrants, with many only a few days or weeks from having arrived in the country. And while Immokalee may be the first destination for many recent immigrants, most will not remain here for long. The turnover in our community is unparalleled, as workers are lured away daily by the call of higher wages and more favorable working conditions in just about any industry other than the fields.

The CIW has over 2,000 members. Only a handful speak even halting English. Instead, if you stand on just about any street corner in Immokalee you can easily hear four or five different languages—Spanish, Haitian Creole, Mixtec, Kanjobal, Quiche, Tztotzil, and more. In a cultural sense, Immokalee is one of the most cosmopolitan communities in the South, despite the fact that we have only four traffic lights (all on Highway 29, the main road through town), and the biggest store in town is the Winn Dixie supermarket. In fact, Immokalee in many ways represents the changing face of the South today.

Despite its well-earned reputation as hostile territory for labor and organizing, the South is in fact home to several of the most militant organizing efforts in the country today, including the Charleston, South Carolina, dockworker' (Local 1422) struggle and our own campaign here in Florida, a campaign that has included three communitywide general strikes, a month-long hunger strike by six CIW members, a two-week-long march across the southern half of Florida, and, now, a national boycott of fast-food giant Taco Bell spearheaded by the country's poorest workers. Creative, community-based, and highly politicized organizing campaigns are becoming increasingly common throughout the region—UNITE for dignity in Miami, Black Workers for Justice, and the Miami Workers Center all speak to the breadth of a grassroots militancy growing in the heart of the South.

But more than that, today's South is undergoing a dramatic demographic shift that is transforming the low-wage labor sector. In fact, in many ways, today's South has far more in common with twenty-first-century Los Angeles than it does with 1960s Montgomery. That is not to say that race— and in particular the relationship between African Americans and white southerners—does not remain the central axis around which life in the South revolves. It does, but there is also an important new issue in southern reality—the rapid and widespread influx of immigrant workers into the southern labor force—that must be clearly understood and factored into the organizing equation, particularly when the question of labor is at hand.

Today, the South is home to some of the most rapidly growing Latino and indigenous communities in the country. Almost without exception, employment has been the magnet drawing these new immigrants to communities throughout the region. From the carpet factories of Dalton, Georgia, to the poultry plants of Sand Mountain, Alabama, from the watermelon fields of Kennet, Missouri, to the tobacco farms of Clinton, North Carolina, you will find recent immigrants from Mexico and Central America holding a growing majority of the back-breaking, low-paying, union-busting jobs. But the list does not stop there. In construction, health care, landscaping, janitorial, restaurant, and just about any service job you can name—Caribbean, Guatemalan, Salvadoran, and Mexican immigrants are by far the fastest growing sector of the workforce in today's low-wage South. Urban or rural, it's the same story.

In short, Immokalee is a crossroads between the rural poverty of the global South and the promise of a modern job paying a minor fortune in American dollars. It is an employer's dream and an organizer's nightmare. Ethnically and linguistically divided, largely undocumented (with many still in debt to their "coyotes," the people who lead undocumented immigrants across the border and across the country to Florida), highly mobile, dirt-poor,

largely nonliterate, and culturally isolated from the mainstream community of southwest Florida, the Immokalee farmworker community could not be more challenging to traditional organizers armed with traditional organizing approaches.

What's more, farm labor is excluded from the National Labor Relations Act, denying farmworkers the legal rights and protections that have made it possible for almost all other American workers to organize and join unions since 1935. And worse yet (as if that weren't enough), the agricultural labor force in Immokalee is structured as one big labor pool, where thousands of people wake up at 4 A.M. every morning to beg for a day's labor at the central parking lot in town, and where workers pick up paychecks from three to four different companies every Friday evening. This means that virtually none of the major agricultural corporations that operate in southwest Florida have fixed workforces. There is no such thing as "Pacific Land Co.'s workers" or "Gargiulo's crews," there are only Immokalee workers and changing faces picking, planting, and pulling plastic in company fields on any given day. Put all this together, and you have a town where workplace organizing in any normal sense of the term is effectively impossible.

And that is why the country's worst-paid, least-protected workers remained unorganized for so long. Until, that is, about eight years ago, when a small group of workers with experience in organizing back home in Guatemala, Haiti, and Mexico started to bring that experience to their lives as farmworkers here in the United States.

The CIW — A Short History

In the early 1990s, Haiti was undergoing another wave of intense political unrest and violence. The presidency of Jean-Bertrand Aristide, a former priest and fiery leader of the community-based movement to oust the twenty-eight-year dictatorship of the Duvalier family, had been overthrown by yet another military coup, and leaders of the grassroots democratic movement were being killed and jailed throughout the country. As a result, a new wave of Haitian "boat people" set out for the shores of Florida, among them many seasoned veterans of some of the most intense grassroots political organizing in this hemisphere's recent history.

Many of those new Haitian refugees made their way to Immokalee, as there was already a significant Haitian community established here during an earlier wave of immigration in the 1980s. Once in Immokalee, they joined Guatemalan and Salvadoran refugees fleeing war and human rights attacks against peasant organizations in their own countries, as well as an

EN LA MESA DE LOS RANCHEROS —

Them (Ellos) and us (nosotros) at the table of the ranchers. One of the popular education drawings CIW posts around town and uses for discussions.

increasing influx of indigenous immigrants from southern Mexico, many of whom came from the soon-to-be-famous state of Chiapas and had participated in the rapidly evolving Zapatista movement.

A history of struggle united many of these new immigrants, but it was a history that, for the most part, people did their best to forget and leave behind as they scratched out a living in the harsh fields of Florida's tomato and citrus industries. What immigrants found in those fields in the early 1990s was anything but refuge. Violence, wage theft, and modern-day slavery—where entire crews of workers were drawn into debt and forced, by threat of death, to work against their will—were common phenomena. Farmworker housing was a disgrace that hadn't been improved since it was first exposed in the 1960 documentary *Harvest of Shame*, and most workers lived with no phones, no cars, no heat and no air conditioning. Workers picked at a piece rate that hadn't gone up in nearly twenty years. In fact, the piece rate was inching its way down in the early 1990s, little by little, as more and more refugees showed up and the labor market grew increasingly flooded. Benefits, of course, were nonexistent. Farmworkers received no overtime pay, sick leave, health insurance, holiday leave, paid vacation, or pension, and if you tried to organize you were fired with absolutely no legal recourse.

FARM WORKERS

But not everyone had left their tools of struggle at home. A small group of workers, including Haitian peasant "animators" (organizers from the Mouvman Peyizan Papay, Haiti's largest peasant movement) and members of rural organizations from Guatemala, Mexico, and Haiti, began meeting to discuss their new situation as immigrants. These workers were determined to find solutions to some of the most pressing problems facing the Immokalee farmworker community, and to do so they decided it would be necessary to finally "unpack" their organizing experience from their home countries and put it to use here in Florida. From a room borrowed from Immokalee's Catholic church, the workers launched an organizing process that drew directly from Latin American and Caribbean organizing traditions for both its methods and its overall, long-term strategy.

Specifically, these experienced organizers employed three key tools common to their organizing experiences at home to forge a movement for grassroots, democratic, worker-led change here in the United States: 1) popular education, used to provoke participatory analysis of the problems facing farmworkers in Immokalee, 2) leadership development, to guarantee a constantly growing, broad base of leadership in the high-turnover worker community, and 3) powerful political actions, both to serve as an additional tool for building awareness and leadership within the movement, and to create a growing pressure on the agricultural industry to negotiate fundamental changes for farm labor, in the absence of the traditional organizing tools most other American workers have had at their disposal since 1935 to legally compel their employers to the table (signature cards, elections, the NLRB, etc.).

Using these three key tools, the CIW today fights for:

a fair wage for the work we do, more respect on the part of our bosses and a more powerful voice in the industries where we work, the right to organize without fear of retaliation, better and cheaper housing, and stronger laws and stronger enforcement against those who would violate workers' rights, with a particular focus on those employers who continue today to hold immigrant agricultural workers in debt bondage. —CIW literature

Over the past several years, the CIW has made unprecedented material progress for farmworkers in the South. Its most significant accomplishments to date include: winning the first raise in the tomato picking piece rate in over twenty years for thousands of Florida farmworkers (an industrywide raise, ranging from 13 to 25 percent, implemented not just in Florida but in all the East Coast states where the Florida-based tomato growing corporations operate, as well); effectively

Coalition of Immokalee Workers

eliminating wage theft and violence against day-haul farmworkers in southwest Florida's fields; uncovering, investigating, and bringing four major, modern-day slavery cases to successful prosecution in cooperation with the Civil Rights Division of the U.S. Justice Department involving hundreds of farmworkers (and consulting with federal authorities on two additional cases); and causing state authorities to dedicate more than $15 million in new housing funds for farmworkers both in Immokalee and throughout the state of Florida. The CIW's latest campaign, the national boycott of Taco Bell, has raised the problem of subpoverty wages and sweatshoplike working conditions in Florida's fields to a level of national awareness that promises even more significant change in the future.

CIW Methods and Strategy

It may be necessary to elaborate, briefly, on the practical meaning of the three organizing tools mentioned above as they are employed in Immokalee. Popular education is perhaps the best place to start, as it is the heart and soul of the entire CIW program. As the CIW motto goes: "Consciousness + Commitment = Change," and popular education, in many forms, is the way CIW members build consciousness among their fellow workers.

FARM WORKERS

David Hanks

Popular theater: "The Marriage of Queen Cheap Tomato and King Taco Bell" by Art and Revolution and CIW farmworkers.

Popular education is a method of education and organization born in the countryside of Brazil and developed in struggles throughout Latin America and the Caribbean. Several of the CIW's original founders not only had experience with popular education but were trained practitioners of the approach through their community organizations at home. At its heart is the use of "codes" drawings, theater, song, video, stories, and so forth—designed to capture a piece of community reality and to present that reality for reflection in a group. The reflection process is usually led by a worker or team of workers with experience in facilitating participatory discussion.

The objective of popular education is to oblige workers to confront the problems in their community in a form that allows, and in fact actively encourages, even the most reticent workers to participate. It is an approach to what U.S. labor organizers tend to call "political education" that ties complex political issues to the concrete conditions of workers' lives through simple but compelling forms, with an emphasis on images, the best of which spark lively conversations that make their way almost effortlessly to discussion of how to address the problem presented in the image. By making political analysis understandable and facilitating the group reflection in a way that brings peripheral members to the center of the process, it challenges workers to abandon their apathy and isolation, to actively analyze their reality, and to redefine their relationship to the forces that shape their lives. It is education for action, and as such its effectiveness must ultimately be measured by the degree to which it moves the community to take action, fight for change, and win a degree of control over its collective destiny.

Leadership development as practiced in the CIW's work also draws its inspiration from the Latin American and Caribbean organizing experience.

FARM WORKERS

In Immokalee, farmworkers interested in sharpening their leadership skills and learning new tools for working with the community can participate in intensive workshops, lasting from two to seven days, where workers study and practice everything from techniques of popular education to the history of the labor movement, labor and human rights, how to plan and run community meetings, the practice of popular theater, economic and political analysis, and even techniques of video production. Participation in the CIW leadership development process is self-selected and is open to any and all members, from the longest-term veterans to the most recently arrived workers, as one of its primary goals is to constantly broaden the leadership base of the organization. In that way, the CIW is best able to counter the erosion of that base caused by the movement of even the most dedicated leaders out of Immokalee toward better, more stable employment.

CIW staff is composed of workers elected by their fellow workers at the annual general assembly. They are members chosen, on the basis of their demonstrated commitment to the CIW's struggle, to handle the daily functions of the organization. Staff members get hands-on training in important new skills and gain insight into the world of organizing in the United States, including the use of computer technology (through e-mail and the CIW Web site), the ins and outs of the U.S. political system, press outreach, and fund-raising. To guarantee that those elected to the staff remain rooted in farmworker reality, however, CIW members established several key organizational bylaws. Staff salaries are commensurate with farmworker wages, the staff structure is nonhierarchical, and staff members are required to spend a significant amount of time every year working in the fields. The opportunity to work as part of the staff is another excellent form of leadership development open to all members, requiring only their active commitment to the organization and their election by fellow members.

Through this constant emphasis on leadership development, the actual, practical leadership of the organization—in terms of such things as running meetings, planning strategy and developing campaigns, and representing the organization in public forums—is able to remain open and fluid, and is shared by any number of active, informed members. As a result, several CIW leaders—young, immigrant workers, men and women—have been recognized nationally for their outstanding efforts over the past several years. The CIW stands out in its extraordinary focus on immigrant, worker leadership from today's working class.

In a certain sense, it can be said that the CIW has made a virtue of necessity in two important ways, both of which are made necessary by the

FARM WORKERS

David Hanks

Marching against Taco Bell, San Francisco, 2002.

high turnover of the Immokalee community. Because every season—every month, even—brings a significant percentage of new workers to Immokalee, the CIW can never abandon the basic political education process (popular education) that informs and motivates workers to become active CIW members. And because even the most committed leaders inevitably move on to better work in distant states, or back home to their families in Mexico, Guatemala, and Haiti, the CIW must maintain a constant process of leadership development to grow and replenish its leadership base.

From this basis, the CIW has organized various high-profile, aggressive, successful actions since 1995. The first major, communitywide action came as a response to the beatings and abuse of workers in the field which in the early nineties was a widespread practice by many local contractors. When a worker who had been beaten for drinking water without permission came to the coalition with his ripped and bloodied shirt, we responded with a 500-person March to End Violence to the home of the contractor who had perpetrated such a heinous act. Since that time the reports of such intolerable abuses in the Immokalee area has come to an end. Actions since 1995 have included three communitywide general strikes, a thirty-day hunger strike by six CIW members ended by the intervention of former president Jimmy Carter, a two-week, 240-mile march across south and central Florida, and now a national boycott of Taco Bell, a major buyer of tomatoes picked in Immokalee.

The centerpiece of the boycott to date has been the "Taco Bell Truth Tour," a cross-country bus and van tour from Florida to California by seventy workers and thirty students, with stops for rallies and protests in major cities across the way in March 2002. The fifteen-city, seventeen-day tour culminated in massive protests—bringing together allies from across the spectrum, including students, anarchists, labor, community, and religious organizations—in Los Angeles and Irvine, California, home of Taco Bell's corporate headquarters. It was the first major "convergence style" action directed at an individual corporation, resulting in a historic, first-time meeting between executives of a multinational fast-food corporation and the farmworkers who produce the raw materials for their products.

Because farmworkers are exempted from the NLRA, the CIW has had to carry on the tradition of high-profile actions that have become typical of farmworker organizing since the fasts and marches of Cesar Chávez and the UFW in the 1960s and 1970s. Without access to NLRB mediation and the more rational, democratic means of an election/appeals process to compel employers to the table, farmworkers have little choice but to use spectacular protests to bring public pressure to bear on the industry for the right to negotiate for better wages and working conditions.

But the CIW also looks at these actions as opportunities for further conscientization and leadership development, and thus strives to shape its actions so as to maximize those opportunities. As a result, the CIW tends to employ forms of protest that allow the broadest participation by CIW members possible, while favoring long-running, often radical actions that offer ample time and material for reflection and the concerted building of political awareness.

The hunger strike of 1997–1998, for example, was a historic, month-long political statement by six tomato pickers, supported by a committee of several other members that watched over the strikers twenty-four hours a day. Today, many of the participants in that action remain central leaders in the organization. Similarly, CIW strikes have not been specific to one grower but have involved the entire community and have taken on the industry as a whole. This is in part due to the community labor pool structure of the labor market in Immokalee, but also to the CIW's casting of grievances in political as well as economic terms. Because CIW members generally understand and define strikes within the broader framework of human rights, strike actions tend to become events that galvanize the entire community and challenge the basic assumptions of agriculture's oppressive power structure. CIW marches also follow this pattern, with the routes covering several days or even weeks of ten- to twenty-mile stretches by day, followed by public meetings and internal reflections by

David Hanks

The Taco Bell Truth Tour is an example of long-duration participatory tactics.

night. The marches, like most CIW actions, have been radicalizing experiences that cement bonds between members and do much to counteract the forces that atomize the Immokalee community and contribute to its unequaled transience.

Even in the case of the Taco Bell boycott—a form of action that in the past has tended to shift limited organizational resources away from worker organizing to consumer education—the CIW has sought to develop its strategy in such a way as to both ensure broad-based, long-term participation by its members and to contribute to the overall political education process that lies at the foundation of our work.

The Taco Bell Truth Tour is an example of the emphasis on long-duration, participatory tactics. Furthermore, the decision to explicitly link the boycott to the broader movement for global justice, through the focus on building strong ties to the youth and radical sectors that have been at the forefront of that movement and through the "convergence style" actions in front of Taco Bell headquarters, reflects the conscious effort on the part of the CIW to place the farmworkers' struggle firmly within the growing debate over globalization, corporate responsibility, and human and economic rights. The Taco Bell Campaign in general and the Truth Tour, in particular, has helped to galvanize alliances between workers from Immokalee and students from across the nation, and resulted in the

David Hanks

The Taco Bell boycott has the potential to become a landmark campaign for the future of farmworker organizing.

historic first-time meeting between farmworkers and executives of a fast-food corporation.

For workers forced from their countries by economic and political conditions linked, in large part, to World Bank and IMF policies, workers who find themselves now in the United States exploited by a major multinational corporation that profits directly from their poverty, the leap from general strikes in the tomato fields to global mobilizations for economic justice like those in Seattle, Washington, and Genoa, is not a difficult one.

For the movement as a whole, the CIW's experience with participatory, democratic methods of education and organizing not commonly found in the United States, its explicitly political orientation and growing network of ties to the emerging movement for global justice, and its proven track record for developing dynamic, young immigrant leaders from today's working class all speak to the valuable contribution that the CIW could make to the movement as a whole.

Furthermore, the CIW was forged in the heat of a long-term, immigrant worker-led struggle against one of the country's most economically powerful and politically entrenched industries—agriculture. There are many lessons that can be drawn from our struggle when contemplating the organization of immigrant workers in other industries throughout the

FARM WORKERS

region, and many resources developed here that can be employed in organizing efforts outside of the fields of Florida. Indeed, we have done leadership development workshops for immigrant community organizations in the South, there is no reason why the same couldn't be done with organizations in similar populations. If the CIW can find success in an environment as hostile to organization as that here in Immokalee, there is no reason why immigrant workers in more stable, less harsh employment conditions in communities around the country could not do the same—or more.

The Taco Bell boycott has the potential to become a landmark campaign for the future of farmworker organizing. If the boycott is successful in gaining access to the resources of the fast-food industry for the purpose of improving the wages and working conditions of the farmworkers that supply the industry with tomatoes and other produce, it could open up organizing possibilities that have for decades remained mired in a tired stalemate between workers and growers, who for their part claim an absolute inability to pay more and remain in business.

The Capitalist City or the Self-Managed City?

By Tom Wetzel

Tom Wetzel has worked as a gas-station attendant, college teacher, typesetter, and technical writer. He is currently a member of the board of directors of the San Francisco Community Land Trust.

Patterns of capital flows have a visible effect on working-class communities in the United States. Some communities see closed plants, abandoned stores, boarded-up dwellings, scarce jobs. Such are signs of disinvestment. Capital has moved to some other site in the global production line.

In other times and places an inflow of investment fuels gentrification. Upscale condos are erected, houses are rehabbed. Candle-lit restaurants and vintage furniture emporia displace bodegas and used appliance stores. Rents rise as landlords realize they can attract professionals and business people as tenants. An area of "valuable city real estate" is being cleansed of its working-class residents.

HOUSING

Both phases in this process fuel conflict. Squatters occupy vacant buildings. Tenants threaten a rent strike in response to deferred maintenance. Tenant activists push for rent control ordinances in response to rising rents. Antigentrification activists jam planning commission hearings to stop upscale condo projects. At the extreme edge, some resort to the torching of condos under construction.

We can regard all of these as expressions of class struggle over the built environment.

Both gentrification and disinvestment are processes made up of the activities of certain kinds of social agents or institutions. Landlords, developers, and banks all play key roles.[1]

Buildings represent a major investment. For this reason, they are not replaced for many years after they are built. An older area in an American city may have been converted from agricultural land to urban uses in the nineteenth century or early twentieth century. As the lots in a newly subdivided area get built upon, builders and subdividers move outward into more outlying areas in search of new building sites.

A building is like a piece of machinery or a motor vehicle; it depreciates in value over time. The roof may need to be replaced after years of beating back the rain. The building style may go out of fashion. Technological changes such as new standards in electrical or plumbing systems may erode the value of a building.

Some neighborhoods continue to retain their ability to attract professional and business people to live there. Landlords in such areas will have an incentive to upgrade their buildings because they can command rents high enough to generate a good return on that investment.

The housing market tends to sort the population by income into different areas. Racism may add another type of sorting. If an area is increasingly filled by lower-income residents, landlords have an incentive to not maintain their properties. If they were to invest in upgrades, they'd need to charge a higher rent to make this a profitable investment. People who could pay the higher rents may not be willing to live in that neighborhood. So landlords simply "milk" the decaying buildings for rents. By putting off repairs, they can save money to buy other buildings elsewhere.

The process of inner-city disinvestment was particularly prolonged in the United States after World War II. Rising real wages, Federal Housing Administration loan policies, the homeowner interest deduction on income

taxes, corporate decisions to relocate plants to outlying areas, massive freeway construction, white flight; all these things contributed to the outflow of investment into suburbanization and lack of investment in older city areas.

As the urban area grows, the terrain now occupied by deteriorated buildings and a low-income population may be close to areas of concentrated economic activity such as a downtown. Closeness to downtown jobs and interesting older architecture may give the area the potential to attract higher income residents or more well-endowed businesses.

A gap thus emerges between the rents that an area of deteriorated buildings and low-income residents can generate and the potential rents that the area could generate if it were rebuilt or renovated to its "highest and best use." Neil Smith coined the phrase "rent gap" to refer to this phenomenon.[2] When this rent gap becomes large enough, the area may be ripe for a new round of investment. Speculators may begin to buy properties in anticipation of increased market values of properties.

To make investment in new construction and rehab profitable, developers must be able to attract residents who can pay higher rents such as professionals and managers (the urban "gentry"). Once this process gets under way, "landlords will have an incentive to evict low-income residents in favor of more affluent tenants who can afford higher rent."[3] During this phase landlords may want to drive out the lower-income tenants. To do this they may avoid repairs, let the roof leak, and so on.

Banks and other financial institutions turn on the faucet for mortgage and construction loans. Construction of condos and office buildings raise real estate values as other landowners realize that more upscale uses of the land are now possible.

Gentrification in the Bay Area

Gentrification in the Bay Area illustrates how investment decisions by industrial employers can also have an impact on residential areas within commuting distance of job sites. Since the 1970s the high-tech sectors—microchips, Internet equipment, software, and so on—have come to dominate the regional economy. For years the industry has pursued a strategy of locating most of its manufacturing facilities outside the Bay Area. For example, in the mid-eighties Atari moved its video game manufacturing plant to Malaysia in response to an effort by workers to unionize the plant.

  363

This has created a skewed job structure, with a high proportion of high-salaried jobs—in "business development," marketing, design and engineering, and so on. At the same time, closures of food processing plants and decline of maritime shipping and ship maintenance led to a loss of better-paying, unionized jobs. For example, in 1990 the Best Foods mayonnaise plant in San Francisco was closed; the operation moved to Guatemala.

Meanwhile, housing construction in Silicon Valley fell far behind the surging employment rolls. The shortage fueled gentrification of working-class areas (with particular impact on communities of color) from East Palo Alto to Oakland to the east side of San Francisco.

These changes illustrate the link between corporate globalization and gentrification.

San Francisco's Mission District was on the front line of this process in the late nineties. The Mission District had gone through a period of prolonged disinvestment during the post–World War II boom years. The construction of the BART subway under the main commercial street of the neighborhood, Mission Street, had accelerated business flight in the sixties. The disinvestment led to an urban renewal proposal which would have bulldozed the center of the neighborhood. This was successfully fought off, through massive community organizing, with the support of the unions.

By the 1980s neighborhoods to the west and east of the Mission were heavily gentrified. The neighborhood had become the heart of the Latino community in San Francisco. The concentration of many low-income people of color, together with media stories about the crime and gang activities that often afflict low-income areas, had discouraged white professional people moving into the neighborhood. Apartments were still relatively cheap.

Yet the area is centrally located, with easy access to the 46 million square feet of office space in downtown San Francisco. Freeway ramps lead to high-tech job areas to the south of San Francisco. A "rent gap" thus existed between the current rental stream generated by the existing population and potential rents or real estate prices this inner-city real estate might generate if it could be redeveloped for the Bay Area's burgeoning population of professionals and managers.

Several types of social agent pioneered the gentrification process in the Mission District. In the mid-nineties antiunion contractors of the Residential Builders Association began buying cheap land in an old factory district in the northeast Mission to build loft condos.

By 2000 they were selling at a half million dollars a pop. A real estate agent told me that such condos would typically be bought by a young couple, each making $90,000 a year.

The state Ellis Act, passed in 1996, permitted landlords to "go out of business" and empty their buildings of tenants. In the late nineties a speculator could buy a fourplex in the Mission for $500,000, invoke the Ellis Act to empty it, and then sell the units for $250,000 each as a tenancy-in-common.

David Hanks

MAC, a coalition of community and global justice groups, marches on a San Francisco slumlord in solidarity with Quebec City protests of the FTAA, April 2001.

Ellis Act evictions in the Mission District mushroomed from 14 in 1995 to over 660 in 2000. About a third of the Ellis Act evictees in the city were elderly people.

The Mission Anti-Displacement Coalition (MAC) was formed in April 2000 to fight the displacement of the Latino working-class community. A series of defensive struggles unfolded in which gentrifying office or condo projects were resisted, through protests at city planning commission meetings, mass marches, initiative campaigns, illegal occupations of buildings, postering, and agitprop of all kinds.

This led to MAC's campaign to popularize urban planning concepts, and demand community participation in a replan of the neighborhood—counterposing a "People's Plan" to the developers' plans. Demands for affordable housing and defense of blue-collar industrial jobs (threatened by the cannibalizing of industrial areas[4] for offices and condos) have been priorities of the MAC effort.

However, 84 percent of the households in the Mission are renters. Without ownership of the land, the community remains at the mercy of landlords and developers.

Despite the post-2000 dot-com crash and recession, rents in San Francisco are still very high. A union janitor in San Francisco making $15 an hour

HOUSING

can't afford to pay $1,300 a month for a one-bedroom apartment in the Mission.

As each rent-controlled apartment becomes vacant, the rent rises to whatever the market will bear. State law prevents the city from requiring that a controlled rent be carried over to the next tenant.

Over time, the market-driven displacement of the working class from San Francisco will affect the political character of the city. Unions and renters will face a less friendly political climate in a city made up of lawyers, bosses, software engineers, and the like.

A Self-Management Approach to Housing

"The opposite of gentrification," says Peter Marcuse, "should not be decay and abandonment but the democratization of housing."[5] Community land trusts may be a way of working toward this goal.

About 125 community land trusts (CLTs) have been formed in communities in the United States in response to either disinvestment or gentrification. The CLT acquires land to take it permanently off the market and make it available for the use of the community. As a democratic organization, the CLT is intended to empower the community in determining what is done with land in that area. The CLT may rehab existing buildings, build new houses or apartment buildings, or do other types of development work. The typical aims of the CLT approach are:

- Resident control of housing
- Community control over land use and development
- Removal of land and housing from the speculative market
- Making sure that housing remains permanently affordable to working-class people.

The residents own the buildings but the CLT retains ownership of the land. This is how permanent affordability is enforced. The dwellings on the CLT land cannot be sold at whatever price the market will bear. Instead, there is a clause in the ground lease that enables the CLT to buy back the dwelling at a restricted price if the resident wants to sell it. The CLT enforces the community's interest in preserving the affordability of housing.

In recent decades most nonprofit housing development in the United States has been done by community development corporations (CDCs) that build rental housing. These vary considerably among themselves but many are lacking in democratic accountability to the tenants or the

communities where they operate. Generally the tenants in their buildings have the same sort of relationship to the CDC landlord as tenants in private, for-profit rental buildings.

The problem is illustrated by a recent upheaval at Mission Housing Development Corporation (MHDC), a CDC in the Mission District. MHDC's self-perpetuating board decided to reorient away from low-income housing in the Mission toward market-rate housing, including development outside the city. This led to an uprising of the staff, who unionized and demanded resignations of board members and structural changes to make MHDC more accountable to the community and residents in MHDC buildings.

The community land trust model differs from the typical CDC in that it poses the possibility of a self-management approach to housing. We can take self-management to be encapsulated in the following principle:

Each person is to have a say over decisions that affect them and a degree of say in proportion as they are affected.

People who live in a dwelling are more impacted by the decisions about what goes on there than anyone else; so, they should have control over what goes on in their space. But the use of the land and the price of housing affect everyone in the community; so everyone should have a say over this.

The ground lease gives the community some say over what happens with the buildings on CLT land. The decisions that the CLT retains a say over are things that would have an impact on the surrounding community. The community can control the type of use or major changes to the building, and can specify minimum levels of maintenance. If the co-op or homeowner association fails to meet their financial obligations, the CLT can step in.

Home ownership is really a bundle of rights, which provide a variety of advantages. You can control the space where you live, you can customize or remodel the interior to suit yourself. You're freed of the whims or intrusions of a landlord. If you own a stand-alone house, you can build an addition or remodel the exterior, and yard space is available for play, for gardening.

On the other hand, the status of a house as a commodity means that the house can be used as a way to profit from appreciation in market value. In the CLT model, these components of home ownership are separated. First, the land is permanently taken off the market. Second, the right to profit

HOUSING

Come Enjoy The Mission

CLEANER WHITER BRIGHTER TABLECLOTHS

SF Print Collective

through speculative investment is removed by placing a permanent restriction on the resale price of the dwelling. Some of the components of ownership are retained— security of tenure and right of control over your own space.

"You're on your own, Jack" is the traditional approach to housing in the United States. The assumption is that it is up to each household to find and hold onto shelter that is habitable and within their means. Not everyone has the income, skills, and experience to do this with equal success.

If your parents owned the house you were raised in, or if you do financial management as part of your job, you may have bits of knowledge that are useful for success at managing a property. Given the huge inequalities in American society, not everyone has the same opportunity to acquire such knowledge.

Stand-alone co-ops can be preyed upon by unscrupulous contractors or property management firms. The community land trust addresses this issue by organizing guidance and sharing of knowledge for homeowner associations.

Another weakness of stand-alone, limited-equity housing co-ops has been that the co-op members have a self-interest in breaking the restrictions on resale price when they want to sell. Such co-ops exist in the context of the capitalist real estate market, which permits speculative profit-taking. The broader working-class community loses affordable housing when co-op residents convert their building into a market-rate co-op.

CLTs are designed to be a solution to this problem. Community land trusts typically have two classes of membership. One group are the residents who own houses, condos, or shares in co-ops that sit on CLT land. Through outreach and community organizing, the CLT recruits others in the community who are supportive of its goals as well as people who are looking for inexpensive housing.[6]

HOUSING

The owner and nonowner members elect the same number of representatives to the CLT board of directors. The San Francisco Community Land Trust bylaws also requires split votes at membership assemblies, requiring agreement of both groups. The idea is to balance the interests of the residents who own their buildings with the broader community interest. This structure makes removal of restrictions on resale price much more difficult than in a stand-alone coop. The presence of renters and those seeking affordable housing also drives the CLT to continually create new affordable housing.

SFCLT has developed a program for conversion of rental buildings to collective tenant ownership. We propose that renters be allowed to select a CLT to buy their building, do any needed rehab, and sell the apartments to the existing tenants at a price based on their ability to pay. Resale restrictions would ensure permanent affordability.[7]

The self-management potential of the CLT model could be developed in a number of ways.

In *The Production of Houses*, Christopher Alexander describes a project in Baja California in the 1970s in which a group of Mexican families were active participants in the design of the houses that were being built for them. Alexander developed a set of modular design elements that represented various design options, and a technique for integrating their design selections into the construction process. The upshot of the self-design process was that each of the houses was unique, reflecting the particular priorities of the family that was going to live in it.

Given the commitment to self-management, space could be provided for self-managing work collectives. For example, a citywide network of CLTs might decide to provide spaces for a network of worker collective groceries.

The CLT can also be given powers of eminent domain, as has been done with Dudley Street Neighbors in Boston.[8] Instead of an "urban renewal" program carried out by a distant bureaucracy, turning over land to for-profit developers, the neighborhood can control its own development.

The Limits of New Urbanism

The housing crisis in American cities is a sign of market failure. But market-driven investment in the built environment also undermines the livability and environmental sustainability of urban regions.

SF Print Collective

Agents of capitalist development have had a relatively free hand in crafting the contours of urban areas in the United States, with severe ecological consequences. The United States generates about one-fourth of the world's air pollution and greenhouse gases even though it has less than 5 percent of the world's population. The heavy reliance of Americans on the private automobile is at the heart of this. According to one survey, residents of American cities consume:

- Nearly twice as much gasoline per person as residents of Australian cities
- Nearly four times as much gasoline per person as residents of European cities
- Ten times as much gasoline per person as such Asian cities as Hong Kong, Singapore, and Tokyo.[9]

This dependence on the private automobile is rooted in the physical layout of American metropolitan areas. For more than half a century the practices of developers in the United States have been based on the assumption that people would get to far-flung suburban single-family houses, shopping centers, and office and industrial parks by driving cars. This wouldn't have been possible without systematic underpricing of the car.

HOUSING

The cost of maintaining the streets and traffic lights, the effects of noise and emissions on the health of the community or the global climate system, and other social costs aren't reflected in the price of the gas. (Lights at an intersection can consume as much electricity as a house.)

The market transaction at the local gas pump is just between the motorist and the purveyor of gas—social impacts on others are hidden from view. There aren't signs on the gas pumps saying "The refinery where this gas was produced generated a lot of cancer in nearby neighborhoods."

Huge expenditures in streets, freeways, extensions of utility grids, and free parking have subsidized a dispersed, auto-dependent land-use pattern.

Prior to 1920, investment flows into the built environment were tightly linked to investment in streetcar lines. Much of the capital for transit systems derived from real estate profits. Beginning in the twenties, the development industry was able to rely upon mass auto ownership to shift the costs of providing transportation services to motorists and homeowners, through personal car ownership, user fees, and property taxes.

With an increasingly motorized population, developers of retail centers and major retail chains used huge caches of parking and easy auto access as a competitive wedge, undermining neighborhood-oriented retail.

Over time these patterns changed the way of life. It became increasingly difficult for Americans to not rely on driving to glue together the fragments of their lives. The developers' investment practices had built an environment that made not having a car a real liability.

One result is that usage of public transit plummeted. The number of rides Americans take on public transit has dropped to low levels compared to cities in Europe or Asia. For example, 50 annual rides per person in Los Angeles County or the East Bay versus 250 in London.

Since the 1970s the social costs from auto-dependency have become harder to ignore. Motor vehicles are a major contributor to the greenhouse gases that are changing the global climate. Democratic mixing and mingling of people in public space shrivels as people get from place to place in individualized metal pods. A form of transportation apartheid segregates the working poor into underfunded bus systems.

New Urbanism has emerged as one response, promoted as the "Smart Growth" strategy by mainstream, middle-class environmentalist organizations. New Urbanism aims to change the built environment of

American urban areas over time by creating a new regulatory regime for development. New Urbanists propose an increase in density in both new suburbs and older areas while discouraging low-density outward expansion into open land around existing conurbations.

Policies pursued in Portland, Oregon, since the 1970s are a model cited by New Urbanists. Portland created a regional über-government called "Metro" that sets housing targets for the various jurisdictions, encouraging areas to become denser through multiunit housing construction. An urban growth boundary channels investment into the existing urban area.

The architects and urban planners who crafted the New Urbanism advocate a variety of tactics. "Mixed use" is one idea—compacting dwellings in close proximity to (for example, on top of) stores and services so that residents can do many of their errands by walking. "Transit-oriented development" would compact apartments and services in mixed-use developments around stations on high-quality transit systems, such as busways, subways, or light rail lines. The stores or services near the stations encourage people to accomplish some errands on the way to or from transit trips. Focusing the land uses around the transit stop helps to make public transit more integral to the way of life.

New Urbanists can point to studies suggesting that a strategy of making American urban areas denser will tend to reduce ownership and usage of autos. Such studies show that the amount of driving or the number of households not owning cars tends to vary mainly with population density, and to a lesser extent with income. Denser areas typically have frequent public transit, stores within walking distance of apartments, and more people who don't own cars.[10]

The Suburban Dream of the isolated house was a product of the gender caste system of the late nineteenth century. In 1890 only 5 percent of married women worked outside the home for wages.[11] A vision of suburbia as "havens in a heartless world" (for men who could afford it) was built on the unpaid labor of women. In the twenties the corporate elite pushed home ownership for skilled male workers as a political strategy to make them less likely to strike. Labor radicals in that era feared that a mortgage would be a ball and chain, tying workers to the system.

The isolated suburban house, with no services or stores within walking distance, no longer fits well with the changes in American family patterns over the past several decades, such as the high divorce rate. Today women must work outside the home, and they want a more varied public life. In an urban environment now built around the car, the big increase in women

working for wages since the sixties has driven increases in traffic density.

Changes in American life thus give a certain salience to the New Urbanist proposals. In preference surveys where people are shown slides of streetcar-era urban neighborhoods of tidy, compact housing and pedestrian-oriented Main Street shopping districts, and are also shown slides of

SF Print Collective

contemporary suburban environments of malls and houses fronting multicar garage doors and large lawns, majorities prefer the older pattern or its New Urbanist clone.[12] Hundreds of groups around the country now advocate New Urbanist solutions to make their cities more livable.

There is a problem here: Who will have access to the newly constructed housing? And isn't a policy that promotes private, for-profit investment in urban working-class neighborhoods a strategy for gentrification?

Defenders of New Urbanism refer to the sort of "inclusionary" zoning used in Portland.[13] This refers to tax breaks and zoning changes to encourage multiunit rental housing as well as requirements for a certain percentage of "affordable" units—typically 10 to 15 percent.

However, developers are likely to chose areas to invest where people making higher incomes want to live. This will enable them to charge higher rents or sell high-profit condos. Either developers will pass over decaying inner-city areas or, if there is potential for gentrification, tokenistic inclusionary zoning will not prevent market-driven displacement.

Lacking any program for democratization of land use, and no way of ensuring access of all income levels to affordable housing and urban amenities, the New Urbanist vision is in danger of being merely a facade, a set of vague slogans to legitimize the agendas of capitalist developers.

"Transit-oriented gentrification" is the label that the Urban Habitat Program has applied to some developments in working-class neighborhoods around BART stations. BART and the local redevelopment agency in Richmond crafted a $60 million project to build 200 townhouses around small shops on a sixteen-acre site next to the BART station. "The project

HOUSING

should benefit the common working class and people of color of my community," asserted Joe L. Wallace, a local activist. "However, right now the project is more of a gentrification threat because it is being tailored to the middle and upper income classes."[14]

On the other hand, there are no guarantees that new investment in "transit villages" will magically appear in decaying inner-city areas just because rail or busway stops are installed or planning policies are updated. The barriers to profitable reinvestment may prevent this.

The problem is illustrated by the Blue Line—a Los Angeles MTA light rail line built through Watts and Compton. The facility, opened in 1990, has attracted very high patronage by working-class people of color who live in surrounding areas. In 1993 the city of Los Angeles adopted a land use and transportation policy that contains many of the New Urbanist proposals.[15] But in a dozen years of operation virtually nil new housing or transit-oriented development has occurred in neighborhoods around most Blue Line stations. A decayed physical environment, toxic wastes from defunct industrial plants, obsolete zoning, a large low-income population, and perceptions of high crime are among the factors that deter for-profit developers. Nonprofit community developers in the area point to the lack of subsidies for community-based development such as affordable housing or neighborhood services.[16]

On the other hand, at the north end of the Blue Line, the Staples Center/Convention Center complex has driven a gentrifying influx of investment. An antigentrification struggle has emerged, with the Figueroa Corridor Coalition fighting the displacement of low-income tenants.

Like their right-wing "free market" opponents, New Urbanists do not challenge capitalist control of investment in the built environment.[17] What is needed is a more bottom-up, grassroots approach that increases community participation and control over land use. Democratic control over land and investment is needed to facilitate revitalization of decayed areas and to prevent displacement of low-income residents.

Rebuilding American urban areas to make them more pedestrian—and transit-oriented, to reduce the U.S. slurping of fossil fuels, is a desirable goal.

Promotion of community land trusts, tied in with enhanced public transit, could be part of a strategy for pursuing these aims. Grassroots groups can demand that cities, redevelopment agencies, or transit agencies provide funding and land to enable CLTs to develop mixed-use affordable housing

around stations or bus tranfer points. A program linking transit improvements to affordable housing and community control over economic development could be part of a program supported by transit rider groups, tenant activists, and labor groups.

Class Politics and the Self-Managed City

Antigentrification protests, rent strikes, and squatting buildings are examples of what I called class struggle over the built environment. Working-class politics can't be reduced to the politics of the labor movement but derives from the various strands of struggle that emerge from working-class communities; that is, communities of people who aren't bosses and whose life prospects are shaped by selling their time to employers.

Nonetheless, labor or workplace organizations are an important potential force for change because the system can't function without the work people do every day.

A weakness of the American labor movement is the domination of most national unions and large, amalgamated locals by rigid, professional cadre hierarchies that don't work the jobs that the members do. The professional cadre will tend to disfavor mass mobilization and militant struggle because of its risks to the union as an institution, and because it puts the rank and file into the center of the action. The power and careers of the hierarchy are based on their relative monopolization of expertise and levers of decisionmaking.

A different kind of industrial organization is needed to develop the capacity and self-confidence of workers for making their own decisions, controlling their own lives. Collective action and self-management of the struggle by the rank and file are crucial to developing a movement that workers can feel is "theirs."

In the past the labor movement in the United States has made major forward strides only during periods of mass upheaval, as in the years before World War I and the thirties. During such periods new types of organization tend to be created. A new labor rebellion would pose the possibility of new self-managed worker organizations emerging.

Since the emergence of the "new social movements" (of women, racial minorities, gay people, the disabled, enviros) in the 1960s–1970s period, a number of the organizations these movements generated came to be dominated by professional/managerial cadres. Because class

HOUSING

circumstances shapes the life prospects of women and people of color, for example, the needs of working-class women or workers of color are often not adequately addressed by such organizations. My earlier discussion of New Urbanism illustrates how environmental organizations sometimes ignore the impacts of their proposals on working-class communities.

Women, people of color, gay folks, and the disabled have specific concerns that also reflect their class situation. There is no impermeable barrier between the "new social movements" and class politics.

To be a force for change the working class needs to be more than just a heterogeneous collection of population groups. Solidarity is at the heart of working-class politics. Solidarity implies concern for others in a context where they are in struggle against those who dominate them in some way, and where it is understood there is at least the possibility that you might require their solidarity in the future.

Development of an intraclass alliance presupposes some process by which the concerns of specific groups can be communicated to, and become the concerns of other groups, thus expanding the boundaries of their solidarity. The concerns specific to women or people of color, for example, need to become concerns of other organizations such as unions or housing groups.

An important milestone in the development of the working class into a more cohesive force are unifying moments, situations where much of the population is drawn into thinking of themselves as "us" versus "them." The general strikes in San Francisco, Toledo, and Minneapolis in 1934 were unifying events that shaped class consciousness in that period in the United States. What if, for example, the unions in California were to organize a mass march of tens of thousands on Sacramento to protect public workers against cuts, and to defend the communities they serve?

Class politics includes struggles around needs not adequately met through the market—affordable housing, public transit, democratic media, universal health care, good low-cost child care, and protection of the environment. Movements around such social goods can help to bring together a variety of sectors of the population.

Movements can and do make demands on the government for social goods that augment inadequate wage income. Concessions can sometimes be won through protest and struggle because the government must maintain a facade of "representing everyone" in order to maintain its legitimacy.

High-quality, low-fare public transit is a social good that can provide access to all that a city has to offer—jobs, housing, entertainment, medical offices, and so on. A point to cheap fares is to ensure that everyone has equal access no matter how low their income is.

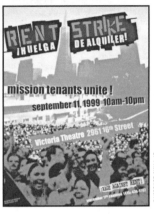

SF Print Collective

Neoliberals, on the other hand, propose privatization and competing services for public transit. This program has been disastrous when carried out in Great Britain and Santiago, Chile.[18] Competing services degrade accessibility because of the lack of seamless connectivity between all the operators. Private competition leads operators to creaming off a more affluent clientel, leaving areas and groups underserved.

Flexibility and ease of access for transit riders requires a network that is a single, comprehensive system of reliable, frequent services, with low fares and free transfers. A bewildering array of private operators who may go out of business next week creates barriers to travel flexibility and access for riders. This is why public transit was historically regarded as a "natural monopoly." In practice the main aim of transit privatization in the United States has been to drive down the wages of transit workers.

These considerations lead some to defend statist central planning.[19] But this also has its problems: It subordinates the transit workforce to an authoritarian hierarchy, leads to management empire-building, and disempowers low-income bus riders who get overcrowded and inadequate services at high fares.

However, there is a third model for public transit based on direct negotiation between workers and riders. This would presuppose the creation of an organization through which the transit workers would manage the transit system.[20] Many of the decisions in the day-to-day management of a transit system mainly impact the workers. The principle of self-management says people are to have control over the decisions that impact them. Self-management of the transit system avoids a bloated managerial hierarchy.

But many of the decisions about the operation of the transit system directly impact the riders—cleanliness and safety, reliability and frequency of service, fares. To empower the riders to have a say over these

HOUSING

377

decisions a riders' council could be created to negotiate with the workers' organization over the issues that impact riders. The direct worker/consumer negotiation model could be applied to other social services such as health care,[21] education, and public utilities.

Applying this to my earlier discussion of community land trusts, we could envision a CLT negotiating construction with a nonprofit construction workers' co-op.

Direct worker/consumer negotiation points us in the direction of a global aternative to capitalism. Participatory economics (ParEcon) is a vision of a nonmarket, socially-owned economy based on grassroots participatory planning and direct negotiation between workers and consumers.[22] The building blocks of a participatory economy are self-managing bodies such as workplace councils and neighborhood assemblies. The neighborhood bodies provide the channel for consumer input.

In ParEcon people in their councils develop proposals for what is to be produced. Both individually and in groups we figure out what we want to do at work or to consume. These proposals filter outward through organizations over a larger geographic scope, depending on where the proposals would have impact. Through a give-and-take process the proposals would be refined to develop comprehensive agendas for what is to be produced. The essence of ParEcon, says Michael Albert, is "a cooperative, self-managing negotiation of collective well-being rather than a top-down or competitive pursuit of narrow advantage."

For cities, ParEcon poses the possibility of a horizontal, self-managing regionalism in planning investment in public goods such as transportation and other infrastructure and in meeting social needs such as housing, child care, and health care.

The way that we organize today helps to determine future possibilities. Self-managed mass organizations are necessary if the working class is to develop the self-confidence, skills, and self-organization that would enable it to emancipate itself from subjugation to an exploiting class.

Building self-managed institutions (CLTs, media collectives, etc.) and developing mass organizations (such as unions) through which rank-and-file people can self-manage their struggles is prefigurative in the sense that it points beyond capitalism, towards the Self-Managed City.

Notes

[1] My rather schematic account here draws a lot on Neil Smith, *The New Urban Frontier: Gentrification and the Revanchist City* (1996).

[2] Ibid.

[3] Todd Harvey et al, "Gentrification and West Oakland: Causes, Effects, and Best Practices," 1999 (http://comm-org.utoledo.edu/papers2000/gentrify/chapter2.htm).

[4] MAC, "The Hidden Costs of the New Economy: A Study of the Northeast Mission Industrial Zone," October 2000 (http://www.medasf.org/reports/NEMIZ_Report.pdf).

[5] Peter Marcuse, "In Defense of Gentrification," *Newsday* (December 2, 1991).

[6] Much of my discussion of the community land trust model draws upon John Emmeus Davis, "Beyond the Market and the State: The Diverse Domain of Social Housing," in *The Affordable City* (1994). The Institute for Community Economics (http://www.iceclt.org/) has played an important role in the development of the Community Land Trust model.

[7] See http://www.sfclt.org.

[8] Peter Medoff and Holly Sklar, *Streets of Hope: The Fall and Rise of an Urban Neighborhood*.

[9] Peter Newman and Jeffrey Kenworthy, *Cities and Automobile Dependence: An International Sourcebook* (1989).

[10] John Holtzclaw et al, "Location Efficiency: Neighborhood and Socio-Economic Characteristics Determine Auto Ownership and Use—Studies in Chicago, Los Angeles, and San Francisco," *Transportation Planning and Technology*, (March 2002); also John Holtzclaw, "Using Residential Patterns and Transit to Decrease Auto Dependence and Costs," 1994; and "Smart Growth—As Seen From the Air: Convenient Neighborhood, Skip the Car," (2000).

[11] Dolores Hayden, *The Grand Domestic Revolution*, 13.

[12] See Reid Ewing, "Is Los Angeles Style Sprawl Desirable?" *APA Journal* (winter 1997).

[13] Arthur C. Nelson et al., "The Link between Growth Management and Housing Affordability: The Academic Evidence," Brookings Institution Center on Urban and Metropolitan Policy (February 2002).

[14] Quoted in "There Goes the Neighborhood: A Regional Analysis of Gentrification and Community Stability in the San Francisco Bay Area," Urban Habitat Program, 1999. A massive project promoted by the Daly City redevelopment agency near the Daly City BART station is subjected to critique in "Smart Growth: Smart of Not?: Debunking the Myths of Sustainable Growth" by Neighbors for Responsible Development (http://home.earthlink.net/~tomroop/index.html). Neither of these projects exhibit the architectural or urban planning features that would make New Urbanists happy. But architectural or zoning rules do not prevent gentrification or disinvestment.

[15] "Land Use/Transportation Policy," adopted by the Los Angeles City Council, November 2, 1993. Council File No. 93-0478.

[16] Anastasia Loukaitou-Sideris and Tridib Banerjee, "The Blue Line Blues: Why the Vision of Transit Village May Not Materialize Despite Impressive Growth in Ridership," University of California Transportation Center Report No. 425; also "Transit-Oriented Development in the Inner City: A Delphi Study," *Journal of Public Transportation* (2000).

[17] For another Left critique of New Urbanism, see Bill Resnick, "Reconstructing Cities, Restoring the Environment: New Urbanism versus Mobile/Agile Capital" in *Not for Sale: In Defense of Public Goods*, ed. Anatole Anton, Milton Fisk, and Nancy Holmstrom.

[18] Paul Mees, *A Very Public Solution: Transport in the Dispersed City.*

[19] Ibid.

[20] A historical example would be the United Public Service Collective, which ran the subway, streetcar, and bus lines of Barcelona during the two and a half years of the Spanish civil war.

[21] Milton Fisk advocates the direct worker-consumer negotiation model for health care reform in *Toward a Healthy Society: The Morality and Politics of American Health Care Reform* chap. 6.

[22] See Michael Albert, *Parecon: Life After Capitalism.*

The Other California

By Ruth Wilson Gilmore and Craig Gilmore

Ruth Wilson Gilmore is a professor at the University of Southern California, and an activist with Critical Resistance, California Prison Moratorium Project, and the Central California Environmental Justice Network. Ruthie works with grassroots groups around the United States, and speaks and writes widely on issues of social and economic justice. Golden Gulag, her book about the expansion of California's prison system and opposition to it, is forthcoming from U.C. Press.

Craig Gilmore is an organizer with the California Prison Moratorium Project and active in the Central California Environmental Justice Network, the Real Cost of Prisons Project, and Education Not Incarceration.

Riding along a two-lane highway in California's southern San Joaquin Valley, it's easy to mistake the landscape for one out of the Third World. Mile after mile of agriculture for export—fruit trees, tomatoes, nuts, melons, mega-dairies, and alfalfa line the numbered roads that cross the

photo top: Gilmore and Gilmore

Valley. The world's largest cotton producer, J. G. Boswell, is at the intersection of Whitley Avenue and Highway 43 in Corcoran. The San Joaquin produces more grapes, peaches, tomatoes, nectarines, almonds, and pistachios than anywhere in the world.

Most of the production takes place on plantations, huge plots of land owned by multinational corporations or prosperous families, and farmed with state-of-the-art equipment and low-wage workers. A visitor can look across hundreds and hundreds of acres without seeing any homes.

At nightfall, one can see another part of the Valley's peculiar landscape—huge facilities whose night lights can be seen for dozens of miles across the flat, mostly dark Valley landscape. These plants, that clearly run 24/7, are not food processors or packers. They are prisons holding the strange fruit of California's globalized economy.

California has built twenty-three massive prisons in the last two decades, prisons that hold from 4,000 to 6,000 people each. The majority of those new prisons are clustered in the southern San Joaquin—the others scattered across other parts of the state's agricultural, timber, and mining lands.

Over the last ten years or so, small rural communities have organized to fight against the siting of prisons in their towns. The story of how the building of those prisons is part of globalization and how the fight against them relates to other struggles is the subject of this essay.

The Other California

In 1999 one west Valley resident put it this way: "The other night I was listening to the news on television, and they were talking about the economy, and most notably they were talking about the economy here in California. Things are booming. Unemployment is down. Everything is great. And you know, I wondered how that washed here in Mendota, because in Mendota I feel like we live in the other California."

He pointed out that Mendota, like a lot of Valley towns, had been "passed over" in the state's remarkable economic boom of the 1990s. Unemployment for the town's 8,000 residents hovers around 35 percent and over half the town lives under the poverty line. The town's groundwater is saturated with salts and agricultural chemicals because of years of irresponsible irrigation and pest control practices in the fields around Mendota, forcing all residents to buy bottled water to drink and cook.

Mendota is not unique. In fact there are many Valley towns with all these problems and more. Both Earlimart and McFarland, respectively just north and south of the Tulare/Kern County line along Highway 99, have epidemic cancer clusters among their children, caused, it appears, by pesticide exposure—direct spraying on kids in the fields with their parents, pesticide drift into residential neighborhoods and schools, and pesticide residues in the drinking water.

The accumulation of chemical fertilizers and pesticides over decades has poisonously polluted the water and soil. The water table is dropping rapidly as farms and new subdivisions pump more water from the aquifer than scarce rainfall can replenish. And the air quality is as bad as any in the country. Kern, Fresno and Tulare Counties rank as the third, fourth, and fifth worst air nationwide, according to the Environmental Protection Agency.[1]

While the statewide unemployment rate ran around 5 percent through most of the 1990s, Valley counties averaged 12 to 16 percent, and towns within those counties suffered rates 2 to 3 times higher than that—in places as high as 50 percent. But that is not to say there is no wealth in the Central Valley. Fresno and Tulare Counties have ranked no. 1 and no. 2 in gross agricultural production worldwide for years, generating billions of dollars in agricultural income yearly. Fresno, Tulare, Kings, and Kern also rank high when assessed for capital investment: as we've noted, it costs a lot in machinery and irrigation to farm these bountiful acres.

In a sense, "globalization" is to urban California what "the farm crisis" is to rural parts of the state. To people in rural communities like Mendota, urban and suburban dwellers are a little late understanding something that's been going on for some time. The centralization of productive agricultural lands in fewer and fewer hands, pressure to produce single crops that compete in a world market (even if consumed relatively nearby), a labor system that makes no allowance for needs other than maximizing profit, have defined facts of the state's agricultural economy for decades; and now those pressures are all the more intense.

As farmland ownership becomes increasingly centralized, one of the less visible casualties are the small towns that served small farmers as places to bank, to shop, to dine out, to get equipment repaired, and to socialize. Fewer farm owners means fewer customers with the income to support those towns. Greater mechanization in the fields means fewer farm workers spending even the little they are paid. The flipside of the farm crisis for these towns has been the emergence of regional shopping centers, financed with national or international capital and filled with national chains. Locally owned businesses are going under. Already frail,

PRISONS

"rural communities" in Clyde Woods's words, "move from a permanent state of crisis toward social and financial collapse."[2]

Many farm towns suffering the loss of their business and tax base due to the forces outlined above turn to the state for help. For the last couple of decades, the state has offered prisons.

The Prison Industrial Complex and Globalization

The counter-revolution of the capitalist entrepreneur today can only operate strictly within the context of an increase in the coercive powers of the state. The "new Right" ideology of laissez-faire implies as its corollary the extension of new techniques of coercive and state intervention in society at large.[3]
—Toni Negri

While California's prison-building boom of the last two decades has been what one state administrator called "the biggest prison building program in the history of the world," other U.S. states and other countries are also building prisons at a breakneck pace. That the "free trade" of the globalization era should bring with it massive increases in cages for the unfree is no coincidence.

Throughout the past twenty years both critics and boosters of the new globalization predicted the demise of the state as a player of any importance. Contrary to the neoliberal propaganda coming from both major U.S. political parties, the state has not withered away. Indeed, in many parts of the world, most notably in the United States, prisons and policing have provided a solid basis on which states are reorganizing themselves to help shape these times.

State budgets don't shrink, but human and environmental care does. The new relations of financing, production, and distribution we call globalization are necessarily also forces that disorganize previous relations. All that was solid melts before our eyes. Structural adjustment names a wide variety of changes in how states act. As the state withdraws unemployment and health insurance and allows rents and food prices to be driven up and wages driven down in the name of the free market, it expands policing and prisons.

The "creative destruction" of capital shatters communities whose means of reproducing themselves are poor and fragile due to decades of disinvestment, political disfranchisement, and social-spatial isolation. Capitalism is always changing (or "creating") in order to continue to grow

PRISONS

by controlling the mixture of land, finance, materials and machinery, and labor. One sort of innovation involves making new kinds of products (cell phones or genetically modified organisms), or making old products seem new (fancier cars or colorless beer). Another kind of change (the "destruction" part) involves making old or new products under new circumstances. The quest for new circumstances

Protests outside of California's growing prison-industrial complex.

signals that capital will reorganize its participation in the landscape. In some cases capital's reorganization means capital flight, in which factories move from cities to suburbs, or from closed-shop to antiunion states, or from the United States to the market side of trade barriers in the industrialized world (such as France), or to labor-rich, money-poor Third World *maquiladoras* within free-trade zones. In other cases, capital's reorganization takes the form of more machines and fewer workers in the same place.

We don't have space to argue in detail all the connections between the prison boom and globalization, but there are a few points we'd like our readers to consider.[4]

First, capital, with some kind of state connivance, has abandoned a generation of workers whose labor is not currently needed, people who are shut out of the kind of work their parents performed, and people (numbering around 2 million in the United States) who are more valuable to the system as prisoners than as workers. If, as Peter Linebaugh points out, "accumulation of capital means accumulation of the proletariat," then capital flight leaves behind it an abandoned, surplus proletariat: a workforce without work.[5] Places that have large numbers of surplused workers—inner cities, California Valley towns—also have surplus land: townscapes made derelict by the changes in the forces and relations of capitalist production outlined in this paragraph.

Second, as the state reinvents itself by developing in ways amenable to capital reorganization, corporations that made billions on projects financed with state debt (bonds) look for ways to maintain those lucrative flows of public money. The firms that designed and built schools, highways, canals, hospitals, and universities from the 1950s to the 1970s, and the banks that put the multimillion-dollar bond deals together to finance that construction, are now designing, building, and financing prisons.[6]

PRISONS

Third, the free flows of capital around the globe depend on the far less free movement of labor. What makes the movement of factories worth the cost is the fact that labor's movement is limited, and that limitation is enforced by policing and prisons. State coercion is also crucial in attempts by local capital (real estate, labor contractors, transport) to attract and retain multinational capital investment by using the local police and military to discipline the local labor force and keep wages as low as possible.

Finally, places whose capacity to reproduce themselves—to feed and house and educate and enjoy themselves—has fallen sharply look desperately for help. Any group of desperate buyers find sellers knocking soon enough. In California's San Joaquin Valley, stories of Dust Bowl towns blowing away are still part of family lore among the Valley's black and white Okie descendents. Most of the Valley's working people are themselves, or are descendents of, long-distance migrants pushed from former homes by many kinds of devastations: the defeats, indentures, dust bowls, death squads, and disinvestments characterizing 150 years of uneven continental, hemispheric, and pan-Pacific relationships. Memories of displacement intensify the desire to stay put. What's offered are toxic waste dumps, barely regulated power plants, waste-to-energy incinerators, and more prisons.[7]

Stopping Prisons, Reclaiming Place

What the government tries to do is to bring prisons into low-income barrios. They come to our barrios promising us all kinds of things; they tell us we will have employment, that our barrios will prosper. But our experience tells us that this is not true. —Juana Gutierrez, Madres del Este de Los Angeles

From Tehachapi to Tonopah (see map) the landscape suffers deepening devastations. From the planned nuclear waste dump at Yucca Mountain to the planned Delano II prison, governments and corporations dump toxic projects on the most vulnerable and least visible parts of the country.

In 1983, the California Waste Management Board hired a high-priced Los Angeles public relations firm to study where the state might locate waste incinerators. Cerrill Associates was asked to study not geology or hydrology, neither air flow patterns nor earthquake faults. Rather they were asked, "to assist in selecting a site that offers the least potential of generating public opposition."

The Cerrill Report suggests that companies target small, rural communities whose residents are low-income, older people, or people with

SAN JOAQUIN VALLEY PRISONS

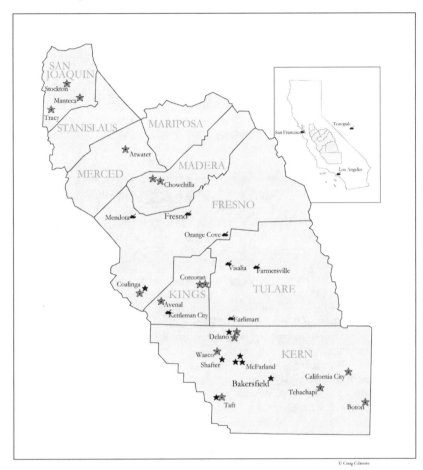

★ Prison (13 state operated, 4 federal, average population: 5,000 prisoners)

★ Community Correction Facility (state prisoners, run by corporations or municipalities, average population: 500 prisoners)

 City

10 20 30 40 50 miles

NOTE: Map does not include state camps, juvenile facilities, or municipal jails.

only a high school education or less: communities with a high proportion of Catholic residents; and communities whose residents are engaged in resource extractive industries such as agriculture, mining, and forestry.[8]

It might be coincidence that California's prison-building frenzy began the year Cerrill released its report, and that the state's new prison towns match the criteria in that report—rural, poor, Catholic, agricultural, modestly educated.

However, the rural towns targeted for incinerators and prisons have not been so compliant as the Cerrill Report hoped. Resistance has sprung up in town after town, in the manner of urban activism springing from unanticipated kitchens and corners.

In California both the environmental justice movement and activism to stop prison construction find roots in the work of the Madres del Este de Los Angeles. In 1985 a group of four women and two men began to organize to stop the state from building a prison in Chicano/Mexicano East Los Angeles. After nine years of organizing, the Madres forced the state to shelve the project. During those nine years, MELA also organized to stop an oil pipeline that was to cut through the barrio, and a hazardous waste incinerator targeted for the neighboring town of Vernon.

> You know how we did it? Knocking on doors and talking to the people. Telling them, "Join us." Especially women, talking to other women. Sometimes, men don't allow women to become involved in community problems. I would go door-to-door and ask women to come out. Some would. Some would not. Sometimes their husbands would say, "Don't go. That woman is crazy." But in the end even they became crazy, because they joined our marches. They saw the power of our marches and of our victories.[9]

Las Madres organized marches and protests every Monday for nine years, successfully fighting off the state and major oil companies. All evidence shows that the success of Las Madres drove the state to a strictly rural prison-siting strategy.

Towns all over rural California targeted for new prisons organize and fight back too.[10] What sparks those fights varies slightly from town to town, but like the Mothers of East L.A., they begin with a small group, more women than men, wondering how the planned prison will affect their families and communities.

California's standard prison siting practice follows this scenario. Department of Corrections representatives talk privately and quietly with

PRISONS

town officials and leading businesspeople. If the town leaders like what they hear, they work with the state to push through site selection and such public meetings as are required by law. The Golden State's practices aren't unusual; indeed, the *Encyclopedia of American Prisons* warns, "One of the most difficult and potentially adverse events in the site selection process is premature disclosure of a proposed project [a prison] resulting in negative community reaction."

The predictable "'negative community reaction" is well founded. Prison peddlers sell their wares as recession-proof, clean industries, whose multimillion-dollar payrolls and purchasing can lift any town from the economic doldrums. Most places do not, as a rule, start out by criticizing the ethical implications of basing an economic recovery on holding people in cages for part or all of their lives. Most U.S. residents of all nationalities and races accept the propaganda put forth by elected and appointed governmental officials, and all forms of media. Crime (like communism or terrorism) is a problem that can only be solved by prison (war)—even though the evidence shows (1) what counts as crime changes over time, and (2) places with more imprisonment have more of what's called "crime" than places with fewer humans in cages. On top of the moral wrong, it also turns out that prison towns haven't prospered from their new industries.

California's twenty-three new prisons offer prospective prison towns plenty of evidence. A few examples:

Corcoran has two massive prisons holding in sum 11,000 prisoners; the town's free-world population (that is, residents not locked in prisons) has remained fairly at just under 9,000 since before the first of the prisons was built in the late 1980s. Before the first prison opened, about 1,000 of Corcoran's residents lived in households whose incomes put them below the poverty line. Ten years later, after the state spent around $1 *billion* in Corcoran for the construction and operating costs of the two prisons, nearly 2,000 people lived beneath the poverty line. When the prison advertised two clerical positions with a starting wage of $17,000, 800 people lined up waiting for the employment office to open so they could apply.[11]

Avenal is a town of 12,000, half of whom are in the state prison. The prison uses so much scarce water that the town has none to offer other prospective developers. And the prison's lack of positive effect on the town's retail trade is shown in the fact that sales tax revenues (a measure of local economic activity) has declined to about a third of what it was before the prison opened.

California built Tehachapi's first prison in the 1930s and substantially expanded it in the mid-1980s. In the decade following expansion, over 700 locally owned businesses went out of business. The driving force? Big low-price "box stores" like Wal-Mart, and national chains like McDonald's, locate in regional malls and small towns, draining reinvestment like leeches while providing low wages and no benefits. The low-wage, low-benefit "new jobs" brought in these chains didn't make up for the jobs lost in locally-owned businesses destroyed.

The prison industry works to reduce the risk that local opposition to a new prison can develop. In Tehachapi, the city council announced a new prison hospital project two days before Christmas, and scheduled the council vote just two weeks later. In Mendota, the Federal Bureau of Prisons (FBoP) published its 1,000-plus-page environmental impact statement, detailing the effects of a planned five-prison complex on the community, only in English. This, despite the fact that 95 percent of the town's 8,000 residents are Chicano, Mexicano, or Central Americanos, and most speak Spanish at home. The FBoP held public meetings about the EIS in English without a Spanish translator. There is as much disinformation as information spread through the community, attempting to persuade that the prison will cost locals nothing and will provide jobs, local housing growth, more trade at local businesses, and so forth. And finally, some who oppose the prison are threatened with loss of jobs, eviction, or both.

While local fights look different from place to place, they have a few features in common.

First is that vital to antiprison grassroots organizing is what Laura Pulido calls "place-based identities."[12] Such identities can be progressive or reactionary. The shared meaning of a place helps shape the ways that residents describe and understand themselves in the world. Place is a fluid creation of personal and group histories of struggles and work, of investments emotional and financial, of migrations in and out, of culture and change, of births and deaths. When residents ask what a prison means to their community, they are asking among other things what meanings sustain that community now, and what they're willing to fight to maintain or enhance.

A pillar of identity in many rural communities is the sense that the rest of the country neither knows nor cares about their struggles. As a result, many rural folks view with skepticism claims that "prisons are recession-proof, nonpolluting industries." As one Tehachapi activist noted, "When they told us how great the new prison would be for our town, I wondered, if it was that great, why wasn't L.A. or San Francisco getting it?" After

Student march for Schools Not Jails.

their victory in the late 1990s stopping the proposed prison/hospital, Tehachapi activists took aim at the box stores and other national retail and fast-food chains that swept into town in the wake of prison expansion during the late 1980s.

In Farmersville, a tiny Tulare County town facing a proposal from a private prison company, the city council met opposition from both the local United Farm Workers *and* local growers and ranchers—one of the few times that these traditional antagonists organized on the same side of an issue. A UFW march from the union headquarters connected with a march of high school students coming from the school in front of City Hall. Whatever the differences between growers and the UFW, they agreed about the importance of maintaining local agriculture at the core of the town's economy.

Often the question of who's local and who's an outsider takes on great importance. During a public meeting about a proposed prison complex in Orange Cove, speaker after speaker began by establishing his or her link to the town. As in many agricultural towns, local growers live outside the city limits, and many prison boosters portrayed them as "outsiders," despite their having in many cases farmed in Orange Cove for generations. Those of us who come in to help local activists organize are inevitably

PRISONS

labeled as "outsiders" as well, a term applied only rarely to the prison bureaucrats or even the national chain stores.

Prison boosters in Orange Cove played up the fact that the local growers were mostly white and mostly resided outside the town limits to suggest that the antiprison movement was interested mostly in maintaining the low-wage, racially segregated agricultural labor market.

In struggle after struggle, the question of whose town it is comes to the front. Prison development highlights both the questions of who will benefit and who makes decisions—questions of economic justice and local democracy—all of which are framed within concerns about what the nature of life in the community will be or can be. The antiprison movement strongly resembles the environmental justice movement, and like it insists that the relations between land use and local democracy are essential. In other words, it is because communities appear to lack the power to resist toxic incinerators or prisons that they get them. And it is because they appear to lack the power to resist mass incarceration that they are arrested and imprisoned.

So the goal becomes not simply to prevent a prison's siting and building, but through that process to help build local democracy and economic justice. To achieve that goal, activists must move beyond place-based identities toward identification across space, from not-in-my-backyard to not-in-anyone's-backyard. The challenge facing activists is to find the work that can expand senses of place and identity beyond simple localism and move toward a greater understanding of how our lives and our homes are connected globally in numerous ways.

It should be noted that there are competing ideas of how we are connected, and that a variety of political models of globalization compete in rural areas. It appears that organizers using anti-immigrant and racist models have made considerably more headway than the Left in much of rural America.[13]

The concentration of prisons in rural areas creates the prospect that local politicians begin to identify incarceration with prosperity (or at least survival). As a result, votes for harsher sentences, less parole, more behaviors criminalized, are less about public safety than about maintaining growth in the local industry. In rural California, that prospect is already a reality, as the state's powerful prison guards' union works tirelessly at the state and local levels to maintain a steadily increasing flow of new prisoners through control of the state's legislature and of county district attorneys.

Delano—the future site of Delano II.

Gilmore and Gilmore

Writing about the increasing disparities in income, wealth, and quality of life between rich and poor in the overdeveloped world, A. Sivanandan calls poor areas "replica[s] of the Third World within the First. And it is that one-third society, asset-stripped of the social and economic infrastructure that give it some sense of worth and some sense of mobility, that provides the breeding ground for fascism."[14]

As rural California towns face their uncertain futures, they see a number of not so appetizing options: industrial agriculture, huge prisons, national retailers, and food chains. Those fighting prisons find new allies and new alternatives. Central to the alternative vision is that local autonomy and local well-being can be achieved only through identification and alliance with the not-local. Or to put it another way, that globalization, considered as ever-stronger links between people separated by distance and culture, is inevitable. The question before us is what sorts of relations we can establish and who sets the terms for them.

One of the central tenets of our organizing has been to persuade people that security and prosperity won't come as a result of more policing or more imprisonment. Where we can make our case, we stop the growth of the prison industrial complex in the literal sense of preventing the construction of more cages. Those cages link in an immediate and material way desperately poor urban and rural communities; people from the

PRISONS

hyperpoliced poorest urban areas are locked away in rural prisons. That link provides activists a chance to connect life and death, day-to-day struggles in different places, and therefore to make connections among different places.

Conclusion

When we explain with stories and statistics that a new prison won't bring prosperity to a poor town, one question is asked at every meeting. "If prisons don't work, what will?" Our poorest urban neighborhoods and rural towns are ready for an answer to that question. The political challenge facing them and their allies resembles challenges facing peasants and workers in southern Mexico, coastal Nigeria, Indonesia, or anywhere else people fight to get out from the yoke of globalization. The problem will not be solved by delinking from the rest of the globe, but rather by radically democratic redistribution of control over the material resources needed to maintain and improve their lives.

Acknowledgments

Thanks to all those in rural California and elsewhere who are fighting back; the battles can be long, rough, and lonely. This essay is only a sketch of their remarkable work. Our crew of "outside agitators" has included Jean Caiani, Eric Ettlinger, Michelle Foy, Sarah Jarmon, Sonja Sivesind, Peter Spannagle, Ashle Fauvre, and Abby Lowe, the compañeras of California Prison Moratorium Project. Thanks also to Joe Morales and the rest of the Center on Race, Poverty and the Environment; John and Rosenda Mataka and all the rest of the Central California Environmental Justice Network; Bradley Angel of GreenAction; Yedithza Nuñez, Michael Murashige, Laura Pulido, Babak Naficy, Celeste Langille, Kassie Siegel, Brigette Sarabi, and the Western Prison Project and the Prison Activist Resource Center. Particular mention should be made of Tracy Huling, whose advocacy against rural prison siting has been crucial, and Rose Braz and the remarkable group of activists who work with Critical Resistance who have logged thousands of dusty miles with us.

Notes

1 For a brief but incisive overview of the Valley's current state, see "The Broken Promised Land," Gray Brechin; *Terrain* (summer 2002, 33, no.2).

PRISONS

[2] Clyde Woods, *Development Arrested: Race, Power and Blues in the Mississippi Delta*. See also Walter Goldschmidt; *Small Business and the Community: A Study in Central Valley of California on the Effects of Scale in Farm Operations*.

[3] Toni Negri, *Revolution Retrieved*, 1988.

[4] For more detailed versions of the relations of prison growth to globalization, see "Globalisation and US Prison Growth" Ruth Wilson Gilmore, *Race and Class* 40 (2/3 1998–1999); Ruth Wilson Gilmore, "Race and Globalization," in *Geographies of Global Change*, 2nd ed., P. J. Taylor, R. L. Johnstone and M. J. Watts, eds., 2002, and Julia Sudbury, "Transatlantic Visions: Resisting the Globalisation of Mass Incarceration," *Social Justice*, 27, no. 3 (Fall 2000).

[5] Peter Linebaugh, *The London Hanged: Crime and Civil Society in Eighteenth Century England*.

[6] Ruth Wilson Gilmore, *Golden Gulag* (University of California Press, forthcoming).

[7] Rural California is not manufacturing running shoes or sportsware because the local agricultural powers don't want any competition in the local labor market. But the common notion that clothing makers have relocated to the global South ignores the explosive growth of Los Angeles as a world-class sweatshop center. It is no shock that L.A. County, with the highest concentration of hyperexploited labor in the state, would also have among the highest rates of arrest and conviction. L.A. provides a textbook example of the relation between policing and labor markets.

[8] Luke Cole and Sheila Foster, *From the Ground Up: Environmental Racism and the Rise of the Environmental Justice Movement*.

[9] Juana Gutierrez, comments during question-and-answers at Joining Forces: Environmental Justice and the Fight Against Prison Expansion. (Fresno Calif., February 10, 2001).

[10] There is a parallel struggle in the state's urban areas led mostly by the families of those arrested and imprisoned with significant organizational aid from longtime community activists. In Los Angeles, for example, Coalition Against Police Abuse, Mothers ROC, and Families to Amend California's Three Strikes (FACTS) have fought to end the endless roundup, and bring policing under community control.

PRISONS

See Ruth Wilson Gilmore, "'You Have Dislodged a Boulder': Mothers and Children in the Post Keynesian California Landscape," *Transforming Anthropology* 8(1–2): 12–38. For more about rural prison siting, see Gilmore, *Golden Gulags* and Tracy L. Huling, "Prisons as a Growth Industry in Rural America: An Exploratory Discussion of the Effects on Young African American Men in the Inner Cities," available at http://www.prisonsucks.com/scans/prisons_as_rural_growth.shtml.

[11] Gilmore, *Golden Gulag,* and Mike Lewis, "Economic Lockdown," *Fresno Bee*, January 9, 2000.

[12] Laura Pulido's groundbreaking work on environmental justice has been crucial in developing the grassroots movement against prison construction and in developing links to the EJ movement. "Place-based identities" is taken from "Community, Place, and Identity" in *Thresholds of Feminist Geography*, J. P. Jones et al., eds. See also her other essays and her great book *Environmentalism and Economic Justice*.

[13] Joel Dyer, *Harvest of Rage*.

[14] A. Sivanandan, "La traison des clercs," *Race and Class*, 37, no. 3.

How One Small Scottish Anarchist Group Toppled the Thatcher Government

An interview by David Solnit with Ramsey Kanaan

Ramsey Kanaan organized in working-class communities in Scotland as part of the Edinburgh antiauthoritarian group Community Resistance and then as an initiator of the Anti–Poll Tax movement that was instrumental in toppling the Thatcher government. He is the founder and a collective member of AK Press, a radical book distribution and publishing worker owned and operated cooperative. (www.akpress.org)

London Riots

DAVID SOLNIT: *The Poll Tax organizing was a successful example of antiauthoritarian community organizing catalyzing a mass movement. In the United States most of us just heard about the London Poll Tax riots. Can you tell me about them?*

RAMSEY KANAAN: On March 31, 1990, there were two marches against the Poll Tax. In London, drawing on folks from England and Wales, we had about half a million participants. In Glasgow, Scotland, about 50,000 people

photo top: Mark Simmons

took part. The London march began as a festive celebration, with kids, families, and all kinds of people. When the march got to Trafalgar Square (a huge square in central London), the police openly and viciously attacked. TV camera footage documents people being knocked over by police horses, getting their heads cracked with eight-foot truncheons, and of police vehicles being driven directly into the crowd at thirty or forty miles per hour. People got pissed and started to fight back. This very quickly escalated from a very defensive reaction—throwing barricades back at police, bottles, rocks, building materials—into a full-scale riot. The South African embassy was set on fire, and the riot quickly spread throughout central London—that is, the prime shopping, downtown, and wealthy areas. The police basically lost control. For that night, people ran amok.

The rioting and looting was very, very targeted. In the papers the next day, there were pictures of rows of parked cars, where the expensive cars were torched and the cheap cars left alone. McDonald's was trashed. The police actually withdrew from the heart of London. But the riot really had nothing to do with defeating the Poll Tax.

What was the Poll Tax?

The Poll Tax was a flat-rate tax levied by local authorities across England, Wales, and Scotland to pay for local services—for the local library, public baths, police, upkeep of the roads, garbage and so on. Its official name was the much more innocuous Community Charge—but an early victory by activists was to popularize the use of the much more accurate—and historically pejorative term Poll Tax.

As in America, voting in Britain is not compulsory; however, you are legally obliged to register to vote. The main way of compiling the tax registry, that is, the list of all the people who had to pay the tax, was through the registry of voters. In effect, if you were registered to vote, you were registered for the tax.

Previously local authorities raised local revenues through property taxes—only those that owned property paid. It was "progressive" in that someone who owned a huge mansion paid more than someone who owned a one-bedroom apartment. The guy who lived in a castle paid tens of thousands of pounds in taxes, whereas the family of four adults in the projects would have paid nothing. At the time, 50 percent of British people lived in rented local authority public housing. Now, suddenly, not only did the resident in the projects have to pay the tax, but pay the same amount as the chap in the castle. Every single adult in Britain had to pay the tax. So a poor four-person household actually paid four times as much as the

guy in the castle. The only people who didn't have to pay the Poll Tax were people in prison and in mental asylums. Oh yeah, and the Queen. Everyone paid the same, whether you were rich or poor.

Registration for the tax started in 1987, and people had to start paying it in 1988. By March 31, 1990, the Poll Tax had been in effect for a couple of years and the movement to overturn it was in full swing.

As in America, the eighties had been a decade of sustained attack on the lives, and organizations, of working people. When the United States had Reagan, we had Thatcher. Unions such as the teachers union and the ambulance workers were systematically smashed. The attacks culminated in a yearlong miners' strike, where the government successfully destroyed a 250,000-member, militant, and powerful union.

The much vaunted welfare state was increasingly dismantled—during the eighties, dental and eye care were no longer free, the system of student grants was replaced with one of loans, and various benefits and eligibilities for unemployment and housing subsidies were whittled away, restricted, and outright abolished for various categories of folks.

We thought the Poll Tax was a huge attack, and a particularly good thing to organize around since everyone had to pay it and hence everyone would not be into paying it!

The Poll Tax was the jewel in the crown of this conservative assault. And like all regressive taxation, a direct attack on the working class. With its implementation, the government felt strong enough to take on everyone, not just certain groups. The last time there was a poll tax in Europe was 1381, which led to the famous English peasant revolt of Wat Tyler and John Ball, which ended up with the king almost being beheaded. The only other place in the world that currently had a flat tax rate on everyone was Papua New Guinea, which was in the process in 1987 of abolishing its tax because it was so unpopular and unworkable.

Community Resistance

What were you doing when the Poll Tax was being planned?

I was involved in a group called Community Resistance in Edinburgh—a city of about 400,000 people. It was a very large and active group, with weekly organizing meetings of up to thirty people. The main focus of the group was strike support and community organizing.

We were going to break the tax by not paying it, by mass civil disobedience, by breaking the law.

For example, back in the eighties on the East Coast of Scotland near Glasgow, a group of women factory workers made lampshades in what today I'm sure would be called a sweatshop. Fed up with working conditions and suffering health, safety, and wage grievances, they joined Britain's largest union, the Trade General Workers Union (TGWU). Once in the union they made their demands of management and when the demands weren't met, they went on strike. The TGWU's leadership refused to support the strike because they said they only recognized strikes of union members with more than twelve weeks' membership. The women had been members eight weeks! Community Resistance heard about this dispute and we contacted them and offered our support.

The main purchaser for said lampshades was Laura Ashley. So we picketed Laura Ashley's store on Edinburgh's main shopping street two or three times a week. We managed, through various anarchist contacts and comrades, to get pickets at Laura Ashley stores across the UK, Europe, and America. After over a year of adverse publicity and pressure on Laura Ashley, the strikers won.

In addition to the strike support work, we acted in solidarity with the struggles of the Asian communities in Glasgow and London; did antiapartheid organizing with independent township committees such as in Alexandra, South Africa. Locally we worked on tenant organizing and preserving unemployment, disability, and housing benefits.

This was a time of insane unemployment. The official rate was over 10 percent. In Scotland for males unemployment ran at 25 percent. By 1986, hence, when the Poll Tax rolled around, we'd been involved in various strikes, community organizing, activism, and more.

First Resistance

What did Community Resistance do about the Poll Tax?

A year before the tax became law, we stopped all other work to focus solely on campaigning against the Poll Tax. In fact, we dissolved

Community Resistance as an organization and divvied up Edinburgh into ten geographical areas, and formed ten Anti–Poll Tax groups.

The first year we put out information. Posting flyers, going door to door, talking to our neighbors in each of the ten areas. The second year when they were getting the actual register of eligible taxpayers, our focus was to try and delay and stall and disrupt as much as possible the garnering of names for the Poll Tax register.

The way they register people is similar to the census. Someone comes to your door and stands on your doorstep and fills out a form for you. How many people live in this dwelling? How many people are over eighteen? What are your names? Sometimes we would intimidate the registrars (part-time workers and students) or convince them that they were doing the work of the devil.

However, refusing to register was a criminal offense. So our advice to people was delay it as much as possible, but it's not worth going to jail, getting a fine, or getting a criminal record. We didn't advise people to refuse to register point blank, but say, I don't live here, I'm only babysitting, or whatever.

Of course back to the origins of the words *Poll Tax*, the main way of compiling the Poll Tax registry was from the electoral roll. During the period of tax registration, in an electorate of 37 million people, 2 million disappeared from the rolls.

The Campaign Spreads

How did Anti–Poll Tax organizing move beyond Edinburgh?

The ten local Poll Tax groups met independently, but also formed a federation together—the Edinburgh Federation. One of the last things we did as Community Resistance was that we produced a packet on how to start your own Anti–Poll Tax group—sample leaflets, posters you could wheatpaste or stick in your window. We said here's how you can contact us to have a public meeting. What to do. Get a local speaker. Get someone from your community. It's also good to have an outside speaker. We said we can come to your town, we can be an outside speaker as someone who has organized a Poll Tax campaign. So we mailed these packets out to all of our contacts. We were one of the first ever Anti–Poll Tax groups to form, but very soon, again, partly based on other anarchists and groups we had contacted, Anti–Poll Tax groups mushroomed all over Scotland and (as the

law was enacted in England and Wales a year later) all over Britain. And groups became regional, and then national federations.

In those tough two years there wasn't much interest from anyone because the public didn't have to pay the Poll Tax. But what we had done was lay the groundwork. With these organizations, these institutions, and these federations in place, when the first bills started dropping through people's mailbox, then, the Anti–Poll Tax movement took off immediately.

Within the first couple of months of people having to pay the bills the numbers had probably doubled. Tripled.

Mass Noncooperation

What was the movement's strategy?

The basis of our campaign was community based—that is, organized where we lived, as opposed to where we worked—but we were going to defeat the tax by not paying it, by mass civil disobedience, by breaking the law. That was the whole focus of our campaign.

Every Saturday we did a table out in front of the local supermarket, giving out information, giving advice; we went door-to-door leafleting—our aim was to leaflet every door every three months—with updates on the campaign, what was going on, legal information, local group contacts, the helpline, and so forth; talking; public meetings; wheatpasting; marches and demonstrations and rallies. While the tax was dreamt up by the national Conservative government, the amount of the tax and its imposition was in the hands of the local authorities, who in Edinburgh, as in most big cities, were Labour. So, every time the local Labour Council would meet to discuss the tax, we would invade the council chambers, disrupt their meetings, and so on.

The basis of defeating the Poll Tax was getting people to not pay their tax. Our organizing strategy was to convince folks that it was okay not to pay the tax, and indeed, that we would ensure that it would be okay for you not to pay it. While it was a criminal offense not to register for the Poll Tax, because of Britain's archaic legal system, it was a civil offense not to pay it. The difference between a civil and a criminal offense is that you cannot go to prison for a civil offense, which was our main godsend in terms of organizing.

This left the local authorities with two ways of actually collecting the tax from those who refused (or as likely, couldn't afford) to pay.

Mark Simmons

The first was garnishing one's wages. This was not an option for the millions of those who were unemployed, and hence unwaged. Most employers—through whom the wages would have to be collected—were unwilling, partly because the tax was so unpopular, to do so. This, ironically, included the government!

The only other recourse, and hence by far the most prevalent, was to send in the bailiffs, as they were known in Scotland, or the sheriffs, as they were known in England. These employees of the local authorities who were empowered to do such things, to evict you for not paying your rent, for example, would come around and seize your luxury goods and hold what was called a warrant sale, or a quick auction, where they would sell off your video, or your television.

By law, sheriffs have to give at least twenty-four hours' notice of when they were coming around to do such a luxury goods "seizure" (called a poinding). So in our leaflets we gave the whole line, saying if you get a letter from the sheriff saying that there will be a sale, call us, we will physically protect you. We will guarantee that the sheriffs will not come and seize your television. And that was the basis of the Anti–Poll Tax movement. We said don't pay the Poll Tax. You won't go to prison and you won't have your goods seized. We will protect you.

Mark Simmons

A poor four-person household actually paid four times as much as the guy in the castle.

So throughout these years of Anti–Poll Tax struggle, across Britain, hundreds of thousands of times sheriffs tried to do these warrant sales, and every single time they were stopped and turned away. Typically, say Person X calls up the local hotline number to inform that the sheriff is coming round tomorrow, at dawn that day, there'd be, say, fifty people standing outside the house, banners hanging out the windows. People singing and dancing and picketing and creating a scene in the street and in the house. Typically the sheriffs would see this facing them and walk away. Occasionally there'd be some violence, perhaps their cars might be smashed up, but more often they would see all the people and just turn away. Of the hundreds and thousands of attempted warrant sales, I'm not aware of a single successful one ever carried out.

Movement Rockets

How widespread was participation in resisting the Poll Tax?

As soon as the bills started coming in, the Anti–Poll Tax movement rocketed. There were 34 million adults in Britain eligible to pay, and 17 million never paid the tax. So 50 percent. That must be the biggest massive law-breaking ever in the history in the world. Half the population never paid it. Not just eventually, but never paid it. Many people obviously couldn't afford to pay it. Its not like 17 million people were out marching and protesting and harassing the sheriff, although many millions of them were, but of course many millions simply couldn't afford to pay. So in terms of popular response, it was easy to organize people. Previously apolitical people: mothers, old-age pensioners, and the like were the backbone of the Poll Tax movement. And of course like many other genuine radical protest revolutionary movements, in many ways the people were far ahead of us organizers.

All kinds of stuff was happening that we weren't involved with, which is as it should be. A friend of mine in another radical group lived across the

street from the offices of the sheriffs. He said every week their windows were smashed or spray painted. It wasn't any of us doing it. We had no idea who was doing it. It wasn't any Anti–Poll Tax group. We had people coming to our local Anti–Poll Tax saying, "come on, let's do it, let's go over to the new police station over there. Let's go burn down the pig station." (Edinburgh police had just built a huge new police station in our area in Edinburgh, that surprise surprise, was notorious very quickly for such community endeavors as deaths in police custody.) And we were saying, "er, no, no we can't do that. Er, how about that new leaflet we were working on."

The struggle took on many different facets. There wasn't a lot of state repression. People were jailed at demonstrations, but we were very large and combative, and there was nothing the state could do about that. There was such mass opposition. The media couldn't say that everyone in Britain is so nice and charming and everyone is paying their Poll Tax. When you walk down the street and everyone has an Anti–Poll Tax poster in the window, it's very obviously not business as usual. Its not picking off an isolated group, or picking off the pensioners, or the disabled, or the nurses, it was this massive attack that garnered an incredibly widespread and pervasive resistance, and they couldn't deal with it on that level. The police never once stepped in, for example, during an attempted warrant sale. My presumption is that they understood if they had tried, there would have been a massive breakdown of the powers of law enforcement. They didn't have the manpower to physically enforce it. To deal with hundreds, probably thousands of outbreaks/disturbances/riots every day, all over Britain. You can't send in the army against the people.

Repression

Did the government crack down on the Poll Tax movement?

There was a lot of repression after the March 31 riot. A few people had to leave the country, and there was a massive witch-hunt. Even back in 1990, surveillance cameras were pretty omnipresent and much of this was photographed and filmed by the media, who either happily or involuntarily turned over their footage. Lots of activists in London were raided. One poster girl for the revolution, a woman with some scaffolding attacking a riot cop with a mask on was turned in by one of her coworkers at the day care where she worked.

But by and large the authorities were largely at a loss. One of the rumors floating around was that someone had hacked into the main computer that kept the Poll Tax register was taking off a registrant every twenty minutes,

and replacing that name with that of a deceased person. We thought nothing of it until shortly after said rumor was reported in the papers, AK Press in Edinburgh received a visit from plainclothes detectives asking us if we had any computers! We of course laughed with glee, and crowed to the detectives that the rumors must be true then! (Needless to say, we didn't let them in as they didn't have search warrants).

Labor and the Party Left

What were the biggest obstacles for the movement?

The difficulties, of course, were many, and did not come from the people, but came from the supposed representatives of the people.

All the other political parties and the trade unions, while of course being ostensibly against the Poll Tax, exhorted their members and supporters to pay the Poll Tax because one can't break the law. You can't do anything illegal, but if you support the Labour Party in four years' time (at the next general election) Labour will repeal it. And the Liberals said, vote for the Liberals and we will repeal it. To their credit, actually, the Scottish Nationalist Party—going through a somewhat atypical courtship with the Left—and the Welsh Nationalist Party both actively supported not paying the Poll Tax.

The various Left gropuscules is where we had the real problems. The Socialist Workers Party (SWP) a Trotskyist group, and until recently a sister organisation to the U.S.-based International Socialist Organization (ISO) initially instructed their members to pay the Poll Tax because the Anti–Poll Tax struggle was community based and not rooted in organized labor—and hence obviously a bourgeois deviation from the class struggle!

Six months later when the Anti–Poll Tax movement was fucking huge, they did a 180-degree turn and launched themselves gloriously into the fray— instructing their members to stop paying the Poll Tax and join the Anti–Poll Tax movement. The other main sect in Britain at the time was the Militant Tendency. As soon as they saw the Anti–Poll Tax movement might be going somewhere they, as they always do, latched on to the movement and tried to take it over, stymie it, and use it as their recruiting ground, or paper-selling ground.

For two years, in Edinburgh, there were only ten Anti–Poll Tax groups, which had been those same ten groups started by us anarchists. Our initial independent groups (and the Federation of Edinburgh groups) didn't have a treasurer, or a secretary, or a president, or any elected officials. So the

Mark Simmons

first thing that the various leftist grouplets did was to pack a meeting, and suggest, "Hey, why don't we have a secretary, or some elected officials?"

To some of the members—and most of the membership weren't anarchists—this didn't seem like a bad idea. Nonetheless, because we were experienced activists, the Militant Tendency and the SWP weren't able to take over any of our groups. But very quickly, they set up new groups, often directly "rival" groups in the same area, which they could control.

Soon, Edinburgh had twenty-one Anti–Poll Tax groups. We still had nine independent groups, and there were another twelve groups in Edinburgh who were controlled by one or another of the different sects. Which meant that suddenly the federation was not working as well. So for a lot of the independent groups, that meant that we ceased working with the federations and started working on our own. Others among the anarchists continued to try to battle with their federation. But it meant that of the twelve elected officials of the federation, seven of them were Militant. And this was replicated throughout Britain. Hence, the head of the All-Britain Federation of Anti-Poll Tax Groups just happened to be the leader of the Militant Tendency. (And whose second-in-command publicly castigated the London Poll Tax rioters and offered to help the police in finding those responsible, and "naming names." This contrasted with a spokesperson from the anarchist Class War Federation, who appeared on the national news the night of the Trafalgar Square Poll Tax riot, and while ridiculing

POLL TAX REBELLION

the idea that Class War, with a national membership of under 200, could have been the instigators of such a massive riot, commended those fighting back against the police attacks as "working-class heroes."

Nevertheless, the active vanguard of the Anti–Poll Tax movement still came from the independent nonaligned groups as we were actually the only ones interested in fighting the Poll Tax—as opposed to recruiting to a party or selling newspapers. The Left still had to run behind us or be exposed for the fakers that they really are. So for example the different leftist groups wanted to focus on the evil Conservative Poll Tax as the creature of the evil Conservative government. Whereas our people were saying it's the local Labour authority that's imposing the Poll Tax, and the Labour authority that's sending the sheriffs around to take your television.

Every time the Labour council would meet to discuss the Poll Tax we would disrupt the meeting so it was never successfully conducted. But the Militant Tendency would try and stop us because they supported the local Labour council. So not only would we have to fight the local police to get into the chambers, but we'd on more than one occasion exchange blows and punches with our local Poll Tax comrades from the Left.

I think the party Left are a huge impediment to organizing for radical change. And it's only because we were able to see that and to fight them off that the Anti–Poll Tax movement succeeded.

It meant that we probably spent as much time fighting the Left as we did fighting the Poll Tax, which is pretty sad.

Lessons

Is there anything you would have done differently in retrospect?

The problems I see are that us anarchist activist types were not as up front as we could have been or should have been about our politics. Although it was very obvious to us why we organized in federations, and so on, it's not necessarily apparent to most. I think that was a huge error. We didn't hide our politics. When we tabled every Saturday afternoon at the supermarket, I would be selling anarchist literature, alongside the Poll Tax information, and local Anti–Poll Tax group stuff, but we didn't push it. We said we are your neighbors and we are against the Poll Tax. (And we were, of course, their neighbors, and we were, of course, against the Poll Tax.) We didn't say we're opposing the Poll Tax because we're anarchists, or we're organizing in this way because we're anarchists or against the state, or we see this as apart of the overall struggle. Indeed, we specifically did not

want to alienate folks by pushing our politics. But if you ask me about our political mistakes, the biggest one was dissolving the anarchist group. We had that level of political and ideological support for each other. We'd been very successful as anarchists of being involved in struggles and initiating struggles. In this case we stopped being anarchist, we became community members and neighbors, and I think that was a huge tactical error, in hindsight. At the time we were very conscious of not being explicit about the political dimension of our politics and that was a huge mistake.

So, for example, with these community groups—if we could stop the sheriffs from coming around like I described earlier, why couldn't we stop them from coming around to turn off your electricity, or stop them from coming around to evict people for not paying their rent, or similar attacks on poor people that happen every day. But we didn't make it more explicit beyond this single-issue campaign. There was some contextualizing— people don't like the government, or the local authority, or the police, but that's not full contextualizing.

This was a huge mistake, in hindsight. As soon as the Poll Tax was repealed, the Poll Tax groups disintegrated. They didn't become other activist groups with a wider focus. And I think that was political failure on our part to impart our politics or do any political education. We were very good at training people, exemplary at passing on organizational skills, at empowering folks. But in many ways we were far behind people in creativity and ideas. We trained people to drop leaflets, post flyers, public speaking, but not any politics behind that. Yes, the Poll Tax was repealed. In many ways, it was a very hollow victory, because it was replaced with the Council Tax, which was a watered-down version of the same tax, and there was very little opposition to that tax, which is still in force today.

The second thing was after five years of organizing we were fucking burned out. There was a huge lull in political activity after the Poll Tax was repealed in 1992. I mean on the radical Left. Five previous years of highly concentrated and in many ways very successful organizing left us all utterly knackered. Not just the anarchists, but the thousands of previously apolitical folks who became the backbone and leadership of the massive Anti–Poll Tax movement.

Get Organized and Do Something

The main lesson I learned from my experiences is the necessity of being organized and doing something. The Anti–Poll Tax movement was literally *created* by a few and it basically brought down fifteen years of Conservative rule. Margaret Thatcher was literally brought down by the

POLL TAX REBELLION

409

Anti–Poll Tax movement. Her failure of the Poll Tax alienated her from her own Party and people, and she was replaced as leader of the Conservative Party by John Major. The reason we were able to do that was because we were organized, disciplined, and we knew what we were doing.

Mark Simmons

And that only came from that previous ten years of doing something. Our skills, our organizations, our attributes and skills we had in community organizing were forged in the struggle. We didn't have to reinvent the wheel.

It's a very touchy subject, but in the Poll Tax we were definitely a vanguard in terms of ideas. We were a leadership in terms of ideas and initiative. We didn't lead the struggle. We were the first people in Britain, us little anarchists sitting in our Monday meetings in the smoke-filled hall, however, to decide that the Poll Tax was a big deal and to organize against it accordingly. And we were the first people to actively try and empower others to do something. We didn't lead the struggle, but we created a model. I think that's crucial. But let's be honest with ourselves. There's nothing wrong with taking a lead. There's nothing wrong with having a good idea and acting upon it and empowering others to do so. That's crucial. In many ways we fell down because perhaps we didn't have enough confidence and belief to further that in the movement we had created. We were happy to take a backseat and try and fight off the Trots.

I think that ideas of anarchism are common sense, and are held by most people, and are easy to grasp by most people. I'm also not interested in selling a party or a particular line. My interest is in people controlling their own lives and empowering people to do so. And getting people organized to control their own lives. And if I can play a part in that, so much the better.

Discovering a Different Space of Resistance: Personal Reflections on Anti-Racist Organizing

By Helen Luu

Helen Luu is a grassroots activist who currently resides in Toronto, Canada. Her interests include liberatory politics, traveling the globe, stuffing herself with good veggie food, biking around the city on her old clunker, drumming with her Asian women's taiko group, obsessing over music, spinning records, and toppling the status quo.

A Budding Consciousness: Discovering a Different Space of Resistance

In the summer of 2000, I was involved with a coalition that organized a demonstration against the Free Trade Area of the Americas (FTAA) at a meeting of the Organization of American States (OAS) in Windsor, Canada. While I shared the general excitement of antiglobalization activists for the successes of the mass convergences that followed the World Trade Organization (WTO) meeting in Seattle in 1999 I was also energized by an emerging critique of the mass protests.

ANTI-RACISM

A few months before, Elizabeth (Betita) Martínez's article "Where Was the Color in Seattle? Looking for Reasons Why the Great Battle Was so White" circulated around the internet after having made its first appearance in *ColorLines* magazine (spring 2000). I read this article with amazement and excitement because it was the first time that someone was publicly bringing up a criticism that many of us people of color (and others) had noticed, and in print no less: the "Battle in Seattle" had been overwhelmingly white, despite the fact that people of color are often the ones hardest hit by global capitalism. It felt like an affirmation.

In Windsor, I remember talking to (mostly white) activists about this criticism and finding that while people acknowledged that there was indeed a problem, barely anyone really did anything to actually address the problem. And so it went that Windsor, too, was overwhelmingly white. This was the turning point for me. Up until then, I had been involved with organizing with a variety of activist groups, within the community and on campus. And most of these, too, had been overwhelmingly white. I was tired of it—tired of feeling like the token person of color, of feeling marginalized even within "progressive" groups and movements, of feeling like certain issues were not being addressed, of feeling like I was by myself in all of this. In many ways, I increasingly felt like I was turning my back on my identity as a person of color, as a former refugee from the South, and as someone whose experience growing up differed so much from most of the people in these groups.

After the Windsor protests, I interned briefly with a union local where I tagged along with organizers who were helping to organize the carriers of a Toronto newspaper. The union organizers were people of color who had immigrated to Canada years ago: Sam, a black man from Nigeria, and Regi, a Sri Lankan woman. The carriers were mostly immigrants from various places around the globe, and some were refugees who were displaced because of the direct or indirect effects of global capitalism in their originating countries. In Canada, they found themselves thrust into a job market and a society that does not favor people of color—particularly not immigrants whose first language is not English—and found that the only kinds of jobs that welcomed them were low-paying and exploitative, such as newspaper delivery.

My major task was to communicate with the many Vietnamese carriers, most of whom Sam and Regi had been unable to adequately communicate verbally with during the past two years of the organizing drive. I've lived in Canada most of my life and due to the pressures of the assimilation processes, my Vietnamese was very basic so I was very nervous. In my broken Vietnamese, I spoke with the carriers about their hopes and fears,

what they thought about their jobs, and what they wanted to see happen. The entire time, I wished and wished that I had not lost so much of my language. I felt really hopeless and sad because here I stood, unable to communicate adequately with my own people!

As I struggled, I watched Regi talking with the Tamil-speaking carriers with ease. I saw that they had developed trust in her because there was no communication barrier. I saw the power of the multilingual newsletter Sam and Regi published that enabled the carriers to share stories, thoughts, ideas, and strategies with each other.

I saw how important all of this was in building a solid resistance, and how important it was to ensure that the organizing being done was inclusive in every possible way. Sam and Regi constantly stressed that those who are facing the oppression (in this case, the workers) be at the forefront of the organizing. Since the Labor movement in Canada still has a ways to go in terms of antiracism within their ranks and with their organizing, I recognize that my experience with Labour may be a rather unique one. Regardless, I learned some valuable lessons from working with Sam and Regi that I will never forget.

After I graduated from university in 2000, I temporarily moved to London. I got involved with Movement for Justice, a group that works on issues of racism such as police harassment and refugee rights, and whose long-term goal is to build a civil rights movement in the UK. This was my first time being directly involved with a group that is predominantly people of color. Sitting in a Movement for Justice meeting one day, I was conscious of the fact that of the people present, about 95 percent were of color and 5 percent white. People were sharing stories of how they have witnessed their neighbors, friends, and family members being brutalized by the police in London just for "walking while black."

The meeting was held in a refugee center in Brixton, an area in south London that is home to many of London's black population, and beginning to suffer gentrification—black people and poor people are being pushed out to make way for rich white folks. Any day of the week, you will see cops walking around or standing prominently in high traffic areas— something you would never see in wealthy areas like Chelsea or Kensington or Notting Hill. The city was trying to implement a program called "Operation Tippett" which, among other things, involves a procedure called Stop and Search. This means that cops have the legal go-ahead to randomly stop anyone on the street and question or search them. Such a procedure in a racist society is never random because it will always mean that certain groups of people, particularly young black males, will be the ones to get stopped most of the time.

ANTI-RACISM

David Hanks

People and liberation puppet in the streets of Washington, D.C. in resistance to the IMF and World Bank.

At the meeting, some shared stories of how getting stopped and searched by the cops is a regular part of their own lives, something they must face every time they step foot outside their door. Some shared stories of how the cops have brutalized them personally, and how other sectors of the (in)justice system did nothing to adequately address this since the (in)justice system is institutionally racist.

One thing is clear: the people who are involved with the Movement for Justice know just how unjust the system is. They know how it affects them every time they get booted from their neighborhoods when the price of living goes up as the rich white folks move in, every time they lose out on a higher job because of their skin color, every hour that their mothers are working as underpaid and overworked nannies for middle-class white women, and every time their friends and relatives from other countries are barred from migrating to the wealthy Western nations by the Western nations. They also know why they, their friends, and their relatives migrated in the first place and that reason is all too often a result of detrimental policies and practices that at the same time benefit the very same Western nations that close their doors to immigrants.

Clearly, it is not just a case of having to be "taught" about the unjust system as so many predominantly white groups seem to believe. Not when you're living it. These people were there at the meeting and taking part in the resistance because the issues that the Movement for Justice deal with

are inherently antiracist. Not having "enough" people of color present is never an issue.

But it goes far deeper than merely having people of color present. As Chris Crass rightfully states in his essay "Beyond the Whiteness—Global Capitalism and White Supremacy: Thoughts on Movement Building and Antiracist Organizing"[1], "we need to be clear that multiracial doesn't automatically mean antiracist." Being merely multiracial does not take apart or even challenge the status quo. Genuine antiracist work involves building alliances and working in solidarity with people of color; it means understanding the ways that unequal power relations manifest themselves in all settings (including "activist" ones) and how they work to oppress some while privileging others; it means looking to people of color as leaders, and not as mere tokens in order to prove how "antiracist" your group is ("We're not racist! Look, we have two Asians in our group!"). It means a whole lot more too, but above all, it means being dedicated to *proactively and consciously* working to bring down the structure of white supremacy and privilege.

Toward the end of 2000, I began dialogue with a few other people—a fellow woman of color and a white male ally—and out of these discussions, Colours of Resistance (COR) was born. It is a grassroots network of people (mainly of color) who actively work to develop multiracial, antiracist politics in the movement against global capitalism. Today, there are COR chapters and COR-affiliated groups and individuals working in various cities across North America, from San Francisco to Gainesville to Toronto to Montreal, and at the time of this writing, our Web site had over 26,000 hits. The COR-affiliated group that I now work with in Toronto came into being as a result of what happened in New York City on September 11, 2001.

Get in the Ring: Power Plays Itself Out

When the planes crashed into the Twin Towers of the World Trade Center —capitalist symbols of the economic and political power of the United States—I felt a deep sense of confusion and despair. Suddenly, I felt like the world had changed. But as I say this, I also realize how privileged I am to be living in the north and to feel shaken by September 11 when such things happen in many parts of the world all the time. I remember my mom making a passing comment about how the World Trade Center going up in flames reminded her of the bombs she saw fall on Vietnam. And so it happened that my life took a turn.

Like many others, I was thrust into frontline organizing against the onslaught of racist attacks and against the impending war. The activist

David Hanks

Two years after the Seattle WTO protests, global justice and environmental justice groups protest PG & E utility companies' environmental racism in San Francisco in opposition to the WTO Ministerial meeting in Doha, Qatar.

work that I presently engage in is largely a result of what transpired in New York City that fateful day in September.

Right after September 11, there were emergency meetings that took place in different cities to deal with the impending war frenzy and racist backlash. As I learned of more and more violent acts being perpetrated against Arabs and Muslims—and those of other backgrounds and faiths perceived to be Arabs and Muslims by sadly ignorant people—I found myself getting in touch with two other women involved with COR to discuss a similar meeting in Toronto. We learned of three other women planning something similar and quickly joined forces with them. Because of the immediacy of the situation, we had very little time to organize and as such, did not come as properly prepared as we should have been.

At our first community meeting, which drew about 250 people, we tried to address the internal dynamics of oppression that exist even within progressive groups by implementing a speakers' list that would allow people of color (especially women) to speak before white people (especially men). Reflecting on this later, I know that the method we haphazardly chose was not the best way to tackle the issue, but the crowd that came to the meeting reacted in a way that made me again see how many supposedly progressive people refuse to critically look at themselves as possible agents of oppression, no matter how good their intentions may be.

ANTI-RACISM

Rather than engaging in a critical dialogue with everyone about their concerns, some chose instead to yell that we were "racists" and that "[we] just don't get it." During the meeting - and the subsequent disastrous one the following week—we could not help but wonder whether we would be treated with such disrespect and outright hostility had we—the facilitators —been men, and particularly older white men. We were six young women: two white, and four of color.

The (Re)Construction of Identity

After the September 11 meetings fell apart, I continued to work with the people in my "outreach group"[2] who cared enough to stick around. People dropped in and out and the resulting group is one I still work with, now known as the "heads Up collective," and now affiliated with the Colours of Resistance network.

The heads Up collective currently consists of five young women of color of different ethnic, cultural, and religious backgrounds, one white Jewish woman, and two white men, with about half of the group identifying as queer. It is recognized and often discussed within the heads Up collective that we are a group predominantly of women of color, and those in the group who are otherwise see themselves—and are seen by the rest of us— as allies. With women of color playing important leadership roles within the group, this is in a sense a role reversal to that which we are taught in society of the mighty (usually white) men leading the way—something that, unfortunately, too many "activist" groups reflect.

In talking about identity, it is important to recognize that identities are very complex, and that they are not fixed "essences" but rather, are very fluid social, political, and psychological constructions; they are *processes*. This more critical conceptualization of identity avoids the all-too-common trap of essentializing identity; that is, it recognizes that identity is not something inherent in us, but is created and re-created by history and political-social situation. As Stuart Hall argues in *Cultural Identity and Cinematic Representation*,[3] identity is not just a matter of "being" but also of "becoming." Similarly, in *Reflections on Race, Class, and Gender in the USA*,[4] Angela Davis conceptualizes "women of color" as a fluid social and political project.

Closely linked with the essentializing pitfall, there is also the danger of homogenizing if the notion of identity is not thought through adequately. While defining ourselves as women of color, we recognize and acknowledge the fact that this category is a heterogeneous one, that we are not all the same. Within the heads Up collective, while the identity "women of color" is a prominent one, we also identify with a variety of

different ethnicities, religions, genders, class backgrounds, and sexual orientations. While recognizing similarities, it is equally important to recognize differences.

However, recognizing the heterogeneous mixture of the group does not mean that we must forgo seeking out similarities among us as well. Identity is a construction that is born of oppression, and later (re)born and reshaped through struggle. The category "women of color" was born out of the marginalization and oppression we face in this society. I had never formally adopted this identity until I first entered university and started to learn more and more about the history and resistance coming out of the space of "women of color".

As such, even while "visible minorities" or "nonwhite people" are created against our will, women of color have reclaimed the box we were dumped into as a politicized identity. This reclaimed identity is also a strategy in survival, empowerment, and resistance, one that acknowledges all of our differences but also connects us in our common histories of oppression, and our struggles against it. As Arlene Stein states in *Sisters and Queers: The Decentering of Lesbian Feminism*,[5] "it is through the process of mobilization that this sense of 'group-ness' is constructed and individual identities are reshaped." This does not imply that we need not think critically about how and where we place ourselves, however. As Angela Davis and Elizabeth Martinez argue in their discussion on coalition-building among people of color,[6] "we need to be more reflective, more critical, and more explicit about our concepts of community . . . How can we construct political projects that rethink identities in dynamic ways and lead to transformative strategies and radical social change?"

Learning the Meaning of Solidarity

After a few weeks of contacting Arab and South Asian community groups, organizations, and mosques to find out how we could assist them, the outreach group quickly learned that our approach was completely wrong. We learned that while our concern and offer of assistance was greatly appreciated, these community groups and organizations were well organized in terms of response and resistance to the racist backlash. They had their antiracist hotlines already set up, support networks already in place, countless educational events lined up, and many more. All they wanted was simply to hear our words of support and for us to be publicly vocal against the racism and war.

Soon after, we decided that perhaps the best way we could support their struggles was to help publicize their events and services. Thus, a biweekly

418

Antiwar march, San Francisco. March 2003.

David Hanks

newsletter called Community Action Notes was born.[7] Of the newsletter, heads Up collective member explains:

> We put out a newsletter every few weeks as a way to link different community groups [of color] that are working around anti-war, anti-racism work, but it's also been a way of putting support listings for people of color especially, and giving space for groups that are doing community work to be heard, to put their words on the page rather than us talking about what they're doing. A lot of groups will speak for groups being targeted right now rather than letting that group speak for themselves, so it's about giving them that space, building solidarity around that.[8]

The notion of solidarity has been key with the heads Up collective since the beginning. We see it as a crucial building block of working within an antioppression framework and see our newsletter as one way that we build and express solidarity with other groups. For us, solidarity involves supporting other people's struggles, acknowledging people's agency and their leadership rather than taking over (that is, knowing when to step back), and above all, acknowledging power dynamics and power structures. We also recognize the interconnectedness of people, their issues, and their relationships as expressed here by two members of the group:

If we're gonna make a definition for solidarity, I would say it's a feeling of compassion for other people's struggles, and understanding your relationship to their struggles, and how your struggles fit into their struggles. I think solidarity is about examining your relationship to power and what your privileges are. Even on a personal level, I think you're sort of addressing that too, because if you want to be supporting somebody, you really have to recognize what your relationship is to their struggle all the time.

Additionally, we see the newsletter in terms of recognizing the importance of simply making people's struggles known. This is significant because of the all too frequent invisibility of resistance in recorded history, particularly the resistance of historically marginalized peoples of all stripes. This is an important basis from which the heads Up collective works:

So for me, solidarity is about my own education and it's also recognizing that folks aren't invisible and trying to learn myself what white supremacy does to cover up the realities of people everywhere, and people of colour everywhere, including our very neighbors. In terms of what we're doing, the kinds of groups that we're trying to do "outreach" to, and what kind of events that we put in the newsletter, I think too often—especially in white activist spaces—these groups are made invisible, as if they're not doing social change kind of work.

Solidarity is also about forging links and building genuine relationships with other people and groups. *Community Action Notes* is one tool that the heads Up collective uses in building these relationships with other communities. By consistently supporting and helping to publicize other groups' events, and supporting various communities' struggles by publishing analyses and informational pieces about these struggles, we are beginning the process of forging real links with other communities. Not only do we hope to build links with other communities ourselves, but we hope that the newsletter plays a useful role in assisting other groups in different communities to network with each other, with the ultimate goal of a multiracial movement brewing in our not-too-distant future.

Today and Tomorrow, No One Is Illegal

While continuing to regularly publish and distribute *Community Action Notes*, the heads Up collective has also been working around issues of immigration and refugee rights. In December 2001, many of us attended a

Democractic National Convention, Los Angeles, July 2000.

David Hanks

demonstration organized by a local predominantly white antiracist group outside of the Celebrity Budget Inn. It is a for-profit motel conveniently located across from the Toronto Pearson International Airport that the Canadian government uses to incarcerate asylum seekers in a dingy wing separated from the motel's paying guests.[9]

That day was a turning point for many of us, seeing this jail-like place where asylum seekers are forced to stay day by day, and for far too many people, month by month. Standing on the other side of the barbed wire and catching a glimpse of some people—*Who are they? What are their names? What are they thinking?*—waving and waving and waving at us from behind a window in the distance, I was deeply touched, especially since my family and I had spent a few months living in a refugee camp in Hong Kong after fleeing from Vietnam.

A few months later, we returned to that very same spot, this time having become involved with the organizing of the demonstration in coalition with two other local groups that are made up of predominantly white members. Unfortunately, this demonstration left a bad taste in our mouths because of marginalization during the organizing process and during the demonstration itself by some members of the other groups. It left us not

ANTI-RACISM

wanting to continue working in coalitions. We turned away for many months, and started plotting our own plan of action.

Today, the process of visiting the Celebrity Budget Inn to actually go inside and communicate with the detainees has begun. It is a slow and painful process because we are just learning the ropes around the issues, but it is one we presently feel fairly confident about. We have begun the important —and sometimes painful—conversations with members of the two groups we initially organized the earlier demonstration with to try and resolve our differences. We do this because we realize that many minds and many hearts are always better than one, and how important it is to work with other groups around this issue if we ever hope to build a mass movement. Tomorrow, we will be taking it further and further, always keeping in mind our criticism against charity without social change, our longer-term goal of movement-building, and our even longer-term goals of abolishing the inhumane practice of detaining asylum seekers, and opening the borders.

Furthering Our Movements: Rethinking Activism, Rethinking "Globalization"

While witnessing and taking part in the "antiglobalization" movement has been exciting and inspiring to me, it has also been disempowering, and it will continue to feel that way until people are serious about challenging and dismantling the racial oppression that has been crippling this movement thus far. There are three important issues that I want to make mention of here.

The first is that the long history of struggle and resistance against capitalist globalization of peoples in the South, and of people of color and indigenous peoples in the North continues to be ignored while Seattle is credited again and again not only by the media, but perhaps more detrimentally by activists themselves, as the official "beginning" of the movement. The fight against global capitalism did not begin with Seattle, nor does it consist only of the mass convergences in the North that we associate with the "antiglobalization" movement. It is important to recognize this, even though we don't always hear about it. Remember that "the revolution will not be televised,"[10] and that means not necessarily always in alternative or independent media either!

Second, it is important to bring into question the meaning of "radical activism." Is it only "radical" when we engage in blockading meetings and get dragged away by the police—which, of course, is something that many people of color face on a regular basis and not just during protests, unlike

the bulk of white activists—or are there other ways of resisting that can be effective and just as "radical," if not more so? Who has the power to decide what is "radical" in the first place and who gets left out because of that definition? In his essay, "Finding Hope after Seattle: Rethinking Radical Activism and Building a Movement,"[11] Chris Dixon challenges activists to rethink radical activism. He writes:

> Too often this concept is defined almost exclusively by white, middle-class men, self-appointed bearers of a radical standard. Rethinking radical activism is about understanding social struggles in broad terms and toppling conventional hierarchies of activist "worth." Equally crucial, it's also about locating and sustaining hope. Overly fixated on mass mobilizations, we can easily lose sight of what's happening around us in our workplaces, households, classrooms, religious communities, neighbourhoods, and local activist groups. Yet these commonplace venues can be just as subversive as street confrontations at major protests, if not more so.

This does not mean that engaging in direct action is not beneficial or something that people of color never do. Among many other examples, the Civil Rights movement in the United States tells us otherwise. What it does mean, however, is that we must take people's history, context, and situations into account when organizing, and that we must constantly engage in a process of rethinking what we mean when we use words such as *radical* or *activist*.

Since I first started becoming engaged in social-change work, I came to a turning point only a few years ago during which I finally started to realize that my work for change circles around bringing down capitalism and fighting against the many ways that capitalism oppresses people. Prior to this realization, I had always thought of issues as separate but I have since come to recognize the ways that all of these issues of injustice—police brutality, the (in)justice system, sweatshops, imperialist and racist war at home and abroad, homelessness, immigration, housing, toxic dumping in poor neighborhoods, gentrification, you name it—are interconnected and how capitalism plays a huge role. It does not make sense to fight against the WTO, the IMF, the FTAA—to fight against "globalization"—and not also against what we consider to be "local" issues, issues that people of color have been building resistance against for decades. Too often, a false line is drawn between "globalization" and "local issues" as if these things could be separated, and as if these things are not integrally connected.

In fighting for a better world, it is important to recognize how our issues are all linked together, and how capitalism and "globalization" leave their

ANTI-RACISM

David Hanks

Tango for Protest, San Francisco.

marks on "local" communities in its myriad forms: gentrification and lack of affordable housing, classist and racist immigration policies, dumping of toxic materials by corporations in poor communities of color and indigenous communities, targeted policing, sweatshop labor by immigrant homeworkers, and the prison industrial complex, to name only a few.

The whole notion of "global" versus "local" also brings to my mind the question of privileged perspective. Oftentimes, issues that we perceive to take place in the South—IMF structural adjustment policies, agricultural cash crops, multinational sweatshops, and so on— are considered to be "global" issues and effects of "globalization" while issues we take notice of at home in the West—immigration, housing, welfare, and the like—are considered to be "local" issues. From whose perspective are issues considered global and local? Does it help to further our movements if we see the world through such a narrow lens? Is it easier on our conscience to fight about issues "over there"[12] than to engage in the struggles of people at home? In ignoring and dismissing these local struggles and issues around which people of color and indigenous peoples have been building resistance for a long, long time, we are only working to further make invisible and marginalize these struggles and the communities who engage in them.

All of these issues have very important implications for the movement (or coalition of movements, as Chris Dixon notes in his essay). Whether we move forward or not, and whether we can truly build and sustain a movement and coalition of movements that is dedicated to ending all forms of oppression, is dependent on how we deal with such challenges, along with many others. It is never easy to face these kinds of challenges, especially not when what is already going on seems so (superficially) positive to begin with. But a movement and coalition of movements that is dedicated to bringing down all forms of oppression simultaneously with challenging global capitalism is the kind of movement we must endeavor to work

ANTI-RACISM

toward if we are truly serious about fighting for a world that is free and just for all. And this is the kind of movement I want to be a part of.

Many thanks to Chris Dixon for his invaluable critical feedback, Josh Lerner for his meticulous editing help, and all members of the heads Up collective for their inspiration and energy.

Notes

1 This article appears on the Colours of Resistance Web site (www.tao.ca/~colours), as well as other Web sites. At the first September 11 meeting, we broke up into smaller working groups to start planning for action: propaganda, outreach, direct support, education, media, and events and actions.

2 Stuart Hall. "Cultural Identity and Cinematic Representation," in *Film and Theory: An Anthology*, ed. Robert Stam and Toby Miller (Malden, Mass.: Blackwell Publishers Inc., 2000).

3 Angela Y. Davis. "Reflections on Race, Class, and Gender in the USA," in *The Angela Y. Davis Reader*, ed. Joy James (Malden, Mass: Blackwell Publishers Inc., 1998).

4 Arlene Stein. "Sisters and Queers: The Decentering of Lesbian Feminism," in *Cultural Politics and Social Movements*, ed. Marcy Darnovsky, Barbara Epstein, and Richard Flacks (Philadelphia: Temple University Press, 1995).

5 Angela Y Davis, and Elizabeth Martínez. "Coalition Building Among People of Color: A Discussion with Angela Y. Davis and Elizabeth Martínez" in *The Angela Y. Davis Reader*, ed. Joy James (Malden, Mass: Blackwell Publishers Inc., 1998).

6 By the time we began publishing our first issue, the make-up of the outreach group had changed (going from a predominantly white group to predominantly women of color), the number of members had decreased, and most of the original members had dropped out while a few new ones replaced them. This is when we officially became "the heads Up collective." Interestingly, the original outreach group was also

mostly female. As a heads Up collective member said to me as she looked around at the different working groups at the first citywide meeting, "all the guys have joined the 'sexy' groups." Sure enough, most of the males were in "direct support" and "events/actions."

7 All heads Up collective quotes come from personal interviews I conducted with some of the heads Up members: Amandeep Panag, Reena Katz, and Niliema Karkhanis.

8 I have recently been informed that because the lease is up soon, the government is planning to close down the immigration facilities at the Celebrity Budget Inn and reopen them in another hotel, also close to the airport.

9 From the 1970s song "The Revolution Will Not Be Televised," by Gil Scott-Heron.

10 This essay appears on the Colours of Resistance Web site (www.tao.ca/~colours), as well as other Web sites.

11 The whole notion of "over there" also seems to falsely imply that we in the North are somehow not connected to the situations of people in the South.

ANTI-RACISM

426

Looking to the Light of Freedom: Lessons from the Civil Rights Movement and Thoughts on Anarchist Organizing

By Chris Crass

Chris Crass is the coordinator of AntiRacism for Global Justice, an organizing and training project of the Challenging White Supremacy Workshops. He works with Colours of Resistance, the Ruckus Society, and heads Up, an antiwar group in San Francisco.

When thinking about organizing, about the possibilities for movement building, about the potential of challenging injustice and fundamentally altering the relationships of power in this society—my mind turns to the Civil Rights movement of the 1950s and 1960s. More specifically, my attention focuses in on Ella Baker and the Student Non-Violent Coordinating Committee who initiated some of the most exciting work that I've ever come across. Today, when I read and hear so many debates, dialogues, and discussions about movement building and "Where do we go from here?", I again look to the insights and inspiration of Ms. Baker and SNCC.

photo top: Orin Langelle

The black liberation struggle and movements for civil rights have shaped the history of the United States. From slave revolts to Ida B. Wells, international antilynching campaign, to the 50,000 women in the National Association of Colored Women at the beginning of the century, to the struggle today against the prison industrial complex: these legacies of resistance are at the heart of liberation struggles in this country. For white organizers, it is key to study these legacies from the understanding that when people of color oppose racism they are also reaffirming their humanity. In a social order built on white supremacy, people of color organizing for justice and dignity challenges the very foundation of this society. This is why struggles against racism have repeatedly been catalysts for revolutionary social change. The challenge for me, as a white organizer, is to apply the insights and inspiration from these legacies to the work that I'm currently engaged in. The mass actions against global capitalism in the last two years have heavily influenced my organizing.

The mass mobilizations in North America opposing corporate power and global capitalism—including Seattle, Washington, D.C., Los Angeles, Philadelphia, and in Québec—have opened up important conversations about strategy, about racism in white progressive movements and the goals of organizing. While these mass actions are connected to a history of resistance over 500 years old, they have served this generation, particularly white activists, as a catalyst for both organizing and reflection on that organizing. In particular, they have created openings for broader movement debate and dialogue. Writings by radicals of color critiquing the whiteness of these actions and the ways in which racism operates within social change movements have presented clear challenges to white radicals working for social change. These challenges and the issues that they bring up are opportunities for growth and learning that white radicals have a responsibility to take seriously and engage with. The questions, possibilities, and challenges coming out of the mass mobilizations become concrete when they are connected to the day-to-day work that makes the mass actions possible.

The critique developed by Elizabeth Betita Martínez in her essay, "Where was the Color in Seattle" needs to be examined for what lessons it has for organizers involved with Food Not Bombs and antipoverty organizing, Earth First! and environmental action, union organizing and economic justice, alternative media like micropowered radio, Independent Media Centers and activist 'zines everywhere, working for immigrant rights and housing, teaching in public schools and free skools, running community gardening and radical art programs, Reclaiming the Streets, working to dismantle the prison industrial complex and support political prisoners, and so on. When the critical analysis and lessons developed out of the

mass mobilizations are applied to the local work that we, as white radicals are doing, then new possibilities and potential is found.

Although there are numerous challenges and complex questions to be struggling with, the goal of this essay is to look at issues of organizing, power, and leadership in relationship to anarchist practice. Anarchism is a political tradition, theoretical framework, and organizing practice that opposes tyranny in all forms and works to build conditions and consciousness for individual and collective liberation. In the United States anarchism has played a leading role in anticapitalist organizing from the Haymarket Martyrs of 1887 who helped organize a mass movement for the eight-hour workday, to Ricardo Flores Magon's organizing of Latino workers for land and dignity, to Emma Goldman's work for reproductive freedom and an end to imperialist wars, to Lucy Parsons and other founders of the Industrial Workers of the World who led strikes and worker sabotage with the goal of a classless society. Anarchist politics and practice have significantly shaped and influenced the global justice movement's analysis, strategy, and vision.

Although the politics of anarchism call for social equality for all people, those who have called themselves anarchists have been overwhelmingly white. In a white supremacist society like the United States one of the most powerful barriers to social change movements throughout history has been white privilege. White privilege is the economic, social, political, and pyschological benefits white people have been given over the course of U.S. history to maintain allegiance to a system that has been robbing most of them. White privilege is the flipside of racial oppression and they both serve to consolidate and maintain power for the ruling class. Additionally, the voices dominating anarchist movement for well over 100 years have been male and this too has shaped much of anarchist thought and action.

This essay argues that anarchists should follow the advice of Pauline Hwang, an organizer with Colours of Resistance, who writes, "Organize from the bottom up, and follow the lead of women and people of colour who are organizing at the grassroots level." With that in mind, there are three immediate challenges that present themselves to white activists generally and white anarchists in particular: understanding and dismantling privilege and oppression based on race, class, and gender; critically examining our understandings of power; and rethinking our conception of leadership. With those challenges before us, let us now look to some of the most dynamic organizers of the twentieth century for both insights and inspiration in doing this work.

David Hanks

Ella Baker, Community Organizing, and Participatory Democracy

Ella Baker, who was born in North Carolina in 1905, was politicized and radicalized by the poverty of the Great Depression. She participated in self-help programs throughout the thirties and developed an understanding and respect for the process by which people take control over their own lives while also protesting injustices.

In the late 1930s, Ms. Baker became a field organizer for the NAACP. She would travel throughout the South and lecture, network, and organize with any one person or group of people she could find. She would stay with local branches and help organize membership drives. She would assist local groups that were having either internal or external problems. However, her overall goal of organizing was to bring the NAACP to the grassroots. As an organizer, Baker believed very strongly in the abilities and the knowledge of local people to address their own issues. She believed that the national organization should serve as a system of support to offer assistance and resources to local campaigns and projects. She believed that organizations needed to serve the grassroots that made the organization strong.

In the early 1940s she became the assistant field secretary for the NAACP and by 1943 she was named the national director of branches. Baker describes her years of organizing with the NAACP and what she tried to accomplish as follows: "My basic sense of it has always been to get people to understand that in the long run, they themselves are the only protection they have against violence and injustice. If they only had ten members in the NAACP at any given point, those ten members could be in touch with twenty-five members in the next little town, with fifty in the next and throughout the state as a result of the organization of state conferences and they, or course, could be linked up with the national. People have to be made to understand that they cannot look for salvation anywhere but themselves."

CIVIL RIGHTS

Baker's organizational style actively worked to keep people informed and empowered, with the goal of people organizing themselves. Baker argued that strong people do not need a strong leader; rather they need an organization that can provide mutual aid and solidarity. Those views on organizing were very different than those of the national NAACP. In fact, Baker became critical of the NAACP's failure to support the development of self-sufficient local groups, as it failed to help "local leaders develop their own leadership potential." In response to the unsupportive stance of the NAACP, Baker began organizing regional gatherings to bring people together and help develop local leadership and organizing skills.

Baker worked to organize and support regional gatherings to both develop people's skills and build communities of support and resistance. This is an example of Baker's commitment to bottom-up organizing that values the work of developing relationships between people and building trust, respect, and power at a grassroots level. She believed in participatory democracy, not just in theory or on paper, but in the messy and complex world of practice: where mistakes are made, decisionmaking is tough, and the process of growth is slow.

In her essay "Ella Baker and the Origins of 'Participatory Democracy', " Carol Mueller breaks down Miss Baker's conception of participatory democracy into three parts: (1) an appeal for grassroots involvement of people throughout society in the decisions that control their lives; (2) the minimization of hierarchy and the associated emphasis on expertise and professionalism as a basis for leadership; and (3) a call for direct action as an answer to fear, alienation, and intellectual detachment.

The call for direct action was one of Baker's main strategies for creating meaningful social change. She argued that it is the people themselves who create change; that not only does direct action challenge injustice in society, but that ultimately individuals confront the oppression in their own heads and begin the process of self-transformation and self-actualization.

She also believed that as people organize, they will learn from their mistakes and successes and become stronger people in the process: people who believe in themselves and feel a sense of their own power to affect the world around them and make history. If there was a shortage of food due to economic injustice, she would help people to provide food for themselves but she would also help organize folks to protest the economic

David Hanks

Affirmative Action protest, UC Berkeley, March 2004.

conditions that deny people food. If the school system isn't providing a satisfactory education, then the community must come together to demand changes and to also provide alternative ways of learning (that is, after-school programs, study groups, tutoring programs, free schools, homeschooling, and so forth). For Baker, direct action was about achieving immediate goals, but it was also deeply connected to developing a sense of power in the people involved. It is this sense of power that would change people far beyond winning the immediate goals and help build a sustainable movement with long-term commitment and vision. It would also hopefully impact people's perceptions of themselves in relationship to the world and open up greater possibilities for happiness and satisfaction.

Ms. Baker had an innovative understanding of leadership, an idea that she thought of in multiple ways: as facilitator, creating processes and methods for others to express themselves and make decisions; as coordinator, creating events, situations, and dynamics that build and strengthen collective efforts; and as teacher and educator, working with others to develop their own sense of power, capacity to organize and analyze, visions of liberation, and ability to act in the world for justice. Miss Baker believed that good leadership created opportunities for others to realize and expand their own talents, skills, and potential to be leaders

CIVIL RIGHTS

themselves. This did not mean that she didn't challenge people or struggle with people over political questions and strategies. Rather, this meant that she struggled with people over these questions to help develop principled and strategic leadership capable of organizing for social transformation.

Baker described good leadership as group-centered leadership. Group-centered leadership means that leaders form in groups and are committed to building collective power and struggling for collective goals. This is different from leader-centered groups, in which the group is dedicated to the goals and power of that leader.

Baker's commitment to participatory democracy led her to resign as the national director of branches of the NAACP in 1946. She moved to New York to care for her niece and became the local branch director and immediately began the process of taking the organization to the grassroots; out of the offices and into the streets.

After the 1954 *Brown vs. Board of Education* verdict declared segregation in public schools unconstitutional, Baker and the local branch started campaigning against segregation in the New York school system. Additionally, after the court decision, Baker and several other organizers formed the group In Friendship, which provided financial assistance to local leaders in the South who were suffering reprisals for their organizing. In Friendship believed that the time had come for a mass mobilization against the legally sanctioned racial apartheid of Jim Crow society in the South. When the Montgomery bus boycott campaign generated local mass participation, national support and international media, In Friendship thought they might have found the spark that they were looking for. The group established contact with the Montgomery Improvement Association, which was leading the campaign, and began taking notes as well as offering support and advice.

Once the campaign came to an end in 1956, with a major victory against segregation on the city buses, In Friendship put forward a proposal to the local leadership of Martin Luther King Jr. and others. Ella Baker, Bayard Rustin, and Stanley Levinson approached Dr. King with the idea of an organizational structure to help network and build a southern movement against segregation. They believed that Montgomery had shown that "the center of gravity had shifted from the courts to community action" and that now was the time to strike. In 1957, the Southern Christian Leadership Conference was founded. The SCLC was intended to be a network of local leaders and communities coordinating their actions and providing assistance to one another. The SCLC was also formed around the strategy of getting more clergy members to involve themselves and their

church communities in the civil rights struggle. SCLC started with sixty-five affiliates throughout the South. The leader of the SCLC was Martin Luther King Jr., but it was Ella Baker who opened and ran the group's office in Atlanta, and she used her connections throughout the South to lay the groundwork for the organization. The two principal strategies of SCLC, laid out at the group's founding conference, were building voter power in the black community and mass direct action against segregation. Baker spent two and a half years as the acting executive director of SCLC. She ran the Atlanta office and traveled throughout the South building support for the organization. The first project was the Crusade for Citizenship, which aimed at doubling the number of black votes in the South within a year. With hardly any resources and little support from the other leaders of SCLC, over 13,000 people came together in over twenty-two cities to plan and initiate the campaign.

During her two and half years of organizing with SCLC, her relationship with the leadership began to wane. Although Miss Baker continued her work building a bottom-up, grassroots-powered organization, others in SCLC consolidated their adherence to the strategy of the charismatic leader-centered group style that formed around King. In addition to this, she was never officially made the executive director during her tenure as "acting" executive director. Baker said that she was never made official because she was neither a minister nor a man. The failure to recognize and respect women's leadership was a major weakness in the SCLC and in other formations of the Civil Rights movement.

Student Nonviolent Coordinating Committee and the Organizing Tradition

In 1960, a massive resurgence of civil rights activism and direct action took place among students who initiated the sit-in movement, which swept through the South like wildfire. Thousands of students participated in desegregation actions in which black and some white students would sit at segregated lunch counters requesting to be served and refusing to leave. The sit-ins were dramatic; they brought the tensions of racial apartheid to the surface and often ended with white violence against the sit-in protesters. The sit-in movement erupted out of previously existing autonomous groups, networks, or both that had been forming. They were largely uncoordinated beyond the local level and there were no visible public leaders—it was a self-organized movement. Within a year and a half sit-ins had taken place in over 100 cities in twenty states and involved an estimated 70,000 demonstrators with 3,600 arrests. Ella Baker immediately realized the potential of this newly developing student movement and went to

IMF-World Bank blockade. Washington, D.C., April 2000.

work organizing a conference to be held in Raleigh, North Carolina, in April 1960.

The conference brought together student activists and organizers from around the South who had participated in the sit-in movement. There were 200 delegates out of which 120 were student activists representing fifty-six colleges and high schools from twelve southern states and the District of Columbia. As the conference was organized by Baker and she was the acting executive director of SCLC, the leadership of SCLC hoped that the students would become a youth wing of the adult organization. However, Baker, who delivered one of the keynote speeches at the conference, urged the students to remain autonomous, form their own organization, and set their own goals that would reflect their militancy and passion for social change.

The Student Non-Violent Coordinating Committee was born out of the Raleigh conference. SNCC (pronounced Snick) was run by the students themselves along with two adult advisers: Ella Baker and Howard Zinn. It would become one of the most important organizations of the sixties. They played a major role in the Freedom Rides, another direct-action tactic that dramatically protested segregation. Its organizers started the "jail no bail" strategy of filling the jails and refusing to pay bail until segregation was

ended. SNCC also played a principal role in Freedom Summer in Mississippi. That campaign followed their strategy of grassroots community organizing that took them into some of the most formidable areas of the South.

Ella Baker has been referred to as both the midwife who helped deliver SNCC and the founder who helped articulate the base principles from which the group developed. For instance, SNCC was committed to group-centered leadership, to mass direct action, to organizing in the tradition of developing people's capacity to work on their own behalf, and to community-building that was participatory and involved local people in decisionmaking with the goal of developing local leaders. In looking to the lessons of Ella Baker's organizing strategies, it is useful to look at SNCC to see how these concepts were experimented with and applied. From the examples of SNCC, we can draw both insights and inspiration for the work that we are doing today.

Charles Payne writes in his book *I've Got the Light of Freedom*:

> SNCC may have the firmest claim to being called the borning organization [as in inspiring and helping shape other organizations]. SNCC initiated the mass-based, disruptive political style we associate with the sixties, and it provided philosophical and organizational models and hands-on training for people who would become leaders in the student power movement, anti-war movement, and the feminist movement. SNCC forced the civil rights movement to enter the most dangerous areas of the South. It pioneered the idea of young people 'dropping out' for a year or two to work for social change. It pushed the proposition that merely bettering the living conditions of the oppressed was insufficient; that has to be done in conjunction with giving those people a voice in the decisions that shape their lives. As SNCC learned to see beyond the lunch counter, the increasingly radical philosophies that emerged within the organization directly and indirectly encouraged a generation of scholars and activists to reconsider the ways that social inequality is generated and sustained.

One model of organizing in SNCC was the Freedom School used in Mississippi. The Freedom Schools prioritized political education informed by daily reality to connect day-to-day experiences with an institutional analysis. The Freedom Schools focused on building leadership and training organizers. SNCC envisioned the schools to operate as "parallel institutions" or what many anarchists refer to today as

CIVIL RIGHTS

"counterinstitutions" or a "dual power strategy." Charlie Cobb, who first proposed the creation of the Freedom Schools, said that the schools were to be "an educational experience for students which will make it possible for them to challenge the myths of our society, to perceive more clearly its realities and to find alternatives and ultimately, new directions for action." Curriculum at the schools ranged from "Introducing the Power Structure", to critiques of materialism in "Material Things and Soul Things," There were classes on nonviolence and direct action as well as classes on economics and how the power structure manipulates the fears of poor whites. The lessons learned from the Freedom Schools can help us to envision programs that educate as well as train people to take action.

Ella Baker devoted her time, energy, and wisdom to SNCC, which came to embody those principles of participatory democracy and grassroots community organizing that she had helped to develop throughout her lifetime as a radical organizer. Both Baker and SNCC struggled to create collective leadership, to engage in activism that empowered others to become active, to generate change from the bottom up, and to experiment with expanding democratic decisionmaking into everyday life.

The history and experiences of SNCC offer much to organizers today, in terms of how we go about our work and how we envision our goals. One organizer from SNCC, Bob Zellner, described being an organizer as similar to a juggling act: "Organizers had to be morale boosters, teachers, welfare agents, transportation coordinators, canvassers, public speakers, negotiators, lawyers, all while communicating with people who range from illiterate sharecroppers to well-off professionals and while enduring harassment from agents of the law and listening with one ear for threats of violence. Exciting days and major victories are rare." Ella Baker described community organizing as "spade work," as in the hard work gardening when you prepare the soil for seeds for the next season. It is hard work, but it is what makes it possible for the garden to grow.

Charles Payne warns us repeatedly to look at the everyday work that builds movements and creates social change and to draw from those experiences in order to learn the lessons for our work today. He writes, "Overemphasizing the movement's more dramatic features, we undervalue the patient and sustained effort, the slow, respectful work, that made the dramatic moments possible."

From here, he develops an analysis of how sexism operates in organizing efforts. He explores why it is that in most histories of social movements, the profound impact of women is rarely mentioned. In the Civil Rights

movement it was women and young people who were the backbone of the struggle. On this Payne writes,

> We know beyond dispute that women were frequently the dominant force in the movement. Their historical invisibility is perhaps the most compelling example of the way our shared images of the movement distort and confuse the historical reality. There is a parallel with the way in which we typically fail to see women's work in other spheres. Arlene Daniels, among others, has noted that what we socially define as "work" are those activities that are public rather than private and those activities for which we get paid. In the same way, the tendency in the popular imagination and in much scholarship has been to reduce the movement to stirring speeches—given by men—and dramatic demonstrations—led by men. The everyday maintenance of the movement, women's work, overwhelmingly, is effectively devalued, sinking beneath the level of our sight.

As organizers today, it is crucial that we look at our own work and consider what activities we place value on. How do we treat the people making the grand speeches and leading the rallies? And how do we treat the people making the phone calls, facilitating the meetings, distributing the flyers, raising money, taking time out to listen to the troubles of other organizers, coordinating child care, cooking all day, patiently answering dozens of questions from new volunteers or potential supporters, or working really hard to make other people in the group or project feel listened to, respected, heard, valued, and supported?

Whose names do we remember and whose work do we praise? As organizers we are not just putting together actions; we are helping to build community, helping to build supportive and loving relationships between people, helping to sustain and nourish alternative values of cooperation and liberation in this fiercely competitive and individualistic society.

This was the strength of Ella Baker's work, a strength that I think we can learn enormously from: her attention to group development. Ella Baker stressed the need to not only politicize and mobilize people, but to consciously develop people's capacities to be organizers and leaders in the long-haul struggle for a better world. While "each one teach one" strategies and training people in the skills of organizing don't grab headlines in the media, it is this work that builds movement and develops a community of empowerment, solidarity, and support that we need in order to transform society. Ella Baker's legacy is one that both inspires and informs our day-to-day efforts. The challenge before us is to make sense of her legacy in relationship to our work today.

CIVIL RIGHTS

Resisting Privilege, Redefining Power, and Rethinking Leadership

At the beginning of this essay I mentioned three immediate challenges that present themselves to white activists generally and white anarchists in particular, and they were: understanding and dismantling privilege and oppression based on race, class, and gender; critically examining our understandings of power; and rethinking our conception of leadership. As a white anarchist, I want to embrace the complexity of these issues, to acknowledge that there are no clear answers, but rather good questions that can challenge us to go further, to break out of what is comfortable and static so that we can open up new possibilities.

First, the challenge of understanding and dismantling privilege and oppression based on race, class, and gender. When talking about privilege and how it relates to one's life, it is important to stay focused on the goal of such reflection. It isn't about guilt or confessing to one's sins. Rather, it is about placing oneself in the matrix of domination that shapes our society. Recognizing the complex nature of where one is placed allows for sharper insights into how your position influences you and how you can take part in dismantling the structures of domination altogether. It is also important to recognize how one's place in society shifts and takes on new meaning in different situations, which pushes us to be more and more aware of these dynamics.

For example, white privilege impacts the ways that white radicals conceive of politics and organizing. I've been socialized most of my life to speak my mind, to take my opinions and thoughts seriously. Teachers, parents, and adults have looked at kids like me as the "future of this country." Pictures of people who looked like me (white, male, and "assuredly" heterosexual) filled the history books, were the important people on the walls, and were celebrated as the smartest and brightest of those who have ever lived. Much of my initial politics was based on rejecting this middle-class culture, rejecting this role of being among the "future leaders of this great country." I had the material privilege to do this comfortably, in terms of money and my parents' house. I say all of this, not because I feel the need to express some sort of guilt, but rather to place myself in both history and society. In this way, I can analyze how my privilege, my location in the matrix, impacts my view of the world, my understanding of myself and my conception of organizing, resistance, and liberation.

My anarchist politics were firmly rooted in a politics of rejection, a refusal to participate in a society based on exploitation, oppression, and massive destruction of the environment, animals, and people. My politics were

CIVIL RIGHTS

summed up by saying, "Fuck all authority." Anarchism is indeed a much more complex body of theory and practice, but this antipower politic, largely based on rejection, has been a strong undercurrent in anarchist thought—certainly in mine. Much of anarchist thought on issues of power, leadership, and organization has been informed by both a brilliant critique of how power operates and of white privilege. One of the most important contributions of anarchist politics has been the analysis of power inequalities and the visions of egalitarian social relationships. One of the biggest shortcomings of anarchism has been, How do we get from here to there? White privilege has been one of the major barriers for anarchists struggling with this question.

The understanding of both power and leadership held by most anarchists has maintained inequalities both within anarchist circles and in our relationships with others. In our rejection of both power and leadership, we frequently work in or create organizations that are breeding grounds for informal hierarchies often defined by race, class, and gender. We have frequently also argued for a complete rejection of organization altogether, advocating for spontaneous revolt, which again breeds informal hierarchies with no means of challenging this behavior. Given this situation, anarchism is one of the most white, often male-dominated political movements in the United States today. Admitting the realities of white supremacy, patriarchy, and heterosexism, I am not trying to isolate the anarchist movement but rather to argue that we need to examine where we are at if we are to seriously think about where we want to go. As a movement we also need to look to the writings and organizing of anarchists of color, women, and queer anarchists for thoughts and leadership about what direction we are already going in and should be going in.

One of the most significant aspects of anarchism is the argument that the ends do not justify the means of organizing. This has generally been thought of in terms of the tactics and organizational structure one uses. Although there is a strong tendency in anarchism to lay out a very simplistic, dualistic framework of good or bad, right or wrong to think about these issues, there is also a large body of theory and practice coming overwhelmingly from anarchists and antiauthoritarians who are women, people of color, queer, or all three. The multiple roles of the state, the ways that power operates, processes for empowerment and self-determination, what group development and collective action looks like and how this informs our organizing are all issues being developed. This is not to say that everything a radical of color or white queer says is brilliant, useful, or right, or that nothing a white, hetero male says is of value. Rather, I'm saying that the voices marginalized in larger society are often

marginalized in mostly white radical movements and that our work is greatly limited as a result. The most radical and realistic perspectives about social change often come from organizers from historically maginalized communities.

How anarchism or radicalism is defined and conceptualized is crucial. For example, defining anarchism as being in opposition to not only capitalism and the state but also to white supremacy, patriarchy, and heterosexism is a move in the direction we need to go. The next step would be to figure out exactly what that shift in thinking means for the ways that we view and act in the world.

How anarchists talk about power is a big issue. For example, the anarchist punk band Crass put forward a slogan that has been widely used and highly popular, "Destroy Power, Not People." The Black Panther Party put forward a slogan that has also been widely used and the highly popular, "All Power to the People." It is not inconsequential that the band Crass was all white people. Although both of these slogans use the word *power*, are they both using the word to mean the same thing? Crass talked about oppressive power: the power of the state to go to war, the power of capitalism to devastate the planet and exploit people. The Black Panther Party talked about power in terms of self-determination. The first demand of the Black Panthers, ten-point party platform was, "1. We want freedom. We want power to determine the destiny of our Black community. We believe that Black people will not be free until we are able to determine our destiny." The Black Panthers, Ella Baker, SNCC, and many, many others (including many anarchists) have argued that the people are the source of power and that we must organize to build collective power to dismantle oppressive power. It is also useful to distinguish between power over others and power with others.

This may sound like a debate over semantics, but it is actually a debate about the ways that anarchists think about the world and the ways that we act in the world. It is also about the ways that white privilege and male privilege have influenced anarchist politics—to speak of antipower rather than building power. This goes deep. Look at, for instance, white anarchist men who say that there are no "power dynamics" within their organizations because no one has or wants power. Or worse still, look at white anarchist men who say that there are no power dynamics because they don't believe in organization anyway and everyone should just "act." These ideas must be challenged, as they fail to see the complex reality of race, class, and gender, or how power and privilege operate on multiple levels. This must be challenged because although white anarchist men might reject power and denounce privilege in theory, we all still live in a society that grants

441

David Hanks

Affirmative Action protest, UC Berkeley, March 2004.

and denies power and privilege on the basis of race, class, and gender. This is why white male anarchists repeatedly say things like, "if women aren't being heard, they should just speak up," or "I'm not the leader, I'm just always doing everything because no one else knows how" (I can't even begin to count how many times I've said something like this over the years).

Helen Luu, an organizer with Colours of Resistance, frames the issue of white privilege as following, "Genuine antiracist work involves building alliances and working in solidarity with people of color; it means understanding the ways that unequal power relations manifests itself in all settings [including activist ones] and how it works to oppress some while privileging others; it means looking to people of color as leaders, and not as mere tokens in order to prove how 'anti-racist' your group is ("We're not racist! Look, we have two Asians in our group!"). It means a whole lot more, too, but above all, it means being dedicated to proactively and consciously working to bring down the structure of white supremacy and privilege."

Toward a Theory and Practice of Antiauthoritarian Leadership

In her groundbreaking book *Black Feminist Thought*, Patricia Hill Collins writes, "Black women have not conceptualized our quest for empowerment as one of replacing elite white male authorities with ourselves as benevolent Black female ones. Instead, African American women have overtly rejected theories of power based on domination in order to embrace an alternative vision of power based on a humanist vision of self-actualization, self-definition, and self-determination." This understanding of power, in conjunction with a critical analysis of how oppressive power operates, is a solid foundation for our work.

Organizing is about building collective power. In the process of building collective power it is also about developing the power that each of us has to act and engage with the world. The ways that anarchists

CIVIL RIGHTS

conceptualize issues of power and politics plays out in the ways that we conceptualize organizing.

Ella Baker talked about and worked from a model of group leadership, of developing the capacities of each person to be a leader to participate in the shaping and making of decisions. She also paid great attention to developing the capacities of people to be organizers, to create a movement based on participation and empowerment. Traditionally, the idea of leadership is based on one person making all of the decisions in an authoritarian manner; a model in which people follow others, often times blindly. Anarchists have been rightfully critical of this model, but our thinking needs to be more complex than this. Furthermore, anarchists are not alone in thinking about these issues. Ella Baker and SNCC, among many others historically, present an approach to organizing that concretely struggles with the question of getting from here to there.

Baker's model of organizing and leadership is firmly rooted in a politics of empowerment. She believed that a movement fighting for social transformation must also be transforming the individuals involved. She believed that people grew and developed through collective work to challenge oppression. She wasn't just talking about the ways that people see the world, but also the place they see themselves in the world; from being acted upon by forces of oppression to acting in the world for social justice. This shift involves learning politics and skills, but also a sense of self and being prepared to act. A leader or organizer in the spirit of Ella Baker is one who actively encourages other people's participation, who works with others to develop skills, confidence, analysis, and ability to take action for the long haul. Leadership in the spirit of Ella Baker and SNCC means not prioritizing the ends over the means, because the means lead you to the ends. Although they were not anarchists, the theory and practice they developed for egalitarian organizing was far more sophisticated than what most anarchists are working with.

The challenge also for a mostly white movement is how to bring people together to not only fight against oppression but to dismantle systems of oppression that grant them privilege. This is a major reason why we need to develop understandings of organizing and leadership. How do we support and encourage self-organization, while also being committed to dismantling white supremacy, patriarchy, heterosexism, capitalism, and the state? As a mostly white movement, that means we are mostly speaking to white people, and when white people have spontaneously demonstrated their rage it has often been directed at communities of color (from lynchings, to rape, to burning down whole towns, to voting overwhelmingly against immigrant rights and affirmative action). White

radicals have a responsibility, at the very least, to play leadership roles in challenging white supremacy in white society.

A theory and practice of antiauthoritarian leadership is a subject full of contradictions, tensions, questions, discomforts, confusion, and uncertainties and that's what I like about it. Being honest about contradictions opens up possibilities for understanding, where denial does not. Furthermore, tensions can be a creative force to develop something new, something uncharted, as opposed to strict guidelines that contain and restrict. By tensions I mean looking at what exists between the binary or dualistic frameworks; the gray areas, the both/and rather than the either/or, where one is multiple. For example, the tension is what exists in the middle, if on one side you had leader and the other side was follower. What exists between these two concepts? What does it mean to be, all at once, a follower, a leader, an individual, a participant in a collective process, someone who is privileged on the basis of race but oppressed on the basis of gender, someone who has experience and wisdom to share with the group and also wants to encourage broad participation in discussions, to know that at all times one can be both oppositional to and complicit with oppression? When all of these different positions and ideas are recognized, rather than denied, then something more creative and dynamic can be developed. I believe that we must be willing to engage with and expand the tools and concepts of leadership. Anarchists need more tools, more concepts to use in our day-to-day work. In looking for insights and inspiration on organizing that prioritizes egalitarian practices, I have looked to liberation struggles from communities of color. Many of these struggles are led by women of color, who are producing many of the most radical and hopeful strategies for social transformation out there.

With that in mind, we should heed the advice of anarchist organizer, Gabriel Sayegh. Sayegh writes in his essay, "Redefining Success: White Contradictions in the Anti-Globalization Movement," "We [white activists] must become active, effective listeners if we are serious about being part of a movement. We must be willing to challenge our selves—our behaviors, actions, and thinking—as much as we are willing to challenge the global institutions of capitalism. This is a difficult task indeed. We can find direction by examining what radical people of color have been doing for centuries—organizing a movement for liberation."

We must be willing to struggle over these complex and difficult questions of theory and practice, but we must do so as we engage in our day-to-day work to transform ourselves in the process of transforming this society. Facing the complexity of reality is one of the most radical acts we can take.

Special thanks to Kerry Levenberg, Clare Bayard, Professor Laura Head, Johnna Bossuot, and Chris Dixon, in particular, for critical feedback on this essay.

Resources

Colours of Resistance Web site: www.tao.ca/~colours

Books on Organizing

Bobo, Kim, Jackie Kendall, and Steve Max. *Organizing for Social Change: Midwest Academy Manual for Activists.*

Naples, Nancy, ed. *Community Activism and Feminist Politics: Organizing Across Race, Class and Gender.*

We Make the Road by Walking: Conversations on Education and Social Change between Myles Horton and Paulo Freire.

On the Civil Rights Movment

Crawford, Vicki L., Jacqueline Anne Rouse and Barbara Woods, eds. *Women in the Civil Rights Movement.*

Payne, Charles. *I've Got the Light of Freedom: The Organizing Tradition and the Mississippi Freedom Struggle.*

On Racism and Anti-Racism

Allen, Robert. *Reluctant Reformers: Racism and Social Reform Movements in the United States.*

Crass, Chris. *Collective Liberation on my Mind,* (available thru akpress.org)

Thompson, Becky. *A Promise and a Way of Life: white antiracist activism.*

CIVIL RIGHTS

445

March for educational justice. UC Berkeley, March 2004.

International Solidarity Movement

By Rachel Neumann

Rachel Neumann is a longtime political activist and writer covering civil liberties and human rights. Her alterego, Auntie Establishment, is the political advice columnist for AlterNet.org.

If you come only to help me, you can go back home. But if you consider my struggle as part of your struggle for survival, then maybe we can work together.
—Aboriginal woman, from the *People's Global Action Manifesto*

In the face of what is called globalization—a world with no borders for capital—let us welcome this vindication of the internationalism of human solidarity.
—Eduardo Galeano, *about the Abraham Lincoln Brigades*

If New York were Palestine, I wouldn't be allowed to travel to the Upper West Side. If New York were Palestine, it would not be safe to live on the fourth floor, surrounded by windows. If New York were Palestine, everyone I know would have a bullet wound or a story about their time in prison. If

photo top: Andrew Stern / www.andrewstern.net

SOLIDARITY

New York were Palestine, the playgrounds and schools would be empty of children. If New York were Palestine, every six-year-old would know the names of a multitude of bullets. If New York were Palestine, the taxi drivers would still brave potholes and traffic, but they would not be allowed to travel to Brooklyn. If New York were Palestine, our monuments would be piles of rubble; our museums would be carefully preserved keys and deeds to properties we could not even visit; and we would have hundreds of thousands of unsung heroes others called terrorists.

On the train, my first day back in New York after traveling in the Israeli-occupied territories, I look at the diversity of the subway riders, all pushed up against each other in a way that is both maddening and inspiring. If everyone here knew what it was like for people there, I think, there would be no choice but for international solidarity.

Of course, the idea of international solidarity is not new. Its seductive call is as old as the first radical political movements. Think of the original hopefulness of the "Internationale," Americans cutting cane in Cuba, and Che's vision of revolution as an unstoppable ocean. Think of those who traveled to Vietnam in the seventies to aid and comfort the "enemy" and those who traveled to Central America in the eighties, accompanying refugees from Honduras and El Salvador. Whether digging ditches, building homes, or acting as human shields—people have always been drawn to resistance wherever it was found. Seeing others resist gives us both inspiration and education. We who can come to share in the struggle, but equally we come to sustain our own spirits.

Between 1936 and 1938, some 3,000 young Americans joined 40,000 international volunteers to defend Spanish democracy against Franco's fascist assaults. They came from every state and their numbers included seventy-five women and eighty African Americans. One-third of all the volunteers in the Abraham Lincoln Brigades died fighting in Spain. They went not just to support the resistance fighters, although they did support them, and not just to observe, although the stories they brought back helped shape our historical knowledge of the war. But they also went primarily to act—to struggle directly against that which they felt could not be allowed to continue.

The latest incarnation of international solidarity combines the passionate spirit of the Brigades, the nonviolent tactics of the freedom bus rides of the Civil Rights movement, and the energy and experience from the large-scale global justice protests in Seattle, Prague, and Genoa. These tactics and strategies are being adapted and transformed by the unique forms of resistance occurring in Chiapas, in Argentina, in Vieques, and in the Israeli-occupied territories.

SOLIDARITY

A Model of International Solidarity

One of the most striking examples of contemporary international solidarity can be seen in the movement to support the Palestinian struggle for self-determination. Born in Bethlehem in the spring of 2001, the International Solidarity Movement (ISM) calls itself a "Palestinian-led movement of Palestinian and International activists." Although it explicitly recognizes the "the Palestinian right to resist Israeli violence and occupation via legitimate armed struggle" it is focused on nonviolent direct action and is committed to the principles of nonviolent resistance. What differentiates ISM from other international solidarity work is the focus on reciprocity; internationals take an active part in the resistance, as observers and economic and physical resources but also in the daily physical struggle to end the occupation. Internationals are trained by local Palestinians and invited to stay in homes and community centers that are connected with the struggle. While the volunteers have brought with them key resources for the movement—including the affinity group structure and the idea of separating actions based on various risk levels—these tactics have been integrated into an already existing tradition of Palestinian nonviolent resistance.

Ghassan Andoni, one of the founders of the ISM, puts it like this: "We are not a social case, and those who do solidarity have to think of that. We are not a . . . humanitarian case. We are a people, who are deprived of the simplest rights to an honorable life. We are in need for help to support us to continue the nonviolent resistance and to continue living, to continue developing and expressing our culture and our identity, and our folklore... We are not beggars. We are not a social case. We are what we are, fighting an occupation that everybody knows."

The group began with a protest against the Israeli occupation of Orient House in East Jerusalem. In August 2001, the first group of internationals arrived. Members of the ISM demolished a roadblock in the village of Al-Khader and protected its farmers from nearby settlers, challenged the roadblock and checkpoint between Jerusalem and Bethlehem, and served as human shields in the village of Beit Jala.

The second delegation of over 200 people arrived in the occupied territories in December 2001. They stayed in Palestinian homes, joined marches to the ever-present checkpoints, helped turn around bulldozers, and accompanied ambulances to the hospitals. The group returned to their home countries committed to spreading the word about the brutalities of the Israeli occupation and building larger international delegations for spring and summer 2002. When the spring group of volunteers came,

SOLIDARITY

Andrew Stern / www.andrewstern.net

Palestinian children holding a demonstration against the occupation organized by the International Solidarity Movement near a construction site of the "apartheid wall" in the West Bank, Palestine. July, 2003.

however, in mid-April, they found themselves in the middle of the largest Israeli reinvasion of the West Bank since the 1967 war. Faced with the intensity of the immediate crisis, the internationals—working with Palestinians—were able to draw attention to the abuses of the invasion. In two of the most publicized examples, internationals were able to bring food, water, and needed medical supplies into both President Arafat's compound and the besieged Church of the Nativity, where Palestinians had been holed up for weeks without adequate food and water. In summer of 2002, over 500 internationals came to the occupied territories for freedom summer, the most coordinated and organized attempt at integrating a long-term international presence as part of the Palestinian struggle.

What Does International Solidarity Look Like?

This is a small glimpse of what international solidarity looks like in the occupied territories. Ten internationals from Europe, the United States, Canada, Japan are working with a group of Palestinians crouched under the barrel of a Makava tank, one of the largest and most indestructible tanks in the world. As it swings, they duck. Finally, a group pastes to the side of the tank: RETURN TO SENDER. The group gets away unharmed.

SOLIDARITY

In the village of Herez, thirty Palestinians are working with their bare hands, crude hoes, and hammers to clear a makeshift roadblock made by Israeli bulldozers. A group of internationals work with them, clearing garbage, rocks, and chunks of cement. Israeli soldiers come almost immediately but, unsure of what to make of the combination of Palestinians and internationals working closely together, leave again. The roadblock remains clear for two days, allowing ambulances, workers, and schoolchildren to go about their days in a semblance of normalcy that is anything but normal in the occupied territories.

One early morning, Caiomhe Butterly, a volunteer from the UK, escorts a pregnant woman whose water has already broken to a hospital in Jenin. On the way into the hospital, one soldier holds his rifle to the woman's stomach and threatens to shoot. Caiomhe puts her body between the butt of the gun and the woman's belly and the woman is finally allowed to enter the hospital.

An armed tank and a bulldozer roll down the street toward a house in Bethlehem. Four Palestinians and four international civilians representing the United States, the UK, Canada, and Israel lay down in the street effectively stopping the advancement. Israeli forces launch tear gas and sound grenades at them but the people in the street don't move. The tank attempts to enter from a different direction, the situation is replayed. Israeli army jeeps arrive and arrest two of the Palestinians and take away the one person from the United States.

Learning from Successes, Building a Stronger Solidarity

One reason the International Solidarity Movement has been successful at building its base, gaining widespread support, and strengthening the resistance to occupation is similar to the reason that the large-scale global justice protests have succeeded: the goal is kept simple and broad, so that many people can participate. There is very little discussion in the International Solidarity Movement of the ultimate solution for the problem beyond the first and most pressing goal—ending the Israeli occupation of the West Bank and Gaza. Instead of requiring that everyone involved agree to particular borders or a final political statement—issues that will need to be decided by Palestinians—participants are asked only to agree to the basic goal—the immediate end of the occupation.

The result has been that organizations have been able to make the connections between their struggles at home and the struggle in the occupied territories. Vieques independence activists recognize a similar pattern of colonization. Prison activists recognize the criminalization of a

SOLIDARITY

The Brass Liberation Orchestra performs at an antiwar action, Bechtel, San Francisco 2003.

David Hanks

whole population and the relationship between the continuous incarceration and harassment of Arab immigrants and the Palestinians' struggle for autonomy. During freedom summer, members of the Free Vieques Coalition, the Coalition for the Human Rights of Immigrants, Malcolm X Grassroots, and the Prison Moratorium Project traveled in an organized affinity group to the occupied territories as part of the International Solidarity Movement. The ability of the solidarity movement to make the connections between poverty and mass incarceration rates in the United States and the prisonlike conditions of the Palestinian people as a whole will be crucial to building a larger model of shared solidarity, when groups support each other's struggle not because it is "right," not because it is "helpful," not even because it is "just," but because it is, ultimately, the same struggle. This is not only important theoretically but practically. Without a strong base tied to local work, solidarity movements tend to flare and die out quickly, moving on to another seemingly more urgent cause.

Passport to Protection

Even as U.S. activists criticize the United States and its role as "police office and protector" of the world, and particularly its role in funding the Israeli military, they rely on their U.S. passports to protect themselves and the oppressed people with whom they work. There are contradictions inherent in a model that depends on using a privilege by the empire. It is a privilege that can, and often is, misused. For example, the presence of American activists in Arafat's compound or the besieged refugee camps becomes more of a story to the U.S. media than what is happening to the Palestinians themselves. The daily dangers and acts of bravery of the Palestinians get less attention than the presence of the internationals whose viewpoint could not be as experienced as someone whose daily experience is occupation. Wherever people travel in the name of international solidarity, the goal should be on highlighting the experiences and voices of the people in struggle. It is necessary to remember that the

SOLIDARITY

Some of the 100,000 Iraqis march in protest of the U.S. occupation to demand immediate elections on January 19, 2004.

Palestinians, the Zapatistas, the U'Wa, and the Argentineans are still, by far, the only experts on their experience.

And, because some governments know the United States will turn a blind eye to human rights abuses, American citizenship is not always a guarantee of protection. American solidarity activists have been killed in El Salvador, East Timor, and Israel. The death of U.S. citizen Rachel Corrie, run over by an Israeli bulldozer in May 2003, is an example. Israeli officials, caught offguard by the internationals during their spring 2002 assault, have begun deporting internationals and refusing them entry into the country and detaining those who make it in. Thus far, over 100 foreign peace and human rights workers have been deported, many have been detained for weeks in Israeli detention centers, and several hundreds have been denied entry into the country.

Strengthening Reciprocity

If our resistance is truly as "transnational" as capital then we must imagine what it would be like if people had the ability to travel as easily as capital does. Right now, with the increasingly restrictive immigration laws and deportation policies of the United States, Israel, Australia, western

SOLIDARITY

453

David Hanks

Globalize Justice Not War! Father Bill O'Donnell (fifth from left) and allies en route to blockade the Pacific Stock Exchange in San Francisco prior to the Invasion of Iraq. A lifelong rebel and well-loved justice worker, Bill died December 8, 2003. Presente!

Europe, it is only the very privileged who can travel as their means of expressing international solidarity. Others are forced to travel only to look for work to feed a family, to escape persecution, or to run from starvation. People's Global Action began in 1998 as a network of people from all continents dedicated to resisting the unfettered spread of global capital. One of the more intriguing ideas to come out of PGA is the eradication of borders. A truly liberatory international solidarity could focus on two fronts—building campaigns at home that made the link between very local and international issues and calling for an end to immigration policies based on borders set up to maintain purely capitalist interests.

In a similar vein, Yazir Henry, director of the Direct Action Center for Peace and Memory in Cape Town, South Africa, suggests that "Solidarity only really exists when it goes both ways." The center holds classes for survivors of apartheid, including former MK soldiers (armed members of the ANC), many of whom spent their whole adolescence fighting and never learned to read or write. They also offer tours for visitors who come to the "New" South Africa, political tours that are as much a matter of reconciliation and remembering for the ex-soldiers as they are about educating progressive tourists. The tour participants are expected to share their own preconceptions of townships, to talk about how being

SOLIDARITY

454

there will change the work that you do. The tours have been a success in that people keep coming and spreading the word about the center, but Henry isn't satisfied. "It can't be one way," he says. "Everyone who takes a tour here should bring one person to their country for a tour there. Why shouldn't these kids, who have only known apartheid and economic apartheid, see New York or Berlin?"

No War No Empire—antiwar activists take on Bechtel corporate office, San Francisco.

One cross-border solidarity success can be seen in the Zapatista caravan of February 2001. After ten years of fighting a war of words from the mountains in Chiapas, Mexico, the Zapatistas organized a bus caravan to the capital to bring their message directly to the people they would meet along the way. They chose, as part of this caravan, to harness the international support that had been bringing volunteers to Chiapas for a decade. Over 500 internationals, from over twenty countries, joined the caravan, traveling the three weeks from San Cristobal to Mexico City, not simply as observers or supporters but as participants in the Zapatista-led caravan. Internationals and Zapatistas rode the buses together, trading stories and jokes into the night, eating the sandwiches thrust through the windows by supportive strangers, learning each others' songs. Participating in all-night conversations in seven or eight languages, facilitated by indigenous leaders, was a lesson for the bus travelers in democracy as well as in international solidarity.

No matter how strong international solidarity campaigns become, traveling is still the privilege of those with the largest resources. Unless international solidarity inspires local struggles in very local communities (whether that community be Brooklyn or Bethlehem) it risks becoming just an "activist vacation"—the latest hot spot to visit, photograph, talk about back home, and forget. If people are only interested in the struggles that happen oceans away and to "other" people, the whole concept of real shared solidarity becomes meaningless. To have reciprocal solidarity, one must know what one is personally and locally struggling against.

Solidarity activists from the First World have value not just as human shields, but also as students of world movements whose lessons can be

SOLIDARITY

brought back home to the center of the empire. Sharing resources, ideas, and struggle, we can learn a lot. While we may need to shout (with our words, our bodies, our art) at those who put themselves above—at the governments, at the cameras—we need to listen to those who have come up from below. We learn, we teach. We listen, we talk. Before she died, Rachel Corrie wrote home: "I am . . . discovering a degree of strength and of basic ability for humans to remain human in the direst of circumstances—which I haven't seen before."

Perhaps one of the lessons that Americans most need to learn is about hope. In one week—and not an extraordinary week— in the occupied territories, nineteen Palestinians are killed. Barbed wire encircles the West Bank. After more then ten years, the Zapatistas are still struggling for food and clean water, as well as for autonomy. In these times, hope sometimes seems misplaced and inappropriate to the level of devastation. But in Palestine and Chiapas, it is hope that leaves me in awe. Despite the deaths, the destruction, the demolitions of homes and livelihoods, people breathe hope. They discuss what art to make, what murals to paint. They have children and raise them as if they will grow up in a world of love. They strategize for liberation and risk their lives to achieve it. Our struggle has many different veins and follows many different paths, but international solidarity is the acknowledgment that is the same hope that lives in all of us—fueling our anger, passion, love, and our pursuit of justice.

CHAPTER 31

From Trotsky to Puppets: Other Revolutions are Possible

By Graciela Monteagudo

Graciela Monteagudo is an Argentine organizer and street theater maker and performer who has made theater for the streets during recent mass actions against the World Economic Forum, the School of the Americas, and the G8. She also works with Bread and Puppet in Glover, Vermont. Her use of art and theater for liberation grew out of her work as an organizer for human rights in Argentina. Her recent show "Que se vayan todos, a cardboard piece" is currently touring the United States and Europe..

Giant puppets took the streets, visions of a better world and images of the tools to build it were carried aloft, people drummed, sang, danced and chanted through the streets. For many people, I think especially for people who were stretching their courage to even be out in the streets at all, the march was liberating and inspiring.
— Starhawk describing the World Economic Forum Protest, New York City, February 2002

photo top: Linda Panetta

STREET THEATER

A beautiful street theater piece may have a deep impact on the conscience of those who see it, but that impact will soon fade if it is not reinforced by another artistic or political event. By emphasizing democratic process in the creation of social art, I attempt to help people learn how to do this work themselves. My experience participating in direct actions in the streets and engaging in performances has taught me the importance of democratic decisionmaking and of allowing everyone's voice to be heard, and I believe the process of working with people, either in theater or in direct street actions, is far more important than the artistic product. If the process is democratic, people will learn how to work with others, and that is what I want to achieve.

From Trotsky to Puppets: Some Background

I was born in 1959 in Buenos Aires, Argentina. My mother was a maid for middle-class families and my father owned a small metalworking shop. As I was growing up, the warmth of the Cuban fire was spreading to social organizations throughout Latin America, and students and workers were organizing, some with theory and strategy, some with pseudo-Marxist tactics and a few guns. And then in 1973, Salvador Allende fell in a blood-bath in Chile, and in 1976 Isabel Perón surrendered the Argentine government to a military junta. Repression, oppression, torture, and disappearances swept the South American continent. I tried to lead a normal life, ignoring, like many Argentines, the fact that 30,000 people were disappeared, 2 million had gone into exile, and the military was running over 300 concentration camps. In 1981, I crossed the Plaza de Mayo, the Argentine center of power, and saw the Madres de Plaza de Mayo and a few small leftist political parties demonstrating. I found out that the Madres were the working-class mothers of people who had in most cases been kidnapped in the middle of the night from their homes. The Mothers were confronting the dictatorship in the streets, and although some of them were disappeared themselves as a result, they succeeded in bringing the issue of brutal human rights abuses by the U.S.-backed military regime to international attention. In 1984, I entered the University of Buenos Aires as a philosophy student and joined the student union as a human rights activist, becoming deeply involved in the struggle against the International Monetary Fund's structural adjustment plans.

The Trotskyist party that I joined out of sheer ignorance was the place where I discovered that abuse of power, authoritarian politics, and corruption were not only predominant in postdictatorship Argentine society but also inside the leftist parties. In 1990, I was violently expelled from the organization, along with twenty of my friends. We began to work on a nonhierarchical collective, ultimately forming a group called La

Naranja. With our anti-authoritarian politics and our democratic methods, we gained a great deal of student support and we were elected as student representatives to the board of directors of the school. We joined with other organizations that were engaged in a similar process, and integrated into a political front called La Mano.

Empire and Profit banner encloses the commons in the Argentine Uprising Pageant. School of the Americas, November, 2002.

Being expelled had caused me to rethink my life and my activism, and after attending an international puppetry festival in Buenos Aires, I started taking commedia dell'arte and puppetry classes with an anarchist artist who also loaned me some books that illustrated the politics of the Soviets toward the leftist opposition. I began to question the theory of the vanguard and instead decided to focus my efforts on democratic collaborations. La Naranja helped organize direct-action resistance to the economic and social policies of the International Monetary Fund and the World Bank (which included the privatization of the educational system, a plan that would make education unaffordable for all but a small minority of Argentines). At the same time, I started to work on creating big puppets and performances.

In 1994, while performing puppet shows for homeless children in Bahia, Brazil, I met the Vermont-based Bread and Puppet Theater, and felt that I had found the school of street theater I needed. Through thousands of hours of rehearsals, and with the collaboration of artists from all over the world, Bread and Puppet has mastered the technique of street theater with profound political content and outstanding aesthetics. Hardworking and well organized, the group builds hundreds of puppets and performs locally and internationally, creating as many shows as possible each year on issues such as human rights, poverty, labor, ecology, politics, and relationships of power.

Shortly after this meeting, I moved to Vermont and joined the company. I was impressed with their level of organization—in one week they taught approximately 100 volunteers a complex show, *The Passion of Chico Mendez*, staged in a format that they call a "passion play," inspired by the Catholic tradition of the Stations of the Cross. Each scene was set in a

different space, and a brass band took the audience from one scene to the next. Each group rehearsed separately, with all the scenes coming together during the final rehearsals.

After working as a full-time company member for a year, I had the opportunity to direct one of the scenes of the same play when we performed it at the International Festival of Arts and Ideas. By observing Peter Schumann, Bread and Puppet's artistic director, and the work of senior puppeteers as they directed the shows, I learned how to incorporate hundreds of people who do not define themselves as artists into huge street shows and pageants.

I was in awe of Peter, though I became increasingly critical of the company's hierarchical structure. Still, despite the fact that Schumann has final say on artistic decisions, there is a lot of space in the earlier stages of rehearsal for creation and collaboration, and from that environment has come a long list of amazing cultural insurrectionists and popular artists. Bread and Puppet has deeply influenced the visual and the performance aspects of protest in the United States, and puppeteers in the anticorporate globalization movement have learned from their techniques and are experimenting with new ways of leading horizontal creation processes.

Street Theater Actions in Argentina

In 1996, after working for a year and a half with Bread and Puppet, touring in all kinds of spaces and for all kinds of occasions, I returned to Argentina to coordinate the creation of a street puppet show to be performed at a protest to commemorate the twentieth anniversary of the most brutal and violent dictatorship Argentina has ever endured.

Tamar Schumann, an American dance theater director, and I traveled to Buenos Aires to work with a group of activists organized by people I had formerly worked with in La Naranja. In group discussions and intensive rehearsals we came up with a simple dance and puppet piece designed to move along with the protest march, honoring the resistance of the Argentine people, especially the Madres de Plaza de Mayo.

We built huge cardboard hands, created simple costumes, and had one stilt-walker who wore a death mask and a military uniform and carried the U.S. flag. This character dragged a dummy dressed as a worker with a paper bag on its head behind him, a symbol of the disappeared. Women in white tunics held the large hands, representing the Madres de Plaza de Mayo, whose distinctive symbol is a white scarf on their heads. Characters

Linda Panetta

Graciela enters with the Esperanto *(hope) contingent that includes birds of liberation with the names of those in prison for resistance to the School of the Americas, November, 2002.*

with Carlos Menem (who was then the president of Argentina) masks danced with shovels, as if burying the disappeared. The women dressed in white would lift the dummy up in the air and subsequently lose him to the Carlos Menem character, evoking the fact that Menem, like many other politicians, was trying to bury the memory of our disappeared. The action repeated itself over and over again, symbolizing a struggle over the human rights issue: would the military and the politicians, with the aid of the United States, prevail over the people and force them to forget the repression, or would the people, led by the Madres de Plaza de Mayo, rescue the memory of the disappeared and honor their struggle? The question, like the actual situation, was left unanswered.

Apart from Tamar and myself, there were no professional performers in the group. However, we were able to create an interesting street theater piece through a democratic process of discussions. Although I very much wanted to direct, I limited myself to suggesting the characters and gave some ideas on how to use the hands. Tamar choreographed the piece, and rehearsals were interrupted several times when proposed movements seemed to imply a statement that contrasted with the message intended by the activists. Whenever that happened, Tamar and I would facilitate a democratic discussion until we all could agree on a movement that reflected the message of the group. This process helped clarify our

   461

STREET THEATER

Linda Panetta

Mothers of the disappeared followed by hope perform at the Argentine Uprising pageant at School of the Americas, Ft Benign, Georgia, November, 2002.

analysis of the repression and how it served the different sectors of society. The process also helped the organizational efforts of La Naranja, as it introduced them to people who were not interested in doing activism without an artistic outlet, and also enabled them to work with and bond with people in a way that no meeting or assembly would allow.

Personally, I was able to integrate two worlds: the Bread and Puppet techniques of creating street theater and working with large groups of people who do not self-define as artists, with the activist world where creation can be a horizontal, nonhierarchical attempt and art can be used as a tool for direct action.

We went back to Buenos Aires in 1998, this time to work with another group called HIJOS, made up of the children of the disappeared, along with a group of young activists from my former school, led by my friends from La Naranja. Tamar and I worked with them to create a street performance for a demonstration in front of the home of a police officer, Miguel Osvaldo Etchecolatz, who had been in charge of several concentration camps in Argentina during the dictatorship. He was also responsible for the disappearance of sixteen high school students. The kidnapping and disappearance of these children, who were protesting to demand an inexpensive bus fare, is known as the Night of the Pencils. The

demonstration was going to be called "Escrache a Etchecolatz." *Escrache* is a slang word for "expose," and in an *escrache* thousands of people get together and make a lot of noise to alert the neighbors that a mass murderer lives among them.

Among the Left in Argentina, HIJOS has a privileged status since they are the actual children of the disappeared. Many of them witnessed the violent abductions of their parents, and some saw their parents tortured or killed. Some were illegally adopted as newborns by families connected to the military after their mothers were killed. I admired their courage and their zeal. Two weeks before Tamar and I arrived, one of their *escraches* had been violently attacked by the secret police. This didn't deter the HIJOS demonstrators, but it did heighten their awareness of risk and safety. As a result, very few of them actually participated in the performance, but they did provide us with a place to work and gave us a prominent space during the protest.

On the day of the protest, the HIJOS banner opened the march, followed immediately by approximately fifty performers with oversized cardboard pencils who engaged in a dance in which ten characters with Etchecolatz masks. The Etchecolatz characters would push the performers with the pencils down and then a little later, the performers with the pencils would regroup and use their pencils to make the Etchecolatz characters fall. The scene repeated itself over and over again. When the protest arrived at Etchecolatz's building, his bodyguards threw a tear gas grenade from the tenth floor and dropped heavy objects onto the crowd. Everyone disbanded, regrouping in a short while to hear the organizers make speeches. In the end, the police attacked the crowd with tear gas and everybody scattered. When the performers ran from the police, they dropped their props, leaving the huge pencils lying in the streets, and late that night a friend saw one of them being dragged away by a homeless woman.

Insurrection, Repression, and Street Theater in Argentina

In July 2002 I returned to Buenos Aires once more, this time with David Solnit of Art and Revolution. Six months earlier, Argentina had been the site of a spontaneous uprising against the IMF and the country's entire political and economic system. The civil society was united under the slogan *Que Se Vayan Todos*, "They All Must Go," meaning that every politician from every party should leave, along with the supreme court, the IMF, and the multinational corporations.

STREET THEATER

Linda Panetta

The people wanted to decide their future for themselves. They created popular assemblies, in which people met to discuss their situation and possible actions, utilizing a direct democracy process. The demonstrations and actions never let up while five successive governments fell in two weeks.

When David and I arrived six months later, the popular assemblies of Buenos Aires were smaller, but they had begun to organize takeovers of buildings and empty lots. We built puppets in a bank that had gone bankrupt three years earlier, which the neighbors had now taken over, cleaned up, and established as a space for organizing and for popular arts and culture. Another assembly had taken over an abandoned clinic and started a free health care program for people at the over eighty factories now being run by workers.

Aníbal Verón, an organization of the unemployed that had recently endured a brutal repression of one of their *piquetes* (road blockades), was organizing for a day of street protest against state terrorism. The three neighborhood assemblies we visited all wanted to participate in the protest, and we decided to create a street theater piece with giant puppets and props. We facilitated workshops with these assemblies and also with the unemployed workers and their children, in their own neighborhoods.

We built dozens of puppets with several different collectives that in turn collaborated with the assemblies, street theater groups, radical students, and feminist and autonomist groups.

The process was far from smooth, and I was constantly aware of the reality that we had a very small budget for street theater in a country faced with a brutal spiral into poverty and hunger. In the past, many of the radical activists and organizations who did work in poor communities had refused to feed people as part of their organizing for fear of attracting those who were hungry but perhaps unwilling to commit to the struggle. This might have made sense in Argentina before the collapse of December 2001, but now the progressive organizations were working to help people to feed themselves.

Since the mid-1990s, groups of unemployed workers had been organizing road blockades, a strategy they used to force the government to pay the meager unemployment subsidies that were always on the verge of being cut off. As Pablo of the Aníbal Verón group explained to us, when the workers had had jobs, they would picket the factories for their right to a decent salary. Now, deprived of that job and collective bargaining power, they used the picket (*piquete*) to block roads to stop the circulation of goods. In this way, they got the attention of the government and the multinational corporations who are responsible for their plight.

Pablo told us that the *piqueteros* (organizations of the unemployed) had organized *ollas populares* (soup kitchens) and day-care centers where they fed the children, and they had coordinated microenterprises where they made bricks, manufactured crafts, and recycled clothing.

We participated in the *olla popular*. Sharing meals with our friends in Aníbal Verón and sometimes spending the night had a tremendous effect on me. I couldn't get this image out of my mind: Darío Santillán, in utter agony, being dragged out of the train station by the police who had shot him. When they executed him, he had been helping Maxi Kosteki, an artist involved in the *piquetero* movement, who was also shot and killed by the police.

Three weeks before the assassination of Maxi and Darío, Oliver North met with the Argentine government. Shortly afterward, when the *piqueteros* of Buenos Aires announced their intention of doing a road blockade on June 26, the government warned them that such tactics would not be tolerated. On that day, the police attacked the *piquete* coordinated by Aníbal Verón. Two protesters were killed and over a hundred people were arrested, beaten, and tortured at the police station. The hall of the

465

Linda Panetta

Three hundred people performed at the Argentina Uprising Pageant to a crowd of 10,000 in front of the gates to the U.S. military counterinsurgency and torture training school for Latin American military dictatorships, Ft Benning, Georgia.

Izquierda Unida, a leftist political party, was raided. The government waged a forty-eight-hour campaign against the *piqueteros*, accusing them of being violent. Fifty thousand people took to the streets to protest against this state terrorism, and finally the newspapers published the photos that showed how Darío Santillán was executed by the police, bending over the dying body of Maxi Kosteki.

On July 26 around 5,000 people gathered under the Puente Pueyrredón Bridge, the main southern access route into Buenos Aires, where the *piquete* had been attacked by the police the month before. The protest was crowded with dozens of oversized cardboard puppets, built after three weeks of intense discussions and rehearsals. It was the first time I had ever seen this kind of massive presence of puppets and props in a protest in Argentina. I had coordinated the construction of a moving collective mural about the repression, and around those "walls" we staged a show based loosely on a Bread and Puppet piece about the death of Carlo Giuliani at the 2001 WTO protests in Genoa. We were able to successfully convey the message that the *piqueteros* of Buenos Aires are honest families who are struggling against corporate globalization in defense of their right to life, dignified employment, and social change.

STREET THEATER

466

In 2003, a populist government was elected in Argentina. Under the presidency of Néstor Kirchner, as the economic and social condition of the middle class has improved, the *piquete* has lost its social consensus. Though important *piquetero* groups continue to organize major *piquetes*, many groups have given up on that tactic that seemed to have worked well under more blatantly repressive neoliberal governments. Autonomist organizations and others are instead focusing on organizing their microenterprises and working toward self-sustainment.

After reflecting on the situation of the social organizations in Argentina and their creative insurrection against a doomed system, a few friends and I decided to help create the Argentina Autonomista Project (AAP). The aim of the AAP is to improve the information and communication flows within Argentina, and between activists there and the rest of the world. The AAP has a website (www.autonomista.org) with information about the social movements in Argentina and it organizes delegations and internships for people from the United States and other countries who are interested in the struggle for a better world. The AAP is also touring a puppet show to raise awareness of the struggle of the Argentine social movements and establish partnerships with other social organizations.

Theatrical Strategies and Ideologies

In his seminal work *Theater of the Oppressed*, Augusto Boal traces the history of theater from the Greeks to Bertolt Brecht and reflects on the way this practice was taken away from the people, how it was transformed from a celebration of the people to a hierarchical event where a few would be on stage and the rest would be passive spectators. Boal argues that Aristotle's "coercive system of tragedy" shows how moral values and political coercion were forced on the population. Under Machiavelli, theater was used to represent the lives of exceptional individuals, thus further removed from the people.

In bourgeois theater, the individual is portrayed as directing the world. Then, in Brecht's work, social forces are shown to dominate and mold men and women. However, as Boal points out, the Brechtian character is divided, both subject and object. He is the object of surrounding forces and the subject of his own actions. In this way, he can understand and act so that he (and by extension the reader/spectator) can alter himself and improve his situation. Boal claims that his theater complements what Brecht started by destroying the barriers that separate spectators from actors. In Boal's theater everyone is a protagonist, all are necessary in the

STREET THEATER

battle for social change. While Brecht's poetics is that of an enlightened vanguard, where the spectator does not delegate power to the actor to think for him, but does delegate power to the actor to act for him, Boal attempts a poetics where the spectator does not delegate this power at all, but thinks and acts for himself.

I am concerned with how we produce our art, what kind of dialogues we establish when working together, how we deal with power in our own process. I believe that social change will come from people working as a community, and that a community is built when people work together in democratic ways.

When we take our puppets, props, banners, and stilt-walkers to the streets, we are attempting to communicate political messages in ways that not only appeal to the general public, but inspire them to engage their own everyday struggles in new ways. The importance of puppets in the streets was proven during the Seattle protests against the WTO and in other conventions and summits later on. The police seem to understand the impact of puppets and street theater, and they have been very diligent in arresting puppeteers, raiding the warehouses where puppets are being built and confiscating the props and tools used for building them, all in a vain attempt to reduce the power of the protesters. But, as a graffiti in Buenos Aires reminds us, "The enemy is not that huge, we are just looking at it on our knees."

Return of the Tortoise:
Italy's Anti-Empire Multitudes

By Keir Milburn

Keir Milburn is a longstanding political and cultural activist. He has worked with the pop band Chumbawamba for many years. He is currently researching the use of collaborative tools and techniques in the counterglobalization movement and how new decentralized democratic decisionmaking is emerging.

Two thousand or so years ago the Imperial Roman army invented a tactic called the tortoise where a group of soldiers combined their shields to form a shell. This military formation was almost invincible; the tortoise could advance forward, protected from attack, and with its collective armor it outmaneuvered the barbarians who fought as individuals. The tortoise played a part in enabling Rome to become an empire straddling the ancient world, smashing all resistance and swallowing every society it encountered. Now a new empire is emerging, a global empire which engulfs everything it comes across and destroys or soaks up all resistance. In the late 1990s the tortoise reemerged; its strength was still social co-operation but this time its ethos was antiempire.

photo top: David Hanks

IMC

The use of shields and padding by the Italian movement captured the imagination of the counterglobalization movement.

October 24, 1998, was a European-wide day of protest against the death of Semira Adamu, a Nigerian girl killed by the Belgian police. In Italy there was a demonstration against an immigrant detention center in Trieste. The Trieste demonstrators looked different from the usual raggle-taggle of political T-shirts and sensible boots; they wore white overalls with homemade foam and cardboard body armor beneath. Their comical roly-poly appearance belied the fact that they were deadly serious. The white overalls on the front lines had crash helmets and homemade Plexiglas shields. To the amazement of the police the shield-bearers started to group together, a line of chalky white demonstrators overlapping their shields, the rows behind raising their shields above their heads as protection from rubber bullets and tear gas. The demonstration was attacked by police and customs officers, but the front line was able to resist and advance to the fences of the detention camp. There, after hours of alternate clashes and negotiations, a number of people were allowed to enter the camp for the first time and document the inhuman conditions of the prisoners. A month later, on November 15, the camp was closed.

The Tortoise Had Reemerged Out of History

How did this happen? Why did such a bizarre and innovative form of protest resurface? It wasn't because the demonstrators had watched *Spartacus* over and over again; the tactics of the white overalls (the Tute Bianche organization) were the result of ten years of theoretical and political development, a decade that saw the Italian movement become the largest and most vibrant in Europe. Italy's political progress was highlighted by the size and intensity of the protests against the G8 in Genoa in 2001 and by the horrific violence used to repress those demonstrations.

The Tortoise's Head

The use of shields and padding by the Italian movement captured the imagination of the counterglobalization movement. Padded armor

disrupted the distinction between violence and nonviolence, confounding the mass media, which tried to divide protesters into good and bad. Being padded, the demonstrators could achieve their aims without having to fight the police on the police's terms. Though they threw the police and the media off balance, the Tute Bianche's actions haven't always been understood by activists from other countries, and their methods have led to allegations of elitism or pacifism. To understand the Tute Bianche we have to look at what has happened to the Italian Left over the last thirty years—the roots of today's tactics lie in that experience.

In 1977 while Britain was rocked by the Summer of Punk, Italy was experiencing social upheaval on an altogether grander scale. Unlike the rest of Europe, the revolutionary fervor of 1968 didn't come to an abrupt end in Italy, but continued to develop for another decade. A cycle of struggles autonomous from the large Italian Communist Party reached its high point with a series of massive demonstrations based around university and workplace occupations. These events—which came to be known as the Movement of 77—were an explosion of creative energy that sparked new sensibilities and experimental ways of living. Young people no longer had the same desires as their parents did: The jobs for life that the previous generation had fought for now represented a prison of interminable boredom. This generation saw work as an unpleasant chore to be endured, now and then, to finance what they really wanted to do.

In the time liberated from work, young people squatted social centers, they set up free radio stations, and set about self-reducing the cost of living through campaigns to make goods and services a token "political price". The movement was playful and ironic, pricking the pomposity of Italian politics. Large sections of the movement weren't against the use of force—the Left often had to defend itself against fascist groups and the violence of the state. Nor did the movement feel it had to stay within the law: Tactics for reducing prices included mass looting sprees, which were dubbed "proletarian shopping."

The Movement of 77 reached its high-water mark in March when huge demonstrations—sparked by the police killing an activist—seized large parts of Rome and Bologna and held them for ten days. In Rome a gun shop was looted and the guns thrown away. This was a clear pronouncement to the state: "We can get guns if we are forced to." In Bologna there were armored cars on the streets and mass arrests. Against a background of increasing violence from the police and fascist groups, and the emergence of clandestine armed groups in response to these attacks, the movement found itself forced off the creative terrain it had carved out. Suddenly it was locked into a fight it couldn't win. Trapped in a deadly spiraling

embrace with the state, the time and space for creativity closed up. In Italy the 1970s ended with state repression unprecedented in postwar western Europe. The clampdown left hundreds of militants dead and thousands in prison. The movement was crushed, leaving a legacy of defeat, disillusion, and a heroin epidemic.

The trauma of the late 1970s had a lasting effect on the next generation of militants. The use of protected demonstrations has to be seen in this light. The padding was a practical and creative attempt to scale down the violence of the forces of law and order. Italian activists had learned valuable lessons from the repression.

What remained of the movement in the 1980s regrouped around squatted social centers and a few remaining free radio stations. They reflected the more creative side of the Movement of 77, allowing a new strategy of exodus. The movement avoided confronting the state on its own ground but sought to weaken it through defection. This strategy was potentially problematic; it could have led to isolation, a separating from society into an inward-looking ghetto. Some called the social centers of the 1980s Indian Reservations. To understand how the movement left its reservations and grew to its present levels we talked to Hobo, a long-standing activist from a free radio station which had been central to the developments in Italy over the last decade; Radio Sherwood.

As Hobo explains: "Music was very important in the social centers. It was a way to attract people, it provided culture and finance." Music might have kept the torch of radicalism supplied with oxygen but it took a new wave of university occupations in 1990 to fully ignite it and break the spell of defeat. Dubbed the Panther Movement (because it coincided with the escape of a panther from Rome Zoo), the protests revitalized the movement. The protesters were brash and inventive and knew how to manipulate the media. The escaped panther seemed to symbolize the escape from blocked thinking and pessimism.

As Hobo recalls: "Panther brought a real renewal in the social centers, supplying vital energy and wiping out that diffuse sense of defeat. Many new social centers (actually, most of the existing social centers) were occupied in those years by the panther students. The panther movement marked the beginning of the longer process of deghettoization."

This deghettoization was aided by a journey undertaken by Italian activists into the misty jungles of southern Mexico. The Zapatista movement had

In the late 1990s the tortoise reemerged; its strength was still social cooperation but this time its ethos was antiempire.

burst on to the world stage with their uprising on January 1, 1994. It sent shock waves around the globe. To some they looked like a throwback to earlier times but their politics were something new. Inventive, expansive, and undogmatic, the Zapatistas constantly looked outward to defend their revolution. They called an international *encuentro* (encounter) in their jungle stronghold in 1996; thousands attended from every corner of the world. The *encuentro* played an important part in bringing together the counterglobalization movement that Seattle made public. In Italy they built an influential network of groups called *Ya Basta!* (Enough!). Their role was to support the Zapatistas but also to apply the new ways of thinking to the struggle in Italy. The Italians who attended took away a new attitude to politics that gelled well with their own experiences. These included:

- Change the world without taking power
- March with questions on your lips, not with a blueprint for revolution
- Reject the old binaries that had trapped thinking for so long: violence/nonviolence, reform/revolution
- Seek a world made of differences, a world containing many worlds, a world without borders
- Many yeses, one no—our struggles are united by our shared opposition to capitalism

Protected demonstraters had shields and padding but no offensive weapons.

Ghost Town

Italy in the 1990s, like many other countries, experienced a growing disaffection with mainstream politics. The Left with its newly expanded social centers didn't have the playing field all to itself. The anger and powerlessness associated with globalization was seized upon and used by opportunistic right-wing parties to gain power. In Italy the racist Lega Nord (Northern League) were quick to exploit the dissatisfaction. As Hobo explains: "Lega Nord was successful, so we started asking why. They collected the protest and displeasure of a lot of people, channeling it into the worst populist platitudes. In most of the cases the roots of this protest were fair, but people were duped. They fed their rage with intolerance and egotism."

In fact, the struggle with the Lega Nord lies at the root of the emergence of the white overall as a symbol. In 1994 the Lega Nord mayor of Milan ordered the eviction of the oldest and largest social center in Italy, the Leoncavallo. The mayor boasted: "From now on, squatters will be nothing more than ghosts wandering about in the city!" Protesters took this description literally: During the demonstrations to protect the Leoncavallo large numbers put on ghostly white overalls and rioted in the center of the city. The symbolism of the white overalls had a powerful resonance; it made visible those who had been ignored but it took a further rhetorical connection to launch the Tute Bianche as an Italian-wide movement.

The Italian Job

In Italian the phrase *tute blu* (blue overall) is the equivalent of blue collar in England and America: *tute blu* represents the traditional manual worker. But work has changed. The introduction of information and computer technologies has made work seem more immaterial and ghostly. Work is less about making material goods and more about providing services, knowledge, and culture. The emphasis is on producing changes in the way people think or feel. Even in industries producing something physical like cars, the material part seems to be less important than the intangible bits like the concept and the brand. The lifestyle the car represents has now become the pivotal point. The experience of work has changed. Jobs are more precarious and insecure, with short-term contracts, self-employment, and frequent job changes. Work now seems to invade the whole of life. The distinction between work time and leisure seems to be breaking down, in an age of home computers, mobile phones, endless advertisements, and constant shopping we're always at work and work is never finished. It's as if the whole of society has become one giant factory.

When Italian theorists began examining the new work experience, the contrast with the *tute blu* was too tempting: the new marginalized workers, the unemployed and temporary workers formed the bedrock of the social centers. Tute Bianche started to be linked to the new work experiences. In November 1998 a national white overalls day was declared with demonstrations outside the stock exchange, council chambers, and employment agencies. The wearing of white overalls swept through Italy with many of the Ya Basta network adopting the Tute Bianche dress and politics.

Hobo explains: "The Tute Bianche experience started from research [mainly conducted by Toni Negri and Maurizio Lazzarato] on "immaterial work"—a new concept that helped investigate some major changes happening in society. There's been a continuous feedback between these intellectuals and the movement. The Tute Bianche struggled for the extension of rights to nonworkers; linking the political to the social, putting bodies and lives center stage. These times are too historically different from previous phases; we have to try new roads and constantly verify them with theory."

This new movement and thinking was brought together at a 1998 conference of social centers, where they agreed a series of proposals known as the Milan Charter. According to Hobo, "The charter talked about the need for plural participation in this mass movement, with wide and rich differences. . . . So they proposed the creation of a network organized by Tute Bianche. The critical point was that the movement must exit the losing loop of 'conflict—repression—struggle against repression'. The aim was to enter a different scene; where social conflict can bring positiveness and start a new loop of 'conflict—projects—broadening of the sphere of rights'. "

This was an attempt to break away from the margins, to bring an end to the paralysis of purity. Hands were going to get dirty but just how dirty was controversial. The charter talked of the need to get recognition of their rights in all areas of society, even in government, though it was important to the Tute Bianches not to focus too much on the latter. In

David Hanks

San Francisco Bay Area residents march from the Italian Consulate in opposition to the repression against the movements in Genoa and the killing of Carlo Giuliani, July 2001.

their view the state had become less powerful as it was overcome by global capitalism. It was out in wider society that the real battles were to be fought, but unfortunately the state still remained an important point of repression. The movement had to manage its relationship to the state as a means of defense. For instance, sympathetic mayors and Members of Parliament were encouraged to attend demonstrations to make it difficult for the media to demonize the protesters. Some of those linked to the movement even stood in local council elections, occasionally getting elected. All of this was heresy in a tradition that prided itself on its autonomy. In many ways it was an admirable refusal to be hemmed in by political orthodoxy, but the tactic had the potential to blunt the movement's opposition to hierarchy and parliamentary politics. To Hobo it was worth the risk:

> The point was: let's start from this and try to acquire some rights that can be extended overall. I can't say if this is a good strategy, I can only see the results and in my opinion they confirm the initial bet. We have been able to bring members of parliament to Belgrade and Ramallah to give voice to the movement, we have been able to bring them to detention camps for immigrants and close them . . . but above all, we can move from a defensive role and try to propose what we want. We have to fight hard (and Genoa was a dramatic example) but we can't easily be pointed out as isolated thugs. Even the right-wing journals are forced to refer to us as a

social movement. They can talk about violence, radicalism, whatever, but they have to admit we represent a part of this society.

Of course there wasn't complete agreement with the new flexibility. In a very schematic way, we can say that there was a part of the movement oriented towards investigating and interpreting the changes in the world—in politics, in society and in production; while there was another part tied to orthodox Marxism and to an unaltered ideology, which simply couldn't accept any contact with institutions. The social centers split, between those who subscribed to the Milan Charter and those who didn't. The controversy was hard. They called us traitors and we called them pointless . . . maybe it's not completely decided, but now it's much softer. In those years we've shown that we didn't abandon the conflict, in fact the struggle has increased.

Another point of innovation and controversy was the relationship between the movement and the media. Hard lessons had already been learned about the way media attention can drag the focus of a movement away from its chosen terrain. When the Red Brigades emerged in the 1970s many activists thought it tiny and irrelevant compared to the size and vitality of the Movement of 77. But terrorism acted like a media black hole, sucking in attention and setting the terms on which politics were seen and conducted. The essential point was that we don't exist outside the media and we must be in charge of our relations with it.

Protected demonstrators had shields and padding but no offensive weapons. Their tactics were transparent. The ridiculous foam padding meant that they could only push and use weight of numbers—this made it obvious that any violence must come from the police. In fact, looking ridiculous, disrupting expectations, and mixing up signals was a powerful tactic against the media. A popular Tute Bianche chant was "Here—we come, Bastards, here we come" sung to the tune of "Guantanamera" while advancing with open hands towards the lines of riot police. The unofficial Tute Bianche salute was waving a little finger at the police—a way of saying "here it is, come and break it."

Another tactic has been to manipulate the press. Luca Casarini, a Tute Bianche spokesperson, has said: "We have analysts working on communication methods, we know what to do to make people talk about us. If a journalist from *Il Giornale* (right-wing newspaper) calls me and asks me for a headline I tell him: 'In Genoa we'll declare war on the powerful of the world,' and he makes a headline out of it. Or else we spread the rumour of the mouse-men that are now digging galleries through Genoa's underground, and they buy it."

ITALY'S DISOBEDIENTS

477

This was a dangerous game to play. A declaration of war made before Genoa backfired when the G8 leaders decided to reciprocate.

Genoa and Beyond

The fruits of this new thinking are there to see in the innovative and expanding protest movement in Italy. The first successful padded demonstration was the storming of the Aviano air force base during the Kosova war; other successes have included the dismantling of an immigrant detention center, a water-borne protest against anti-immigrant naval patrols, and accompanying the Zapatistas on their glorious meander to Mexico City. But it's in the international counterglobalization movement that the Tute Bianche's politics have really made a mark. The sight of the mass ranks of Michelin men with shields and inflatables at the Prague anti-IMF demo brought the Tute Bianche to international attention. The anti-G8 protests on their home territory of Genoa were to be their biggest test.

With 300,000 on the streets the Italian prime minister Berlusconi responded with escalating violence.

Defensive shields were met with tear gas, indiscriminate beatings, and armored cars driven at speed into the crowds. Worst of all, Carlo Giuliani was shot dead and people were arrested and systematically tortured. It was time for a rethink.

Before Genoa there had been a decision to take off the white overalls for fear they were becoming more of an identity than a tool: "The white overalls were a symbol," says Hobo. "It wasn't useful anymore. I think we have to never grow too attached to symbols, as they have their own cycle of life. Padding and shields are not symbols but technical instruments to reduce pain. Sometimes it's better using them, sometimes not. That's a technical choice."

The events in Genoa seemed to mark the end of a period of development. The Tute Bianche underwent a rethink and changed form. A new movement, the Disobedienti, was formed.

"This development is not just a rename, it's an expansion," explains Hobo. "Casting off the Tute Bianche also represented casting off a presumed role of leadership or avant-garde of a movement. The Disobedients are not only the social centers, they are a multitude composed of all who oppose neoliberalism: many grassroots organizations, some Catholics, sectors of parties . . . the whole range of people who were demonstrating in Genoa. It was time, especially at that moment, to give to this movement the strength to walk on its own legs. All together, all the different parts of mass movement. Thanks to this they couldn't pretend protest was confined only to those in the ghetto. All 'normal' people watching TV know the truth about the violence of the police."

A related but even more diffuse development has been the post-Genoa explosion of social forums across Italy. They are arenas where a wide range of civil society can meet and discuss.

Commemoration at the Italian Consulate. After Genoa performers took over the street in front of the Consulate and held a 6–hour performance protest, community and labor activists held pickets and prevented the unloading of a Berlusconi-allied Italian-owned ship at the Oakland docks, July 2001.

"In each social forum there are social centers, grassroots associations, civic committees, student organizations, pacifist groups, Attac, Rifondazione Comunista (refounded Communists), Verdi (Greens Party), Ya Basta, Cobas (radical trade union), sectors of CGIL (institutional trade union), Mani Tese (a catholic organization), lila (AIDS activists), some gay associations, some independent media, and so on. As for the general struggle, they brought the concept of generalized strike, meaning that the same rights should be extended to nonworkers (students, unemployed, occasional workers, immigrants). There has been complete participation in the recent demonstrations (including the general strike) in all the cities and in the social centers their presence has been very evident."

The problems being worked through are familiar to others in the counterglobalization movement—experimenting with new forms of organization that are relevant to the present. In Italy the buzz-word is the *multitude*; we'll let Hobo finish off:

> The "multitude" concept came from a necessity to overcome the sectarianism of the former extra-parliament groups. The idea is to use networks just as capital does. The force of this movement is really in this networking method: a multitude, not a party. In time it has become a theory that led us to consider the force of difference. We think it's a winning notion, maybe the only way out.

479

Postscript

This piece was written in 2002 but the trajectory it charts has continued and accelerated. Social struggle in Italy has now reached truly gigantic proportions. One march against Berlusconi in 2003 had 3,000,000 participants and one in five Italians are said to have marched against the invasion of Iraq. The last few years have been called "the springtime of the movements" and been compared to the late sixties' wave of protest. There has been a burst of creativity, particularly in the creation of alternative media to combat Berlusconi's monopoly over mainstream TV and print. An exciting development has been the emergence of Pirate TV stations across Italy. Sometimes they exist for only a short period and sometimes with a broadcast range of only a few streets but the infectious idea continues to spread. Ultimately this is a movement of movements and the Tute Bianche experience is only one among many, albeit an important one. There continues to be conflict between different movements and different strategies but those strategies are continually tested in the laboratory of social struggles which is Italy today.

photo top: Jutta Meier-Wiedenbach

The Sound and the Fury: The Invisible Icons of Anticapitalism

By John Jordan

John Jordan's bio: see Chapters 2 and 22.

"Look Dad, there's a picture of that guy that you like." Even my son recognizes Che Guevera's image, pointing to a newspaper article someone is reading on the train. The headline reads: "Clothes that changed the world." It's illustrated by a photo of a supermodel wearing a Che T-shirt. These days, Che's face is everywhere, from pop bottles to key rings—and where once it was an image that may have helped to inspire change, now it has joined the many images that are used merely to aid in selling our world back to us.

Since the 1960s and until recently there was a belief that through clever manipulation one could use mainstream media and the power of an image to influence public opinion. Yippie Jerry Rubin said, "You can't be a revolutionary today without a color television set—it's as important as a gun." But many of today's protesters, brought up in a culture saturated by advertising and branding campaigns, realize, as did the Situationists back

in the 1950s, that "revolt is contained by overexposure. We are given it to contemplate so that we forget to participate."

Radical actions are coopted instantly. For example, "State of Emergency," a new Sony PlayStation game, is billed as an "urban riot game set in the near future, where the oppressive American Trade Organization (ATO) has declared a state of emergency. . . . It is up to you to smash up everything and everyone in order to destabilize the ATO." Sound familiar?

The marketers of capitalism think that the problem with it is simply one of image. Their answer is rebranding to create a new "style" that is more palatable to the critics of capital, a makeover for the apocalypse. The movements' answer to their spell of hegemony and homogeneity is not a counterbranding campaign, nor counterimages, but process: the creation of relationships and spaces that nurture radical diversity.

It's definitely not a makeover that the movements are demanding; far from it. The message that's rising from the streets calls for the fundamental transformation of the entire system. If this global movement, which mainstream commentators find so hard to define, is about anything cohesive at all, it is about the importance of creating spaces for participation, arenas where grassroots direct democracy can take place. It's about people taking control of their everyday lives and collectively deciding the future of their own communities. "Participate, don't spectate"; "listen, don't preach"; "talk to someone who doesn't look like you": these are the cries echoing from Seattle to Bangalore, from Pôrto Alegre to Genoa, from London to San Cristóbal.

At the beginning of 2002, I was one of the many international activists who accompanied the Zapatista caravan as it wended its way through Mexico, strengthening grassroots support for the Zapatistas' demand for the constitutional recognition of indigenous rights. In many of the places we passed through we saw beautifully designed banners depicting Che and the Zapatistas' spokesperson Subcommandante Marcos. These images—young, beautiful Che alongside Marcos in a black balaclava smoking his regulation pipe—seemed somehow to represent two different ways of resisting.

In the masked and unmasked faces we can see the differences between the postmodern politics of plurality and paradox that have taken the lead in the anticapitalist movement, and the politics of personality and singular ideology that dominated the last century or more of struggle.

Zapatista supporters hit the streets of Mexico City.

Jutta Meier-Wiedenbach

Faces define, telling the unique story of an individual; they are the worn relics of specific personalities with particular pasts. A masked face however, does the opposite: as the individual vanishes behind the mask a new personality is revealed. The eyes, because they are all that one can see, speak of what is special about each and every one of us, and yet the mask contains many possibilities. Marcos's black mask becomes a mirror, a mirror for all Zapatistas who are also masked, a mirror for everyone excluded and marginalized by neoliberalism, a mirror that reflects diversity and shatters the illusion of singular ideology. "*Todos somos Marcos*" is a common slogan; everyone can be Marcos but not everyone could have been Che. Che had a biography, a specific history; he fought to take power and be visible. Marcos and the Zapatistas are "fighting in order to disappear." Their image is ephemeral not eternal, their desire is to dissolve power rather than take it, to be catalysts rather than heroes, instigators rather than icons.

At the end of the caravan's journey, Marcos spoke to a crowd of 200,000 people in the symbolic heart of the Mexican state, Mexico City's enormous zócalo: "We are here and we are a mirror," he said. " Not reality, but merely its reflection. Not light, but merely a glimmer. Not a path, but merely a few steps. Not a guide, but merely one of the many routes which lead to tomorrow."

Witnessing the humility of zapatismo is in itself a humbling experience. To imagine this level of openness and dedication to authentic direct democracy in the European activist milieu is sometimes difficult, but without aspiring to it, we will simply return to old forms, which will inevitably lead to sectarianism and the fragmentation of this growing movement which has so much potential.

The fear of many European radicals is that if we open up too much space it will be filled with the reformist policy politics of the NGOs, or by those who think that a benign state can somehow reform capital, or else it will be sabotaged and coopted by the outdated authoritarian leftist parties. But I think there has been a lack of nerve, a failure to take the risk and trust that the radical path is the one that will grow from a truly open and nurturing space.

As eighteenth-century commentator Samuel Johnson famously said, "Courage, sir, is the first of virtues, because without it, it is sometimes difficult to exercise the others." We have to have the courage to let go. The courage to work hard, and then the courage to let things take their own course. We have to have the courage and to believe that a truly radical popular insurrection can and will take place, if only we would just let it. The courage to believe, as the Situationists did, that "our ideas are in everyone's mind."

With the Zapatistas we see a movement that is extraordinarily popular, not only within their own indigenous communities—who ultimately dictate what the Zapatista Army does through consensus decisionmaking during village assemblies—but also within the broader civil society of Mexico and the world. In the last official vote, the "Consulta" of 1999, 2.5 million Mexicans expressed support for the Zapatistas' radical demands.

I'm inspired by the notion of a revolution that listens. I recently read an essay containing Eduardo Galeano's description of how Marcos, the vanguardist urban revolutionary, "went to Chiapas and spoke to the indigenous, but they didn't understand him." The author (not Galeano) goes on to say, "Then he penetrated the mist, learned to listen, and was able to speak." This is the politics of joined hands and interlaced fingers rather than the clenched fist.

This idea of a listening revolution turns preconceived notions of struggle on their head. Zapatismo throws political certainty to the wind, and out of the shape-shifting mist it grasps change; change not as a banal revolutionary slogan, but as actual process. Change as the ability of revolutionaries to admit mistakes, to stop and question everything.

Change as the desire to dissolve the vertical structures of power and replace them with radical horizontality: real popular participation. Change as the willingness to always listen and always be ready and willing to change.

Zapatismo is a living example of how we can open the space, prepare the soil, and through direct democratic dialogue, witness the radical roots growing authentically deep. And so we must have the courage and the heart that is in the root of the word *courage, le coeur*, to build a rebellion that embraces, the courage and the heart to insist on an insurrection that listens. Let's have the courage to demand nothing for ourselves, but everything for everyone. The courage to keep that space radically open, rebelliously inviting, and profoundly popular. Because if we don't, the brutal state repression that is being brought to bear will succeed in weakening and dividing us.

One night while on the Zapatista caravan, I dreamt that Marcos simply disappeared, that he never took off his mask, never revealed his identity, but simply melted back into the mist and was never seen again—a perfect humble ending without the seemingly obligatory martyrdom of revolutionary leaders. An iconoclastic ending for the invisible icon of this movement without icons or ideologies.

> Zapatismo is not an ideology,
> it is not a bought and paid for doctrine,
> it is . . . an intuition.
> Something so open and flexible that
> it really occurs in all places.
> Zapatismo poses the question:
> "What is it that has excluded me?"
> "What is it that has isolated me?"
> In each place the response is different.
> Zapatismo simply asks the simple question
> and stipulates that the response is plural,
> that the response is inclusive . . .
>
> —Subcomandante Marcos

Originally published in a slightly different version in Red Pepper *magazine, September 2001.*

REVOLUTION THAT LISTENS

Photographers and Artistic Contributors

Morgan Fitzpatrick Andrews
began rehabilitating his eyes through
making woodcuts and shadow puppets.
morganfitxp@yahoo.com

Jeff Conant
has been participating in and
documenting liberation struggles
through writing, photography, and
other avenues for over a decade.

Mona Caron
is a San Francisco-based illustrator
and muralist.
www.monacaron.com

Hugh D'Andrade
is a San Francisco-based artist
and agitator.
www.hughillustration.com

Terrence Freitas
is an indigenous rights activist and
photographer from the U.S. who was
defending U'wa land from oil exploration
when he, together with Washinawatok
and Lahe'ena'e Gay, was kidnapped
and murdered by FARC guerrillas in
March 1999.

David Hanks
has photographed hundreds of protests
in the San Francisco Bay Area; his
work is available to social justice
organizations and has been published
in many newspapers and magazines.
photos@davidhanks.org
www.davidhanks.org

Orin Langelle
is a photographer who has documented
indigenous, ecological, and global
justice movements and is codirector
of the Vermont-based Global Justice
Ecology Project
langelle@sover.net

Jason Justice
is an activist graphic designer serving
causes for social and cultural change;
he designed the book you have in
your hands and spends his days and
nights working *toward a "better
looking" revolution!*
jason@justicedesign.com
www.justicedesign.com

Hilary Klein
has lived Chiapas where she worked
with women's cooperatives and
Zapatista communities.
hilaryklein@earthlink.net

Jutta Meier-Wiedenbach
worked as a photographer and with local
human rights organizations in Chiapas
for four and a half years and is active
doing Latin American solidarity work.
meiwie@eudoramai.com

Mariana Mora
is graduate student and a participant in
the struggle in Chiapas, working to
(re)circulate radical images of Chiapas.
mariana_mora@yahoo.com

Oakley Myers
is a photographer and activist who did
extensive photodocumentation of the
Seattle 1999 antiWTO protests.

Linda Panetta
is the director of SOA Watch/NE and a
photojournalist whose work focuses on
cultural, environmental, and human
rights, with a particular emphasis on
conflict zones.
www.OpticalRealities.org
www.soawne.org

Nicolas Pousthomis

is a documentary photographer whose work has won various prizes and is widely shown in Argentina and internationally. His development has been largely influenced by the events of the past few years, in direct involvement with his subject matter, and his efforts are directed toward deepening both his craft and the struggle he documents.
http://stray.linefeed.org/argentinaphoto

Karl Seifert

is a photographer from San Francisco.
www.karlsportfolio.com

SF Print Collective

The San Francisco Print Collective is a community-based political street-art collective that uses provocative graphics to promote public dialogue and to reclaim public space from the highest bidder.
www.sfprintcollective.missionartist.net

Mark Simmons

is a photographer/photojournalist based in Bristol. The images appearing in this book are from a book on the Anti-Poll Tax Campaign (at akpress.org).

Andrew Stern

is a documentary photographer who is also coauthor of the book *We Are Everywhere: The Irresistible Rise of Global Anti-Capitalism* (Verso, 2003).
www.andrewstern.net

Jim Swanson

is a San Francisco artist, illustrator, and animated filmmaker.
www.typesettingetc.com

Seth Tobacman

is a radical comic artist and author of *You Don't Have to Fuck People Over to Survive* and *War in the Neighborhood*.

Florencia Vespignani

These images were created from the heat of the struggle alongside my *compañeros* in the Movement of Unemployed Workers of Argentina. They are the reflection of that daily struggle: the *piquete*, the work, the organizing in the neighborhoods. They are the hope, the sharing, the memory of our assassinated brothers, the struggle in the street.
(email Spanish please):
florenciave@yahoo.com.ar
www.inventati.org/mtd/arte

Eric Wagner

is a veteran computer expert and activist photographer from the San Francisco Bay Area. His photographs have appeared in the *San Jose Mercury News*, *The Progressive*, *Adbusters*, and the center page of *IndyMedia*.
eric@basetree.com
www.basetree.com

Josh Warren White

is a radical photojournalist living in Oakland, California, who publishes books as a member of the AK Press collective, facilitates antiracism workshops as a member of the Active Solidarity collective, and organizes around housing issues.
josh@activesolidarity.net
www.activesolidarity.net